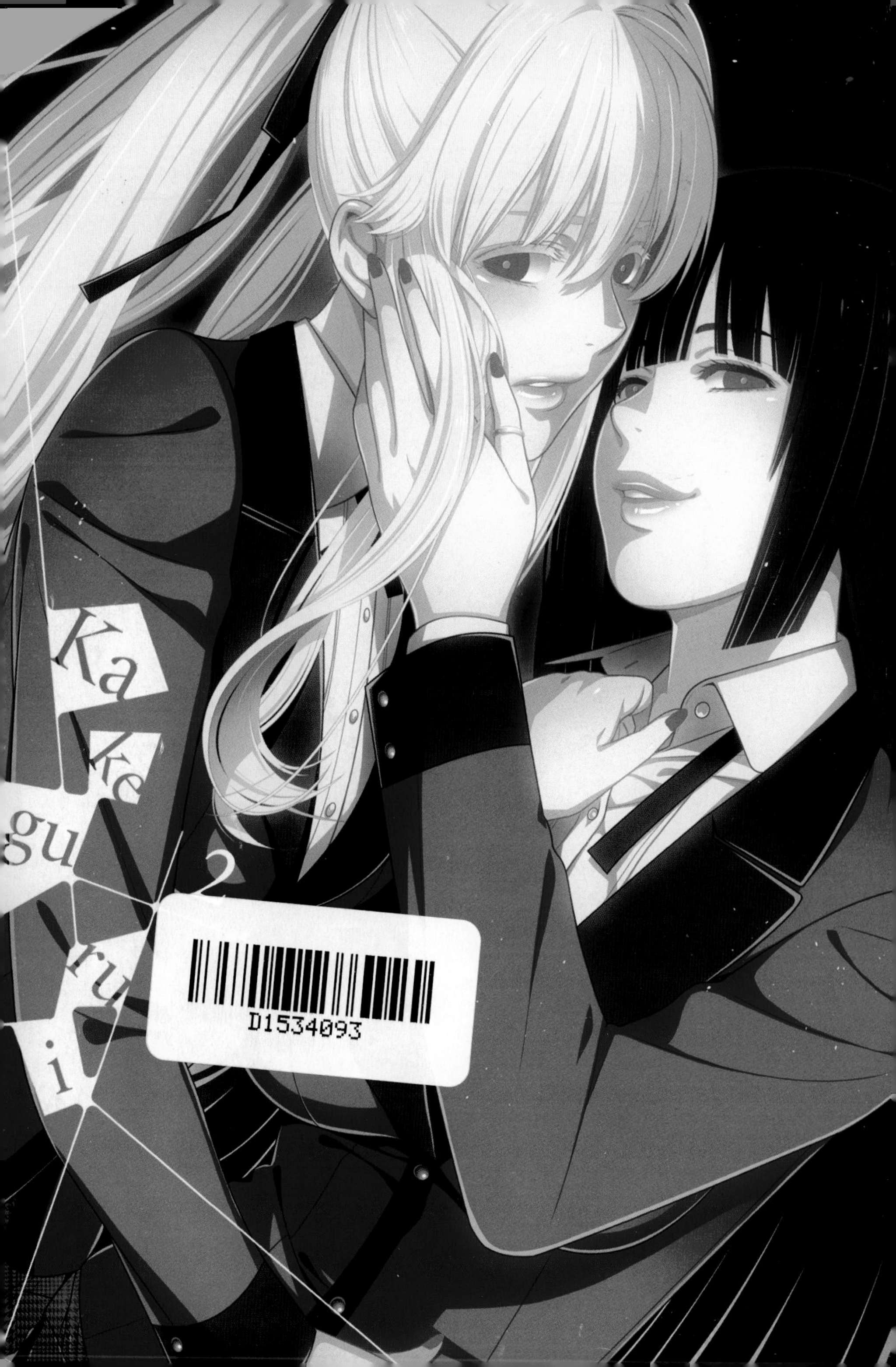
Ka
ke
gu
ru
i
2

②

K
A
K
E
G
U
R
U
I

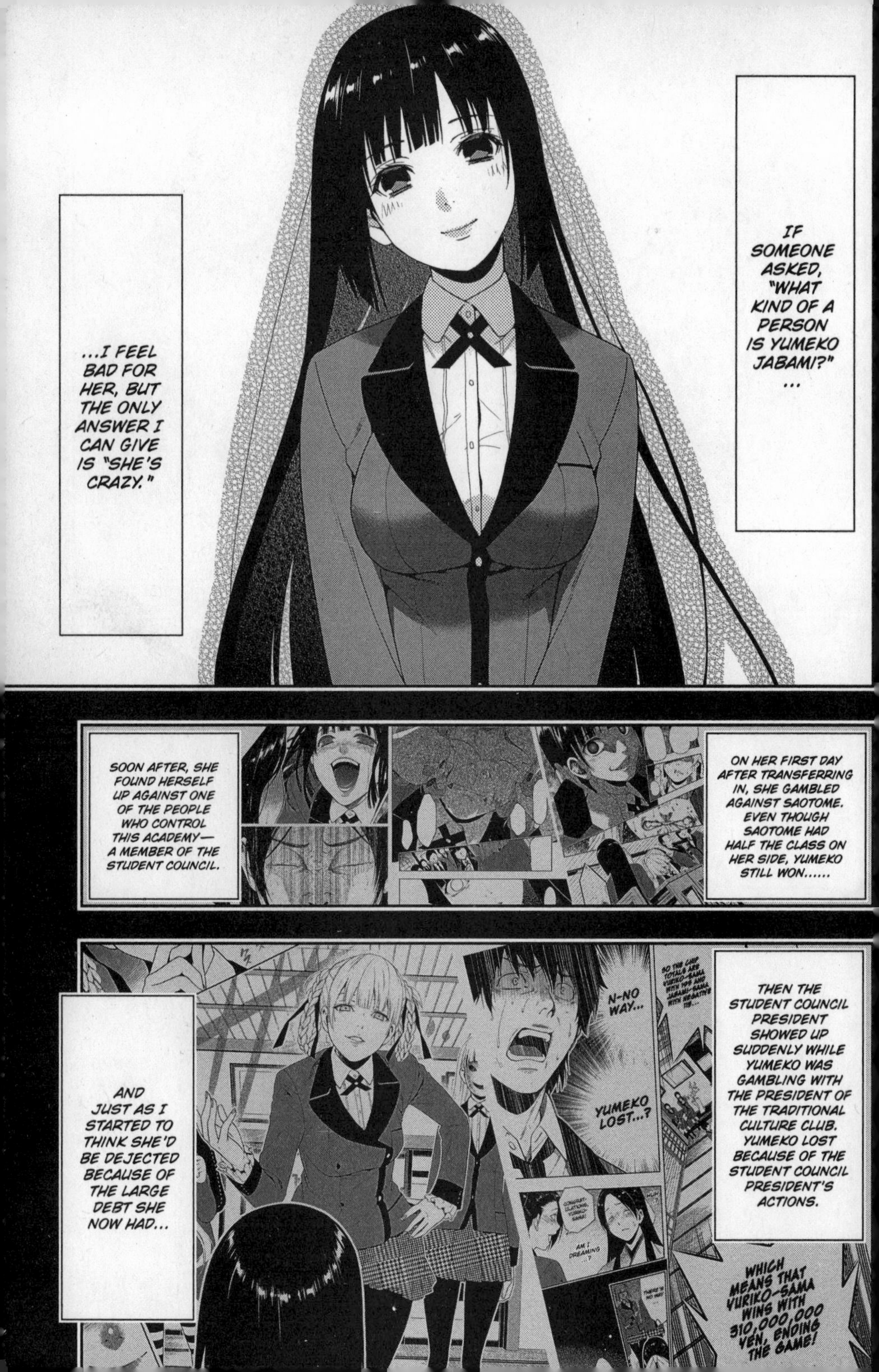
IF SOMEONE ASKED, "WHAT KIND OF A PERSON IS YUMEKO JABAMI?" ...
...I FEEL BAD FOR HER, BUT THE ONLY ANSWER I CAN GIVE IS "SHE'S CRAZY."
ON HER FIRST DAY AFTER TRANSFERRING IN, SHE GAMBLED AGAINST SAOTOME. EVEN THOUGH SAOTOME HAD HALF THE CLASS ON HER SIDE, YUMEKO STILL WON......
SOON AFTER, SHE FOUND HERSELF UP AGAINST ONE OF THE PEOPLE WHO CONTROL THIS ACADEMY—A MEMBER OF THE STUDENT COUNCIL.
THEN THE STUDENT COUNCIL PRESIDENT SHOWED UP SUDDENLY WHILE YUMEKO WAS GAMBLING WITH THE PRESIDENT OF THE TRADITIONAL CULTURE CLUB. YUMEKO LOST BECAUSE OF THE STUDENT COUNCIL PRESIDENT'S ACTIONS.
N-NO WAY...
YUMEKO LOST...?
CONGRATULATIONS YURIKO-SAMA!
AM I DREAMING...?
WHICH MEANS THAT YURIKO-SAMA WINS WITH 310,000,000 YEN, ENDING THE GAME!
AND JUST AS I STARTED TO THINK SHE'D BE DEJECTED BECAUSE OF THE LARGE DEBT SHE NOW HAD...

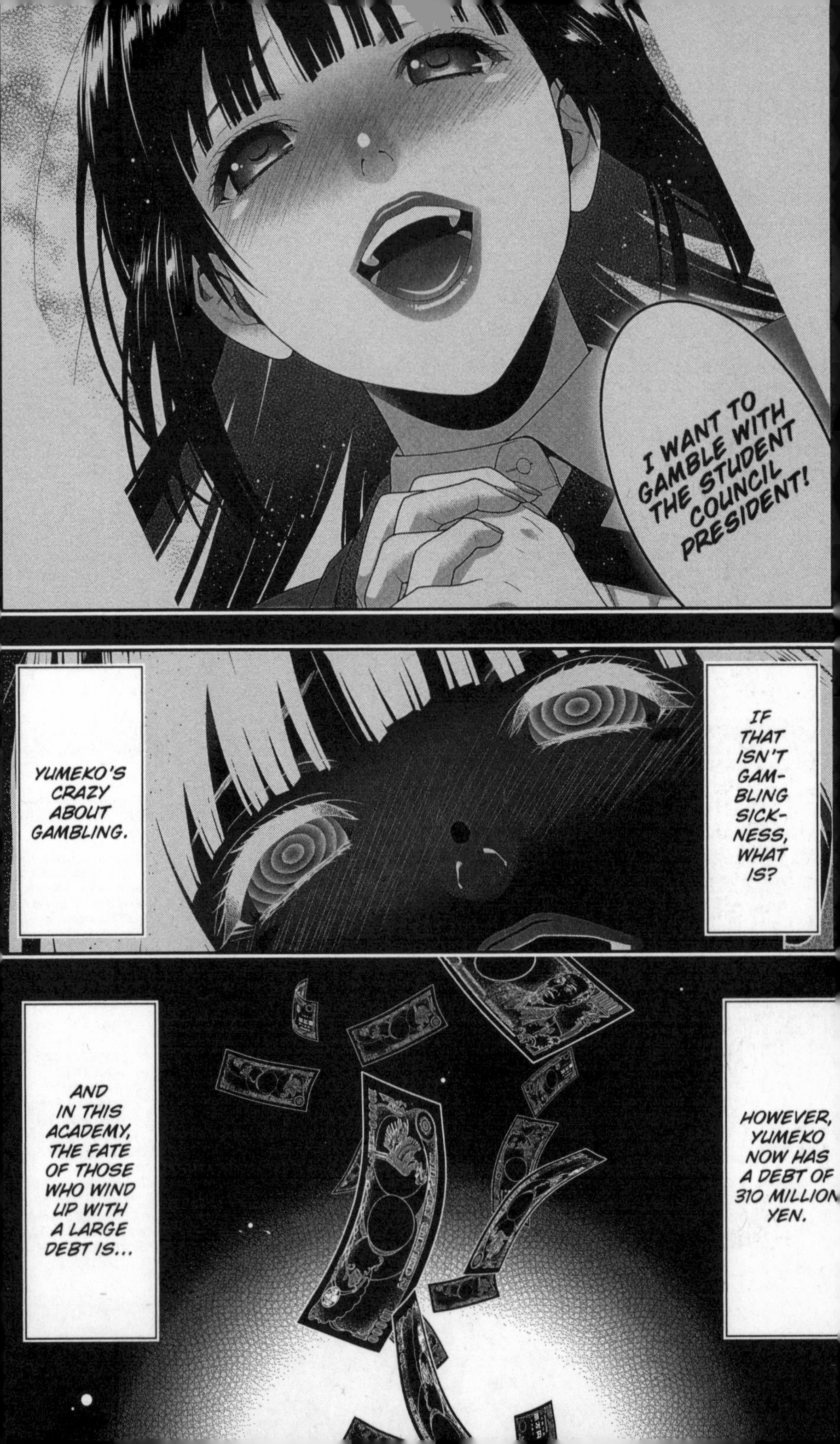
I WANT TO GAMBLE WITH THE STUDENT COUNCIL PRESIDENT!
IF THAT ISN'T GAM-BLING SICK-NESS, WHAT IS?
YUMEKO'S CRAZY ABOUT GAMBLING.
HOWEVER, YUMEKO NOW HAS A DEBT OF 310 MILLION YEN.
AND IN THIS ACADEMY, THE FATE OF THOSE WHO WIND UP WITH A LARGE DEBT IS...

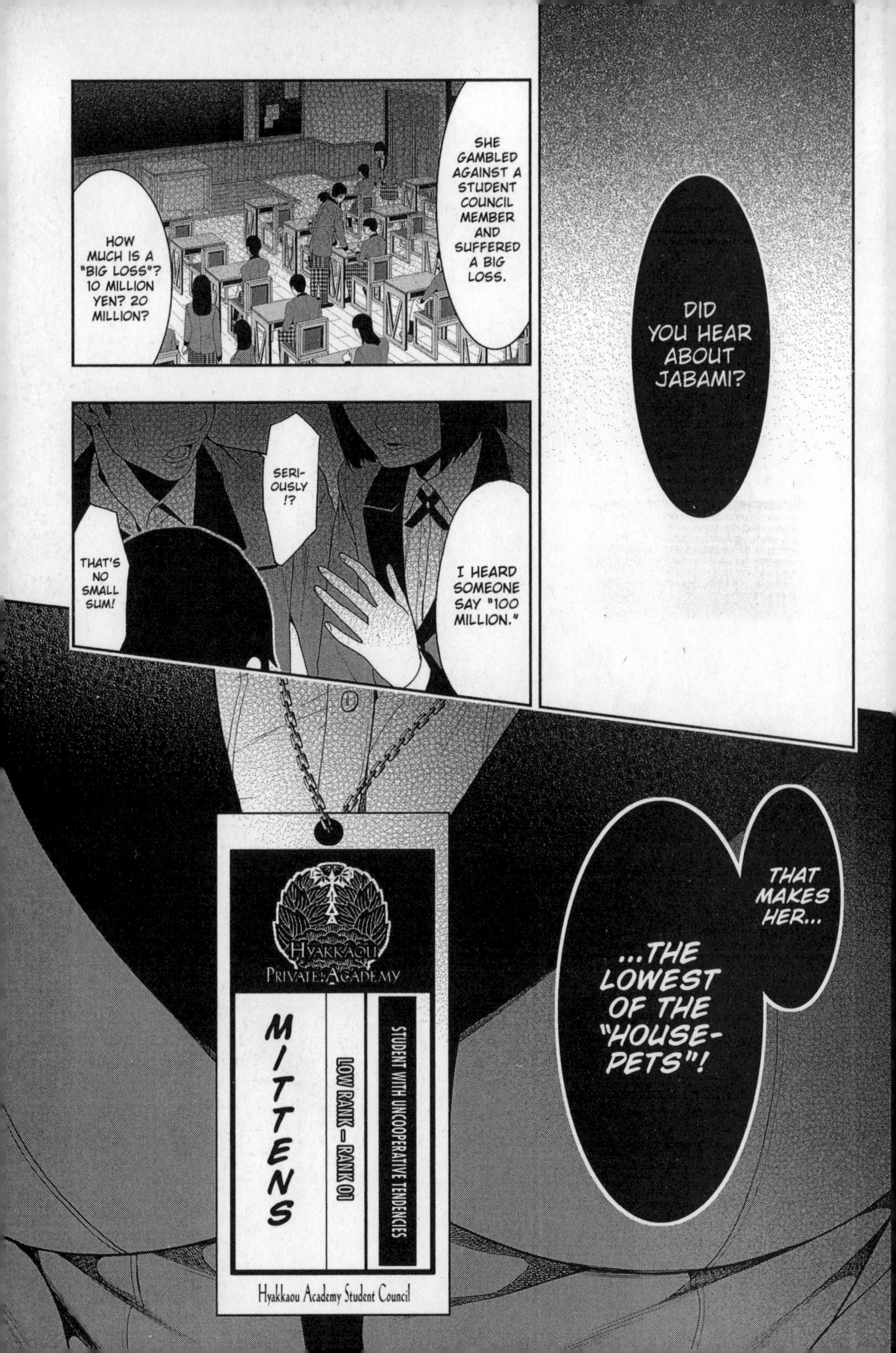

DID YOU HEAR ABOUT JABAMI?
SHE GAMBLED AGAINST A STUDENT COUNCIL MEMBER AND SUFFERED A BIG LOSS.
HOW MUCH IS A "BIG LOSS"? 10 MILLION YEN? 20 MILLION?
I HEARD SOMEONE SAY "100 MILLION."
SERI-OUSLY!?
THAT'S NO SMALL SUM!
THAT MAKES HER...
...THE LOWEST OF THE "HOUSE-PETS"!
HYAKKAOU PRIVATE ACADEMY
STUDENT WITH UNCOOPERATIVE TENDENCIES
LOW RANK - RANK 01
MITTENS
Hyakkaou Academy Student Council

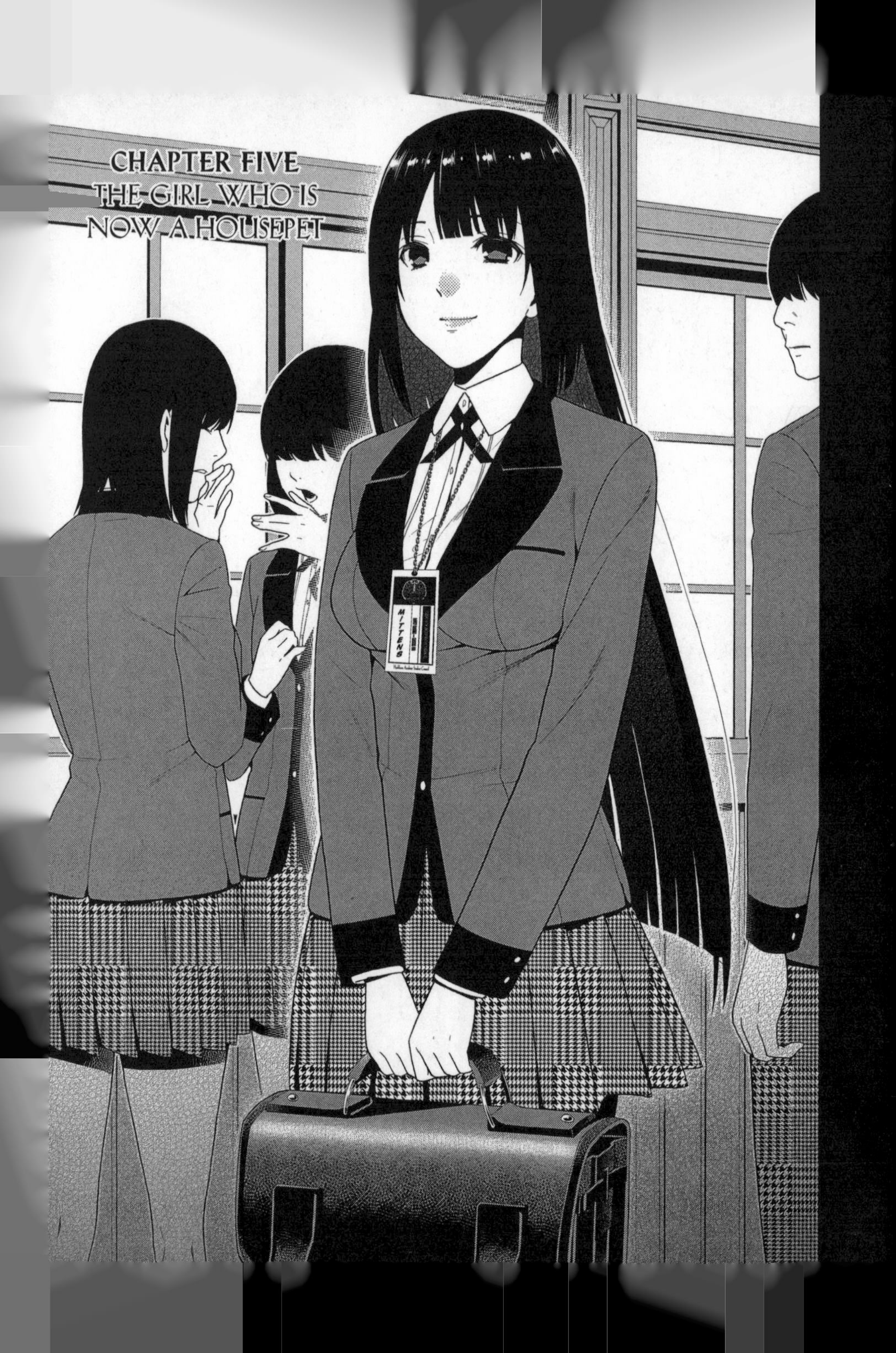
CHAPTER FIVE
THE GIRL WHO IS
NOW A HOUSEPET
MITTENS

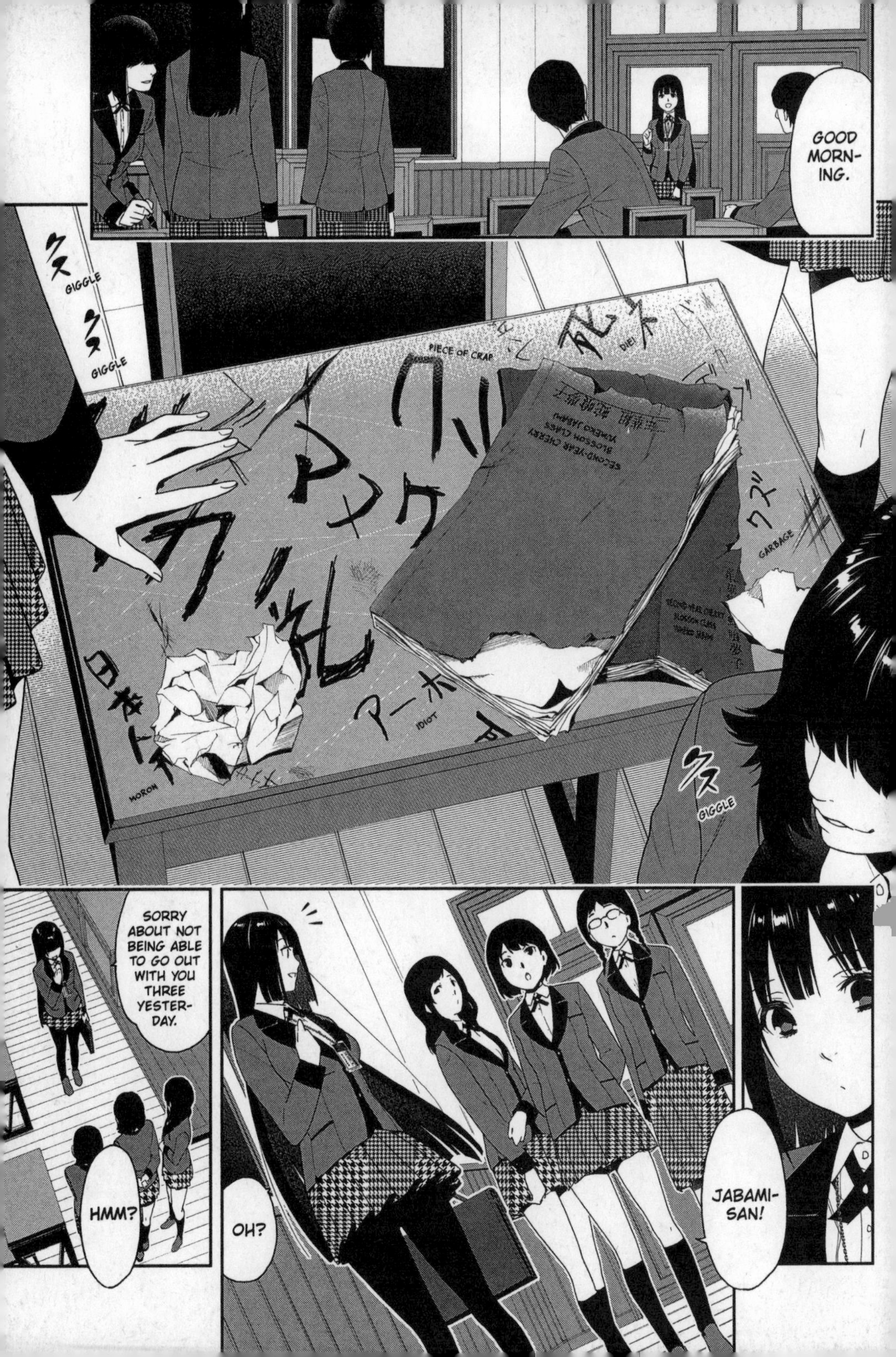
GOOD MORNING.
クス GIGGLE
クス GIGGLE
DIE!
PIECE OF CRAP
SECOND-YEAR CHERRY BLOSSOM CLASS YUMEKO JABAMI
GARBAGE
IDIOT
MORON
クス GIGGLE
JABAMI-SAN!
OH?
SORRY ABOUT NOT BEING ABLE TO GO OUT WITH YOU THREE YESTERDAY.
HMM?

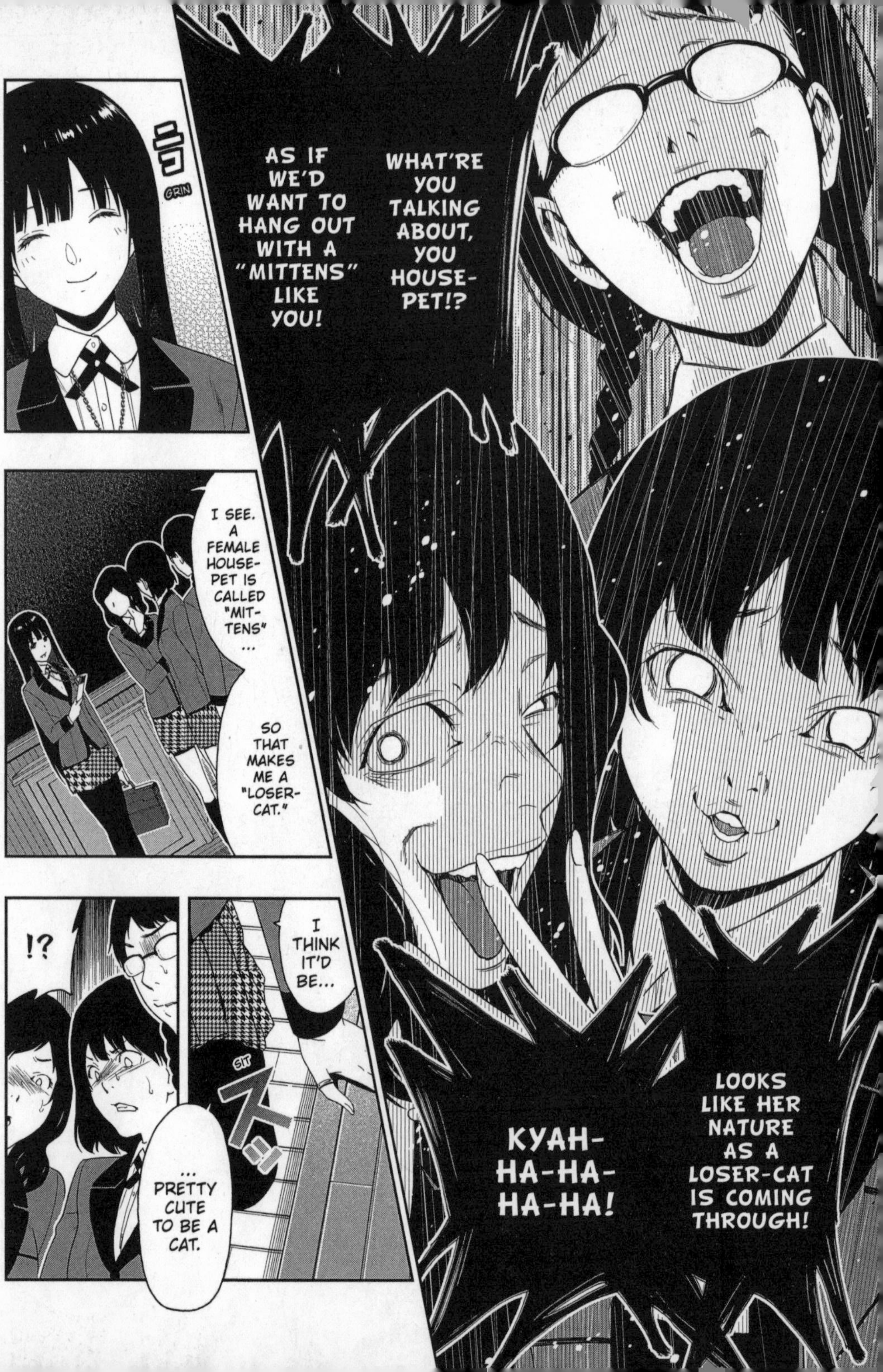
WHAT'RE YOU TALKING ABOUT, YOU HOUSE-PET!?
AS IF WE'D WANT TO HANG OUT WITH A "MITTENS" LIKE YOU!
LOOKS LIKE HER NATURE AS A LOSER-CAT IS COMING THROUGH!
KYAH-HA-HA-HA-HA!
GRIN
I SEE. A FEMALE HOUSE-PET IS CALLED "MIT-TENS"...
SO THAT MAKES ME A "LOSER-CAT."
I THINK IT'D BE...
SIT
... PRETTY CUTE TO BE A CAT.
!?

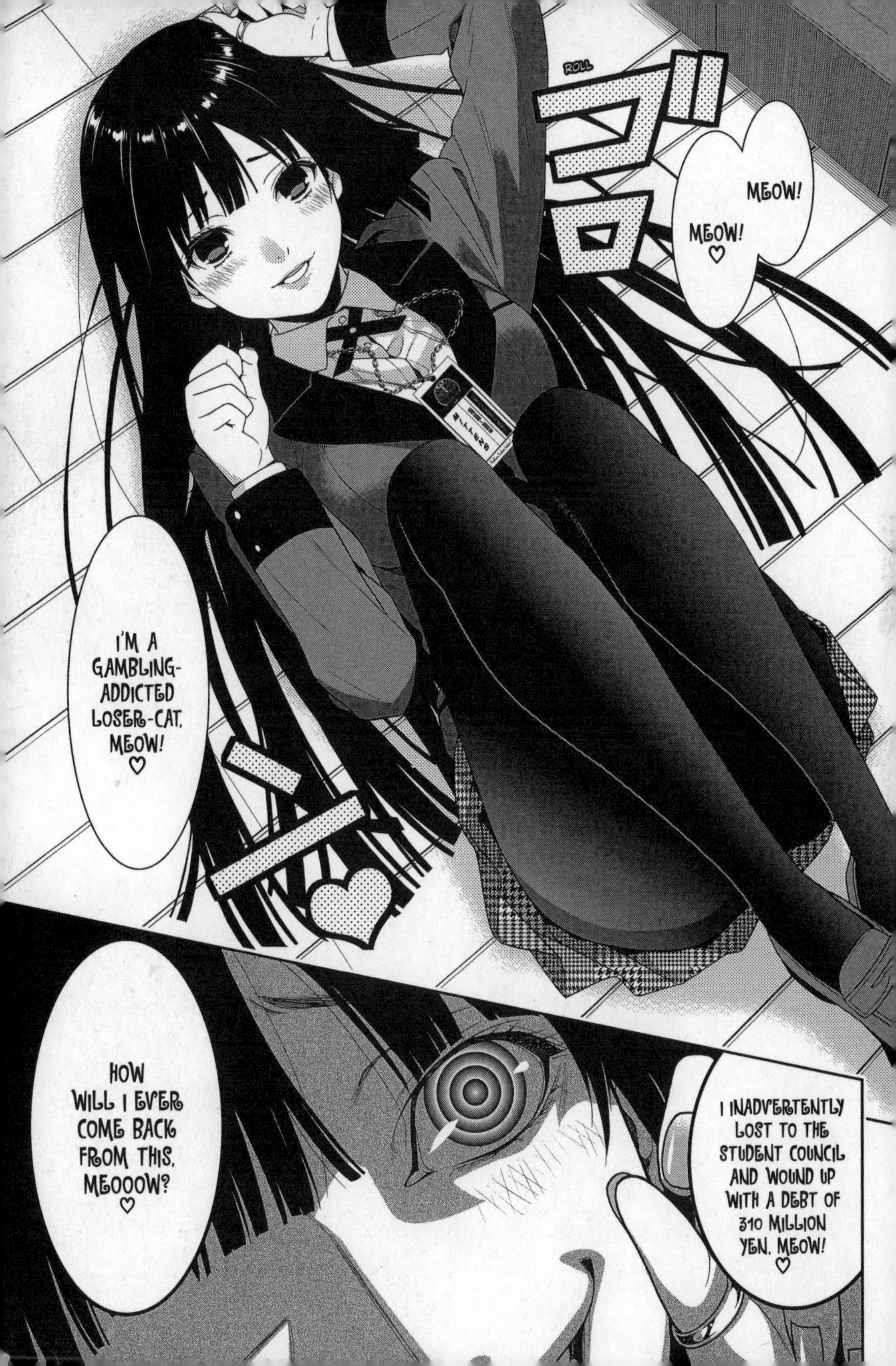
ROLL
MEOW! MEOW! ♡
I'M A GAMBLING-ADDICTED LOSER-CAT, MEOW! ♡
I INADVERTENTLY LOST TO THE STUDENT COUNCIL AND WOUND UP WITH A DEBT OF 310 MILLION YEN, MEOW! ♡
HOW WILL I EVER COME BACK FROM THIS, MEOOOW? ♡

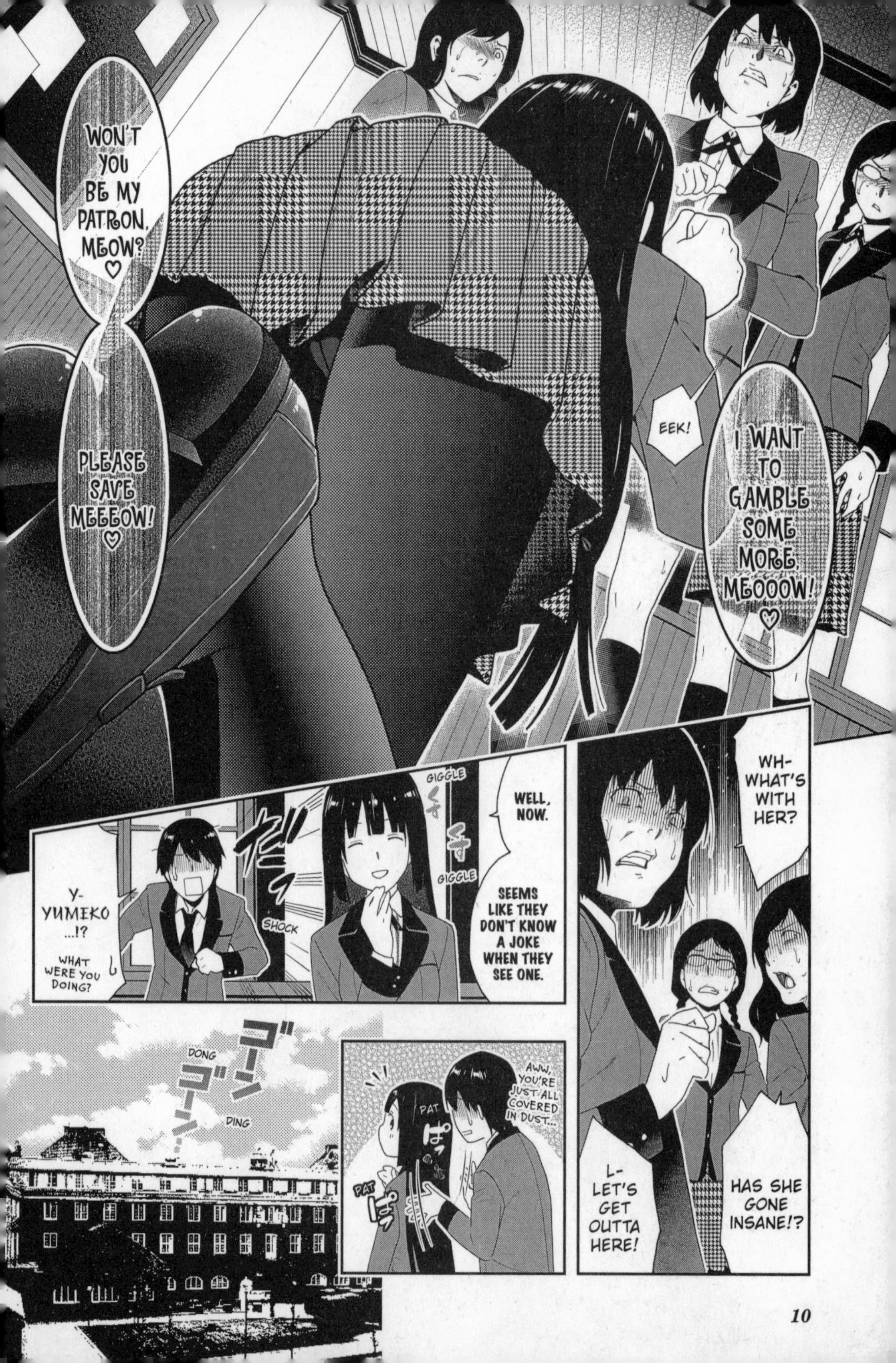
I WANT TO GAMBLE SOME MORE MEOOOW! ♡
EEK!
WON'T YOU BE MY PATRON, MEOW? ♡
PLEASE SAVE MEEEOW! ♡
WH- WHAT'S WITH HER?
HAS SHE GONE INSANE!?
L- LET'S GET OUTTA HERE!
WELL, NOW.
GIGGLE
GIGGLE
SEEMS LIKE THEY DON'T KNOW A JOKE WHEN THEY SEE ONE.
SHOCK
Y- YUMEKO ...!?
WHAT WERE YOU DOING?
AWW, YOU'RE JUST ALL COVERED IN DUST...
PAT
PAT
DONG
DING

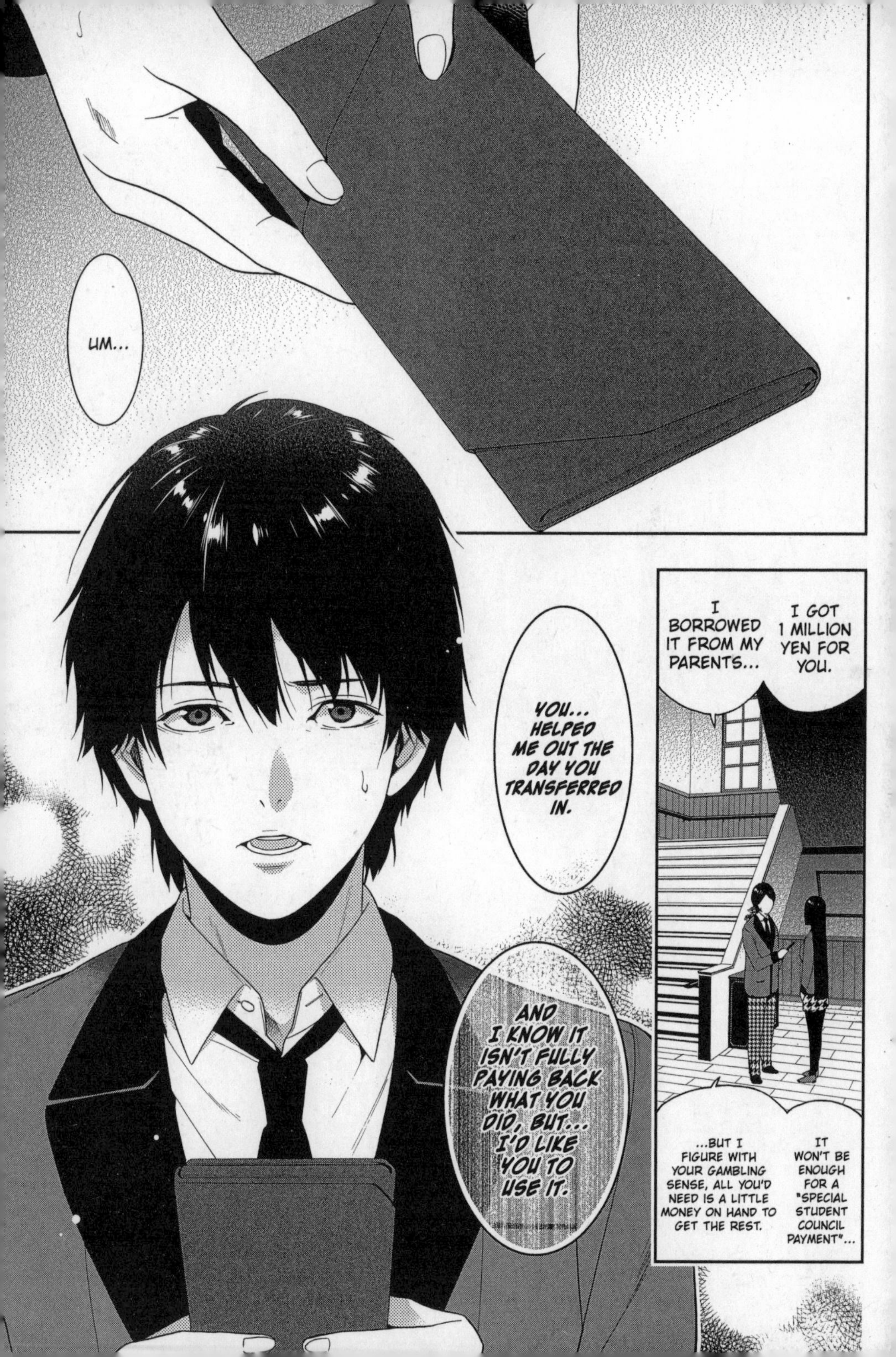
UM...
I GOT 1 MILLION YEN FOR YOU.
I BORROWED IT FROM MY PARENTS...
IT WON'T BE ENOUGH FOR A "SPECIAL STUDENT COUNCIL PAYMENT"...
...BUT I FIGURE WITH YOUR GAMBLING SENSE, ALL YOU'D NEED IS A LITTLE MONEY ON HAND TO GET THE REST.
YOU... HELPED ME OUT THE DAY YOU TRANSFERRED IN.
AND I KNOW IT ISN'T FULLY PAYING BACK WHAT YOU DID, BUT... I'D LIKE YOU TO USE IT.

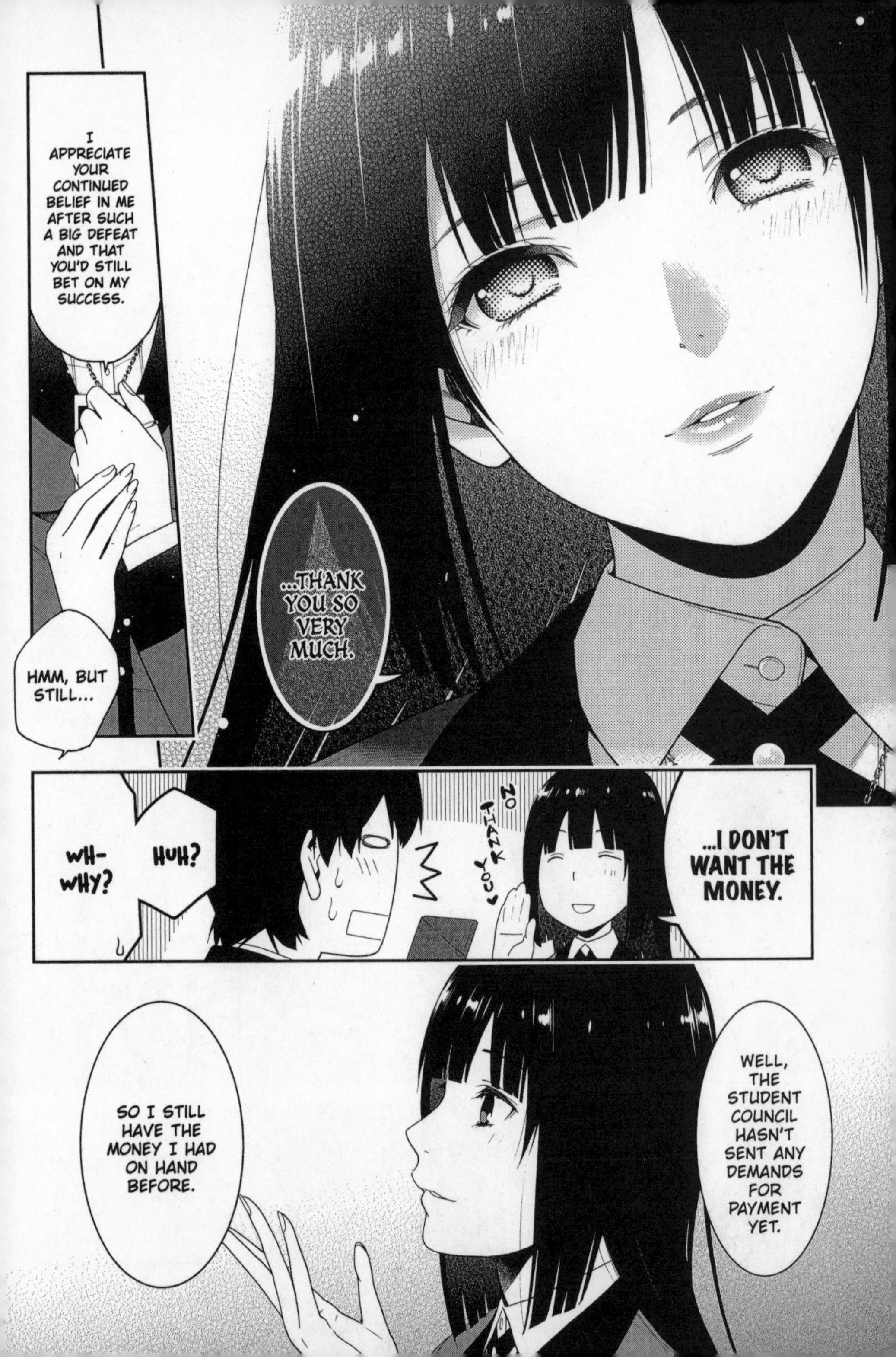
I APPRECIATE YOUR CONTINUED BELIEF IN ME AFTER SUCH A BIG DEFEAT AND THAT YOU'D STILL BET ON MY SUCCESS.
...THANK YOU SO VERY MUCH.
HMM, BUT STILL...
...I DON'T WANT THE MONEY.
NO THANK YOU♥
HUH?
WH-WHY?
WELL, THE STUDENT COUNCIL HASN'T SENT ANY DEMANDS FOR PAYMENT YET.
SO I STILL HAVE THE MONEY I HAD ON HAND BEFORE.

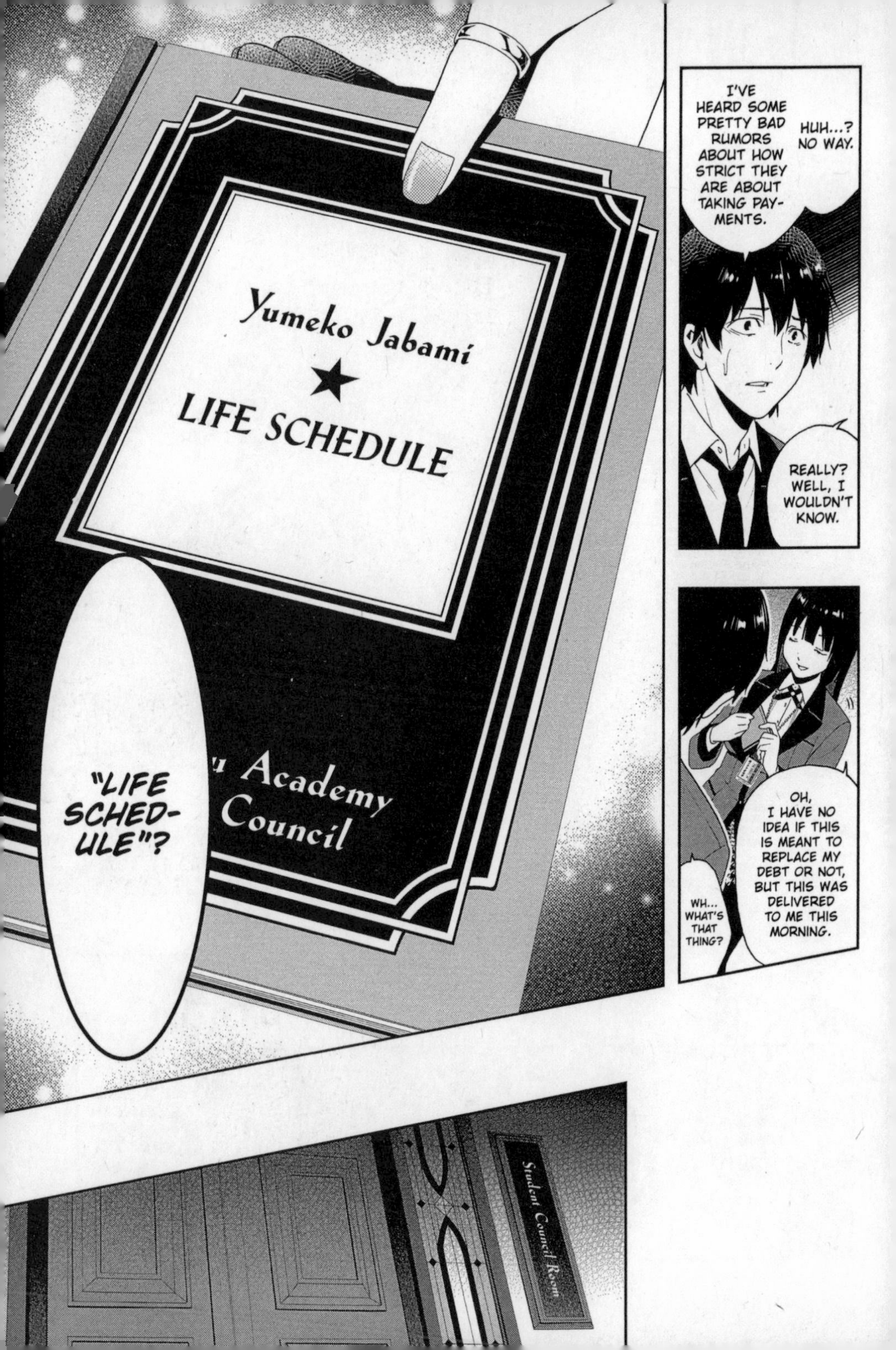

HUH...? NO WAY.
I'VE HEARD SOME PRETTY BAD RUMORS ABOUT HOW STRICT THEY ARE ABOUT TAKING PAY-MENTS.
REALLY? WELL, I WOULDN'T KNOW.
OH, I HAVE NO IDEA IF THIS IS MEANT TO REPLACE MY DEBT OR NOT, BUT THIS WAS DELIVERED TO ME THIS MORNING.
WH... WHAT'S THAT THING?
Yumeko Jabami
★
LIFE SCHEDULE
u Academy
Council
"LIFE SCHED-ULE"?
Student Council Room

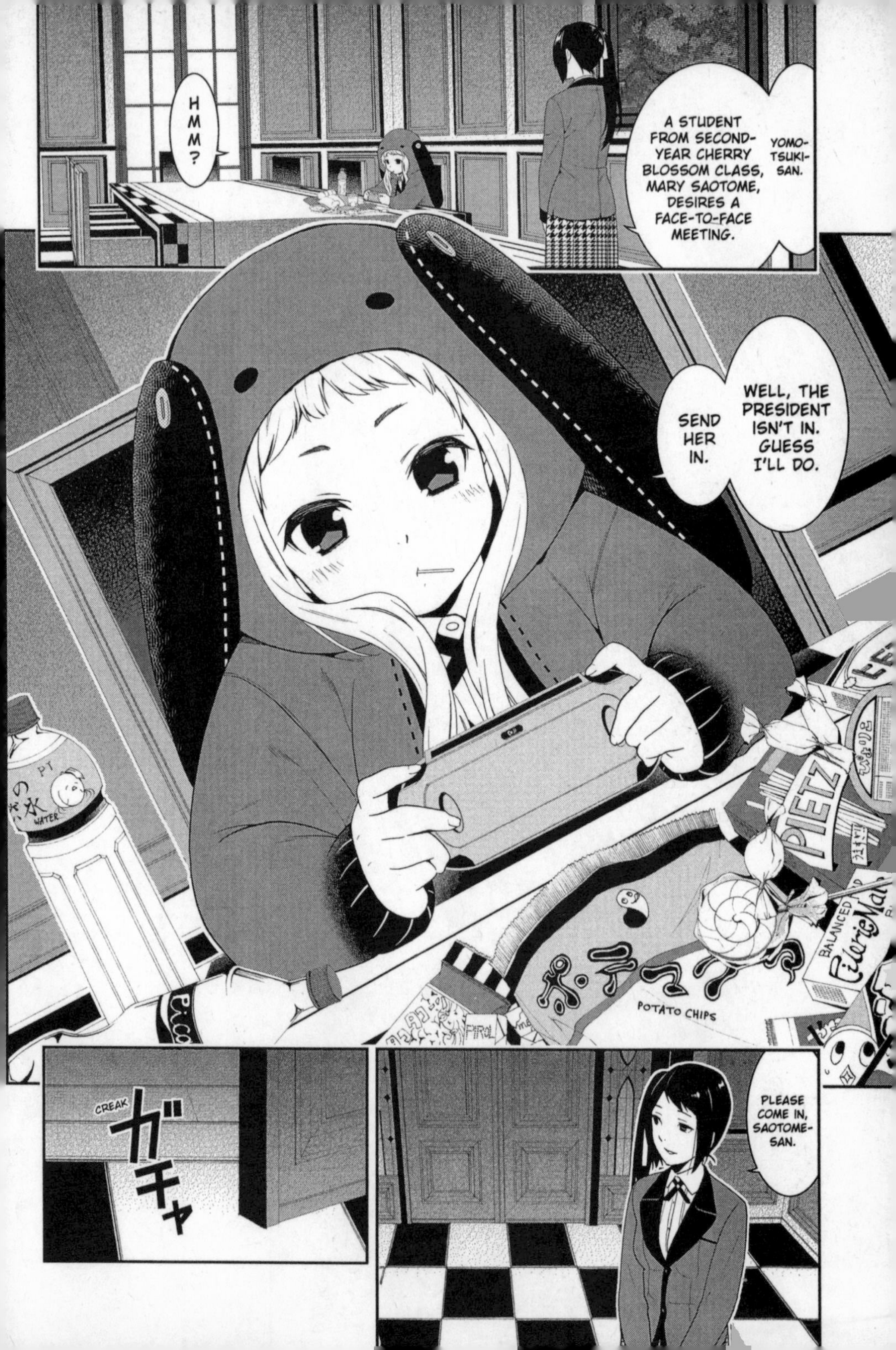
YOMO-TSUKI-SAN.
A STUDENT FROM SECOND-YEAR CHERRY BLOSSOM CLASS, MARY SAOTOME, DESIRES A FACE-TO-FACE MEETING.
HMM?
WELL, THE PRESIDENT ISN'T IN. GUESS I'LL DO.
SEND HER IN.
PIETZ
WATER
BALANCED
POTATO CHIPS
PLEASE COME IN, SAOTOME-SAN.
CREAK
ガチャ

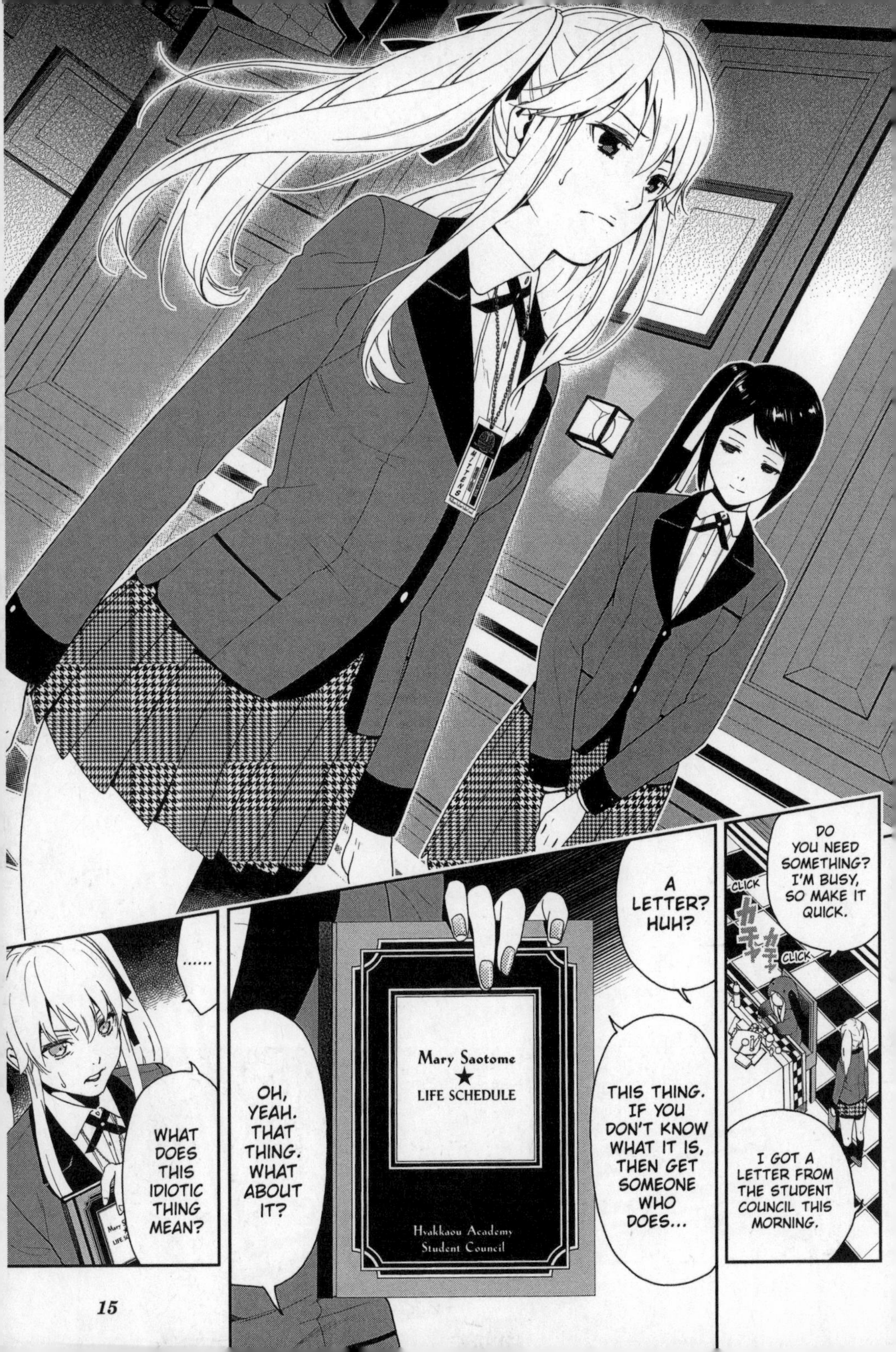
DO YOU NEED SOMETHING? I'M BUSY, SO MAKE IT QUICK.
CLICK
CLICK
I GOT A LETTER FROM THE STUDENT COUNCIL THIS MORNING.
A LETTER? HUH?
THIS THING. IF YOU DON'T KNOW WHAT IT IS, THEN GET SOMEONE WHO DOES...
Mary Saotome
★
LIFE SCHEDULE
Hyakkaou Academy
Student Council
OH, YEAH. THAT THING. WHAT ABOUT IT?
......
WHAT DOES THIS IDIOTIC THING MEAN?

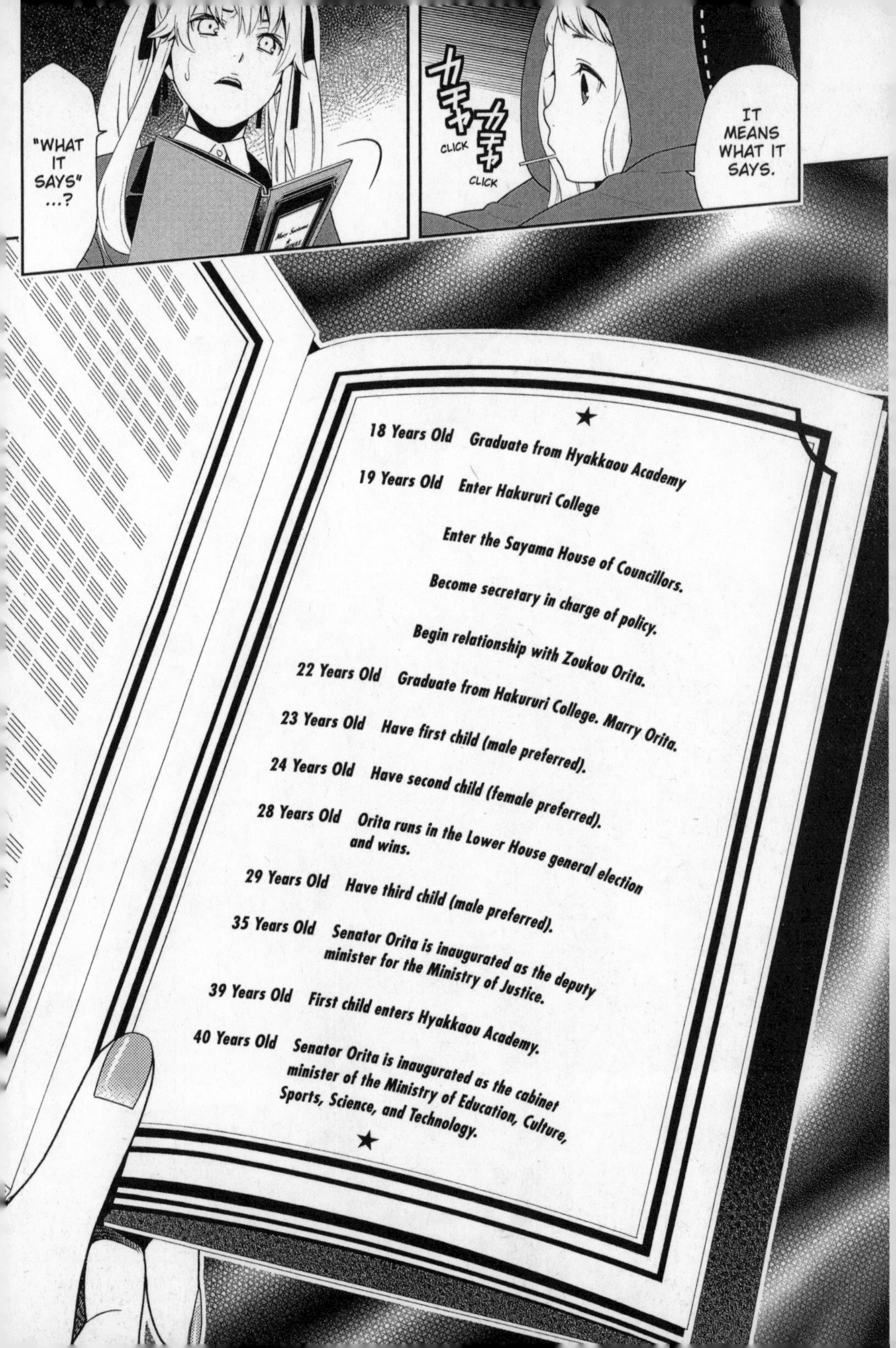

IT MEANS WHAT IT SAYS.
カチャカチャ
CLICK
CLICK
"WHAT IT SAYS" ...?
★
18 Years Old Graduate from Hyakkaou Academy
19 Years Old Enter Hakururi College
Enter the Sayama House of Councillors.
Become secretary in charge of policy.
Begin relationship with Zoukou Orita.
22 Years Old Graduate from Hakururi College. Marry Orita.
23 Years Old Have first child (male preferred).
24 Years Old Have second child (female preferred).
28 Years Old Orita runs in the Lower House general election and wins.
29 Years Old Have third child (male preferred).
35 Years Old Senator Orita is inaugurated as the deputy minister for the Ministry of Justice.
39 Years Old First child enters Hyakkaou Academy.
40 Years Old Senator Orita is inaugurated as the cabinet minister of the Ministry of Education, Culture, Sports, Science, and Technology.
★

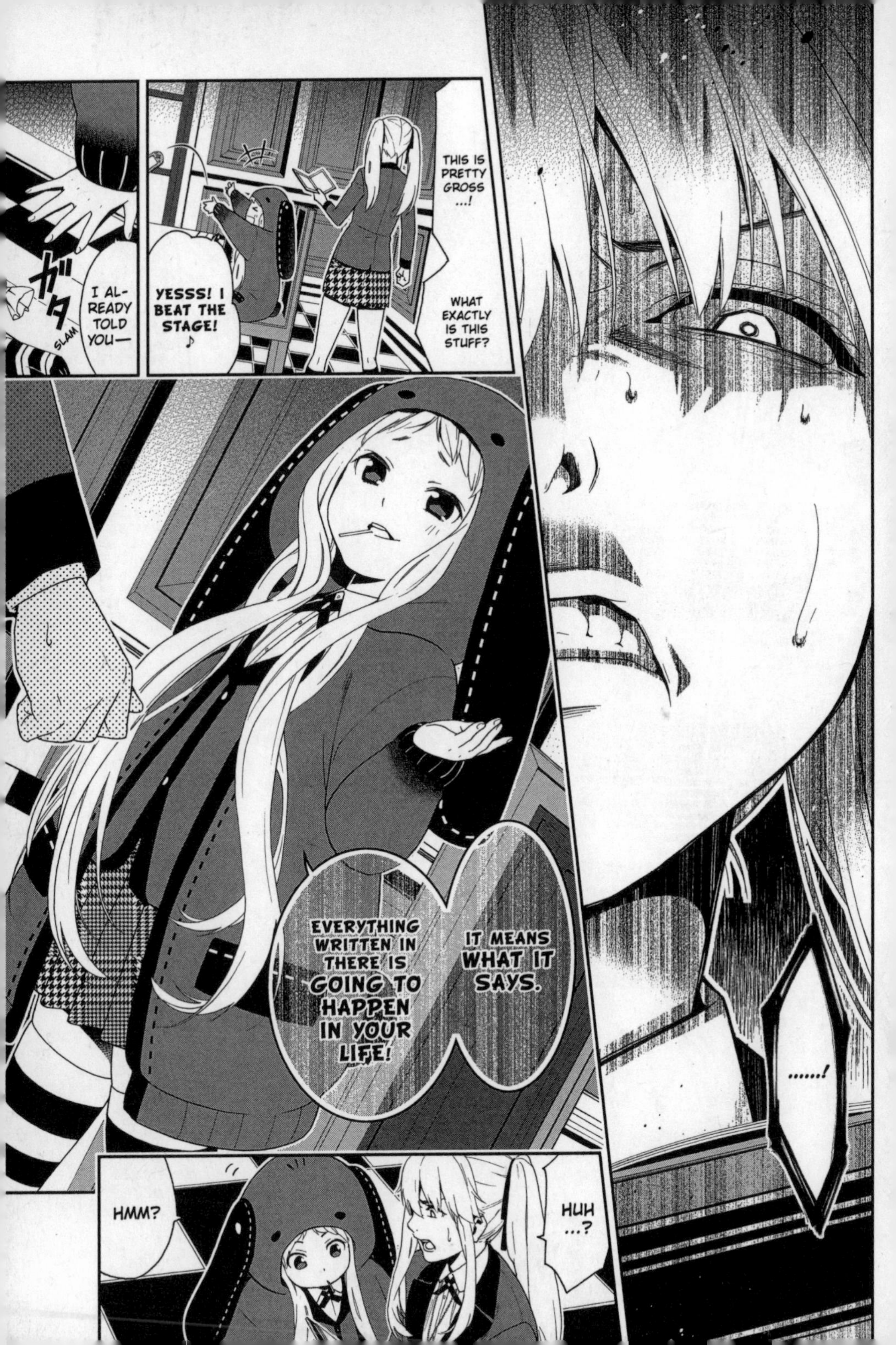
THIS IS PRETTY GROSS ...!
WHAT EXACTLY IS THIS STUFF?
YESSS! I BEAT THE STAGE! ♪
ガタ
SLAM
I AL-READY TOLD YOU—
IT MEANS WHAT IT SAYS.
EVERYTHING WRITTEN IN THERE IS GOING TO HAPPEN IN YOUR LIFE!
HUH ...?
HMM?
......!

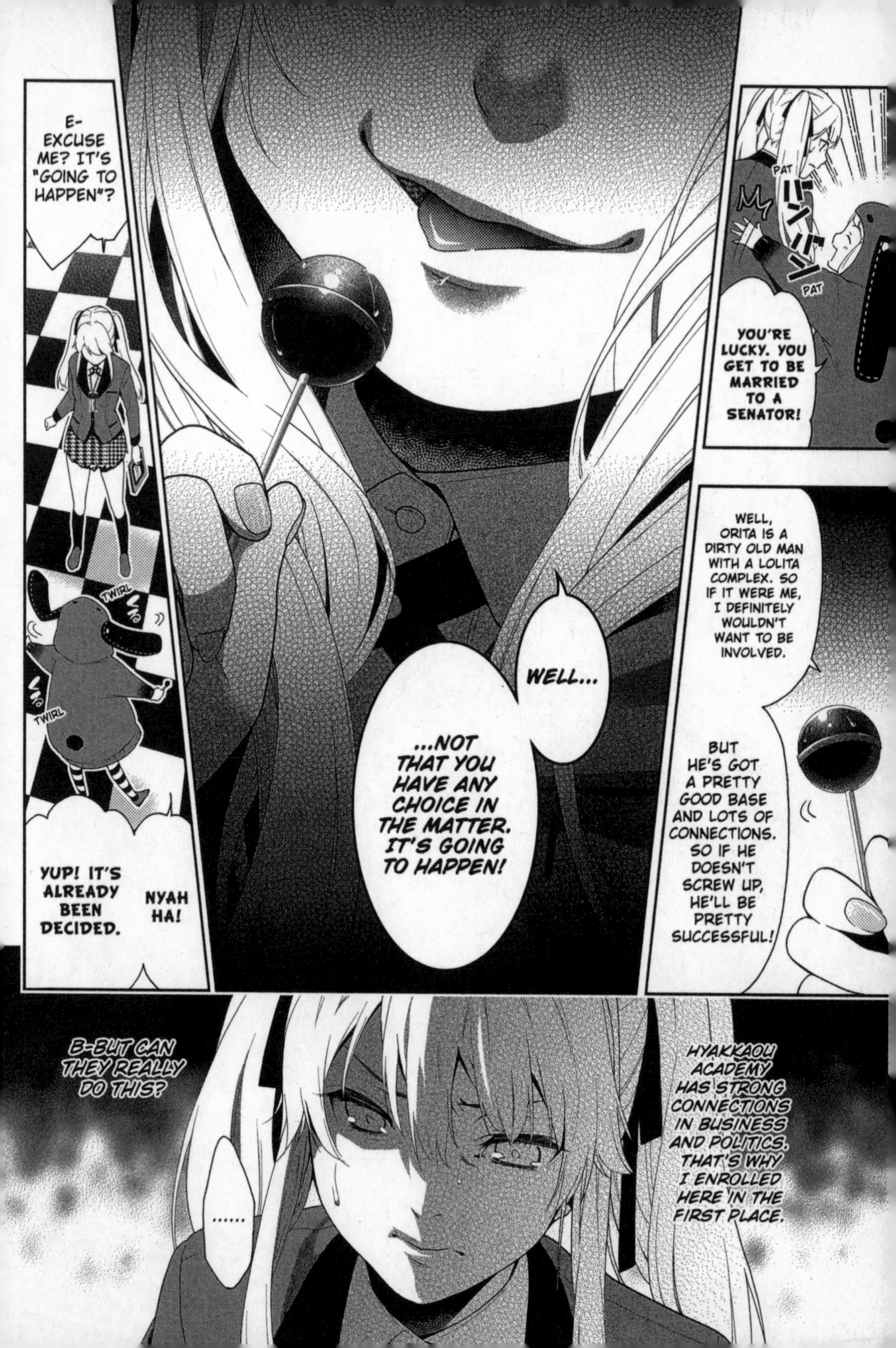
PAT
PAT
YOU'RE LUCKY. YOU GET TO BE MARRIED TO A SENATOR!
WELL, ORITA IS A DIRTY OLD MAN WITH A LOLITA COMPLEX. SO IF IT WERE ME, I DEFINITELY WOULDN'T WANT TO BE INVOLVED.
BUT HE'S GOT A PRETTY GOOD BASE AND LOTS OF CONNECTIONS. SO IF HE DOESN'T SCREW UP, HE'LL BE PRETTY SUCCESSFUL!
WELL...
...NOT THAT YOU HAVE ANY CHOICE IN THE MATTER. IT'S GOING TO HAPPEN!
E-EXCUSE ME? IT'S "GOING TO HAPPEN"?
TWIRL
TWIRL
YUP! IT'S ALREADY BEEN DECIDED.
NYAH HA!
HYAKKAOU ACADEMY HAS STRONG CONNECTIONS IN BUSINESS AND POLITICS. THAT'S WHY I ENROLLED HERE IN THE FIRST PLACE.
B-BUT CAN THEY REALLY DO THIS?
......

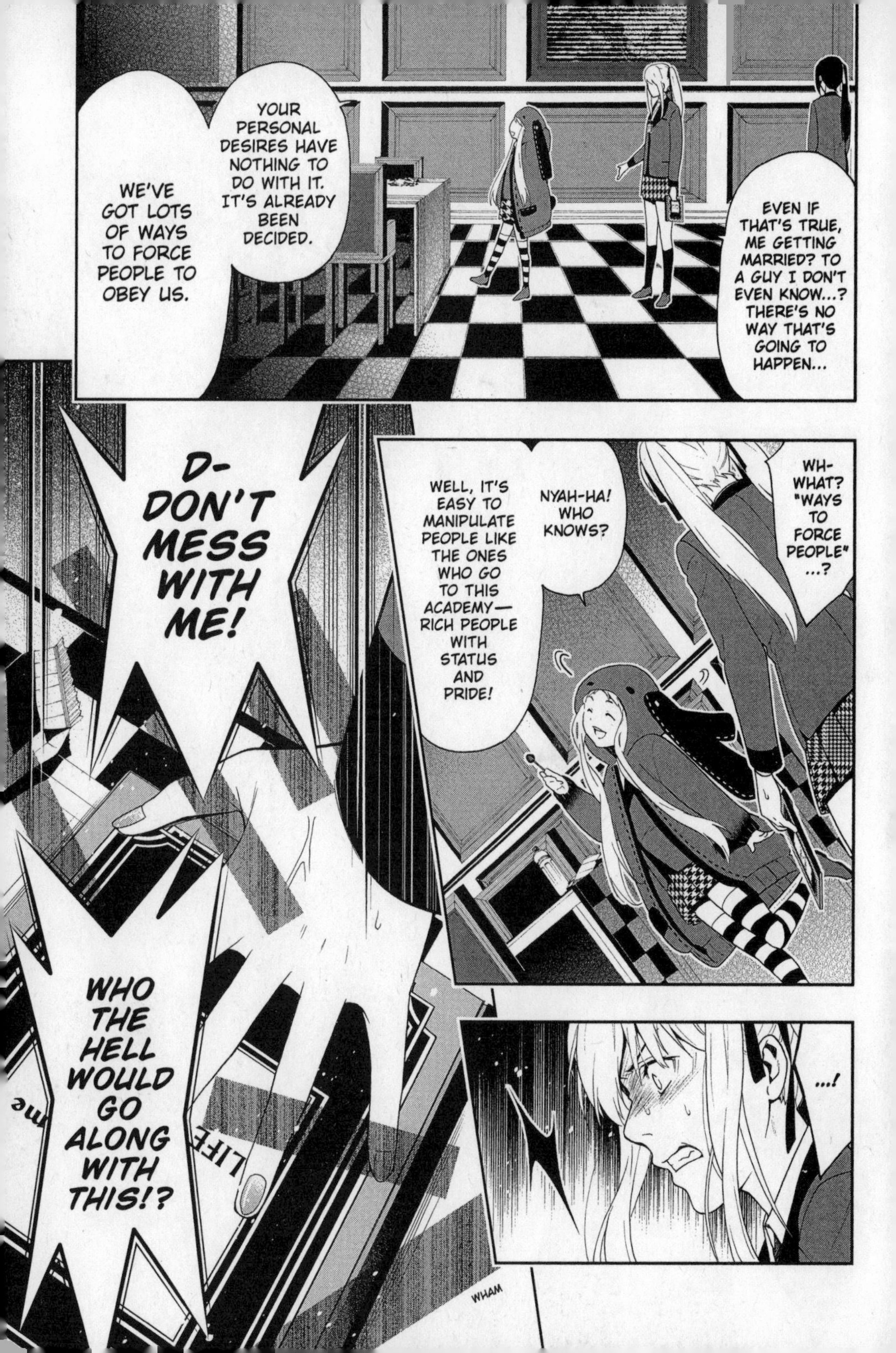

EVEN IF THAT'S TRUE, ME GETTING MARRIED? TO A GUY I DON'T EVEN KNOW...? THERE'S NO WAY THAT'S GOING TO HAPPEN...
YOUR PERSONAL DESIRES HAVE NOTHING TO DO WITH IT. IT'S ALREADY BEEN DECIDED.
WE'VE GOT LOTS OF WAYS TO FORCE PEOPLE TO OBEY US.
WH-WHAT? "WAYS TO FORCE PEOPLE" ...?
NYAH-HA! WHO KNOWS?
WELL, IT'S EASY TO MANIPULATE PEOPLE LIKE THE ONES WHO GO TO THIS ACADEMY— RICH PEOPLE WITH STATUS AND PRIDE!
...!
D-DON'T MESS WITH ME!
WHO THE HELL WOULD GO ALONG WITH THIS!?
WHAM

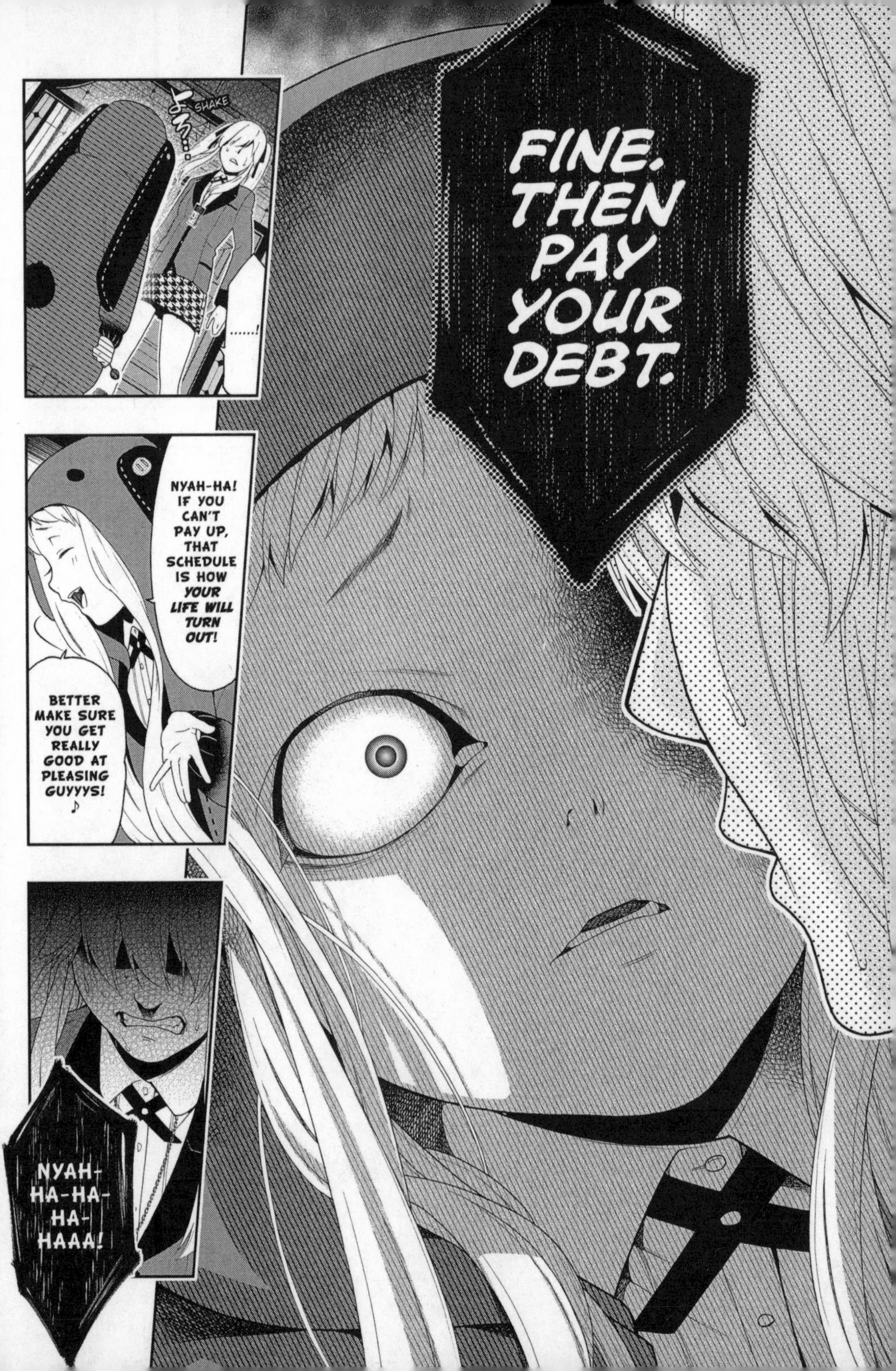
FINE. THEN PAY YOUR DEBT.
SHAKE
......!
NYAH-HA! IF YOU CAN'T PAY UP, THAT SCHEDULE IS HOW *YOUR LIFE WILL TURN OUT!*
BETTER MAKE SURE YOU GET REALLY GOOD AT PLEASING GUYYYS! ♪
NYAH-HA-HA-HA-HAAA!

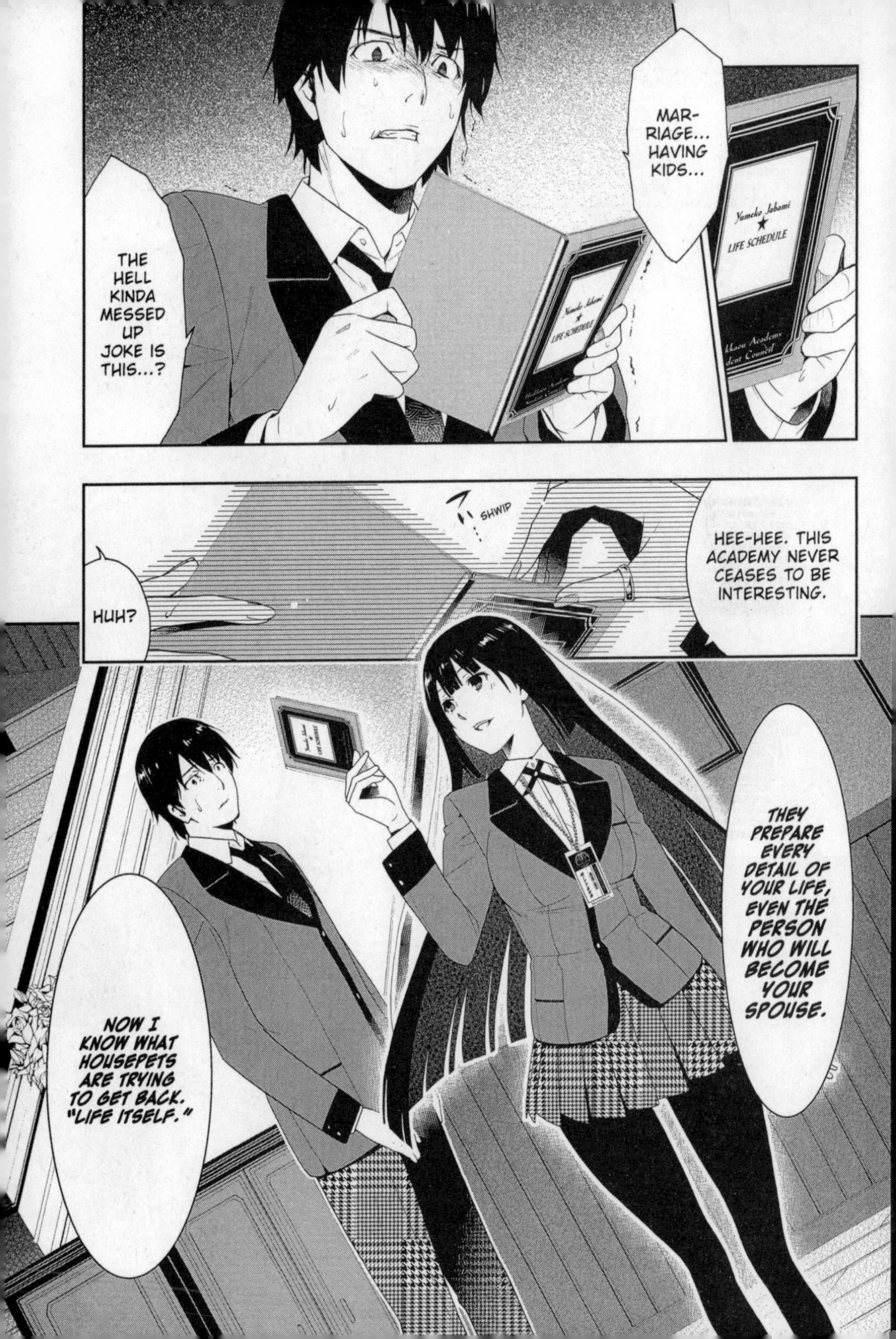
MAR-RIAGE... HAVING KIDS...
Yumeko Jabami ★ LIFE SCHEDULE
THE HELL KINDA MESSED UP JOKE IS THIS...?
HEE-HEE. THIS ACADEMY NEVER CEASES TO BE INTERESTING.
SHWIP
HUH?
THEY PREPARE EVERY DETAIL OF YOUR LIFE, EVEN THE PERSON WHO WILL BECOME YOUR SPOUSE.
NOW I KNOW WHAT HOUSEPETS ARE TRYING TO GET BACK. "LIFE ITSELF."

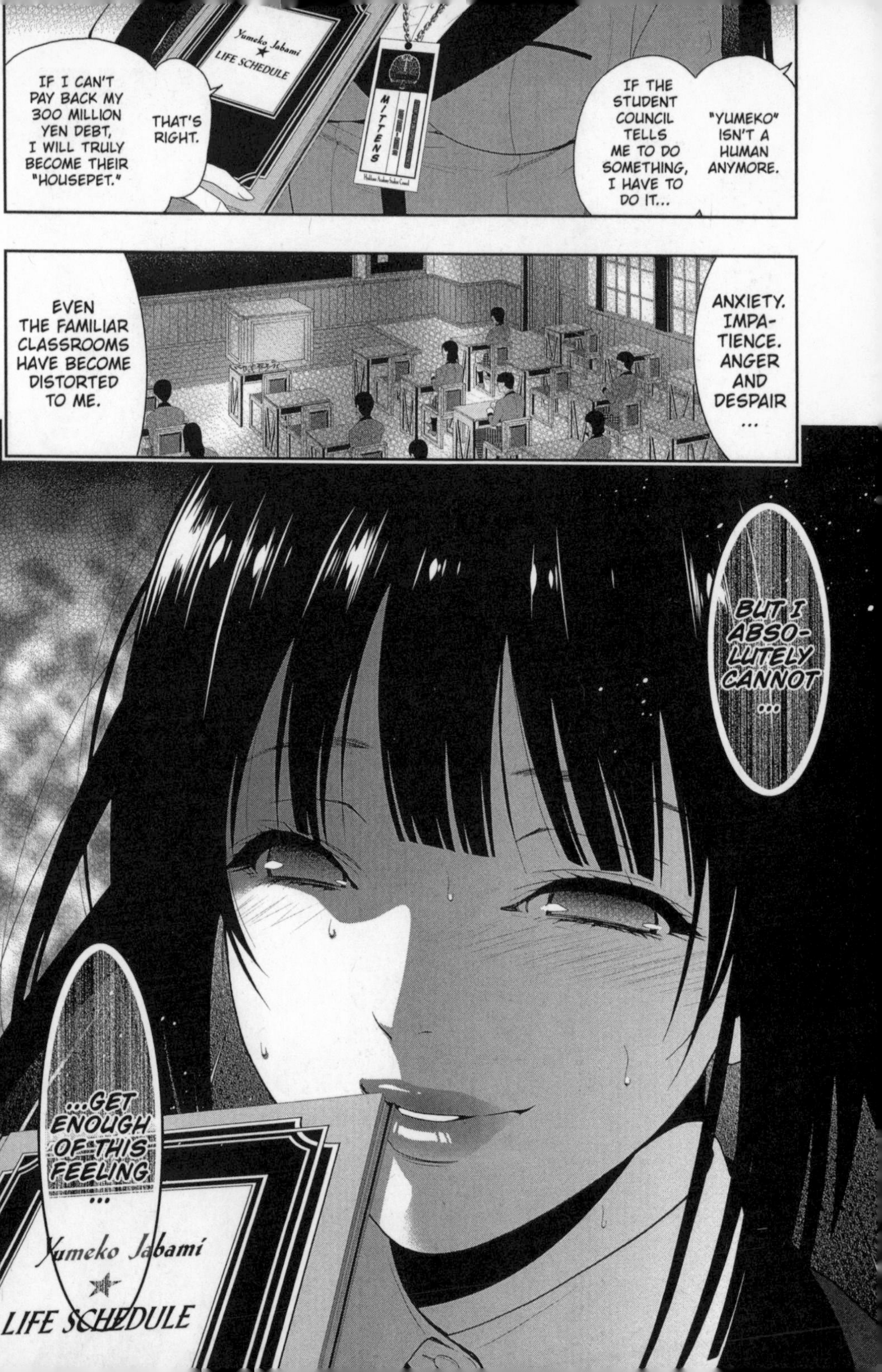
"YUMEKO" ISN'T A HUMAN ANYMORE.
IF THE STUDENT COUNCIL TELLS ME TO DO SOMETHING, I HAVE TO DO IT...
MITTENS
THAT'S RIGHT.
Yumeko Jabami ★ LIFE SCHEDULE
IF I CAN'T PAY BACK MY 300 MILLION YEN DEBT, I WILL TRULY BECOME THEIR "HOUSEPET."
ANXIETY. IMPATIENCE. ANGER AND DESPAIR ...
EVEN THE FAMILIAR CLASSROOMS HAVE BECOME DISTORTED TO ME.
BUT I ABSOLUTELY CANNOT ...
...GET ENOUGH OF THIS FEELING ...
Yumeko Jabami
LIFE SCHEDULE

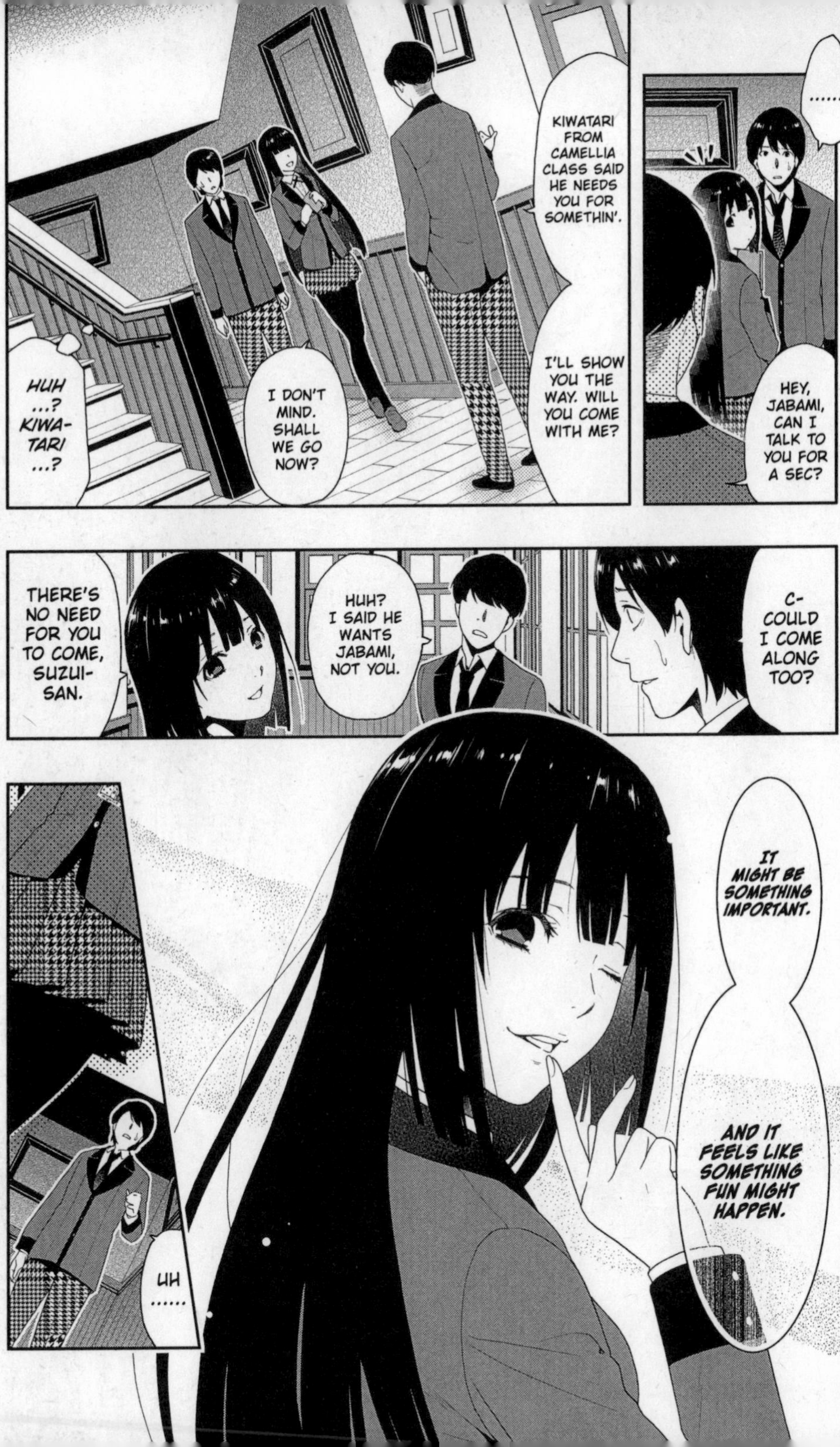
......
HEY, JABAMI, CAN I TALK TO YOU FOR A SEC?
KIWATARI FROM CAMELLIA CLASS SAID HE NEEDS YOU FOR SOMETHIN'.
I'LL SHOW YOU THE WAY. WILL YOU COME WITH ME?
I DON'T MIND. SHALL WE GO NOW?
HUH ...? KIWA-TARI ...?
C-COULD I COME ALONG TOO?
HUH? I SAID HE WANTS JABAMI, NOT YOU.
THERE'S NO NEED FOR YOU TO COME, SUZUI-SAN.
IT MIGHT BE SOMETHING IMPORTANT.
AND IT FEELS LIKE SOMETHING FUN MIGHT HAPPEN.
UH ......

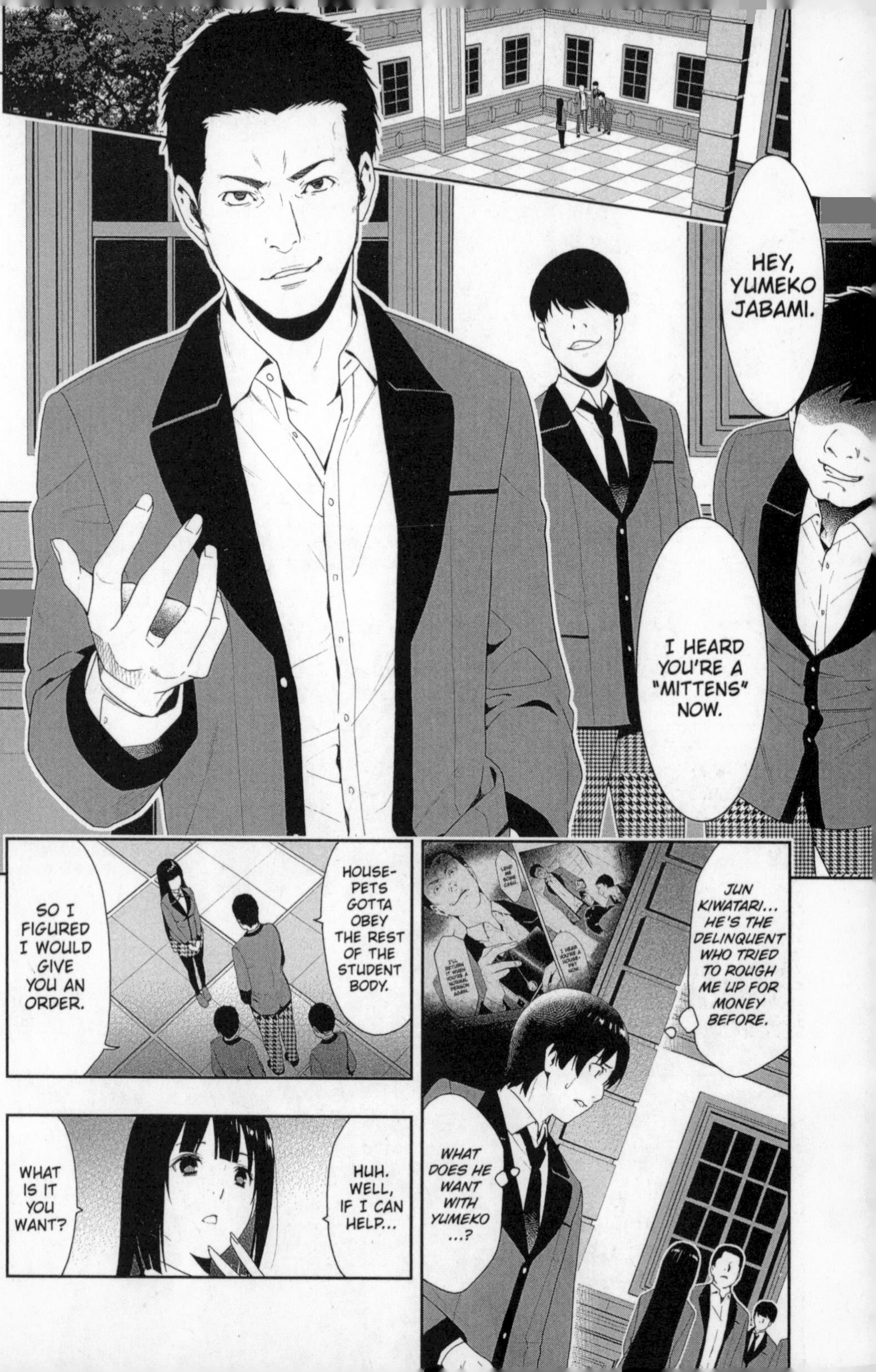
HEY, YUMEKO JABAMI.
I HEARD YOU'RE A "MITTENS" NOW.
JUN KIWATARI... HE'S THE DELINQUENT WHO TRIED TO ROUGH ME UP FOR MONEY BEFORE.
WHAT DOES HE WANT WITH YUMEKO ...?
HOUSE-PETS GOTTA OBEY THE REST OF THE STUDENT BODY.
SO I FIGURED I WOULD GIVE YOU AN ORDER.
HUH. WELL, IF I CAN HELP...
WHAT IS IT YOU WANT?

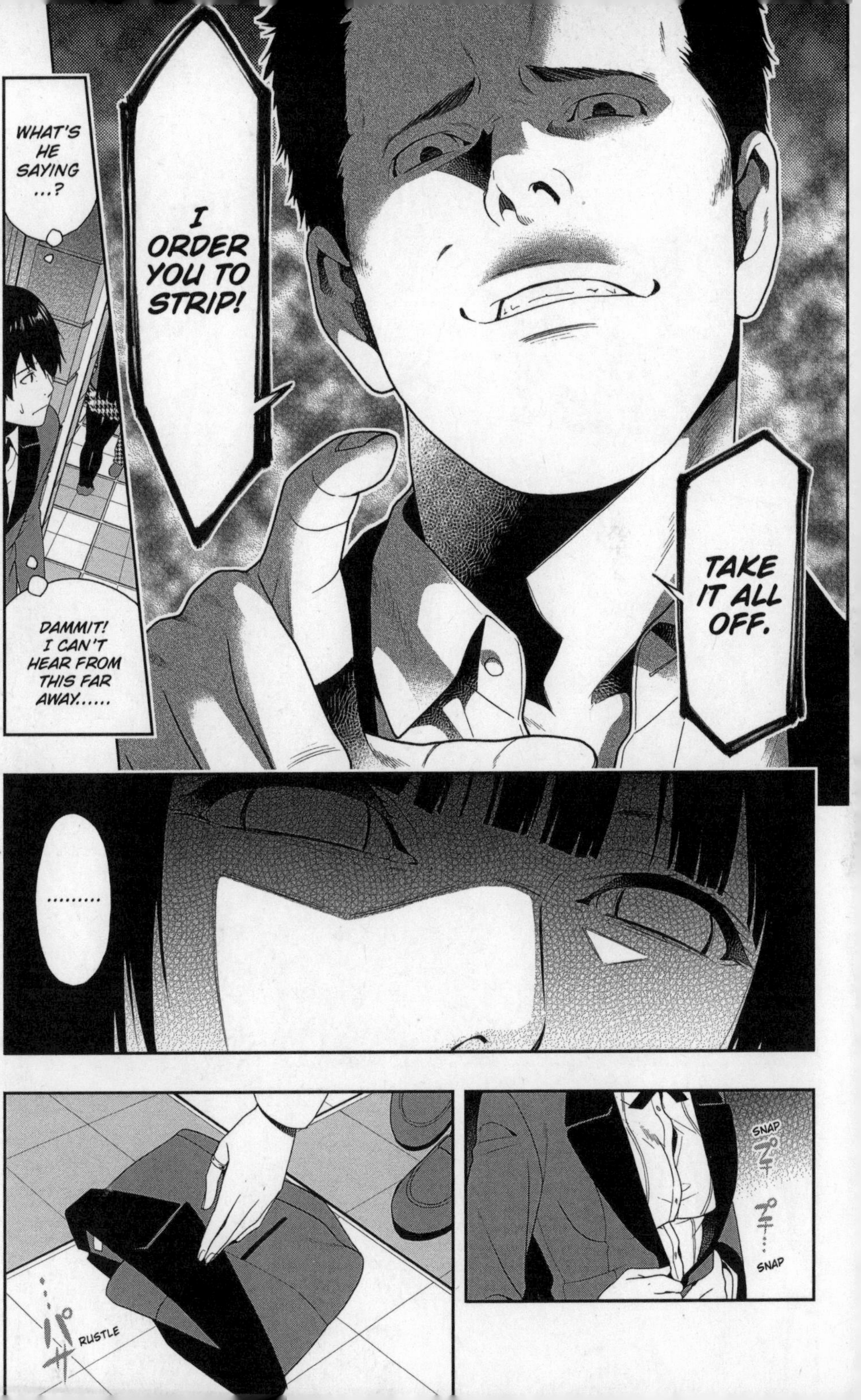
I ORDER YOU TO STRIP!
TAKE IT ALL OFF.
WHAT'S HE SAYING ...?
DAMMIT! I CAN'T HEAR FROM THIS FAR AWAY......
....
SNAP
SNAP
RUSTLE

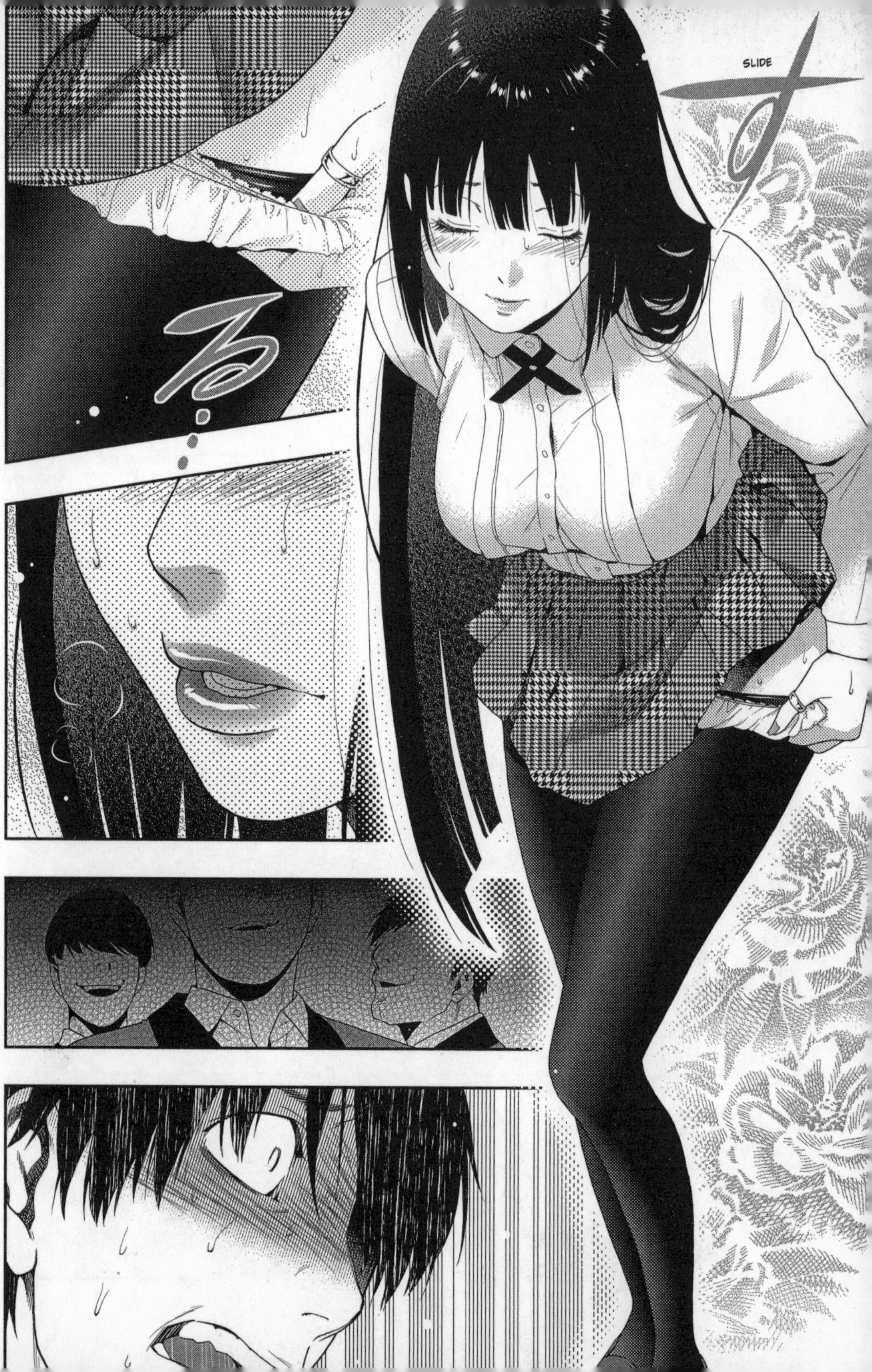
SLIDE

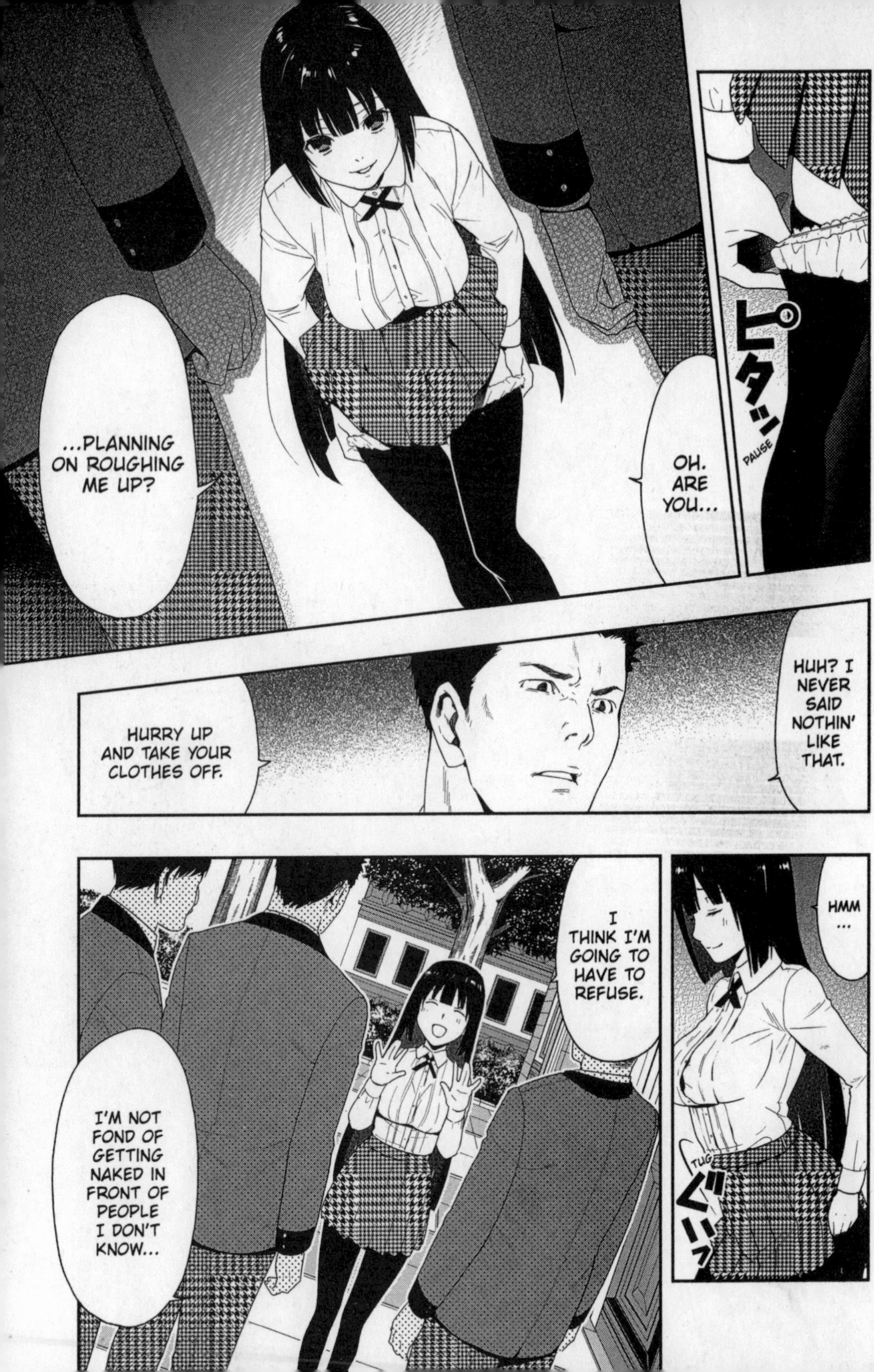
ピタッ
PAUSE
OH. ARE YOU...
...PLANNING ON ROUGHING ME UP?
HUH? I NEVER SAID NOTHIN' LIKE THAT.
HURRY UP AND TAKE YOUR CLOTHES OFF.
HMM ...
TUG
ぐいっ
I THINK I'M GOING TO HAVE TO REFUSE.
I'M NOT FOND OF GETTING NAKED IN FRONT OF PEOPLE I DON'T KNOW...

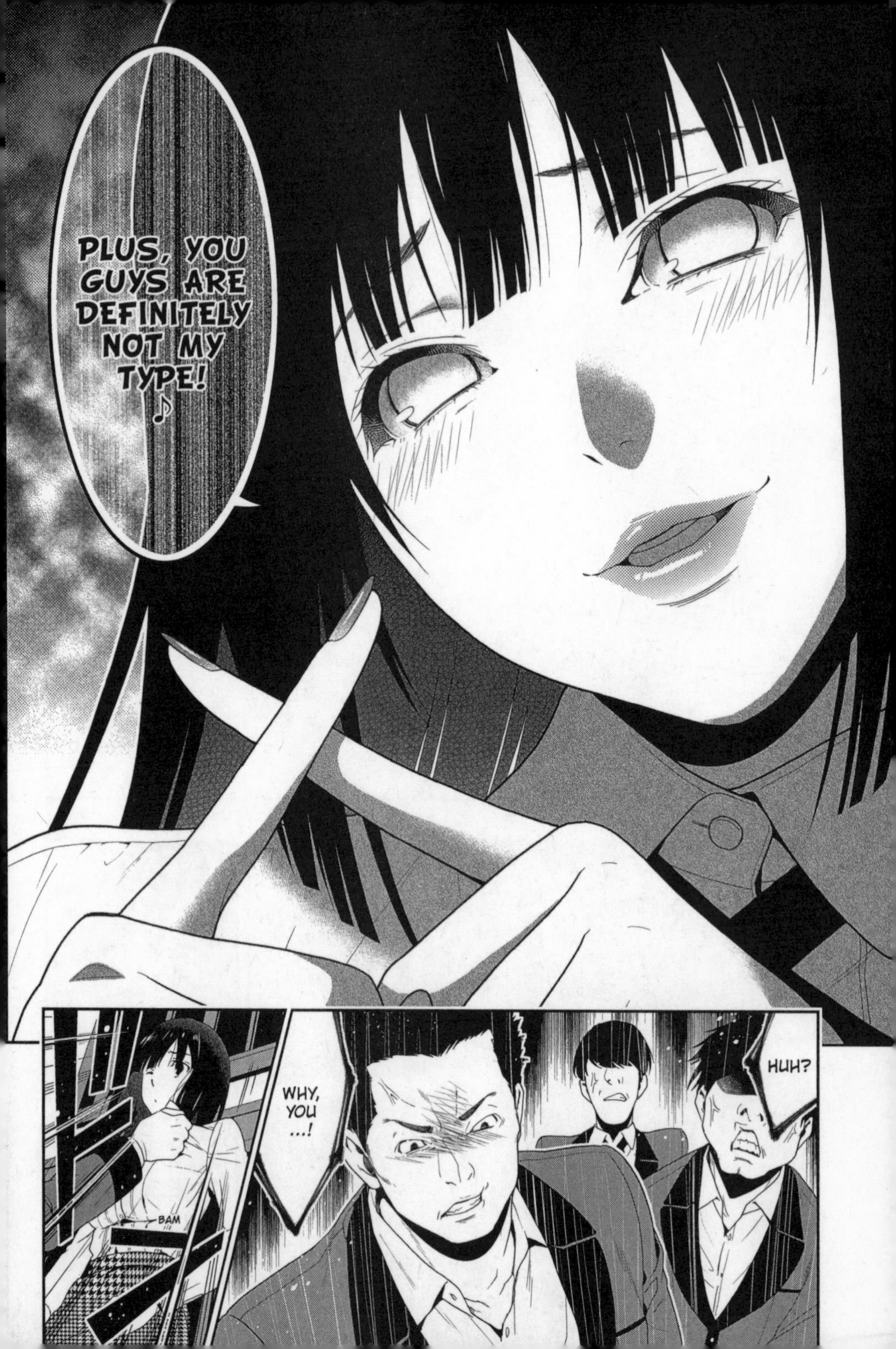
PLUS, YOU GUYS ARE DEFINITELY NOT MY TYPE! ♪
HUH?
WHY, YOU ...!
BAM

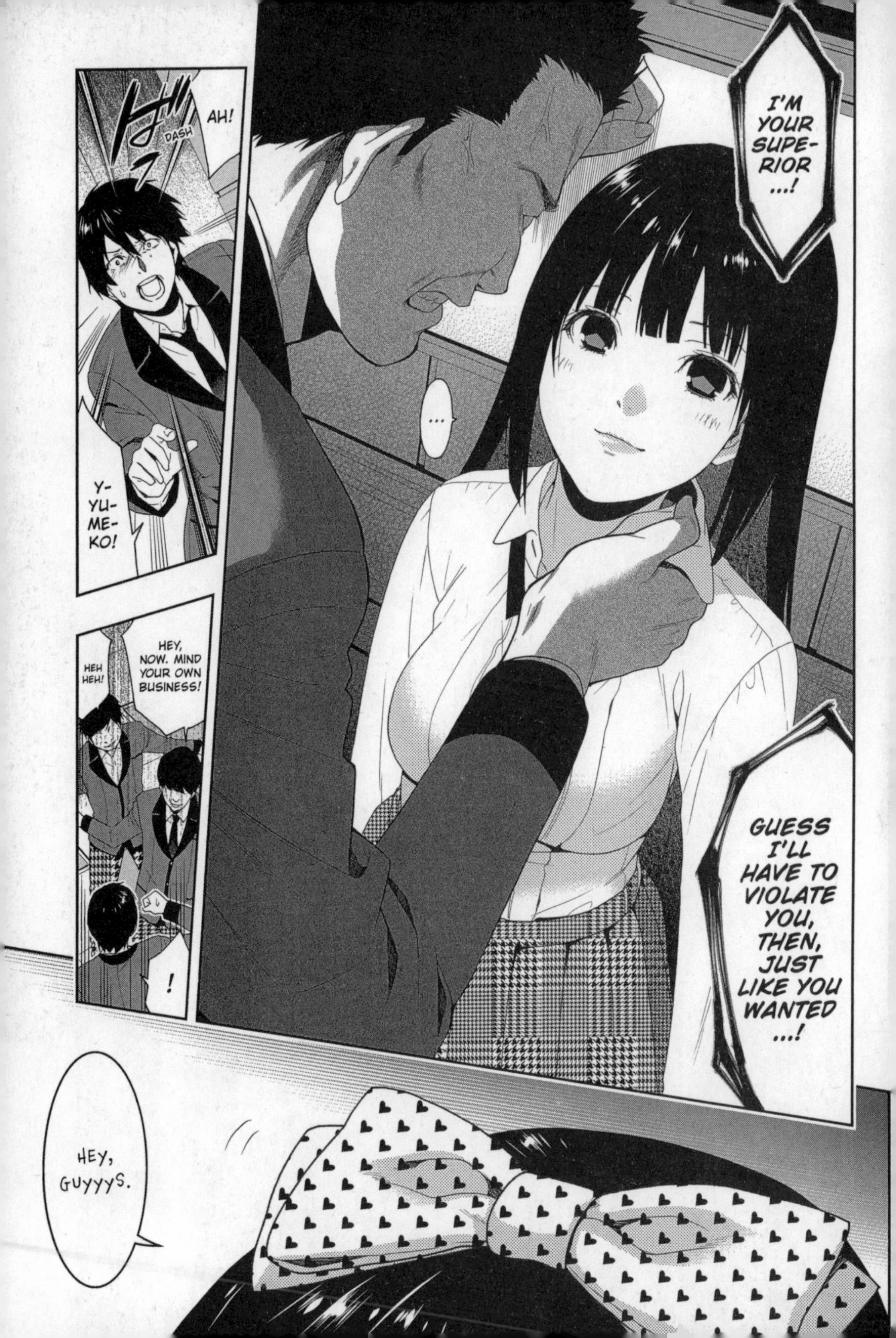

I'M YOUR SUPERIOR ...!
...
GUESS I'LL HAVE TO VIOLATE YOU, THEN, JUST LIKE YOU WANTED ...!
DASH
AH!
Y-YUMEKO!
HEY, NOW. MIND YOUR OWN BUSINESS!
HEH HEH!
!
HEY, GUYYYS.

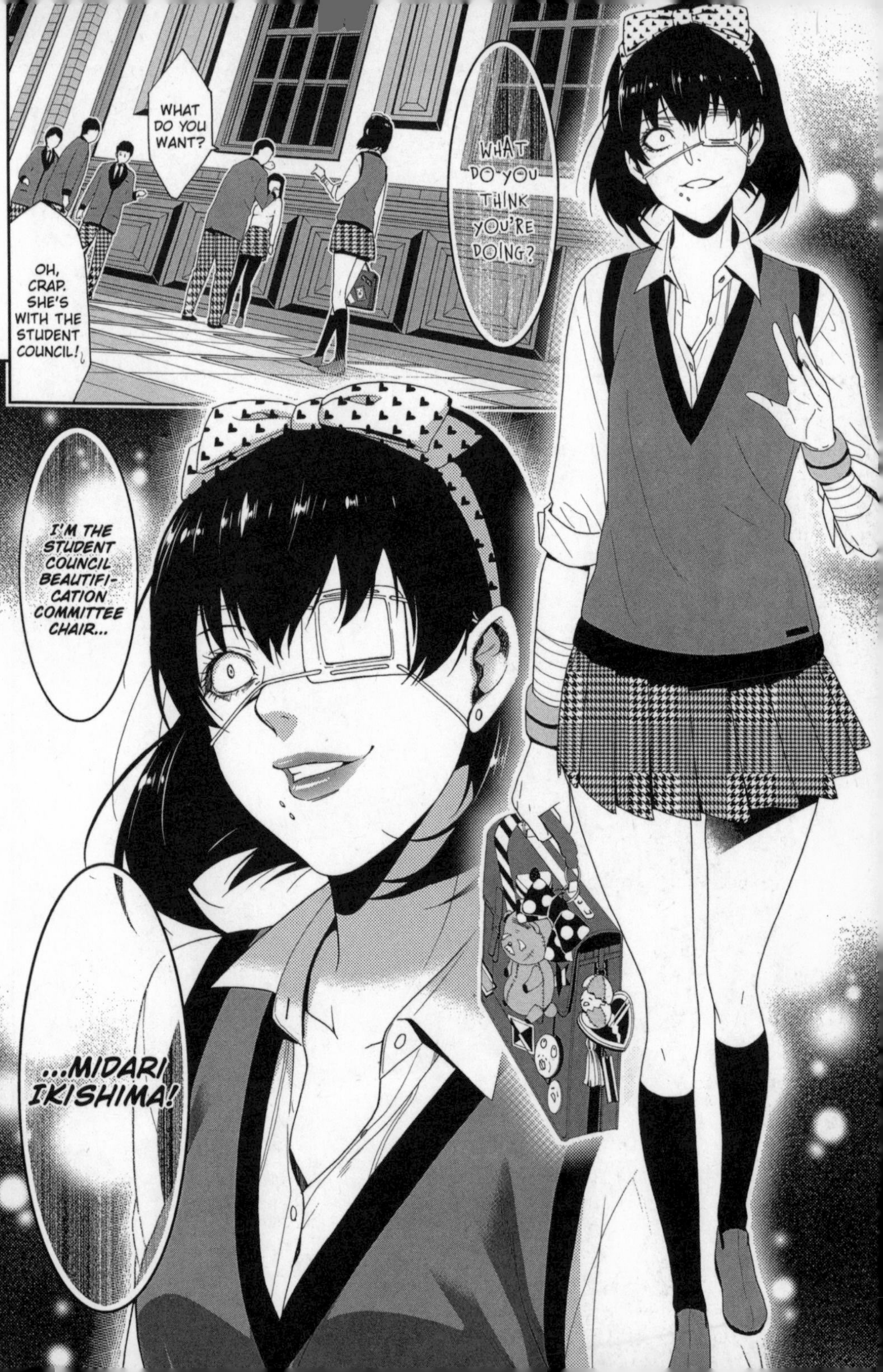
WHAT DO YOU THINK YOU'RE DOING?
WHAT DO YOU WANT?
OH, CRAP. SHE'S WITH THE STUDENT COUNCIL!
I'M THE STUDENT COUNCIL BEAUTIFICATION COMMITTEE CHAIR...
...MIDARI IKISHIMA!

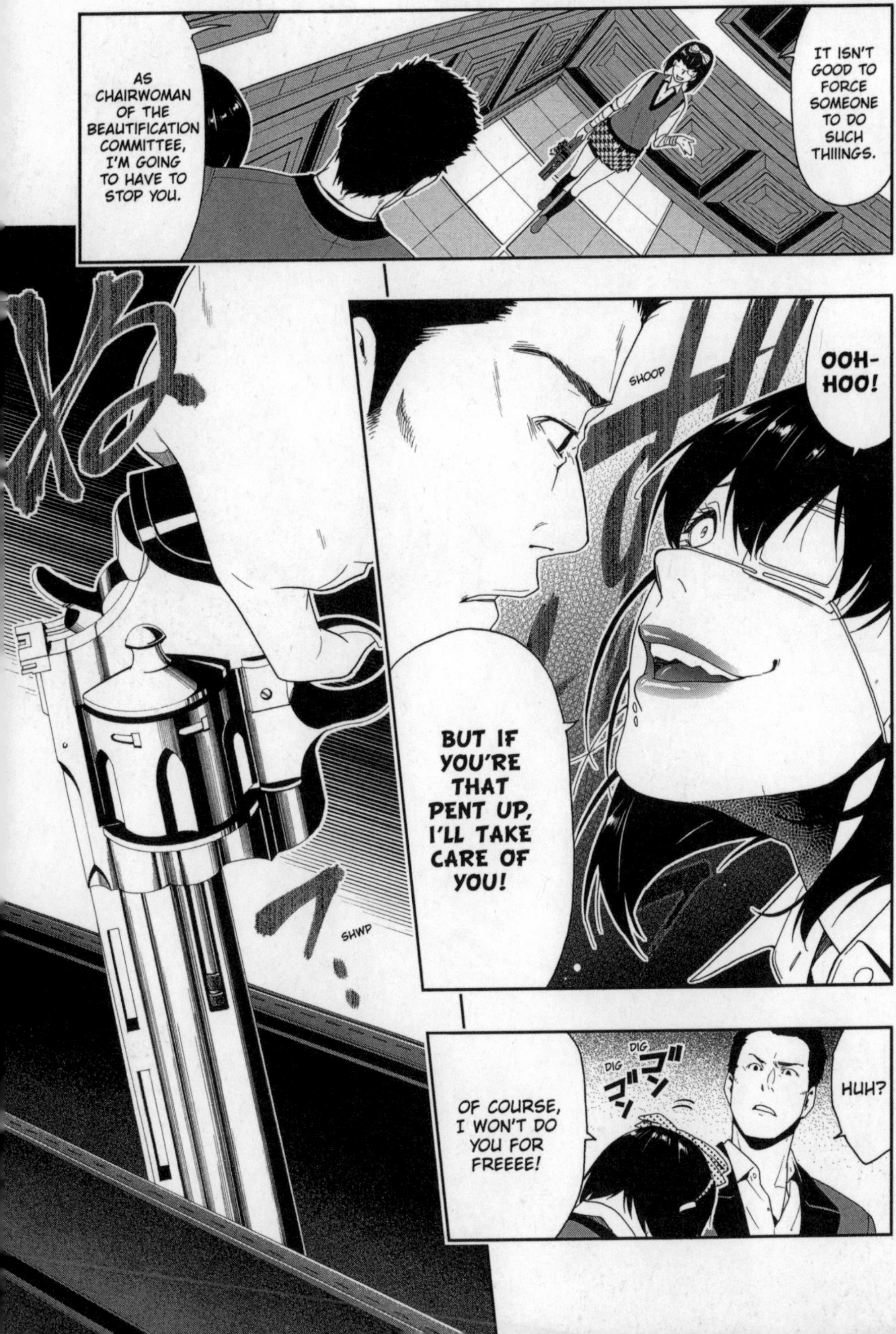
IT ISN'T GOOD TO FORCE SOMEONE TO DO SUCH THIIINGS.
AS CHAIRWOMAN OF THE BEAUTIFICATION COMMITTEE, I'M GOING TO HAVE TO STOP YOU.
OOH-HOO!
SHOOP
BUT IF YOU'RE THAT PENT UP, I'LL TAKE CARE OF YOU!
HUH?
DIG DIG
OF COURSE, I WON'T DO YOU FOR FREEEE!
SHWP

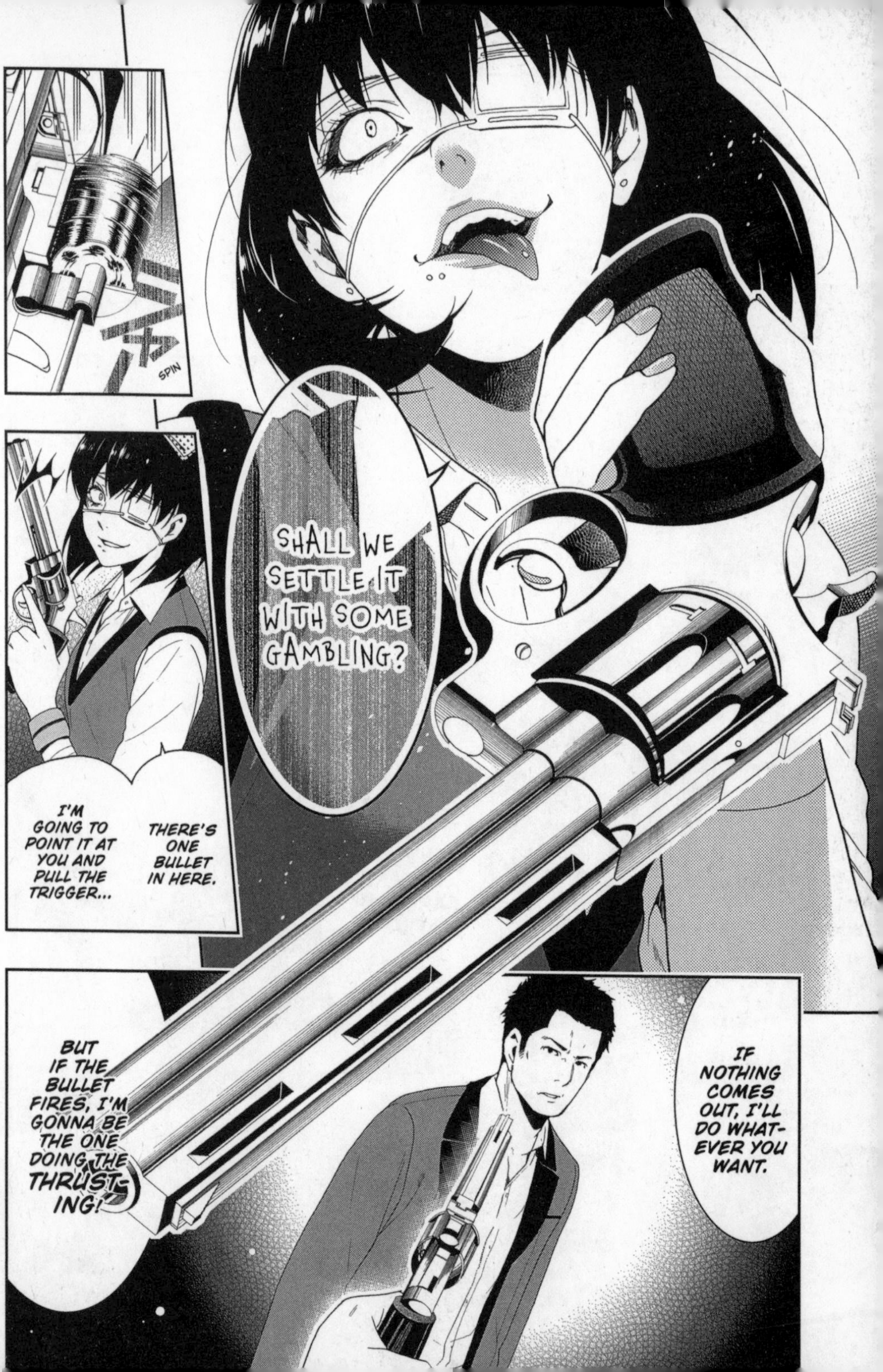
SHALL WE SETTLE IT WITH SOME GAMBLING?
SPIN
THERE'S ONE BULLET IN HERE.
I'M GOING TO POINT IT AT YOU AND PULL THE TRIGGER...
IF NOTHING COMES OUT, I'LL DO WHATEVER YOU WANT.
BUT IF THE BULLET FIRES, I'M GONNA BE THE ONE DOING THE THRUSTING!

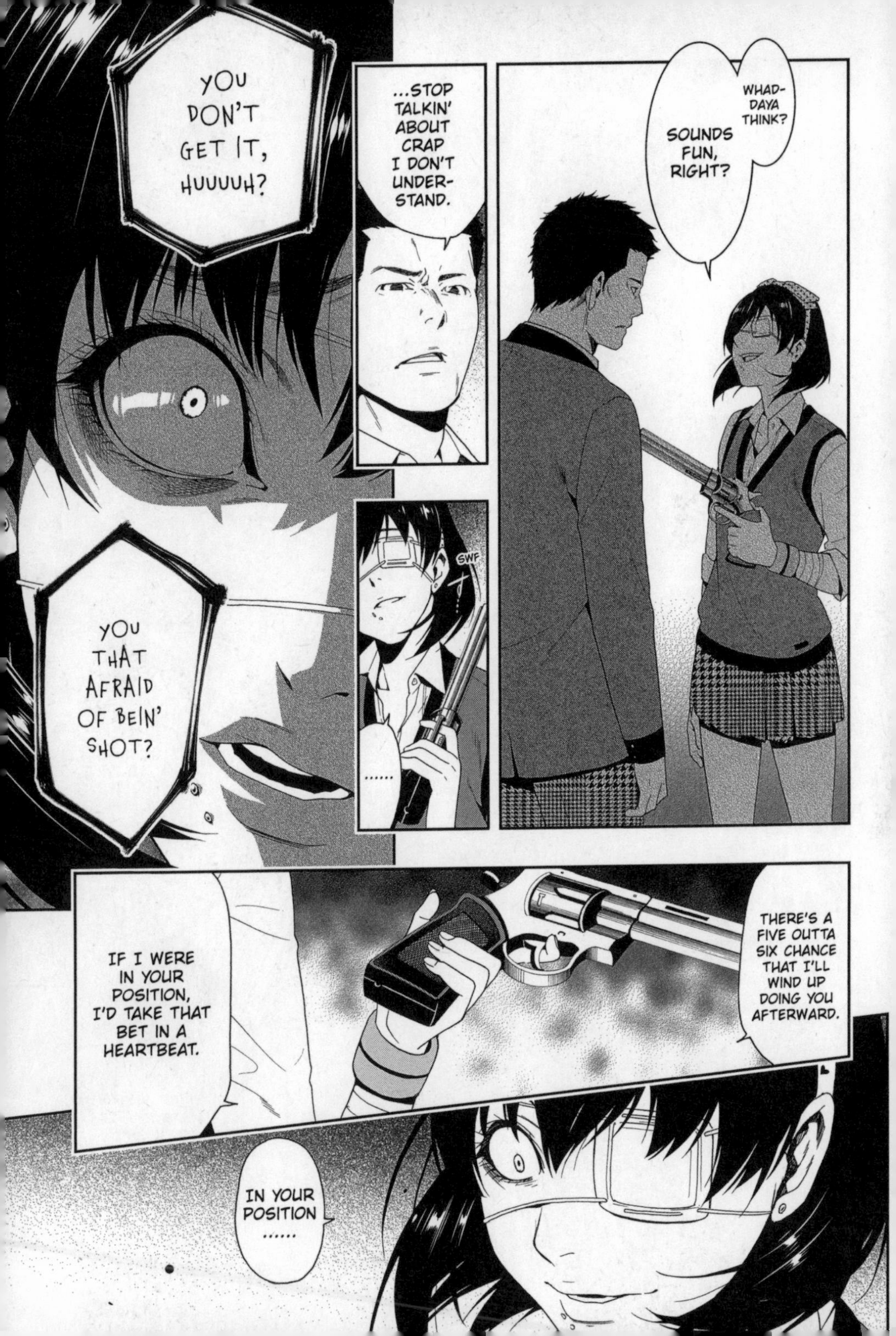
WHAD-DAYA THINK?
SOUNDS FUN, RIGHT?
...STOP TALKIN' ABOUT CRAP I DON'T UNDER-STAND.
SWF
......
YOU DON'T GET IT, HUUUUH?
YOU THAT AFRAID OF BEIN' SHOT?
THERE'S A FIVE OUTTA SIX CHANCE THAT I'LL WIND UP DOING YOU AFTERWARD.
IF I WERE IN YOUR POSITION, I'D TAKE THAT BET IN A HEARTBEAT.
IN YOUR POSITION ......

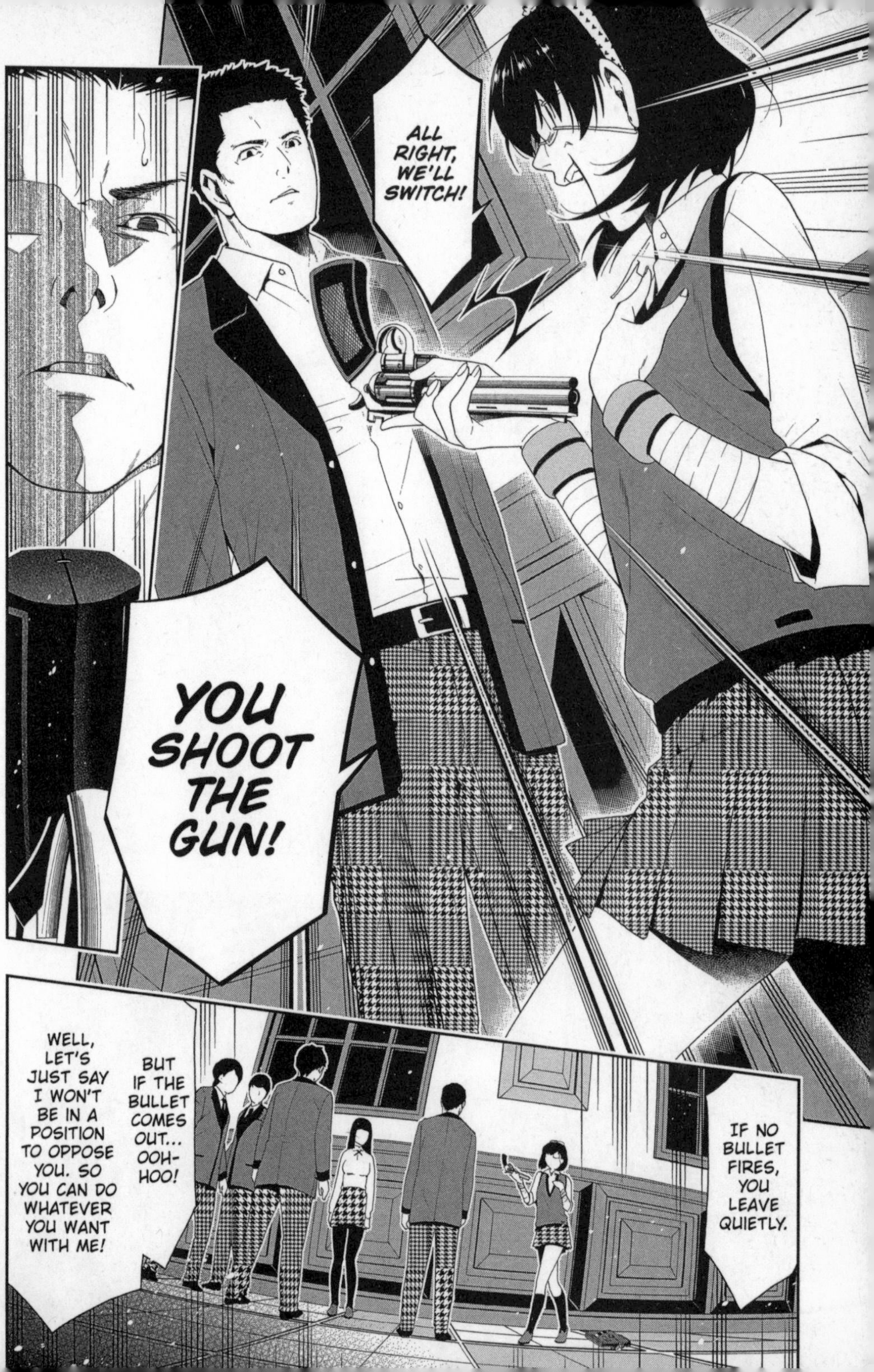
ALL RIGHT, WE'LL SWITCH!
YOU SHOOT THE GUN!
IF NO BULLET FIRES, YOU LEAVE QUIETLY.
BUT IF THE BULLET COMES OUT... OOH-HOO!
WELL, LET'S JUST SAY I WON'T BE IN A POSITION TO OPPOSE YOU. SO YOU CAN DO WHATEVER YOU WANT WITH ME!

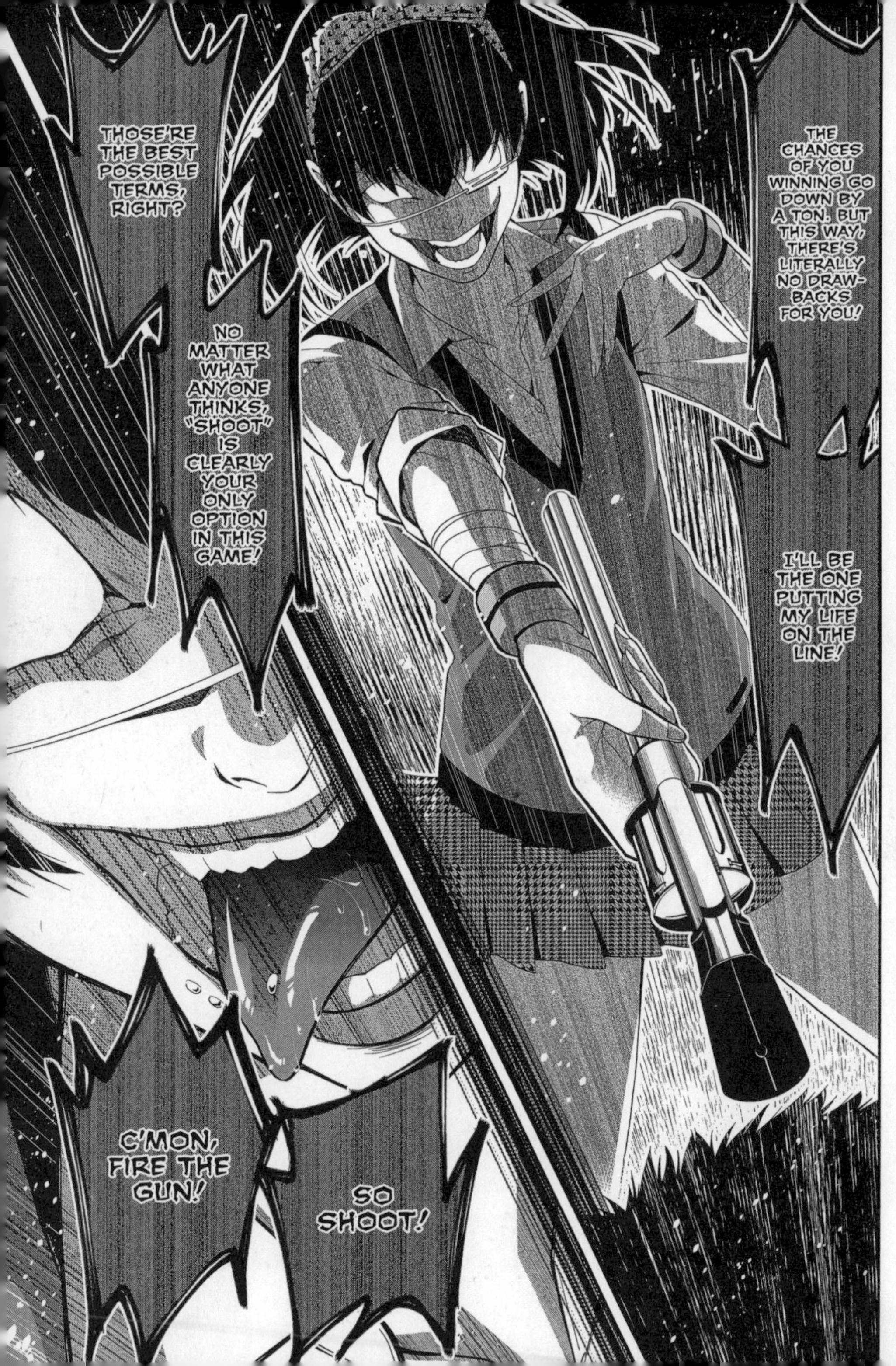
THE CHANCES OF YOU WINNING GO DOWN BY A TON. BUT THIS WAY, THERE'S LITERALLY NO DRAW-BACKS FOR YOU!
I'LL BE THE ONE PUTTING MY LIFE ON THE LINE!
THOSE'RE THE BEST POSSIBLE TERMS, RIGHT?
NO MATTER WHAT ANYONE THINKS, "SHOOT" IS CLEARLY YOUR ONLY OPTION IN THIS GAME!
SO SHOOT!
C'MON, FIRE THE GUN!

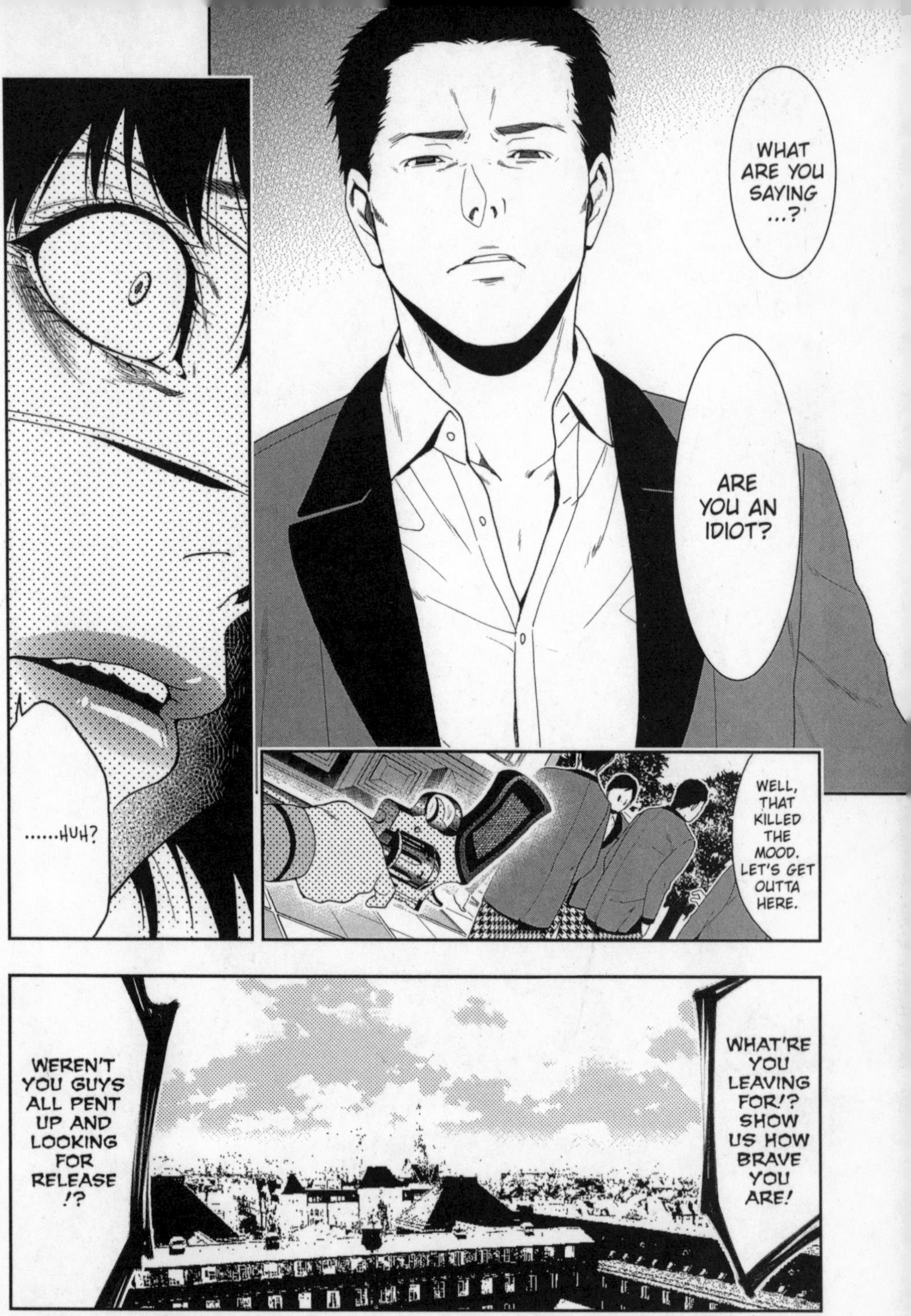
WHAT ARE YOU SAYING ...?
ARE YOU AN IDIOT?
WELL, THAT KILLED THE MOOD. LET'S GET OUTTA HERE.
......HUH?
WHAT'RE YOU LEAVING FOR!? SHOW US HOW BRAVE YOU ARE!
WEREN'T YOU GUYS ALL PENT UP AND LOOKING FOR RELEASE!?

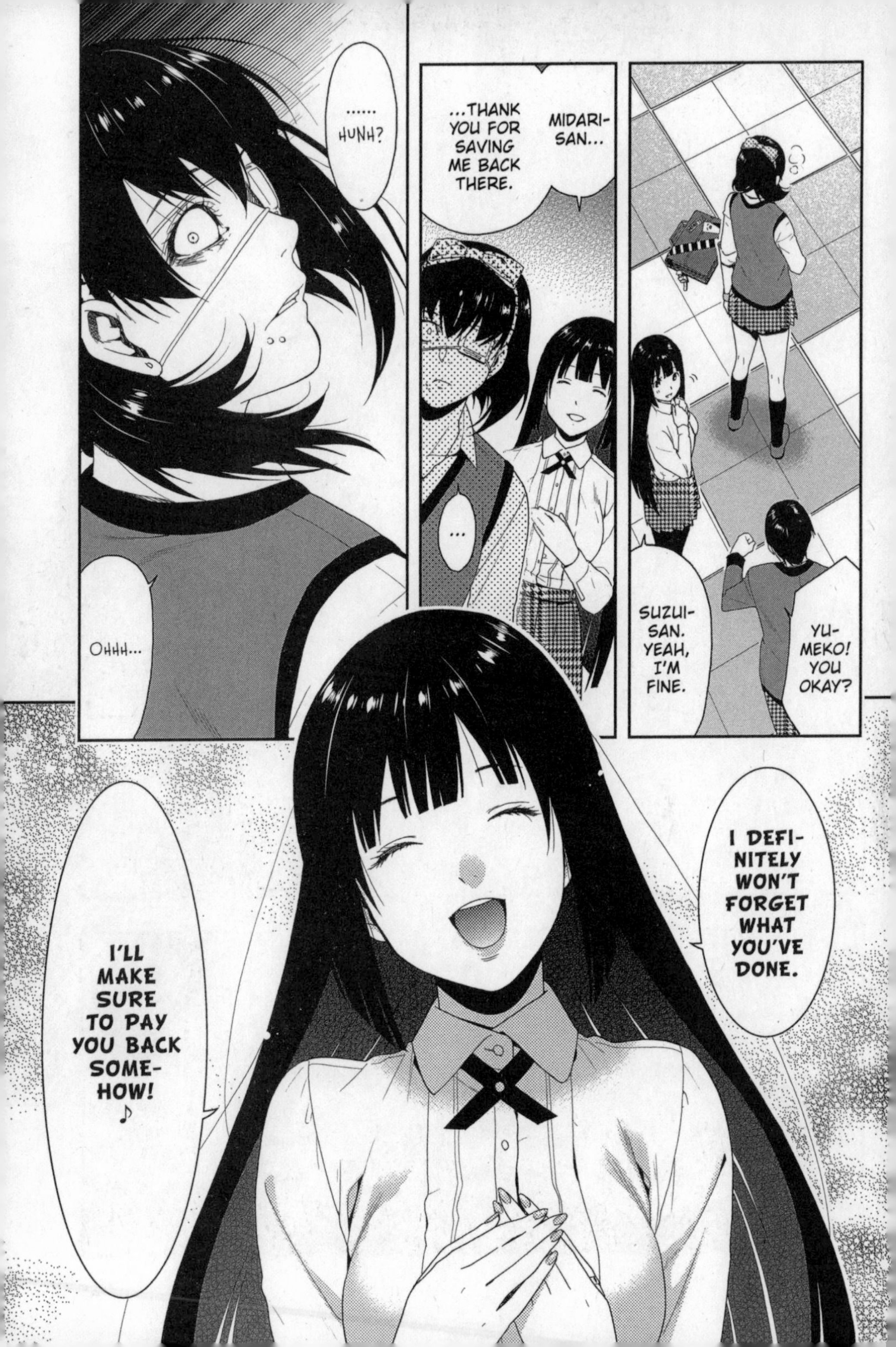
YU-MEKO! YOU OKAY?
SUZUI-SAN. YEAH, I'M FINE.
MIDARI-SAN...
...THANK YOU FOR SAVING ME BACK THERE.
...
...... HUNH?
OHHH...
I DEFI-NITELY WON'T FORGET WHAT YOU'VE DONE.
I'LL MAKE SURE TO PAY YOU BACK SOME-HOW! ♪

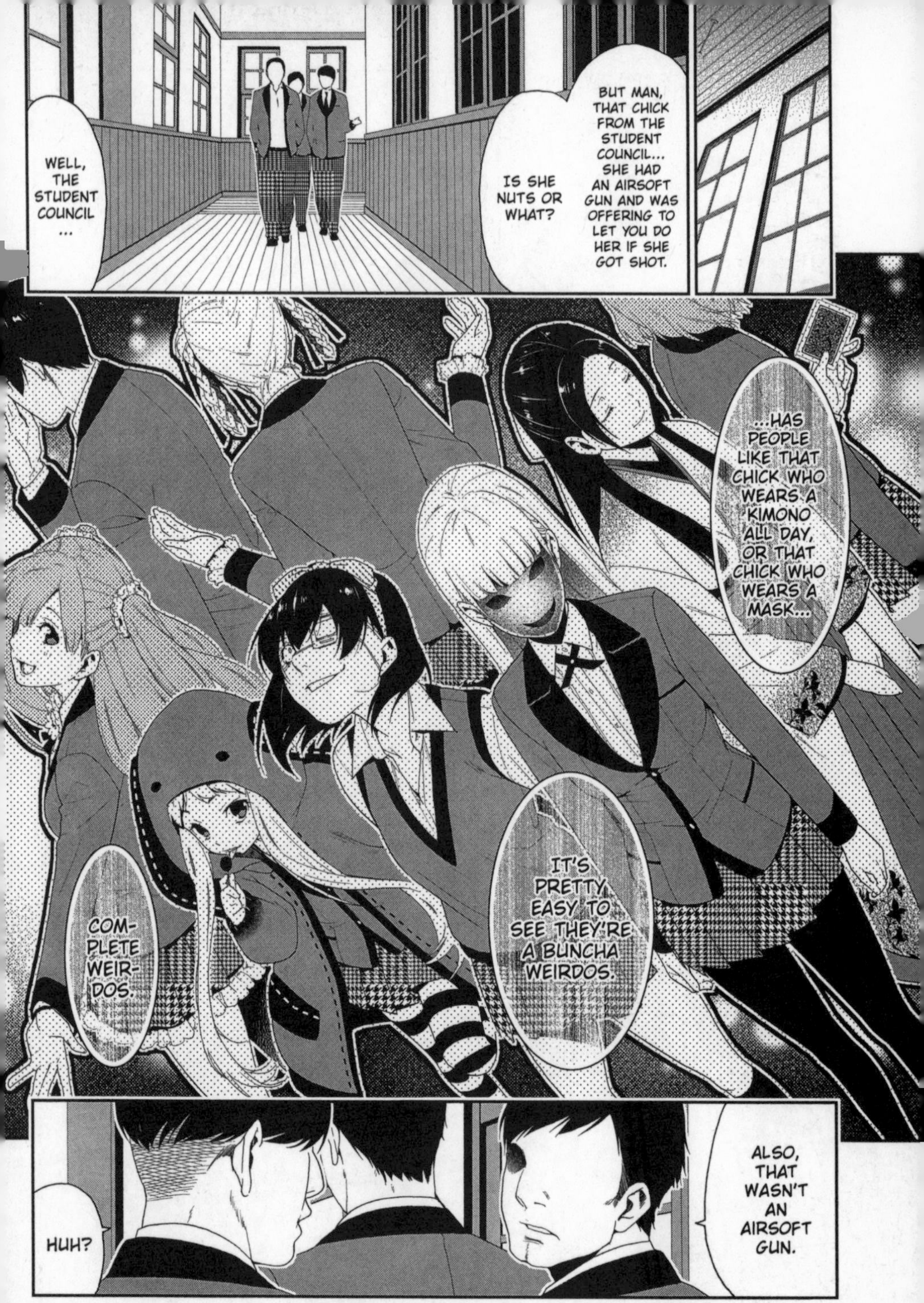
BUT MAN, THAT CHICK FROM THE STUDENT COUNCIL... SHE HAD AN AIRSOFT GUN AND WAS OFFERING TO LET YOU DO HER IF SHE GOT SHOT.
IS SHE NUTS OR WHAT?
WELL, THE STUDENT COUNCIL ...
...HAS PEOPLE LIKE THAT CHICK WHO WEARS A KIMONO ALL DAY, OR THAT CHICK WHO WEARS A MASK...
IT'S PRETTY EASY TO SEE THEY'RE A BUNCHA WEIRDOS.
COMPLETE WEIRDOS.
ALSO, THAT WASN'T AN AIRSOFT GUN.
HUH?

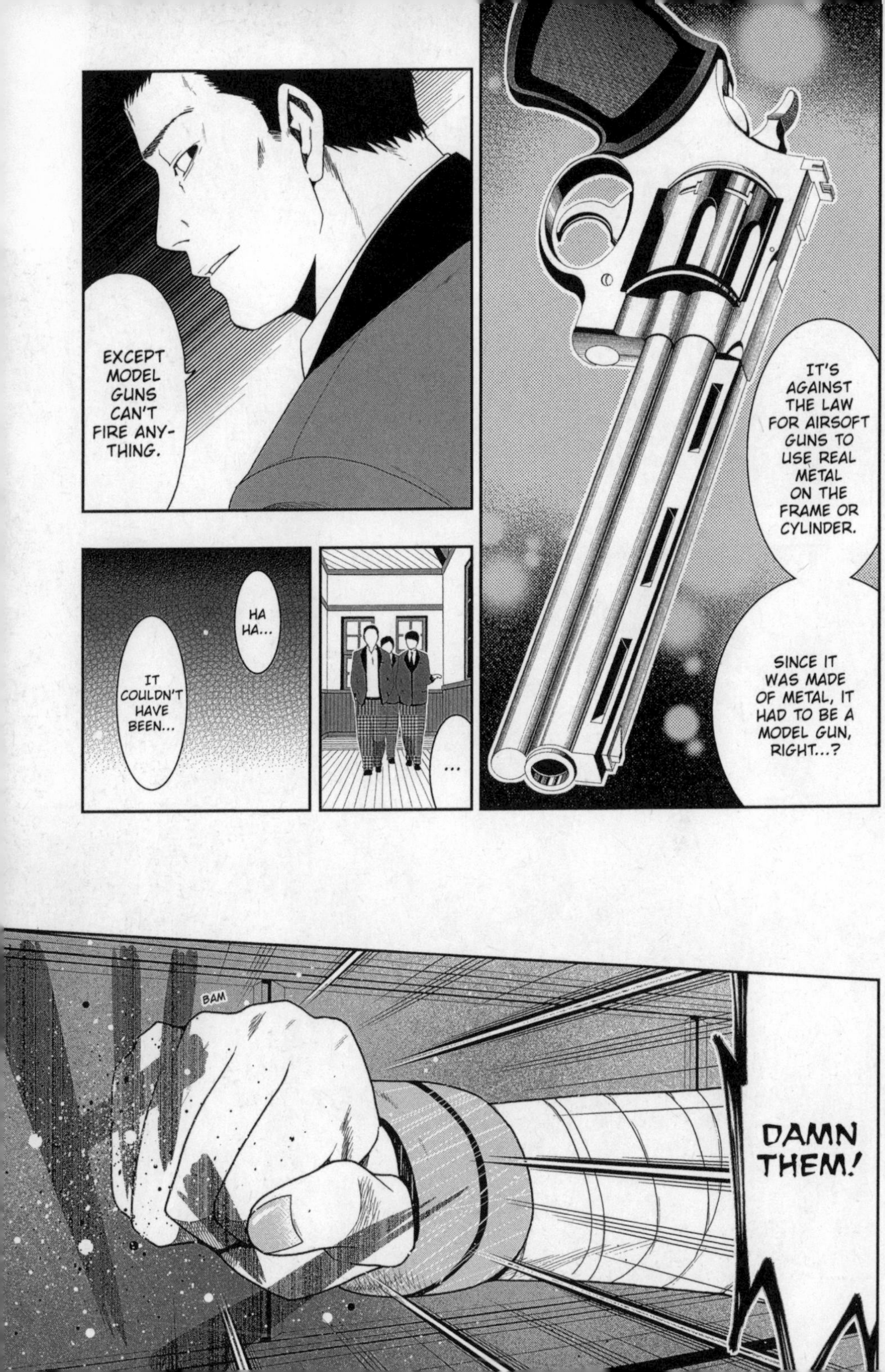
IT'S AGAINST THE LAW FOR AIRSOFT GUNS TO USE REAL METAL ON THE FRAME OR CYLINDER.
SINCE IT WAS MADE OF METAL, IT HAD TO BE A MODEL GUN, RIGHT...?
EXCEPT MODEL GUNS CAN'T FIRE ANY-THING.
...
HA HA...
IT COULDN'T HAVE BEEN...
BAM
DAMN THEM!

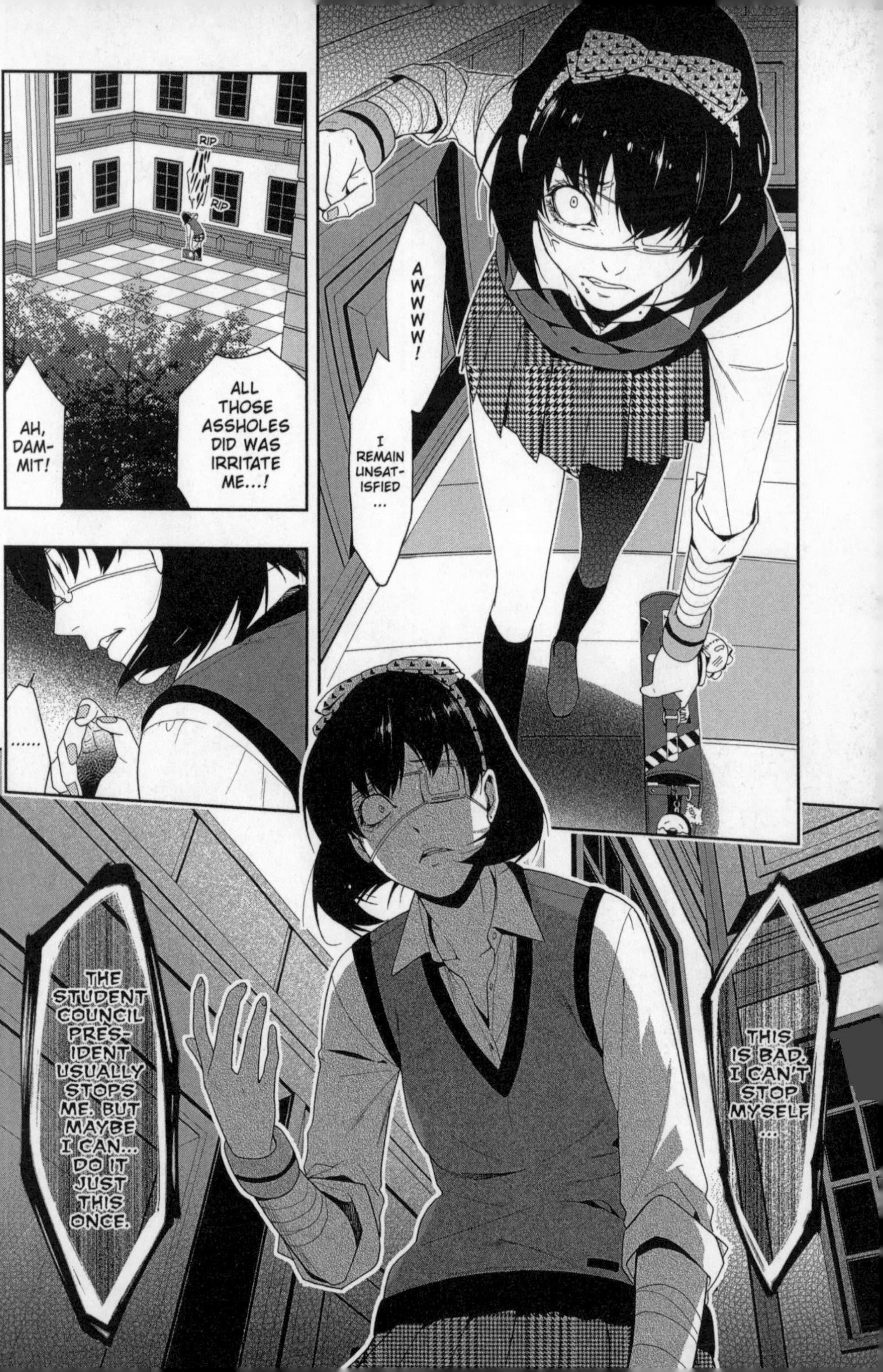
AWWWWW!
I REMAIN UNSATISFIED...
RIP
RIP
ALL THOSE ASSHOLES DID WAS IRRITATE ME...!
AH, DAMMIT!
......
THIS IS BAD. I CAN'T STOP MYSELF...
THE STUDENT COUNCIL PRESIDENT USUALLY STOPS ME. BUT MAYBE I CAN... DO IT JUST THIS ONCE.

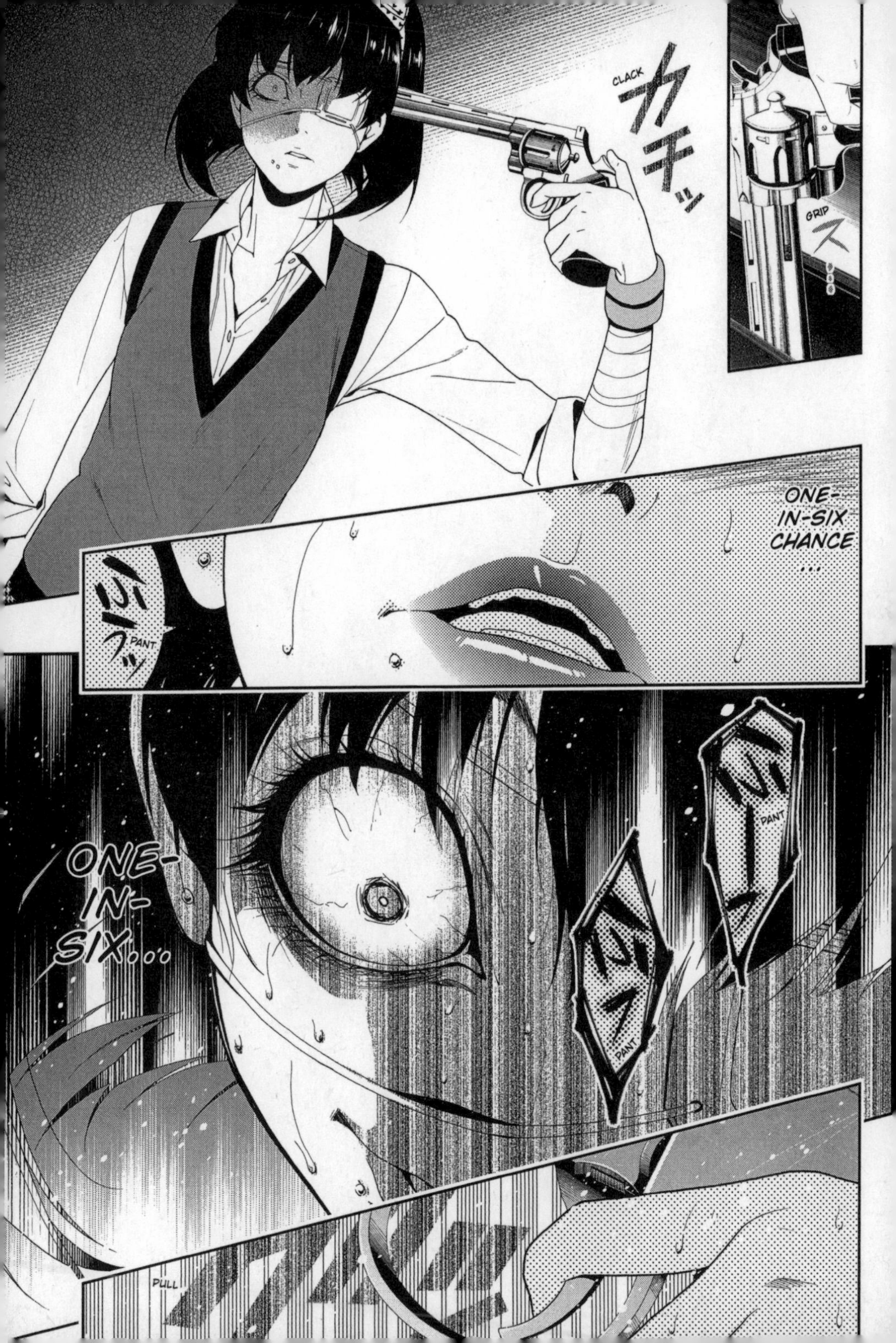
GRIP
CLACK
ONE-IN-SIX CHANCE...
PANT
PANT
PANT
ONE-IN-SIX...
PULL

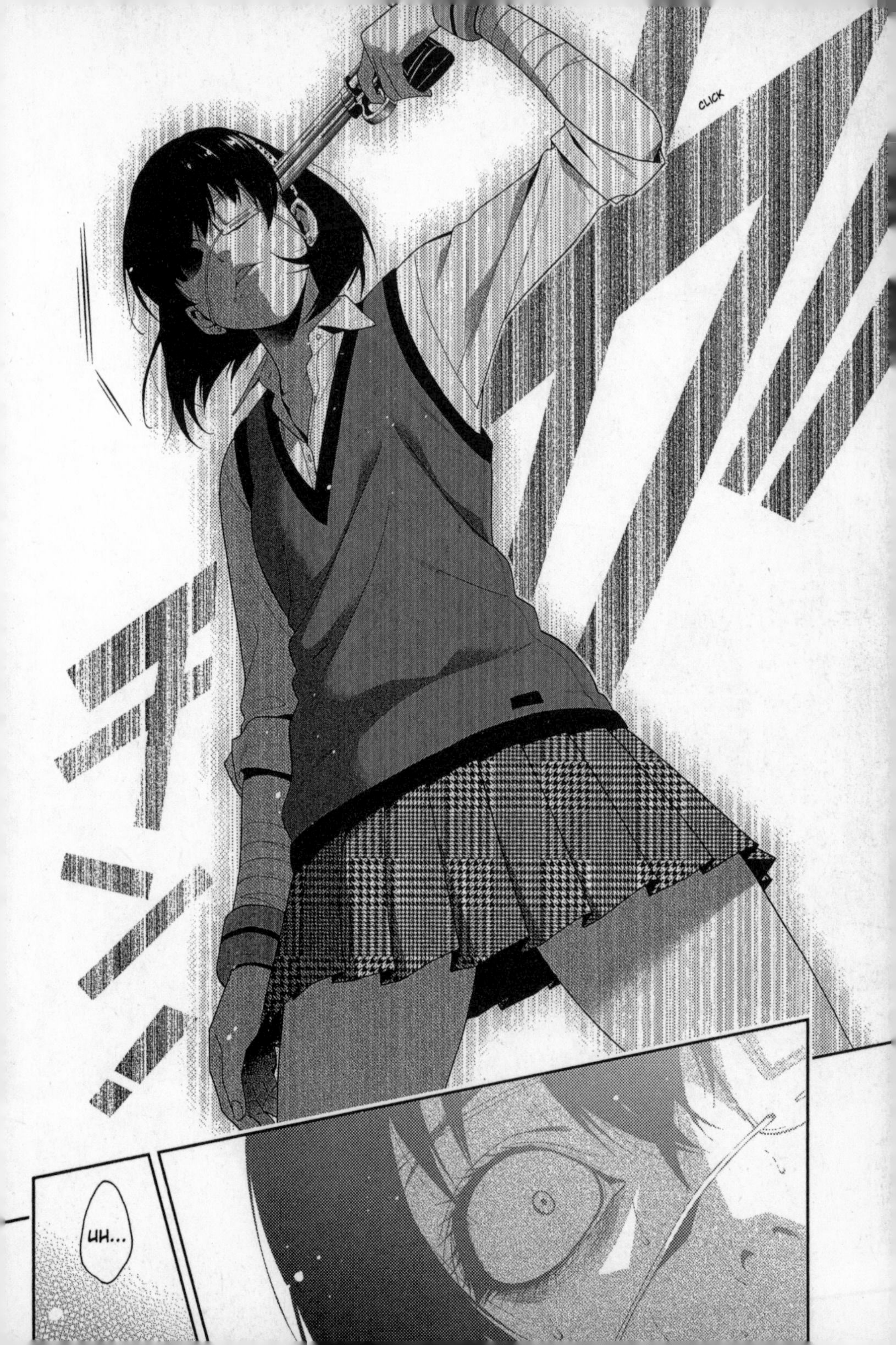
CLICK
UH...

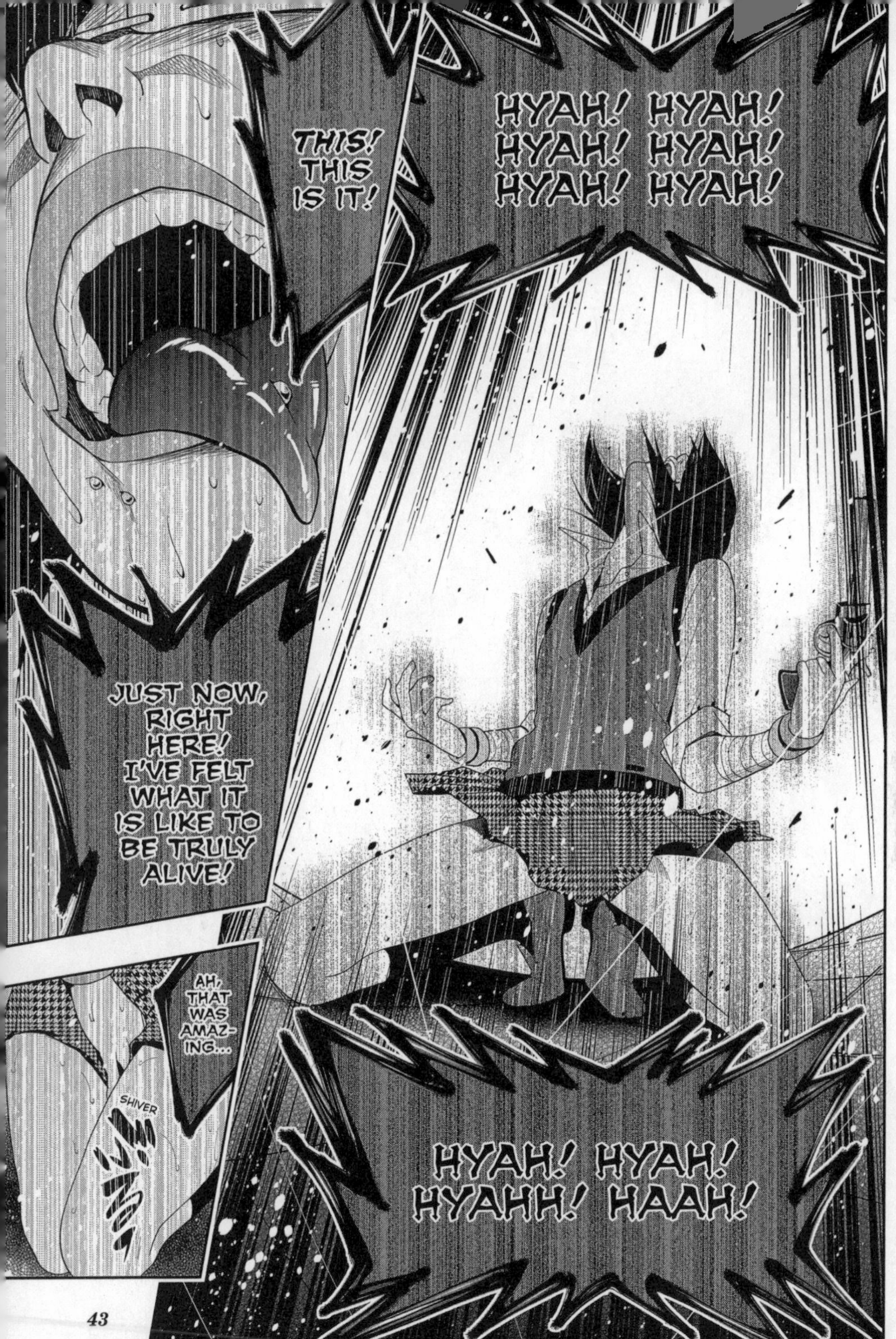
HYAH! HYAH! HYAH! HYAH! HYAH! HYAH!
HYAH! HYAH! HYAHH! HAAH!
THIS! THIS IS IT!
JUST NOW, RIGHT HERE! I'VE FELT WHAT IT IS LIKE TO BE TRULY ALIVE!
AH, THAT WAS AMAZ-ING...
SHIVER

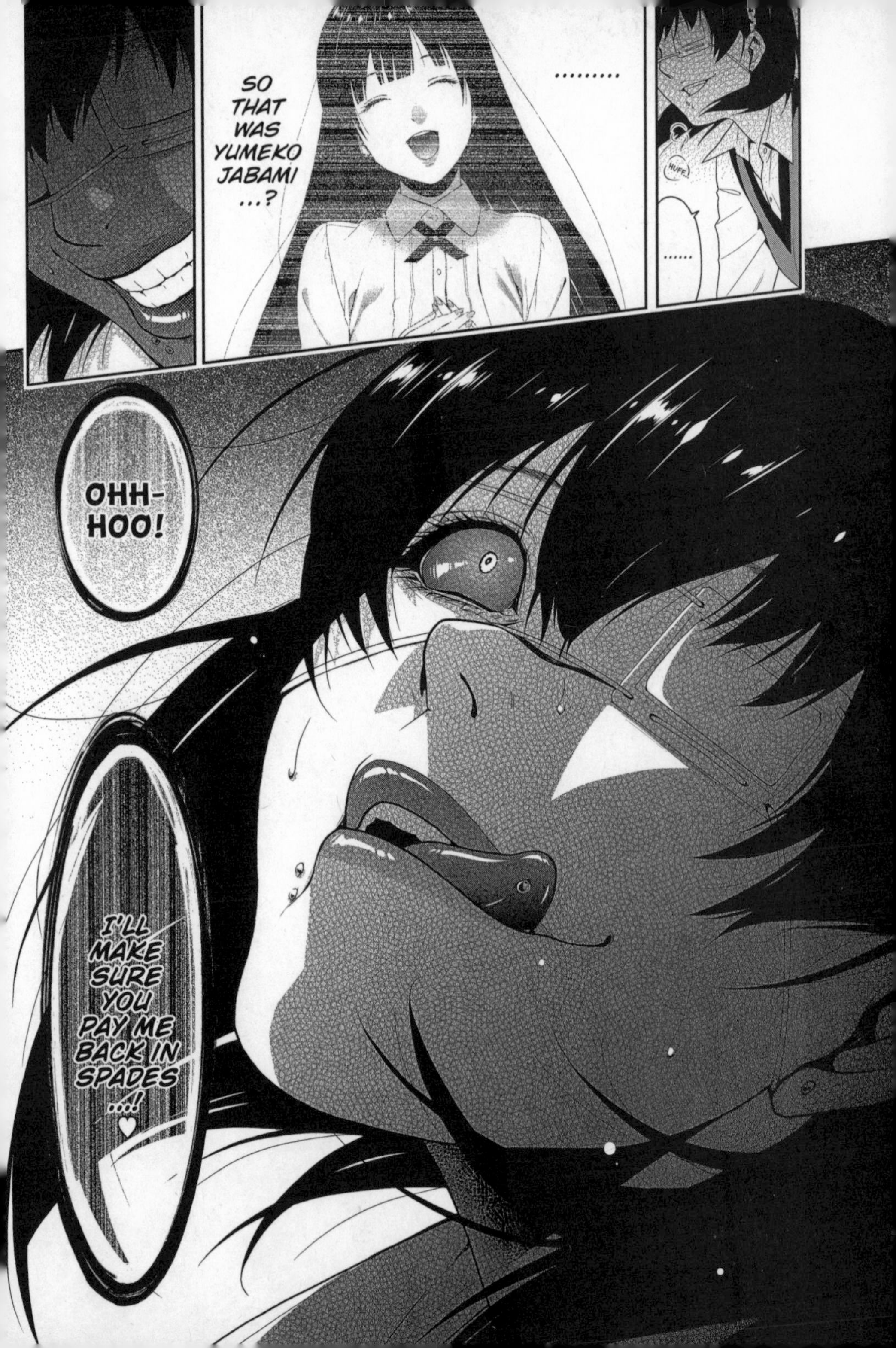
HUFF
......
....
SO THAT WAS YUMEKO JABAMI ...?
OHH-HOO!
I'LL MAKE SURE YOU PAY ME BACK IN SPADES ...! ♥

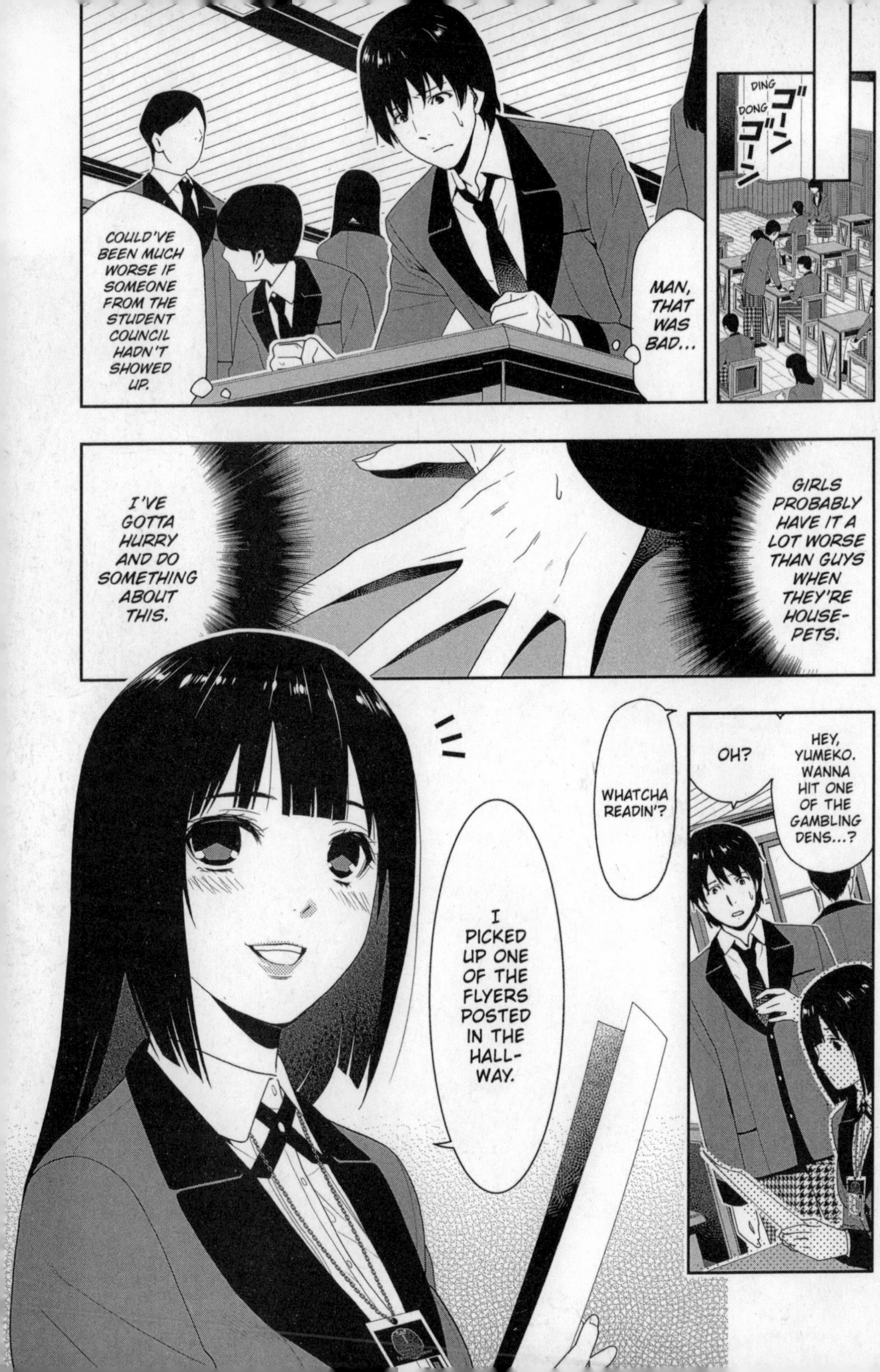
DING ゴーン
DONG ゴーン
MAN, THAT WAS BAD...
COULD'VE BEEN MUCH WORSE IF SOMEONE FROM THE STUDENT COUNCIL HADN'T SHOWED UP.
GIRLS PROBABLY HAVE IT A LOT WORSE THAN GUYS WHEN THEY'RE HOUSE-PETS.
I'VE GOTTA HURRY AND DO SOMETHING ABOUT THIS.
HEY, YUMEKO. WANNA HIT ONE OF THE GAMBLING DENS...?
OH?
WHATCHA READIN'?
I PICKED UP ONE OF THE FLYERS POSTED IN THE HALL-WAY.

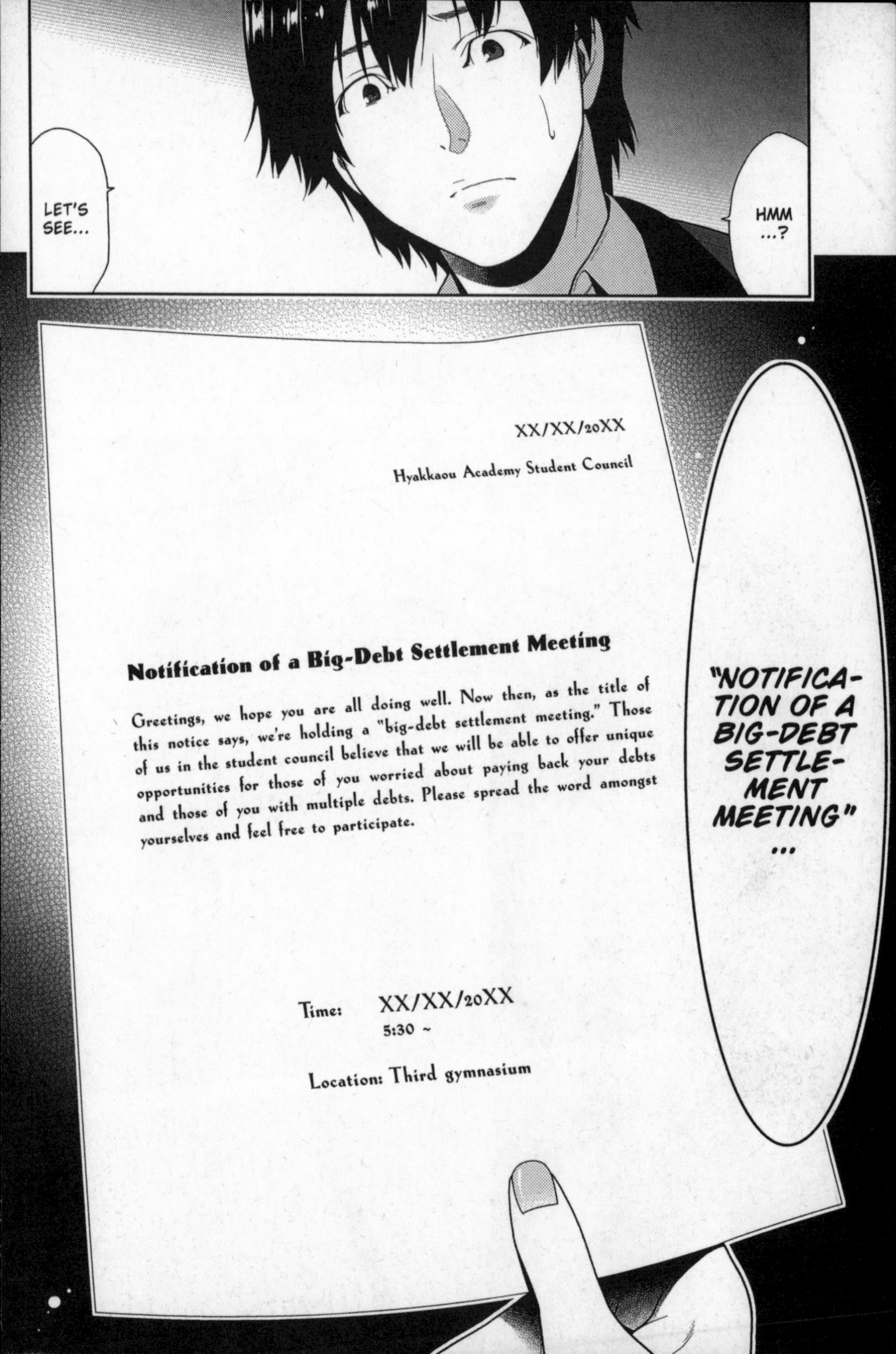
HMM ...?
LET'S SEE...
"NOTIFICATION OF A BIG-DEBT SETTLEMENT MEETING" ...
XX/XX/20XX
Hyakkaou Academy Student Council
Notification of a Big-Debt Settlement Meeting
Greetings, we hope you are all doing well. Now then, as the title of this notice says, we're holding a "big-debt settlement meeting." Those of us in the student council believe that we will be able to offer unique opportunities for those of you worried about paying back your debts and those of you with multiple debts. Please spread the word amongst yourselves and feel free to participate.
Time: XX/XX/20XX
5:30 ~
Location: Third gymnasium

Poker Terms

"Bet" - To wager a certain amount of chips.
"Call" - To wager the same amount of chips as your opponent.
"Raise" - To wager more chips than your opponent.
"Fold" - To quit the game.

KAKEGURUI

— Compulsive Gambler —

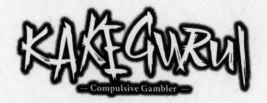

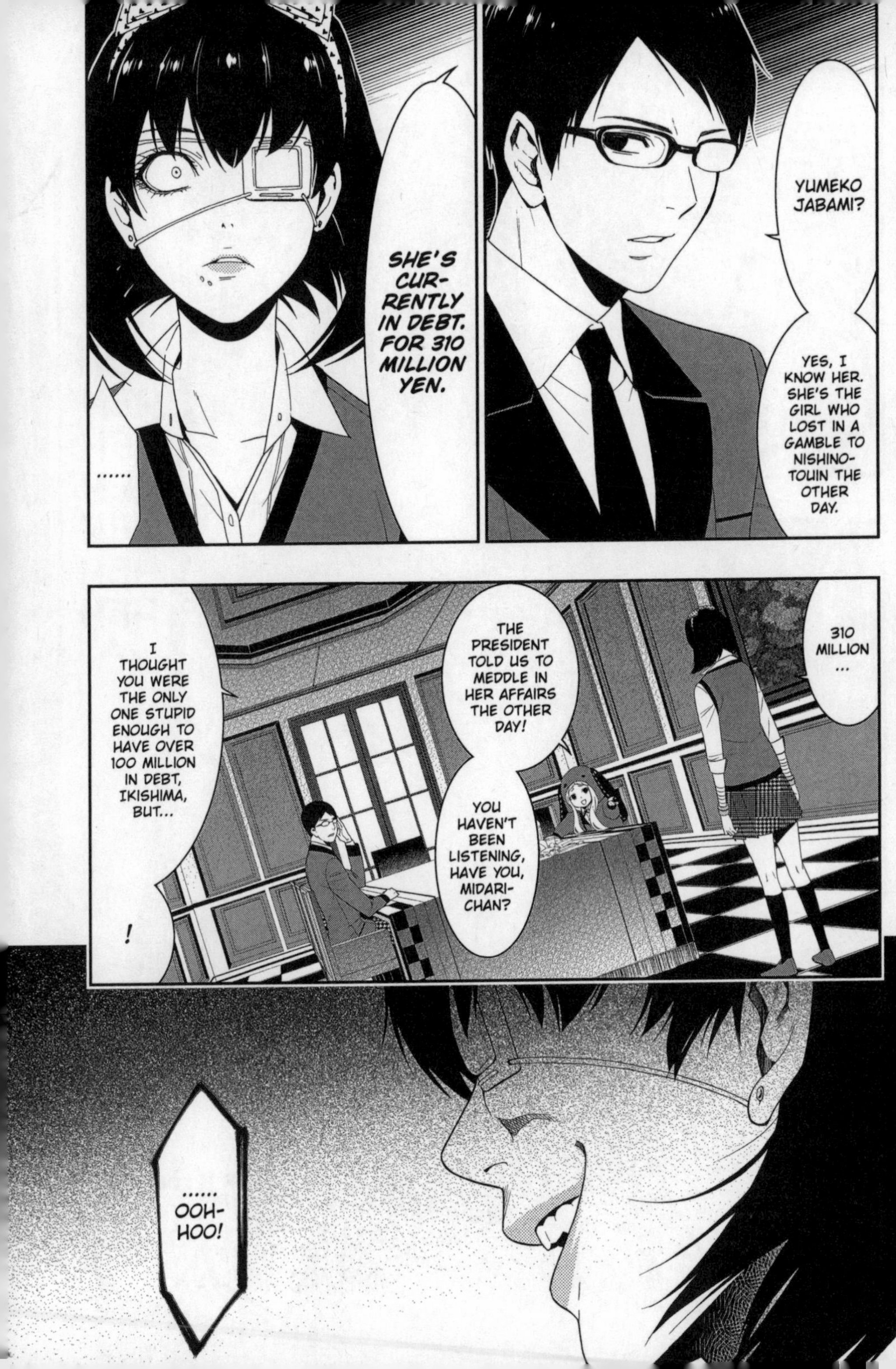
YUMEKO JABAMI?
YES, I KNOW HER. SHE'S THE GIRL WHO LOST IN A GAMBLE TO NISHINO-TOUIN THE OTHER DAY.
SHE'S CUR-RENTLY IN DEBT. FOR 310 MILLION YEN.
......
310 MILLION ...
THE PRESIDENT TOLD US TO MEDDLE IN HER AFFAIRS THE OTHER DAY!
YOU HAVEN'T BEEN LISTENING, HAVE YOU, MIDARI-CHAN?
I THOUGHT YOU WERE THE ONLY ONE STUPID ENOUGH TO HAVE OVER 100 MILLION IN DEBT, IKISHIMA, BUT...
!
...... OOH-HOO!

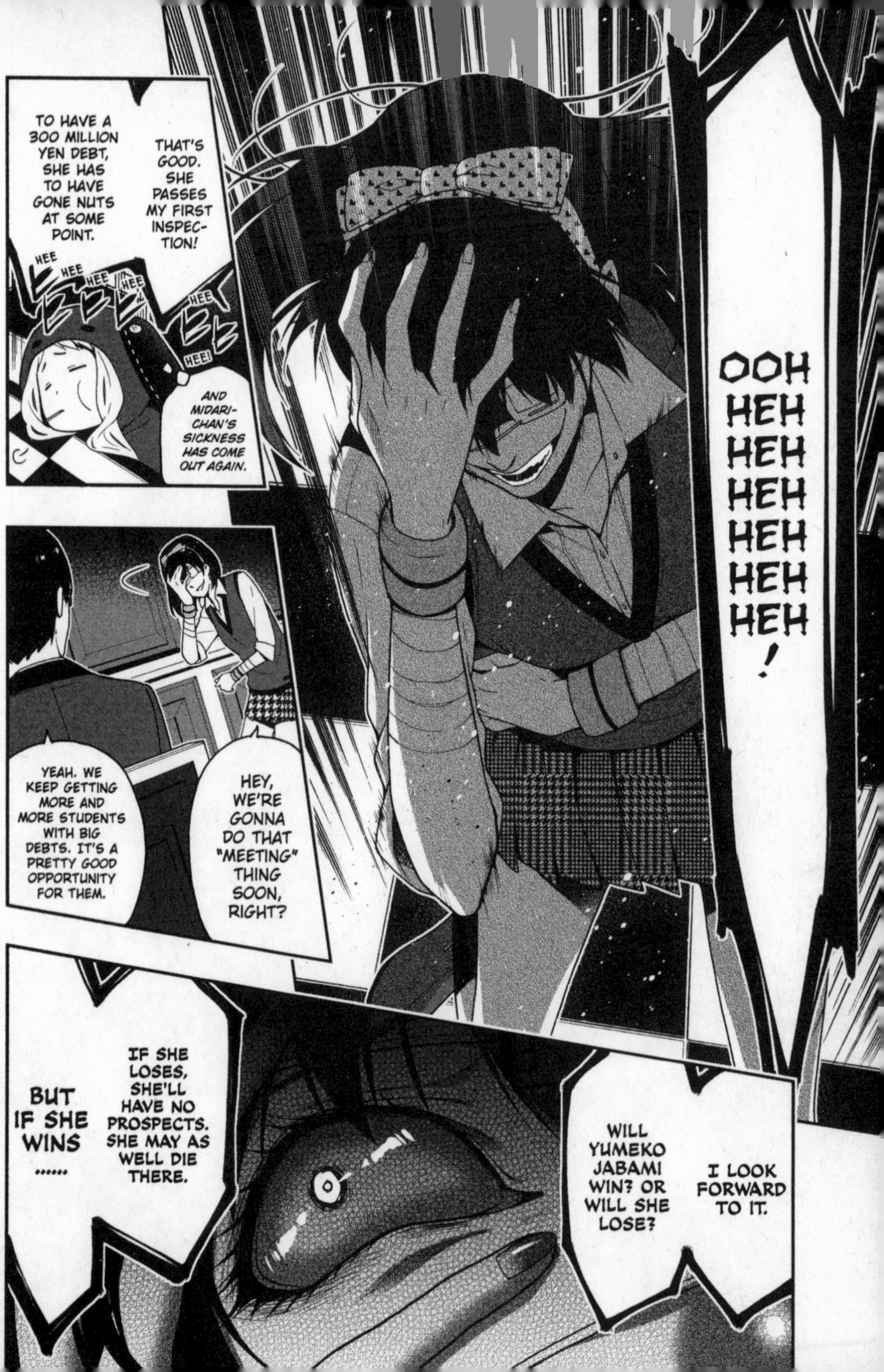
OOH HEH HEH HEH HEH HEH HEH!
TO HAVE A 300 MILLION YEN DEBT, SHE HAS TO HAVE GONE NUTS AT SOME POINT.
THAT'S GOOD. SHE PASSES MY FIRST INSPEC-TION!
HEE HEE HEE HEE HEE HEE!
AND MIDARI-CHAN'S SICKNESS HAS COME OUT AGAIN.
HEY, WE'RE GONNA DO THAT "MEETING" THING SOON, RIGHT?
YEAH. WE KEEP GETTING MORE AND MORE STUDENTS WITH BIG DEBTS. IT'S A PRETTY GOOD OPPORTUNITY FOR THEM.
WILL YUMEKO JABAMI WIN? OR WILL SHE LOSE?
I LOOK FORWARD TO IT.
IF SHE LOSES, SHE'LL HAVE NO PROSPECTS. SHE MAY AS WELL DIE THERE.
BUT IF SHE WINS ......

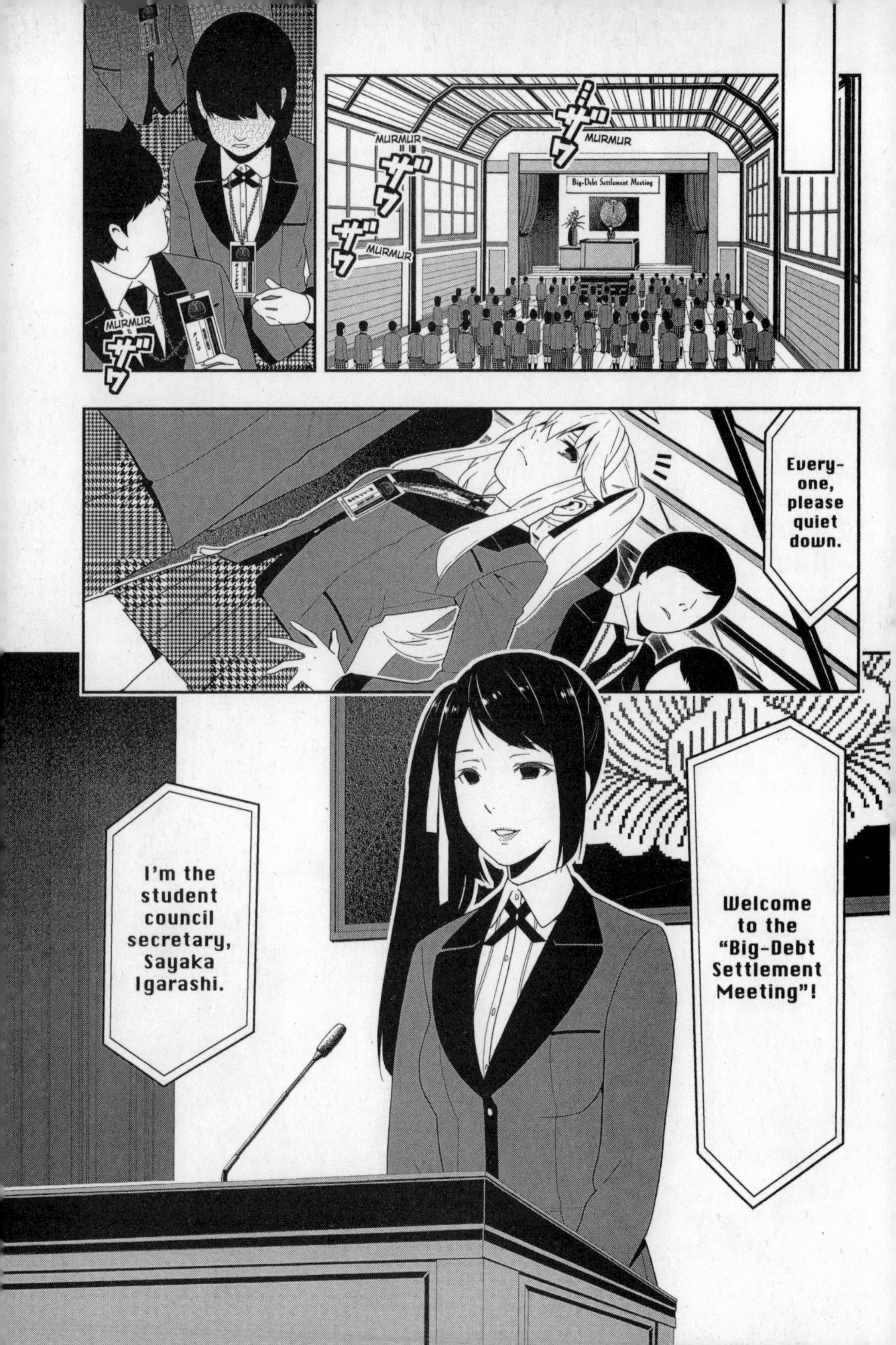

ザワ
MURMUR
ザワ
MURMUR
ザワ
MURMUR
Big-Debt Settlement Meeting
MURMUR
ザワ
Every-one, please quiet down.
Welcome to the "Big-Debt Settlement Meeting"!
I'm the student council secretary, Sayaka Igarashi.

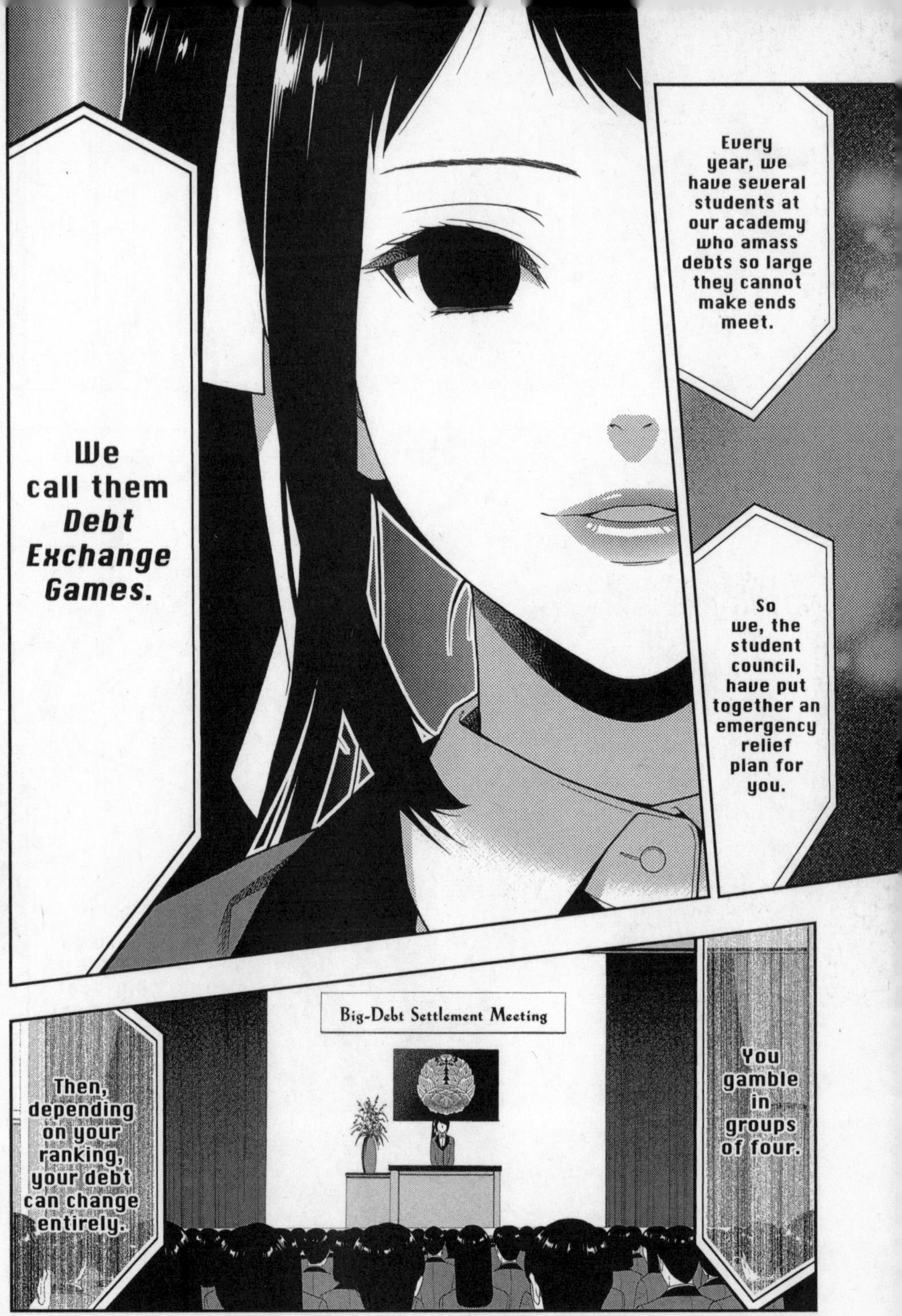
Every year, we have several students at our academy who amass debts so large they cannot make ends meet.
So we, the student council, have put together an emergency relief plan for you.
We call them *Debt Exchange Games.*
Big-Debt Settlement Meeting
You gamble in groups of four.
Then, depending on your ranking, your debt can change entirely.

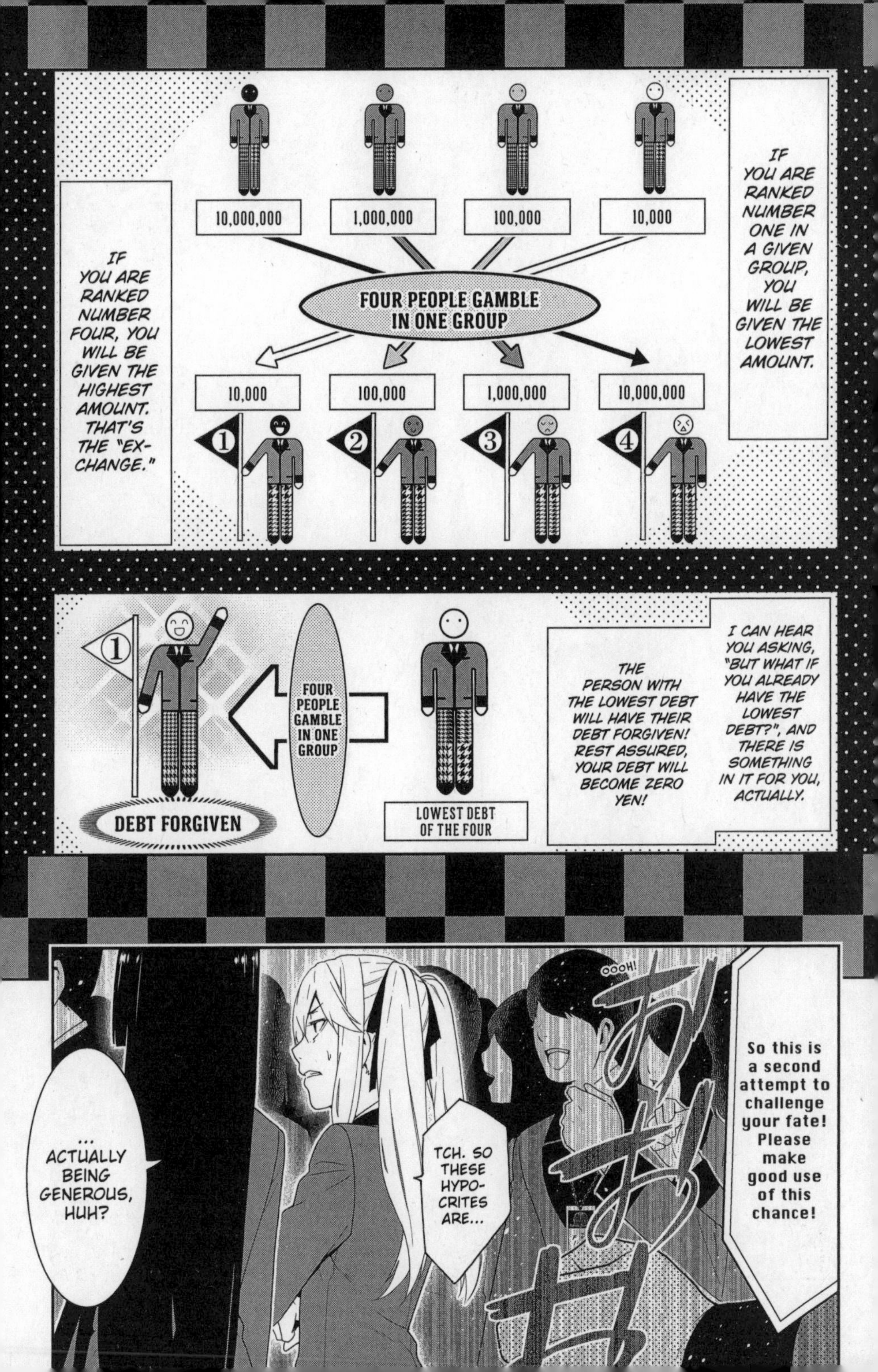
IF YOU ARE RANKED NUMBER ONE IN A GIVEN GROUP, YOU WILL BE GIVEN THE LOWEST AMOUNT.
10,000
100,000
1,000,000
10,000,000
FOUR PEOPLE GAMBLE IN ONE GROUP
10,000,000
1,000,000
100,000
10,000
④
③
②
①
IF YOU ARE RANKED NUMBER FOUR, YOU WILL BE GIVEN THE HIGHEST AMOUNT. THAT'S THE "EX-CHANGE."
I CAN HEAR YOU ASKING, "BUT WHAT IF YOU ALREADY HAVE THE LOWEST DEBT?", AND THERE IS SOMETHING IN IT FOR YOU, ACTUALLY.
THE PERSON WITH THE LOWEST DEBT WILL HAVE THEIR DEBT FORGIVEN! REST ASSURED, YOUR DEBT WILL BECOME ZERO YEN!
LOWEST DEBT OF THE FOUR
FOUR PEOPLE GAMBLE IN ONE GROUP
①
DEBT FORGIVEN
So this is a second attempt to challenge your fate! Please make good use of this chance!
OOOH!
TCH. SO THESE HYPO-CRITES ARE...
... ACTUALLY BEING GENEROUS, HUH?

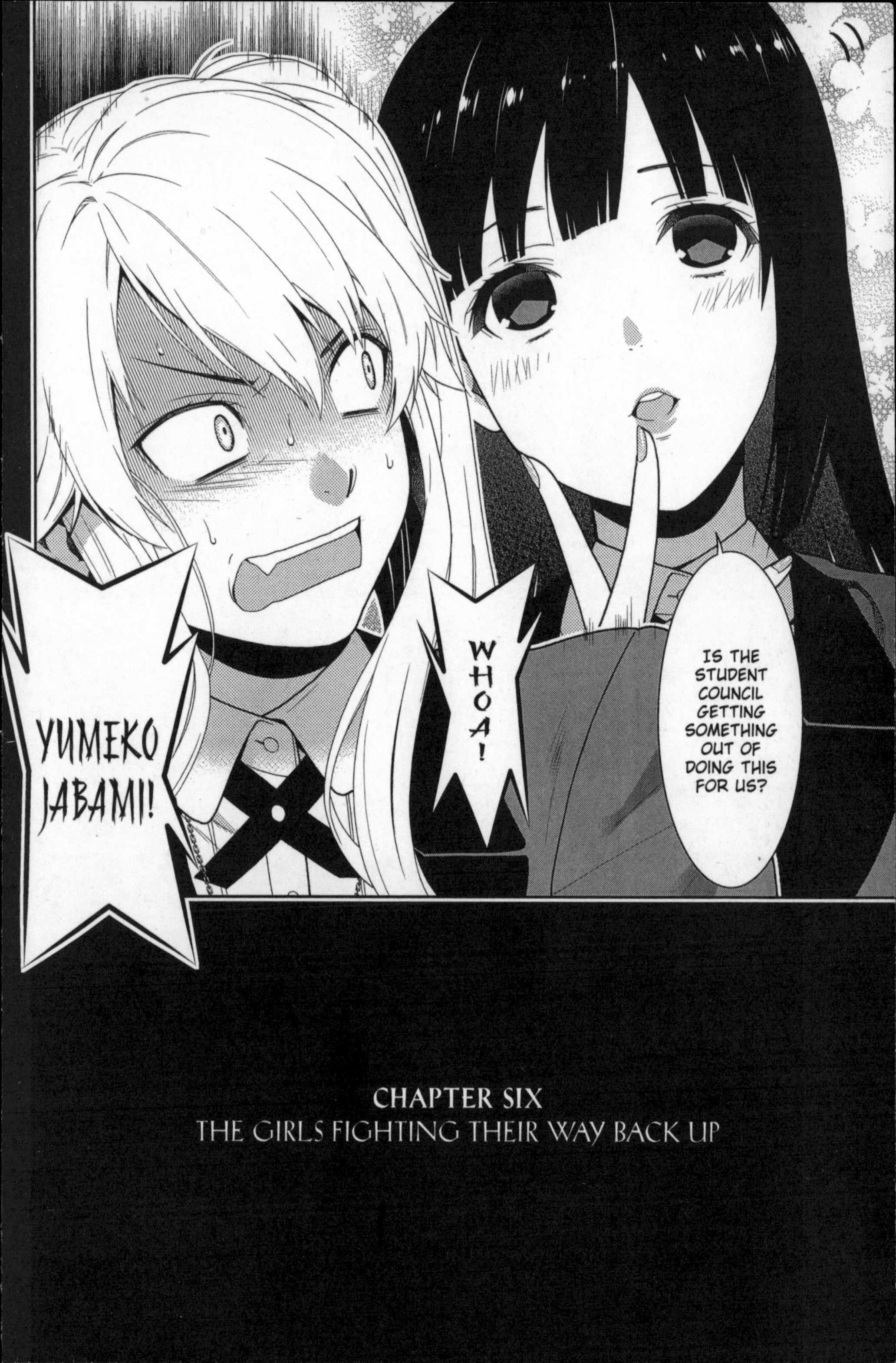
IS THE STUDENT COUNCIL GETTING SOMETHING OUT OF DOING THIS FOR US?
WHOA!
YUMEKO JABAMI!

CHAPTER SIX
THE GIRLS FIGHTING THEIR WAY BACK UP

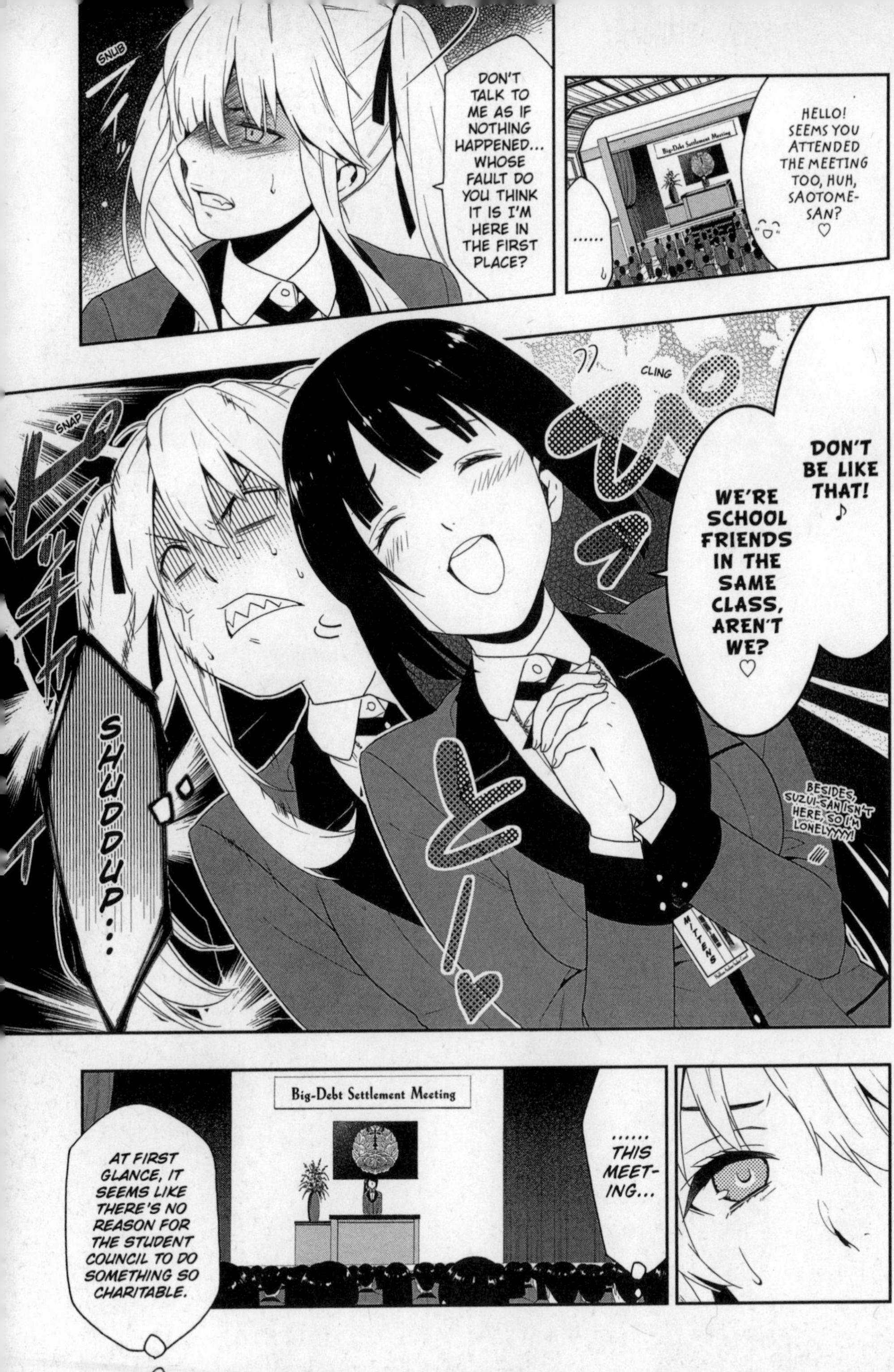
HELLO! SEEMS YOU ATTENDED THE MEETING TOO, HUH, SAOTOME-SAN? ♡
Big-Debt Settlement Meeting
......
SNUB
DON'T TALK TO ME AS IF NOTHING HAPPENED... WHOSE FAULT DO YOU THINK IT IS I'M HERE IN THE FIRST PLACE?
CLING
DON'T BE LIKE THAT! ♪
WE'RE SCHOOL FRIENDS IN THE SAME CLASS, AREN'T WE? ♡
BESIDES, SUZUI-SAN ISN'T HERE, SO I'M LONELYYYY!
SNAP
SHUDDUP...
......THIS MEET-ING...
Big-Debt Settlement Meeting
AT FIRST GLANCE, IT SEEMS LIKE THERE'S NO REASON FOR THE STUDENT COUNCIL TO DO SOMETHING SO CHARITABLE.

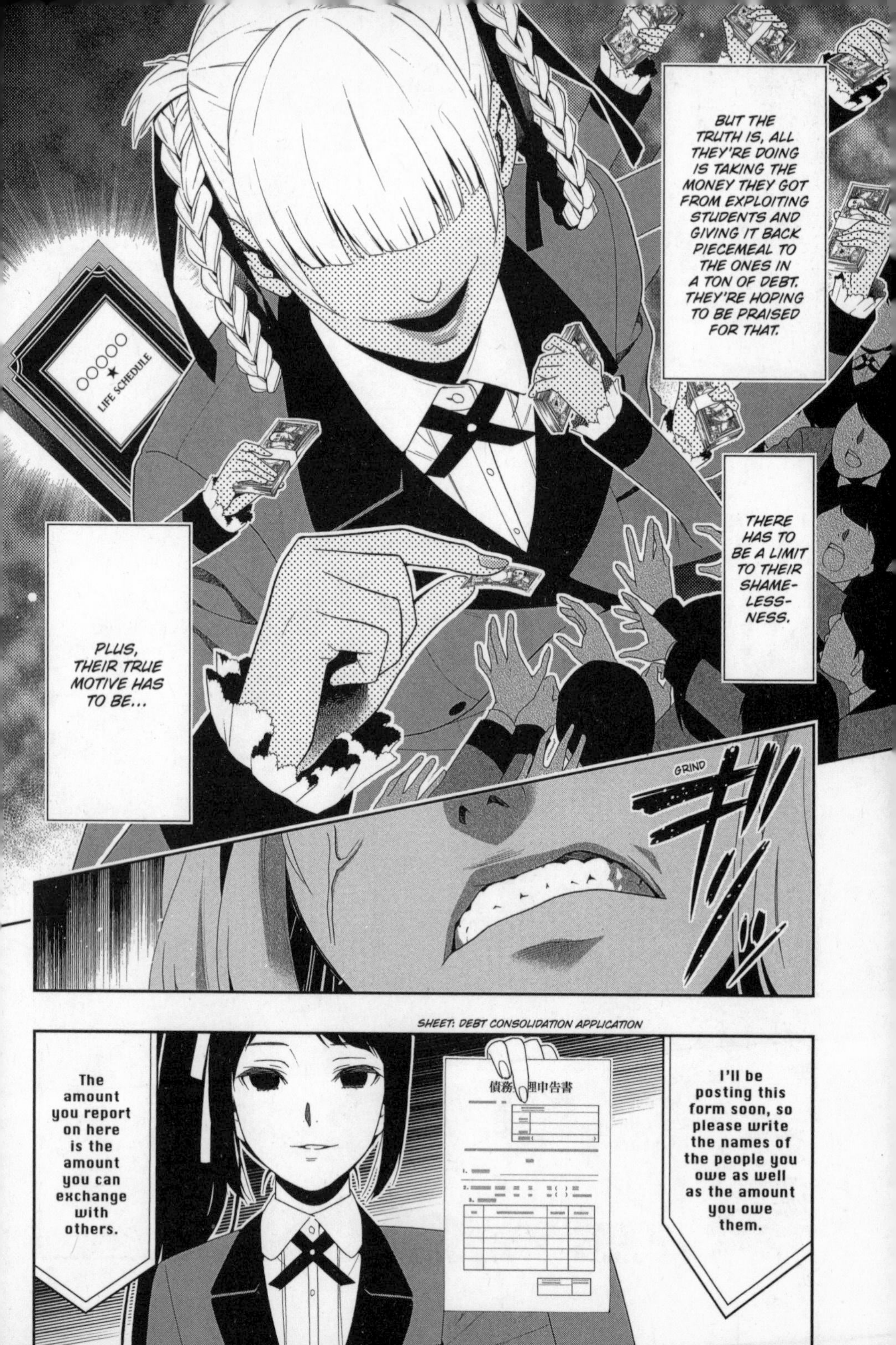
BUT THE TRUTH IS, ALL THEY'RE DOING IS TAKING THE MONEY THEY GOT FROM EXPLOITING STUDENTS AND GIVING IT BACK PIECEMEAL TO THE ONES IN A TON OF DEBT. THEY'RE HOPING TO BE PRAISED FOR THAT.
LIFE SCHEDULE
THERE HAS TO BE A LIMIT TO THEIR SHAME-LESS-NESS.
PLUS, THEIR TRUE MOTIVE HAS TO BE...
GRIND
SHEET: DEBT CONSOLIDATION APPLICATION
I'll be posting this form soon, so please write the names of the people you owe as well as the amount you owe them.
債務 理申告書
The amount you report on here is the amount you can exchange with others.

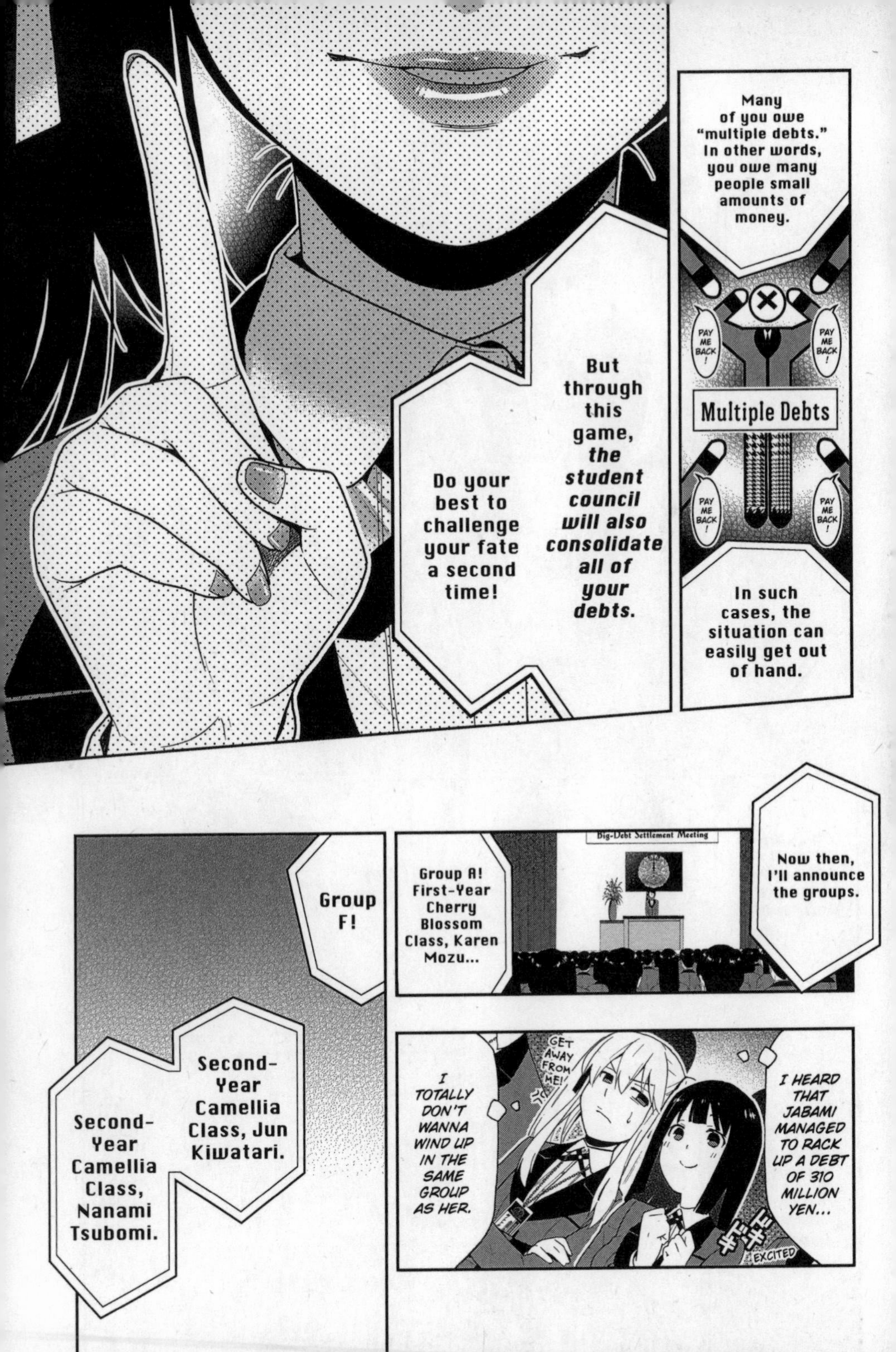
Many of you owe "multiple debts." In other words, you owe many people small amounts of money.
PAY ME BACK!
PAY ME BACK!
Multiple Debts
PAY ME BACK!
PAY ME BACK!
In such cases, the situation can easily get out of hand.
But through this game, *the student council will also consolidate all of your debts.*
Do your best to challenge your fate a second time!
Now then, I'll announce the groups.
Big-Debt Settlement Meeting
Group A! First-Year Cherry Blossom Class, Karen Mozu...
I HEARD THAT JABAMI MANAGED TO RACK UP A DEBT OF 310 MILLION YEN...
EXCITED
GET AWAY FROM ME!
I TOTALLY DON'T WANNA WIND UP IN THE SAME GROUP AS HER.
Group F!
Second-Year Camellia Class, Jun Kiwatari.
Second-Year Camellia Class, Nanami Tsubomi.

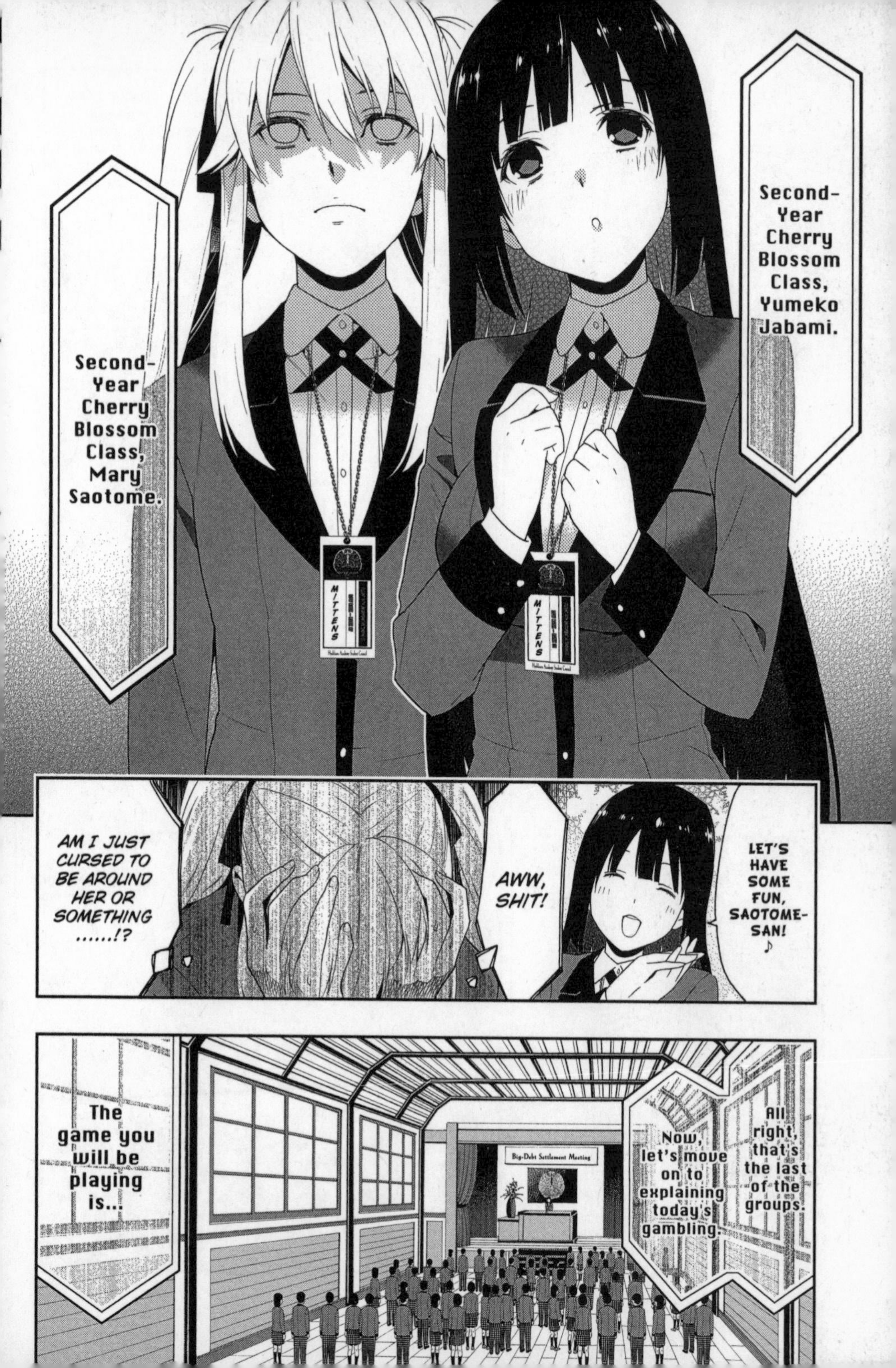
Second-Year Cherry Blossom Class, Yumeko Jabami.
Second-Year Cherry Blossom Class, Mary Saotome.
LET'S HAVE SOME FUN, SAOTOME-SAN! ♪
AWW, SHIT!
AM I JUST CURSED TO BE AROUND HER OR SOMETHING......!?
All right, that's the last of the groups.
Now, let's move on to explaining today's gambling.
Big-Debt Settlement Meeting
The game you will be playing is...

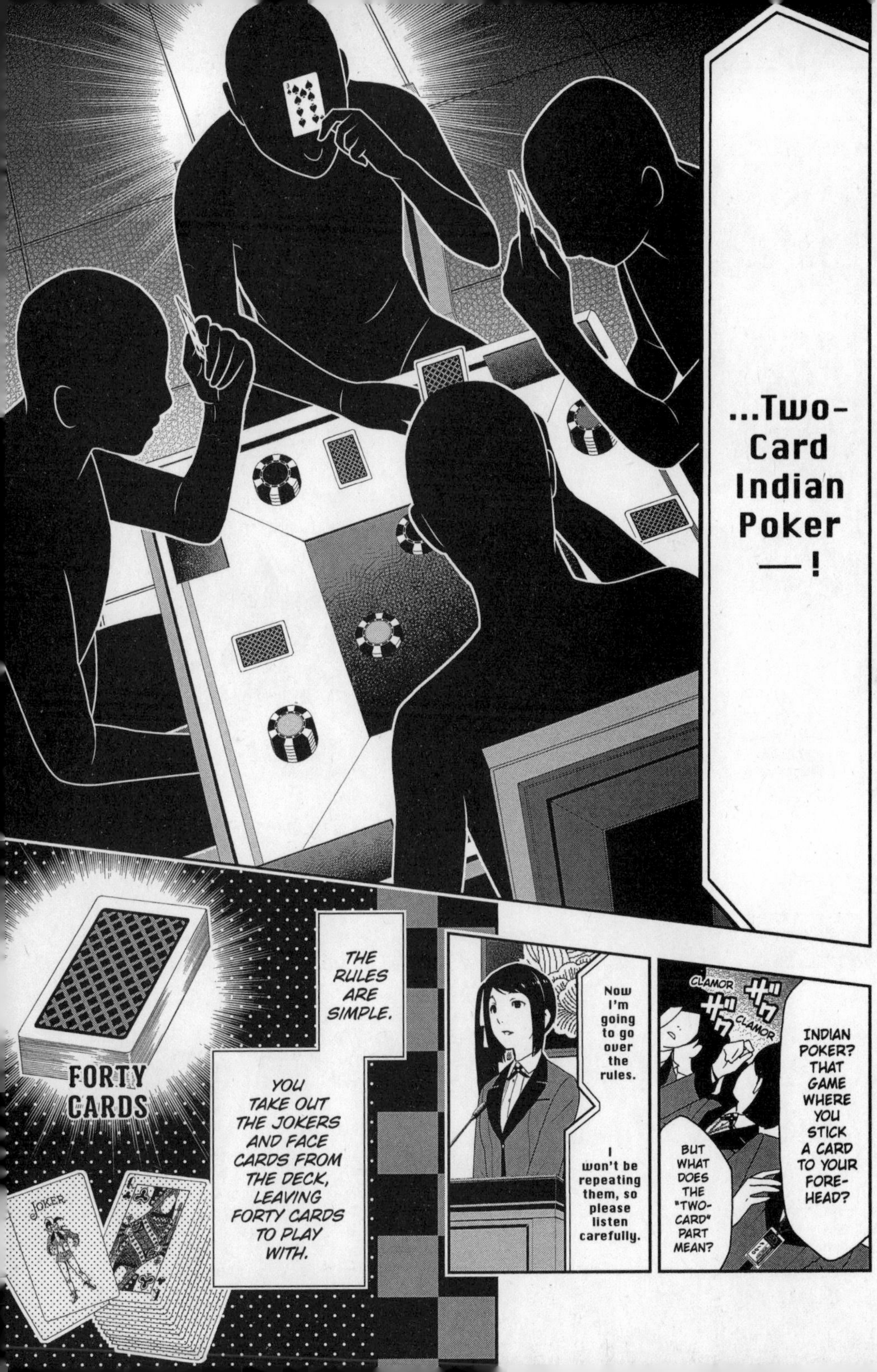
...Two-Card Indian Poker—!
INDIAN POKER? THAT GAME WHERE YOU STICK A CARD TO YOUR FORE-HEAD?
ザワ CLAMOR
ザワ CLAMOR
BUT WHAT DOES THE "TWO-CARD" PART MEAN?
Now I'm going to go over the rules.
I won't be repeating them, so please listen carefully.
THE RULES ARE SIMPLE.
YOU TAKE OUT THE JOKERS AND FACE CARDS FROM THE DECK, LEAVING FORTY CARDS TO PLAY WITH.
FORTY CARDS
JOKER

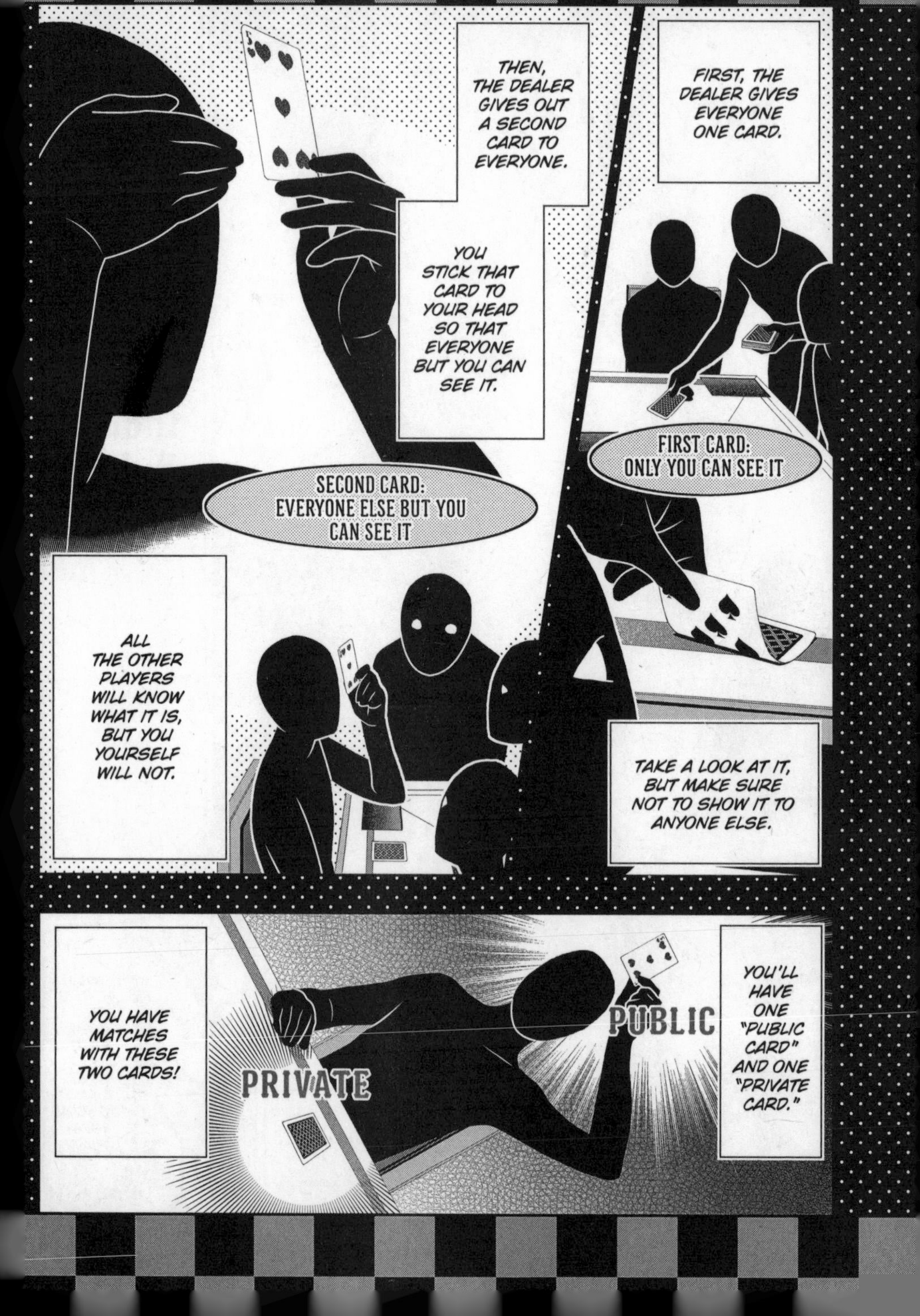
FIRST, THE DEALER GIVES EVERYONE ONE CARD.
FIRST CARD: ONLY YOU CAN SEE IT
TAKE A LOOK AT IT, BUT MAKE SURE NOT TO SHOW IT TO ANYONE ELSE.
THEN, THE DEALER GIVES OUT A SECOND CARD TO EVERYONE.
YOU STICK THAT CARD TO YOUR HEAD SO THAT EVERYONE BUT YOU CAN SEE IT.
SECOND CARD: EVERYONE ELSE BUT YOU CAN SEE IT
ALL THE OTHER PLAYERS WILL KNOW WHAT IT IS, BUT YOU YOURSELF WILL NOT.
YOU'LL HAVE ONE "PUBLIC CARD" AND ONE "PRIVATE CARD."
PUBLIC
PRIVATE
YOU HAVE MATCHES WITH THESE TWO CARDS!

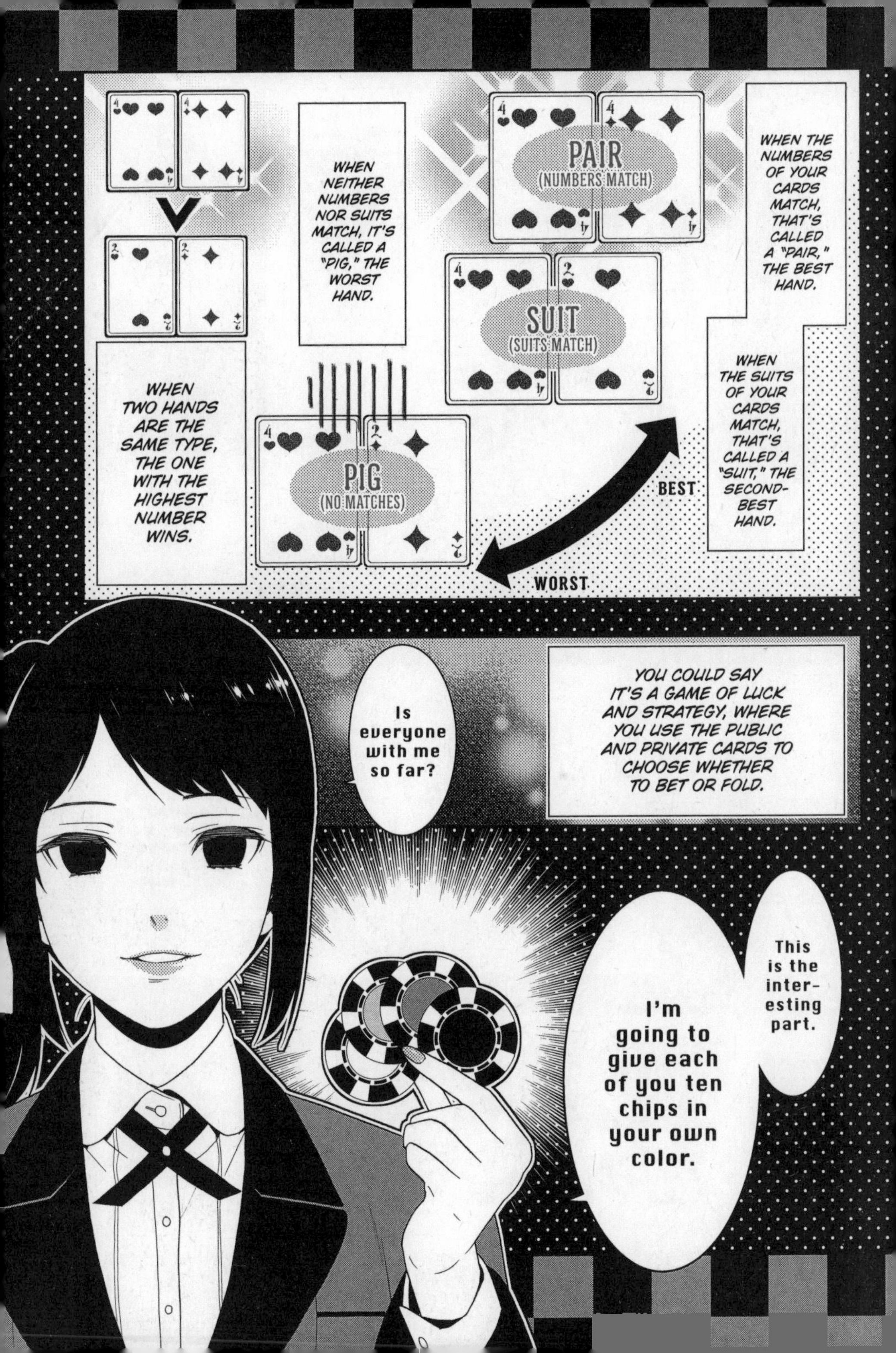
WHEN THE NUMBERS OF YOUR CARDS MATCH, THAT'S CALLED A "PAIR," THE BEST HAND.
PAIR
(NUMBERS MATCH)
WHEN THE SUITS OF YOUR CARDS MATCH, THAT'S CALLED A "SUIT," THE SECOND-BEST HAND.
SUIT
(SUITS MATCH)
BEST
WORST
PIG
(NO MATCHES)
WHEN NEITHER NUMBERS NOR SUITS MATCH, IT'S CALLED A "PIG," THE WORST HAND.
WHEN TWO HANDS ARE THE SAME TYPE, THE ONE WITH THE HIGHEST NUMBER WINS.
YOU COULD SAY IT'S A GAME OF LUCK AND STRATEGY, WHERE YOU USE THE PUBLIC AND PRIVATE CARDS TO CHOOSE WHETHER TO BET OR FOLD.
Is everyone with me so far?
This is the inter-esting part.
I'm going to give each of you ten chips in your own color.

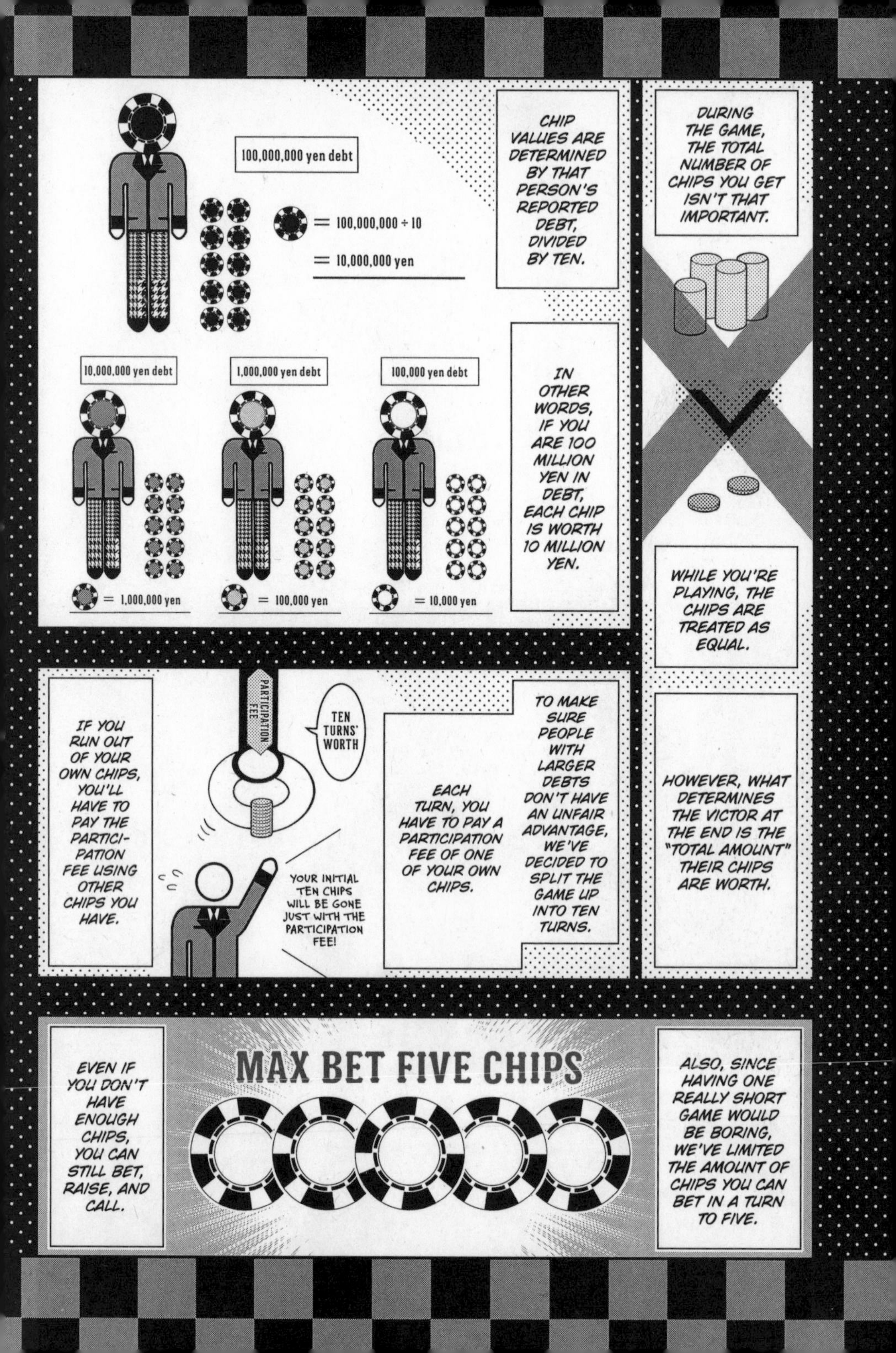

DURING THE GAME, THE TOTAL NUMBER OF CHIPS YOU GET ISN'T THAT IMPORTANT.
WHILE YOU'RE PLAYING, THE CHIPS ARE TREATED AS EQUAL.
HOWEVER, WHAT DETERMINES THE VICTOR AT THE END IS THE "TOTAL AMOUNT" THEIR CHIPS ARE WORTH.
CHIP VALUES ARE DETERMINED BY THAT PERSON'S REPORTED DEBT, DIVIDED BY TEN.
IN OTHER WORDS, IF YOU ARE 100 MILLION YEN IN DEBT, EACH CHIP IS WORTH 10 MILLION YEN.
100,000,000 yen debt
= 100,000,000 ÷ 10
= 10,000,000 yen
100,000 yen debt
= 10,000 yen
1,000,000 yen debt
= 100,000 yen
10,000,000 yen debt
= 1,000,000 yen
TO MAKE SURE PEOPLE WITH LARGER DEBTS DON'T HAVE AN UNFAIR ADVANTAGE, WE'VE DECIDED TO SPLIT THE GAME UP INTO TEN TURNS.
EACH TURN, YOU HAVE TO PAY A PARTICIPATION FEE OF ONE OF YOUR OWN CHIPS.
TEN TURNS' WORTH
PARTICIPATION FEE
YOUR INITIAL TEN CHIPS WILL BE GONE JUST WITH THE PARTICIPATION FEE!
IF YOU RUN OUT OF YOUR OWN CHIPS, YOU'LL HAVE TO PAY THE PARTICI-PATION FEE USING OTHER CHIPS YOU HAVE.
ALSO, SINCE HAVING ONE REALLY SHORT GAME WOULD BE BORING, WE'VE LIMITED THE AMOUNT OF CHIPS YOU CAN BET IN A TURN TO FIVE.
MAX BET FIVE CHIPS
EVEN IF YOU DON'T HAVE ENOUGH CHIPS, YOU CAN STILL BET, RAISE, AND CALL.

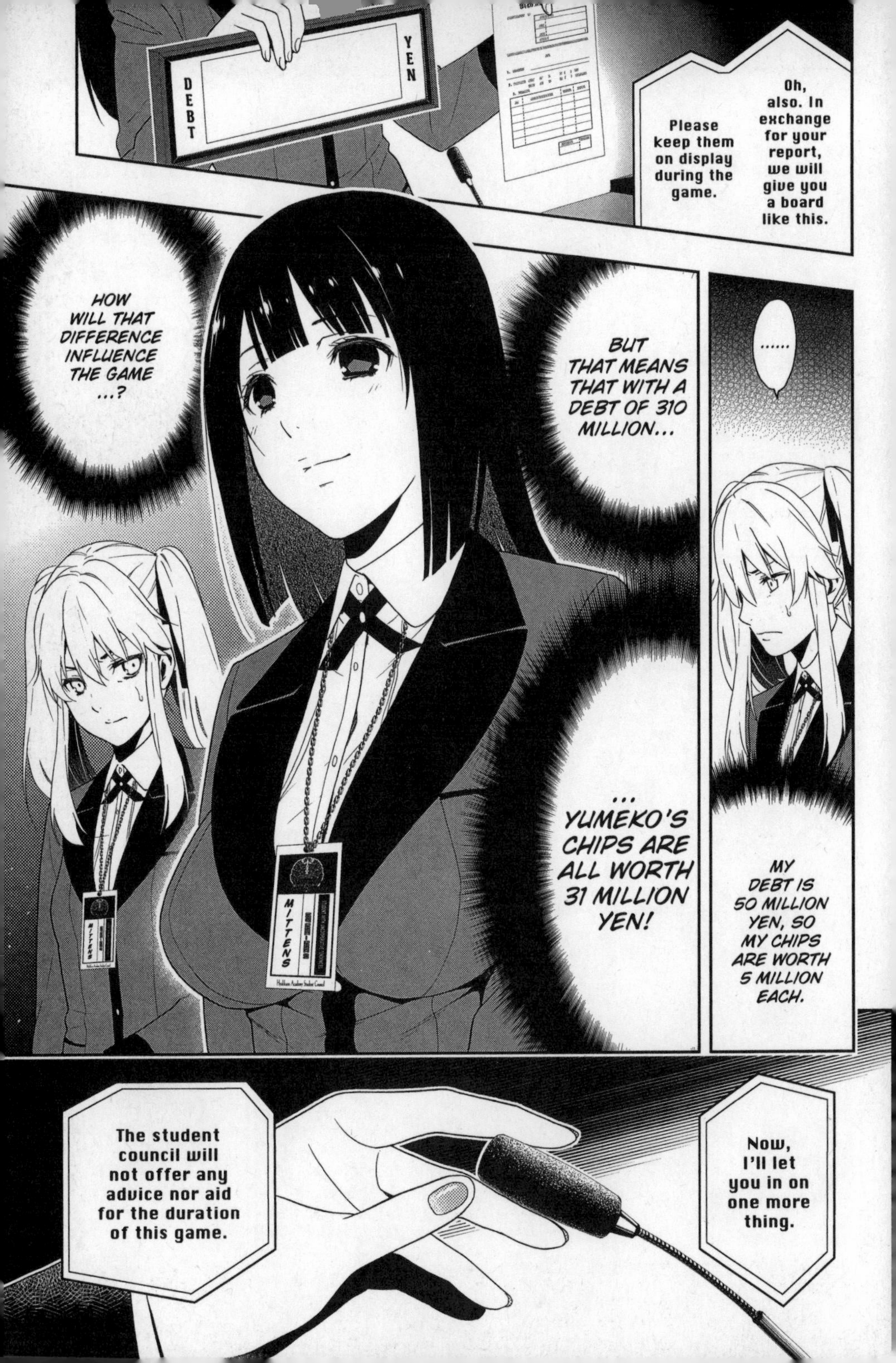
DEBT
YEN
Oh, also. In exchange for your report, we will give you a board like this.
Please keep them on display during the game.
......
MY DEBT IS 50 MILLION YEN, SO MY CHIPS ARE WORTH 5 MILLION EACH.
BUT THAT MEANS THAT WITH A DEBT OF 310 MILLION...
...YUMEKO'S CHIPS ARE ALL WORTH 31 MILLION YEN!
HOW WILL THAT DIFFERENCE INFLUENCE THE GAME...?
MITTENS
Now, I'll let you in on one more thing.
The student council will not offer any advice nor aid for the duration of this game.

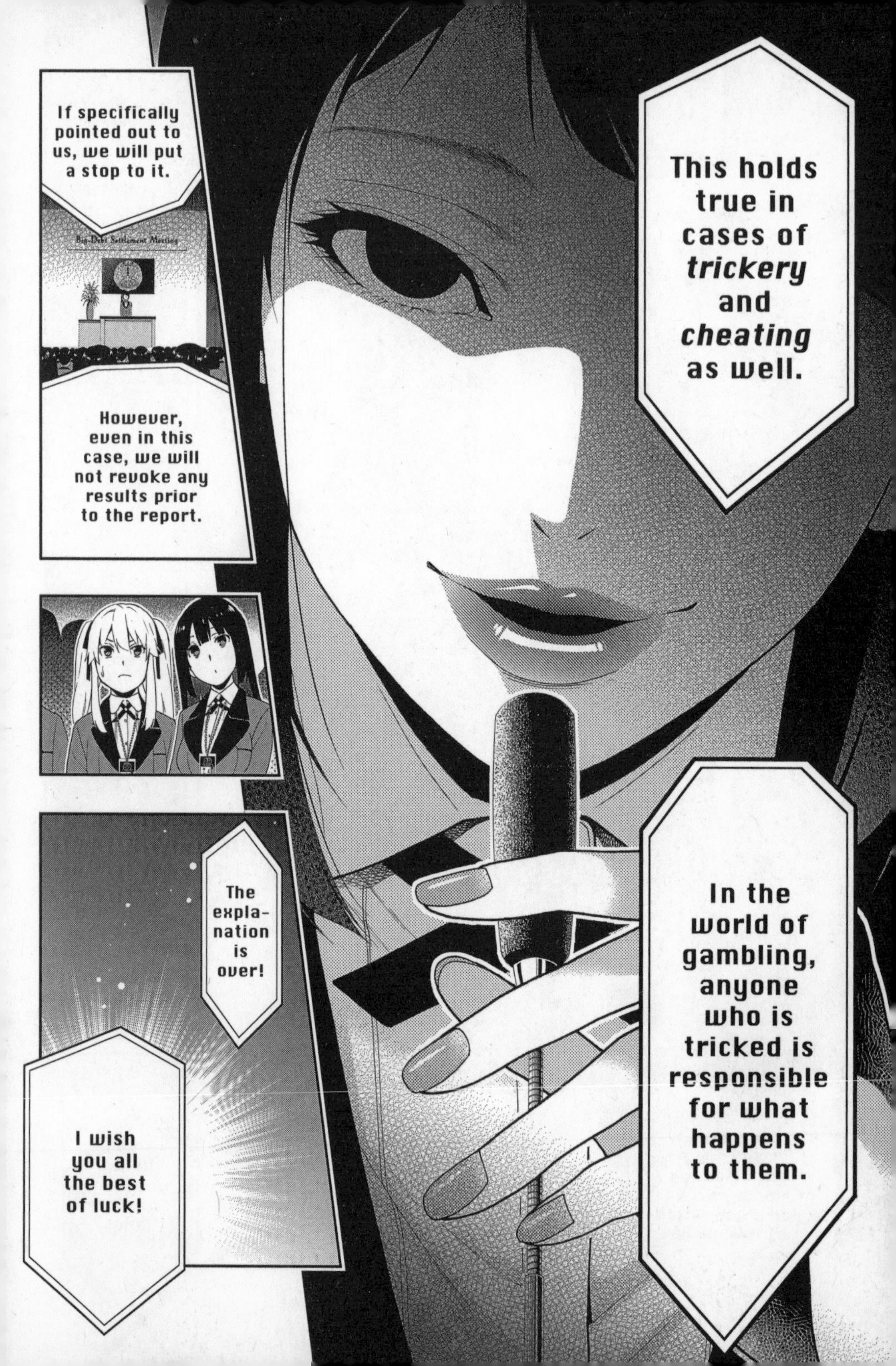
This holds true in cases of *trickery* and *cheating* as well.
In the world of gambling, anyone who is tricked is responsible for what happens to them.
If specifically pointed out to us, we will put a stop to it.
Big-Debt Settlement Meeting
However, even in this case, we will not revoke any results prior to the report.
The explanation is over!
I wish you all the best of luck!

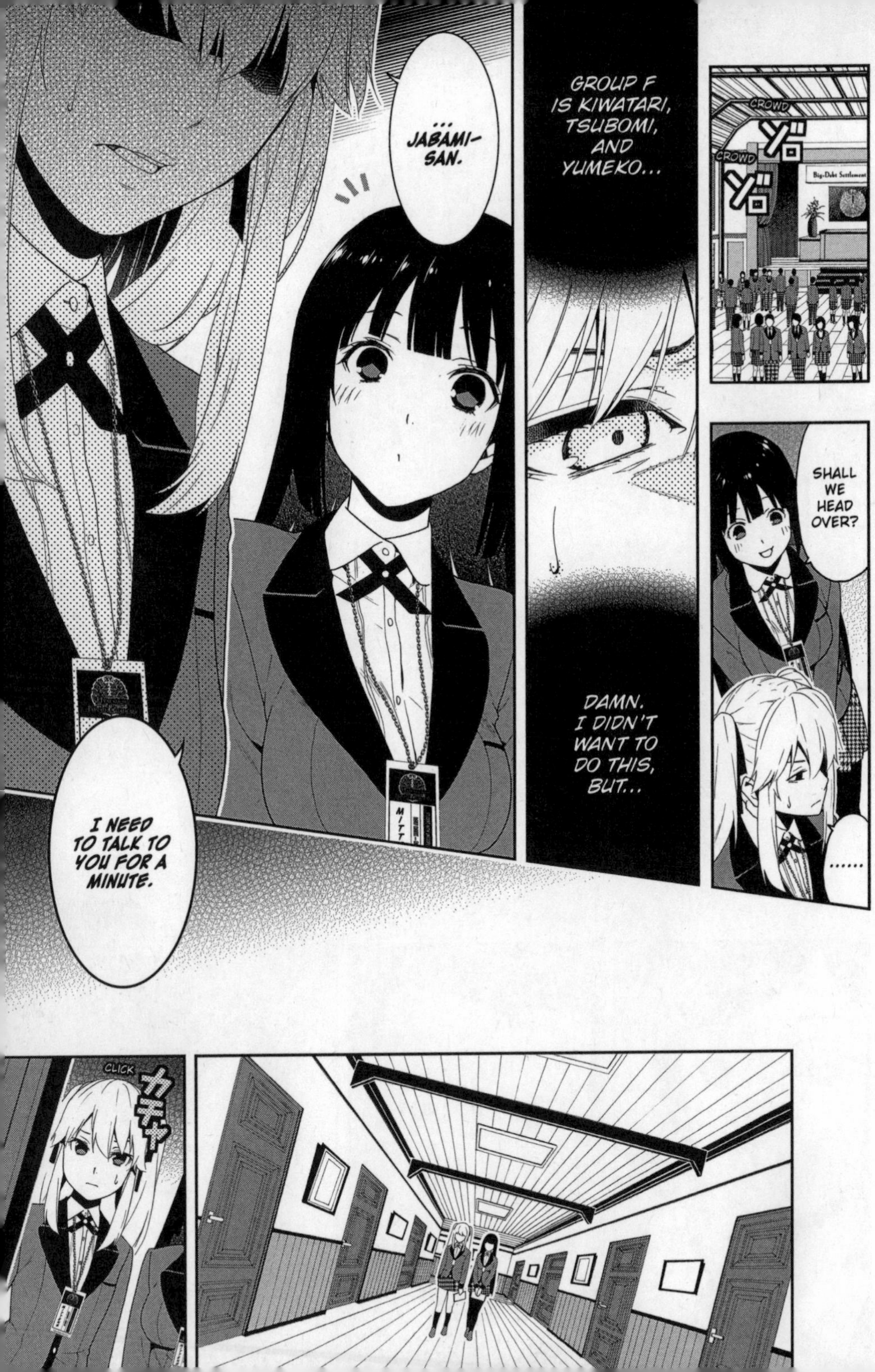
CROWD
ゾロ
CROWD
ゾロ
Big-Debt Settlement
SHALL WE HEAD OVER?
......
GROUP F IS KIWATARI, TSUBOMI, AND YUMEKO...
DAMN. I DIDN'T WANT TO DO THIS, BUT...
... JABAMI-SAN.
I NEED TO TALK TO YOU FOR A MINUTE.
CLICK
カチャ

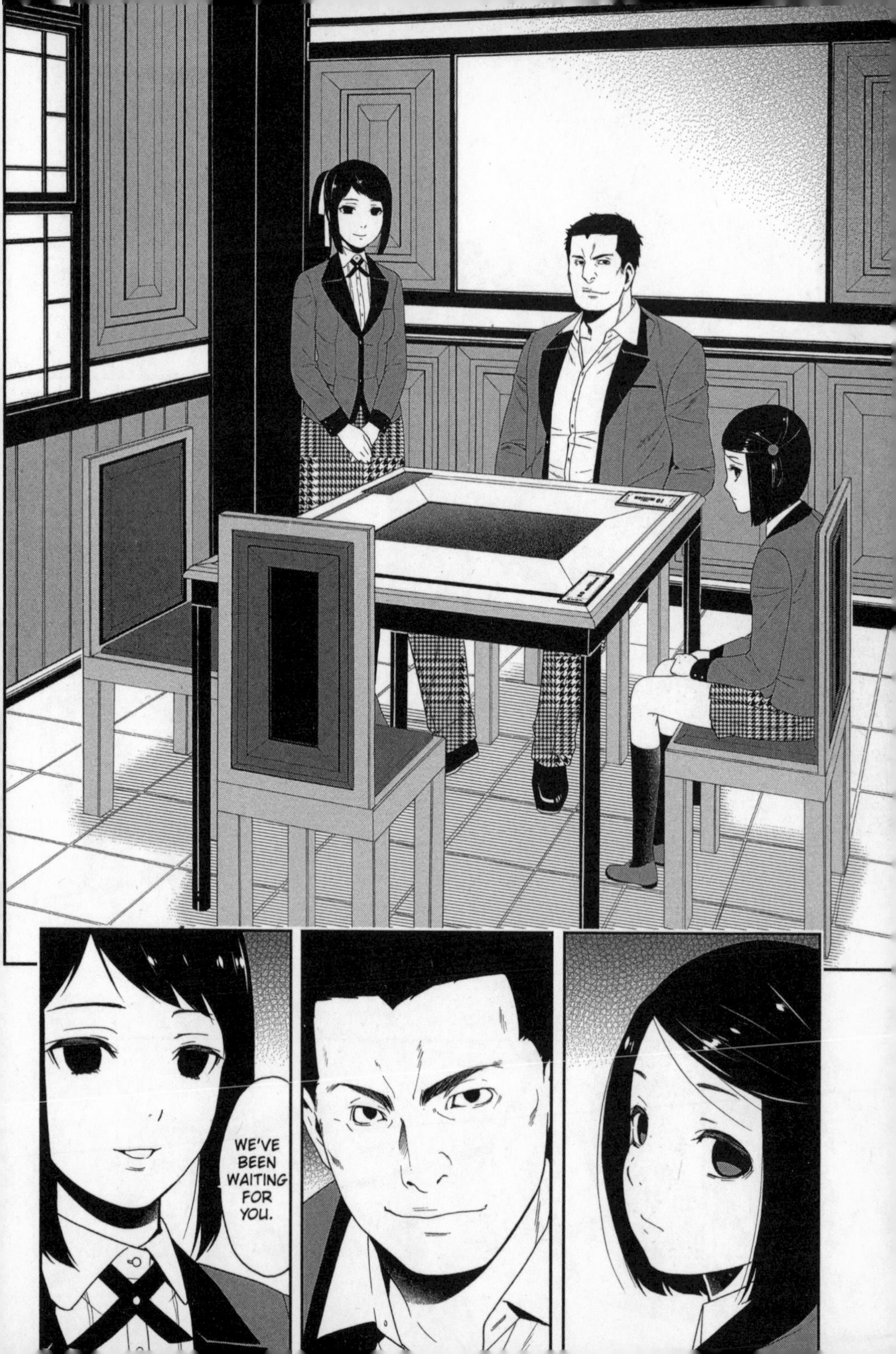
WE'VE BEEN WAITING FOR YOU.

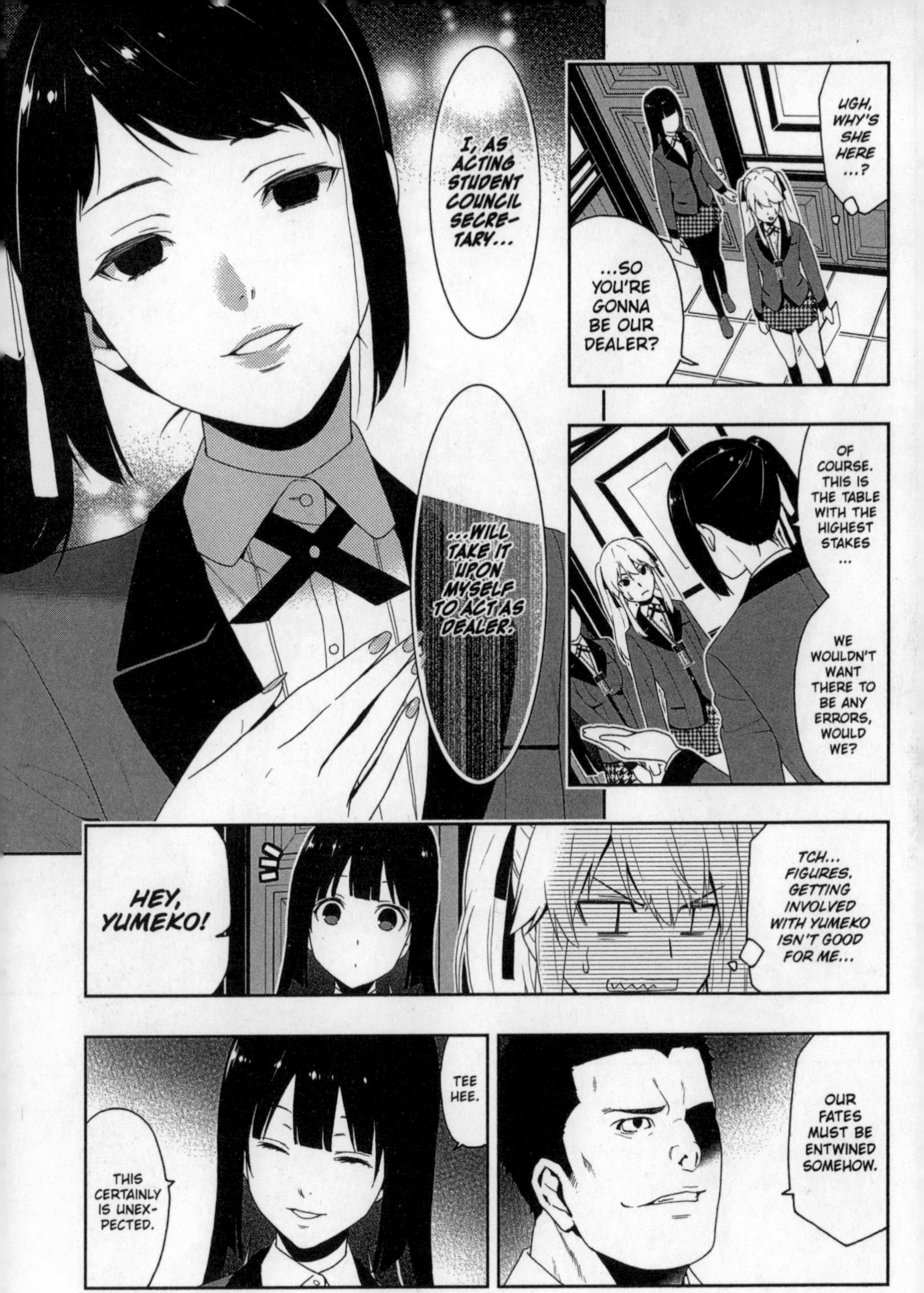
UGH, WHY'S SHE HERE ...?
...SO YOU'RE GONNA BE OUR DEALER?
OF COURSE. THIS IS THE TABLE WITH THE HIGHEST STAKES ...
WE WOULDN'T WANT THERE TO BE ANY ERRORS, WOULD WE?
I, AS ACTING STUDENT COUNCIL SECRETARY...
...WILL TAKE IT UPON MYSELF TO ACT AS DEALER.
TCH... FIGURES. GETTING INVOLVED WITH YUMEKO ISN'T GOOD FOR ME...
HEY, YUMEKO!
OUR FATES MUST BE ENTWINED SOMEHOW.
TEE HEE.
THIS CERTAINLY IS UNEXPECTED.

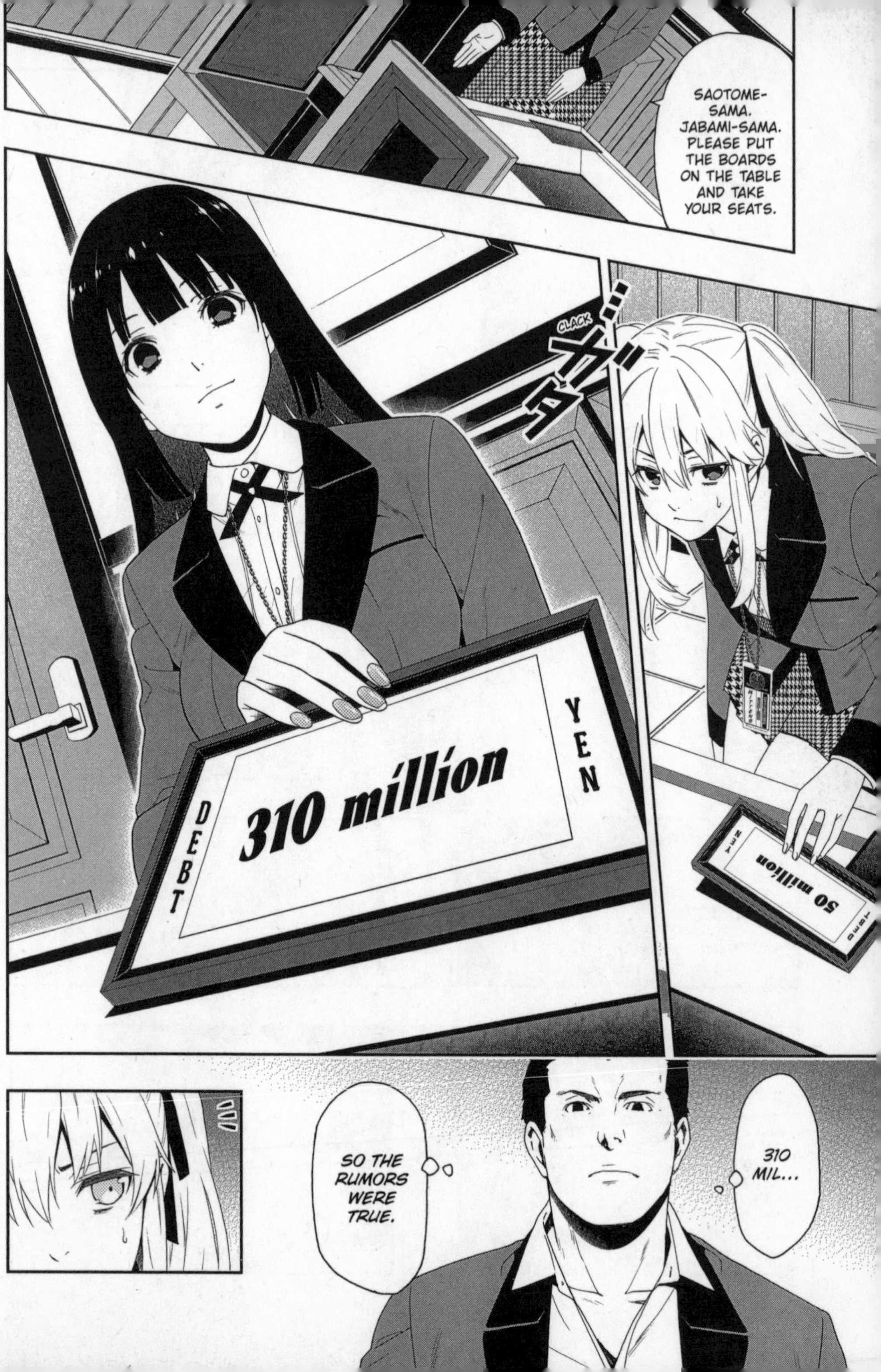
SAOTOME-SAMA. JABAMI-SAMA. PLEASE PUT THE BOARDS ON THE TABLE AND TAKE YOUR SEATS.
CLACK
DEBT
310 million
YEN
50 million
310 MIL...
SO THE RUMORS WERE TRUE.

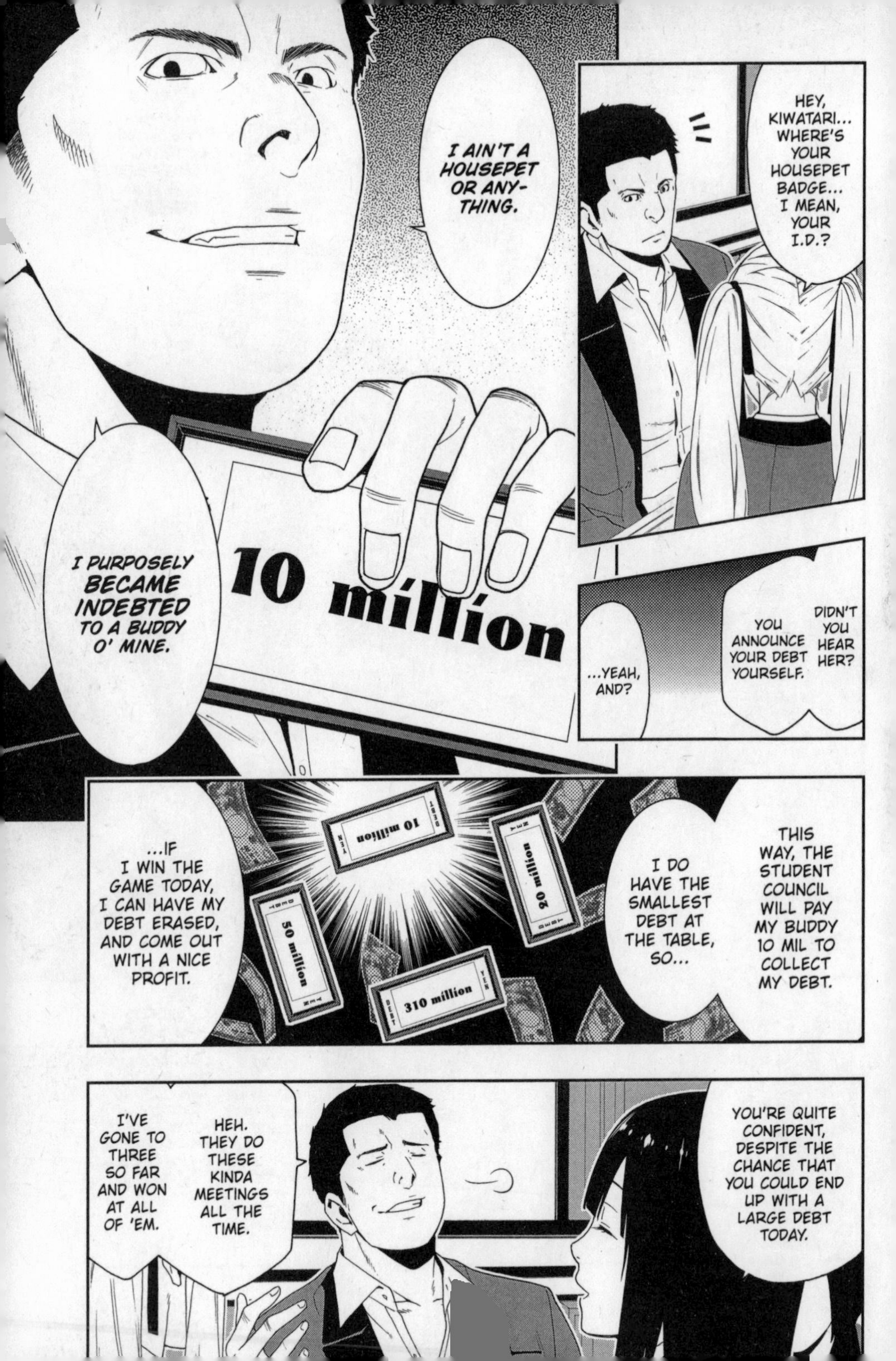
HEY, KIWATARI... WHERE'S YOUR HOUSEPET BADGE... I MEAN, YOUR I.D.?
DIDN'T YOU HEAR HER?
YOU ANNOUNCE YOUR DEBT YOURSELF.
...YEAH, AND?
I AIN'T A HOUSEPET OR ANY-THING.
10 million
I PURPOSELY BECAME INDEBTED TO A BUDDY O' MINE.
THIS WAY, THE STUDENT COUNCIL WILL PAY MY BUDDY 10 MIL TO COLLECT MY DEBT.
I DO HAVE THE SMALLEST DEBT AT THE TABLE, SO...
10 million
20 million
50 million
310 million
...IF I WIN THE GAME TODAY, I CAN HAVE MY DEBT ERASED, AND COME OUT WITH A NICE PROFIT.
YOU'RE QUITE CONFIDENT, DESPITE THE CHANCE THAT YOU COULD END UP WITH A LARGE DEBT TODAY.
HEH. THEY DO THESE KINDA MEETINGS ALL THE TIME.
I'VE GONE TO THREE SO FAR AND WON AT ALL OF 'EM.

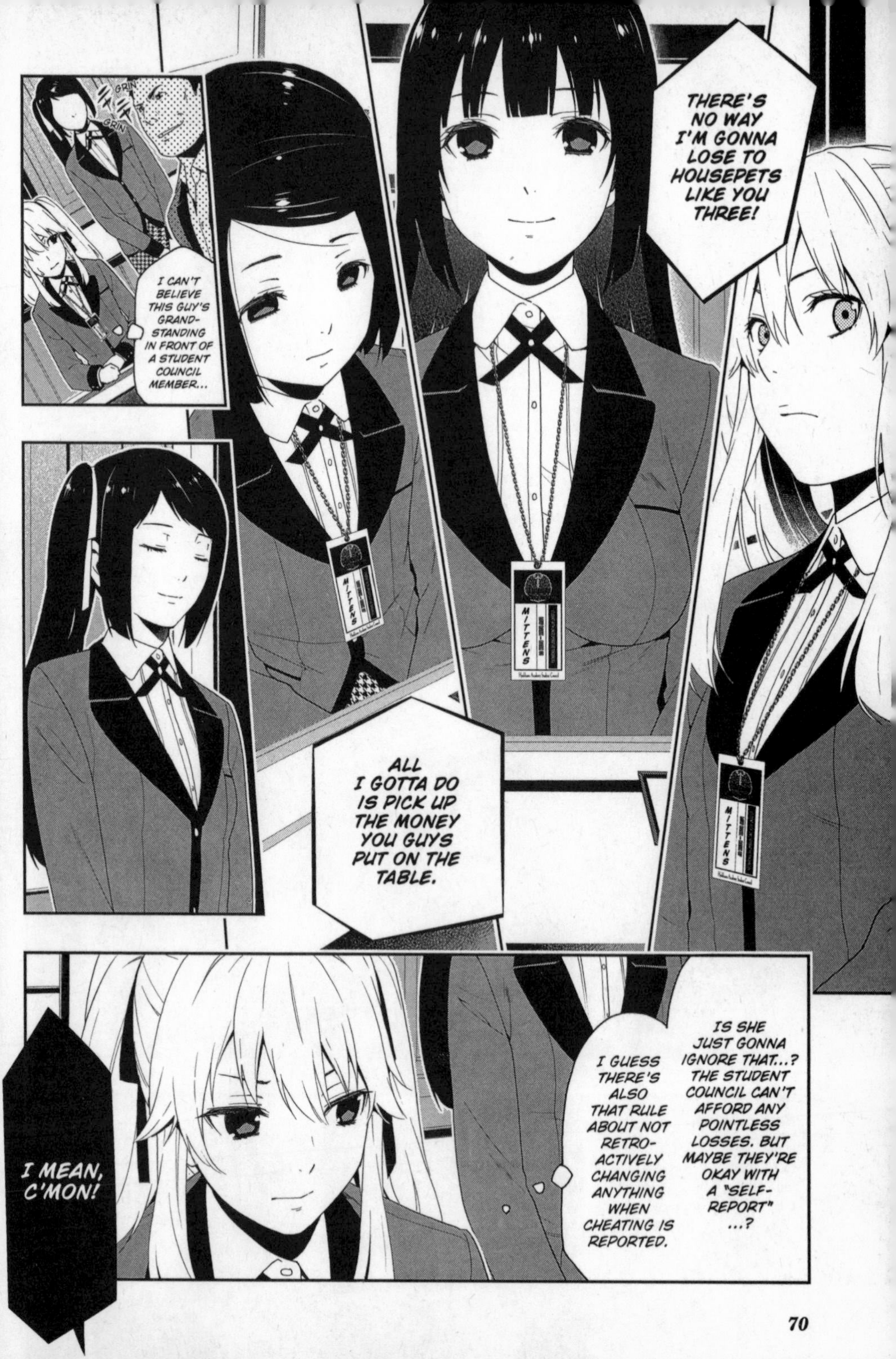
THERE'S NO WAY I'M GONNA LOSE TO HOUSEPETS LIKE YOU THREE!
ALL I GOTTA DO IS PICK UP THE MONEY YOU GUYS PUT ON THE TABLE.
GRIN GRIN
I CAN'T BELIEVE THIS GUY'S GRAND-STANDING IN FRONT OF A STUDENT COUNCIL MEMBER...
IS SHE JUST GONNA IGNORE THAT...? THE STUDENT COUNCIL CAN'T AFFORD ANY POINTLESS LOSSES. BUT MAYBE THEY'RE OKAY WITH A "SELF-REPORT" ...?
I GUESS THERE'S ALSO THAT RULE ABOUT NOT RETRO-ACTIVELY CHANGING ANYTHING WHEN CHEATING IS REPORTED.
I MEAN, C'MON!

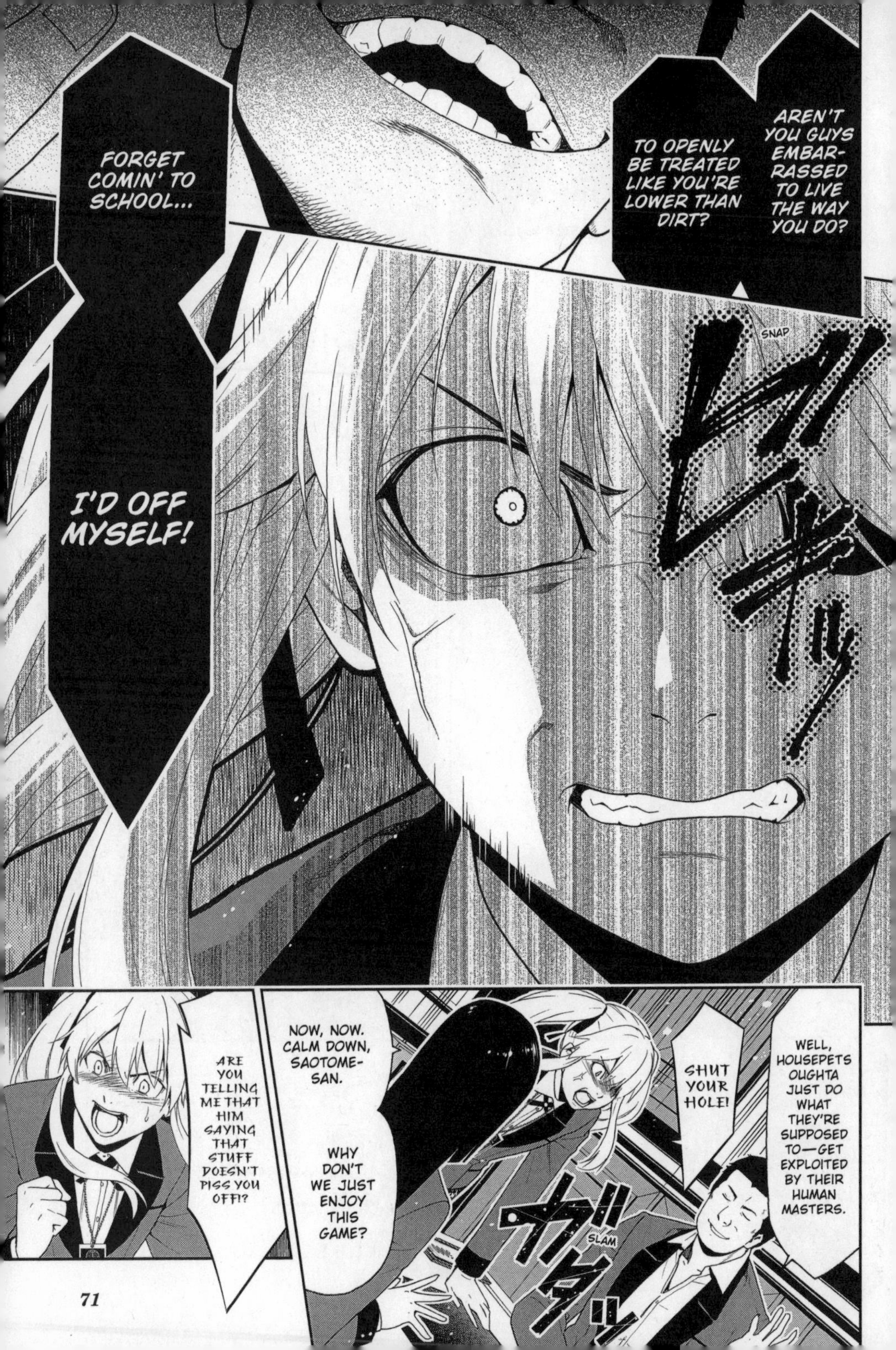
AREN'T YOU GUYS EMBARRASSED TO LIVE THE WAY YOU DO?
TO OPENLY BE TREATED LIKE YOU'RE LOWER THAN DIRT?
FORGET COMIN' TO SCHOOL...
I'D OFF MYSELF!
SNAP
WELL, HOUSEPETS OUGHTA JUST DO WHAT THEY'RE SUPPOSED TO—GET EXPLOITED BY THEIR HUMAN MASTERS.
SHUT YOUR HOLE!
SLAM
NOW, NOW. CALM DOWN, SAOTOME-SAN.
WHY DON'T WE JUST ENJOY THIS GAME?
ARE YOU TELLING ME THAT HIM SAYING THAT STUFF DOESN'T PISS YOU OFF!?

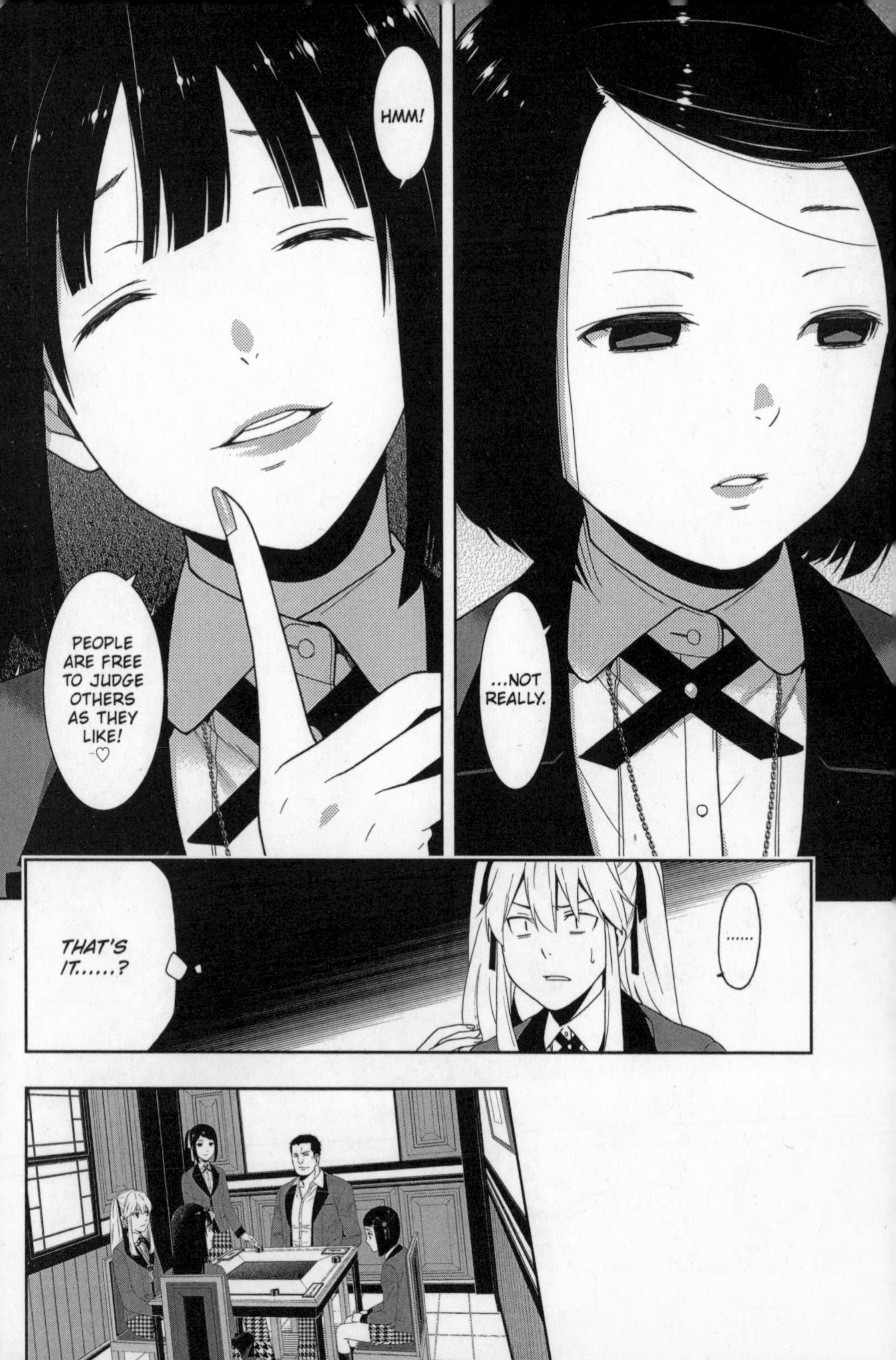
...NOT REALLY.
HMM!
PEOPLE ARE FREE TO JUDGE OTHERS AS THEY LIKE! ♡
......
THAT'S IT......?

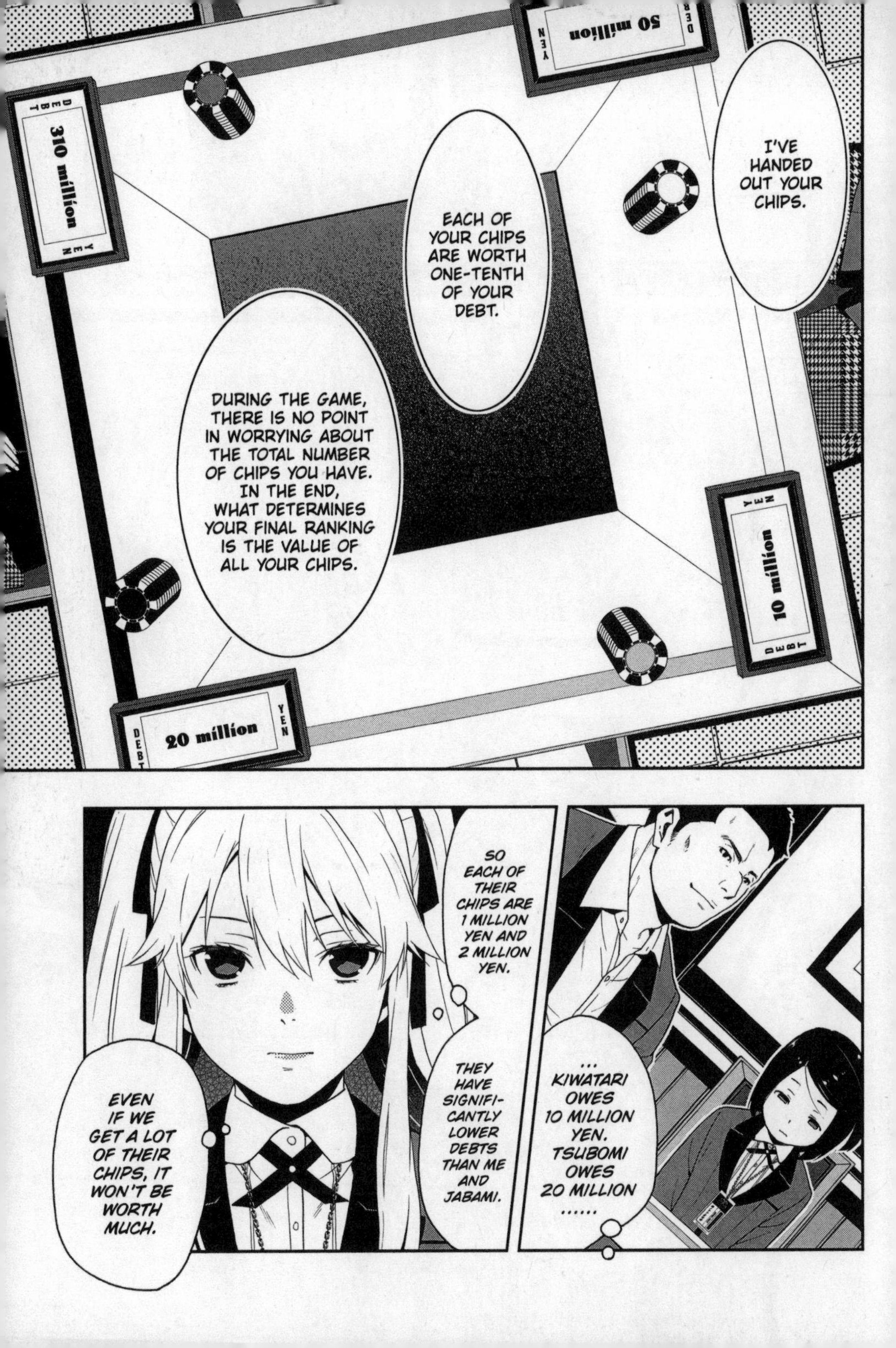

I'VE HANDED OUT YOUR CHIPS.
EACH OF YOUR CHIPS ARE WORTH ONE-TENTH OF YOUR DEBT.
DEBT 50 million YEN
DEBT 310 million YEN
DURING THE GAME, THERE IS NO POINT IN WORRYING ABOUT THE TOTAL NUMBER OF CHIPS YOU HAVE. IN THE END, WHAT DETERMINES YOUR FINAL RANKING IS THE VALUE OF ALL YOUR CHIPS.
DEBT 10 million YEN
DEBT 20 million YEN
... KIWATARI OWES 10 MILLION YEN. TSUBOMI OWES 20 MILLION ......
SO EACH OF THEIR CHIPS ARE 1 MILLION YEN AND 2 MILLION YEN.
THEY HAVE SIGNIFI-CANTLY LOWER DEBTS THAN ME AND JABAMI.
EVEN IF WE GET A LOT OF THEIR CHIPS, IT WON'T BE WORTH MUCH.

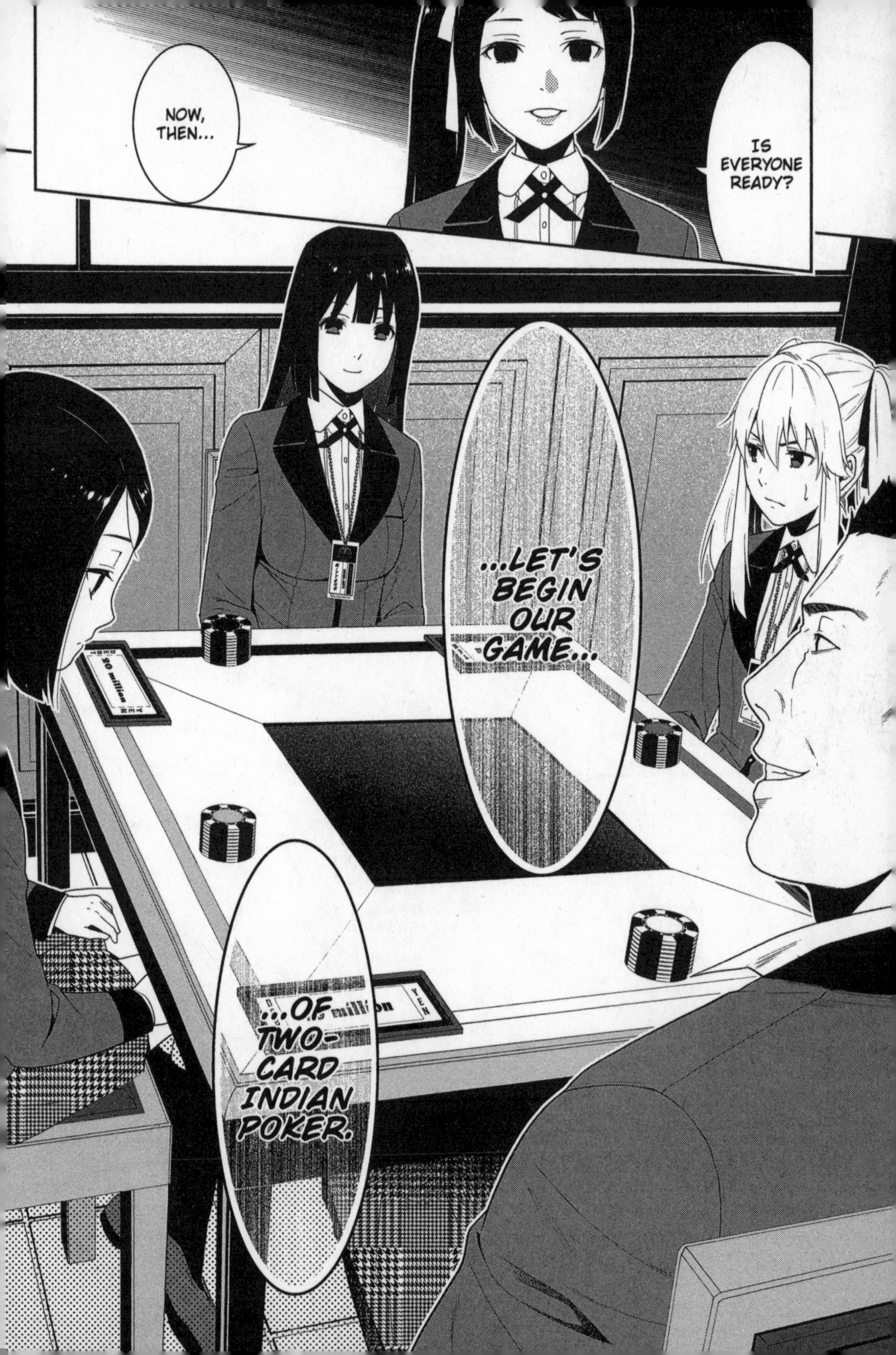
IS EVERYONE READY?
NOW, THEN...
...LET'S BEGIN OUR GAME...
...OF TWO-CARD INDIAN POKER.

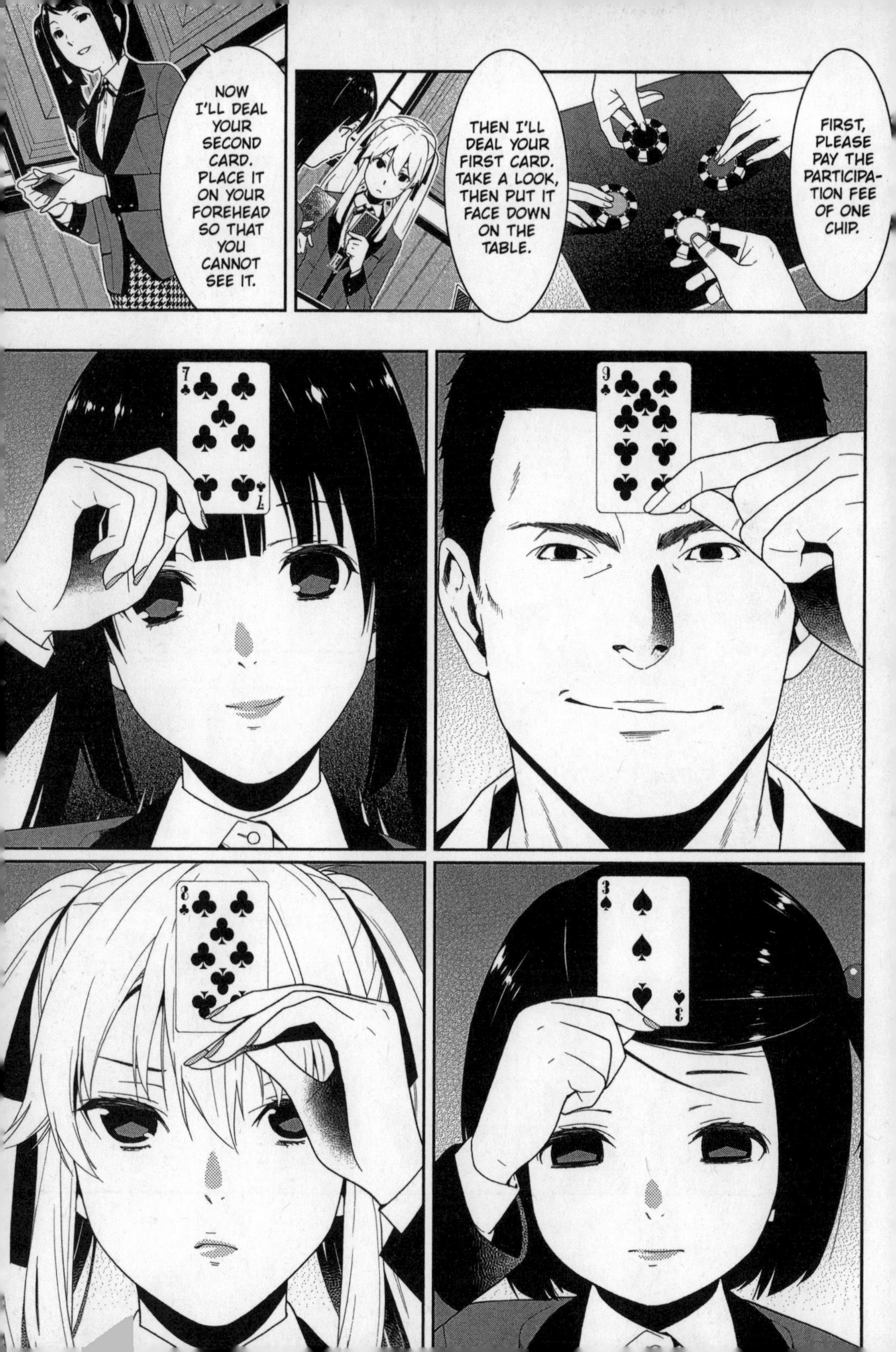
FIRST, PLEASE PAY THE PARTICIPA-TION FEE OF ONE CHIP.
THEN I'LL DEAL YOUR FIRST CARD. TAKE A LOOK, THEN PUT IT FACE DOWN ON THE TABLE.
NOW I'LL DEAL YOUR SECOND CARD. PLACE IT ON YOUR FOREHEAD SO THAT YOU CANNOT SEE IT.

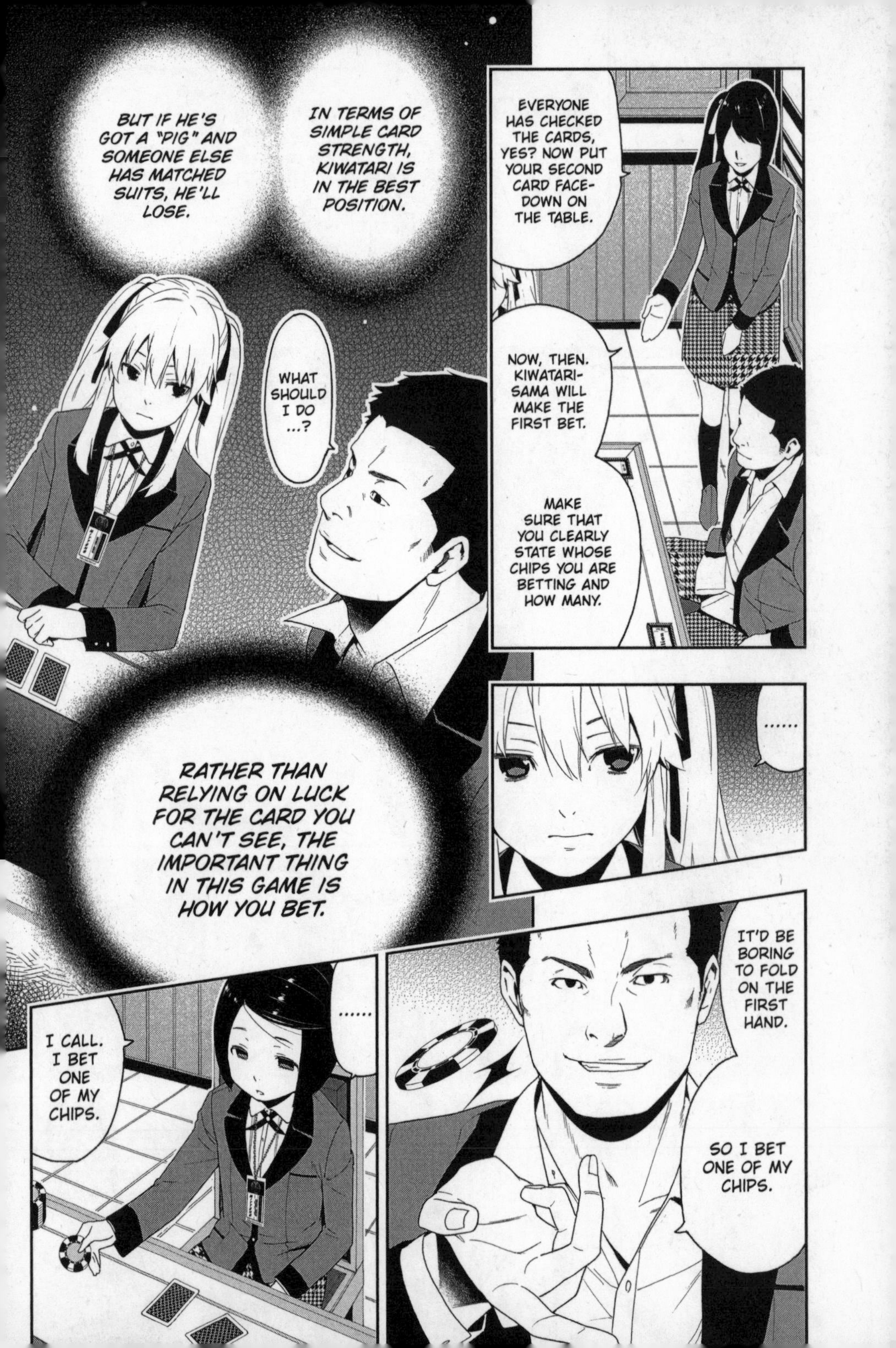
EVERYONE HAS CHECKED THE CARDS, YES? NOW PUT YOUR SECOND CARD FACE-DOWN ON THE TABLE.
NOW, THEN. KIWATARI-SAMA WILL MAKE THE FIRST BET.
MAKE SURE THAT YOU CLEARLY STATE WHOSE CHIPS YOU ARE BETTING AND HOW MANY.
......
IN TERMS OF SIMPLE CARD STRENGTH, KIWATARI IS IN THE BEST POSITION.
BUT IF HE'S GOT A "PIG" AND SOMEONE ELSE HAS MATCHED SUITS, HE'LL LOSE.
WHAT SHOULD I DO ...?
RATHER THAN RELYING ON LUCK FOR THE CARD YOU CAN'T SEE, THE IMPORTANT THING IN THIS GAME IS HOW YOU BET.
IT'D BE BORING TO FOLD ON THE FIRST HAND.
SO I BET ONE OF MY CHIPS.
......
I CALL. I BET ONE OF MY CHIPS.

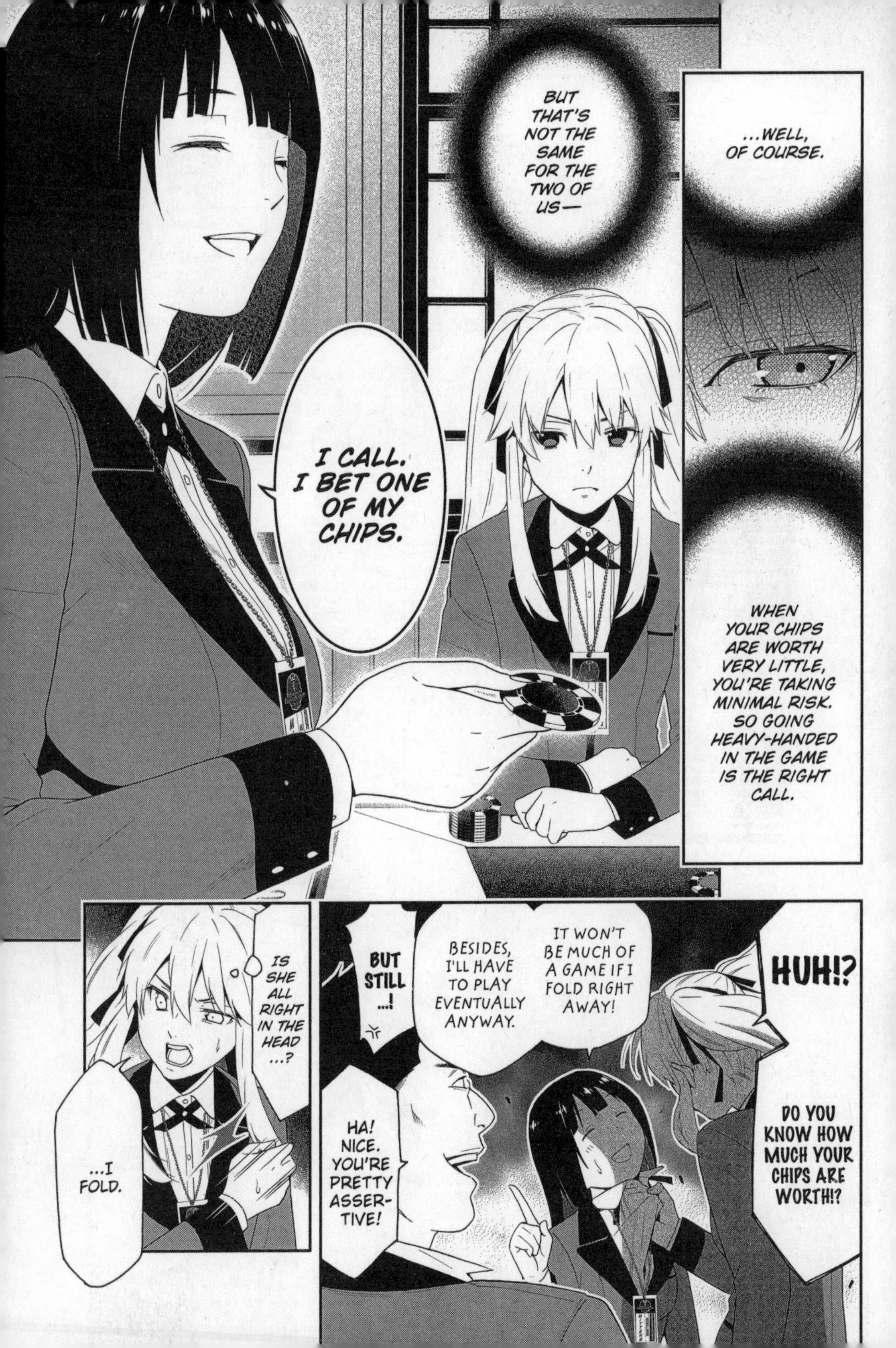
...WELL, OF COURSE.
WHEN YOUR CHIPS ARE WORTH VERY LITTLE, YOU'RE TAKING MINIMAL RISK. SO GOING HEAVY-HANDED IN THE GAME IS THE RIGHT CALL.
BUT THAT'S NOT THE SAME FOR THE TWO OF US—
I CALL. I BET ONE OF MY CHIPS.
HUH!?
DO YOU KNOW HOW MUCH YOUR CHIPS ARE WORTH!?
IT WON'T BE MUCH OF A GAME IF I FOLD RIGHT AWAY!
BESIDES, I'LL HAVE TO PLAY EVENTUALLY ANYWAY.
BUT STILL ...!
HA! NICE. YOU'RE PRETTY ASSERTIVE!
IS SHE ALL RIGHT IN THE HEAD ...?
...I FOLD.

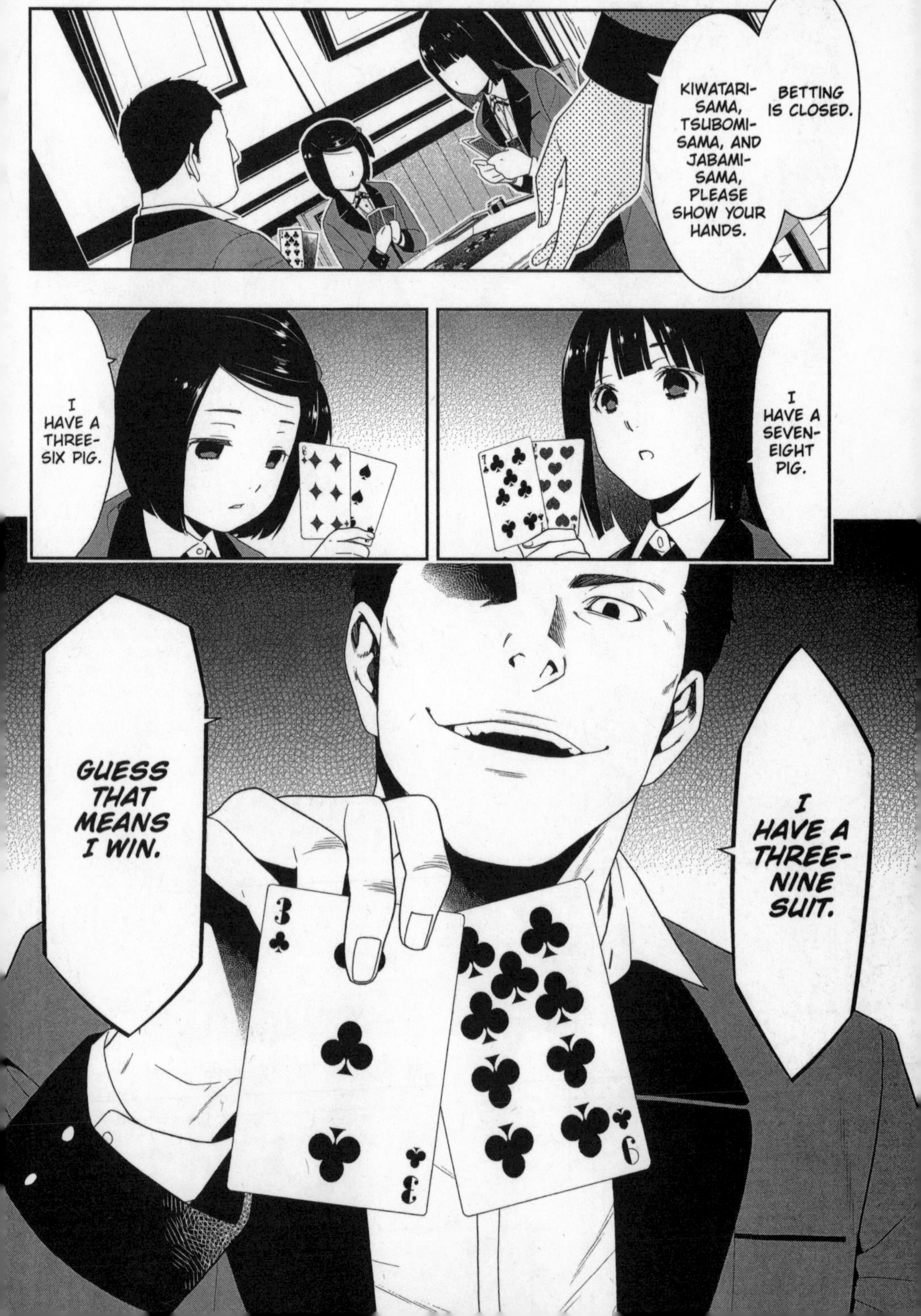
BETTING IS CLOSED.
KIWATARI-SAMA, TSUBOMI-SAMA, AND JABAMI-SAMA, PLEASE SHOW YOUR HANDS.
I HAVE A SEVEN-EIGHT PIG.
I HAVE A THREE-SIX PIG.
I HAVE A THREE-NINE SUIT.
GUESS THAT MEANS I WIN.

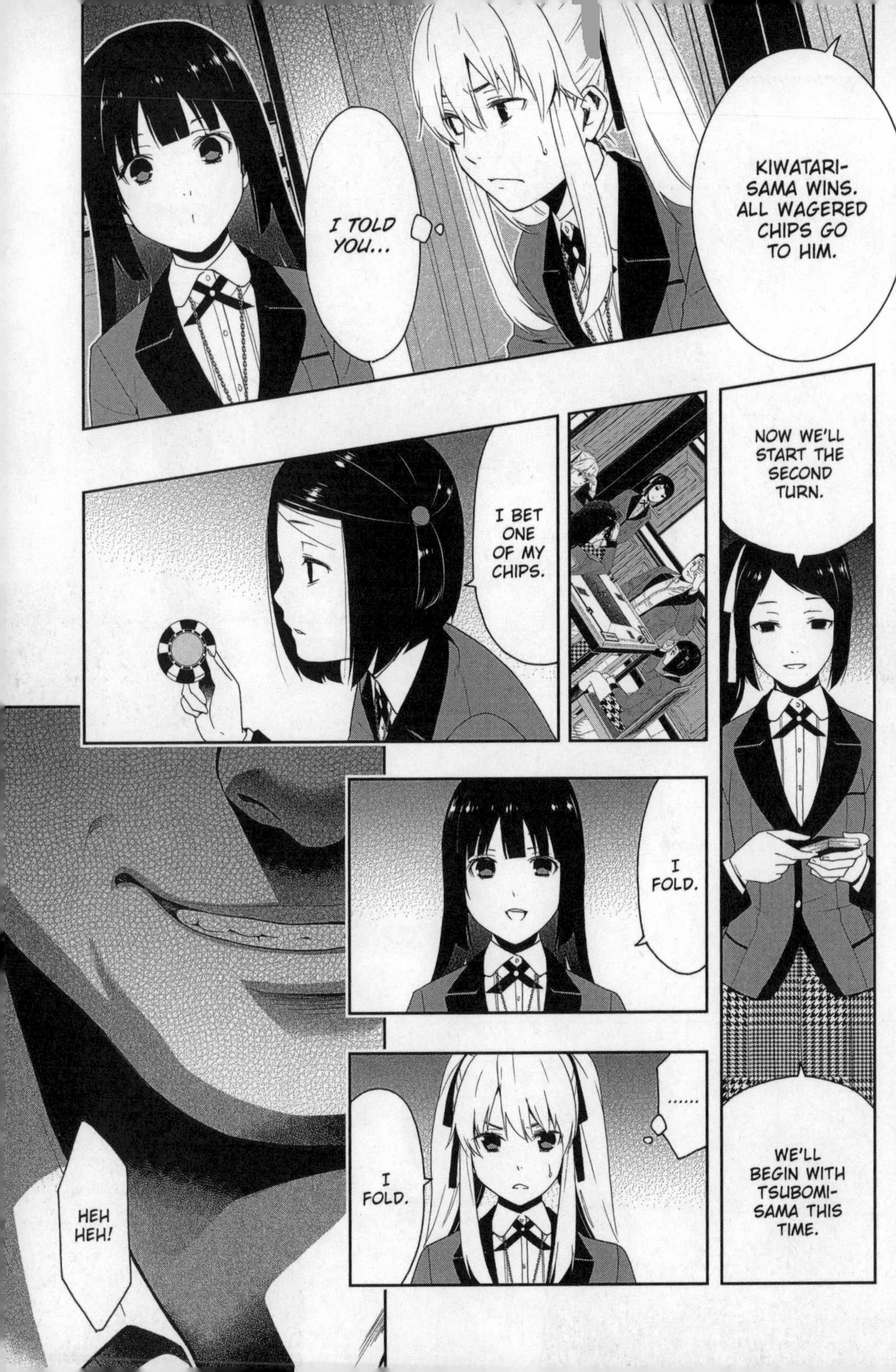
KIWATARI-SAMA WINS. ALL WAGERED CHIPS GO TO HIM.
I TOLD YOU...
NOW WE'LL START THE SECOND TURN.
WE'LL BEGIN WITH TSUBOMI-SAMA THIS TIME.
I BET ONE OF MY CHIPS.
I FOLD.
......
I FOLD.
HEH HEH!

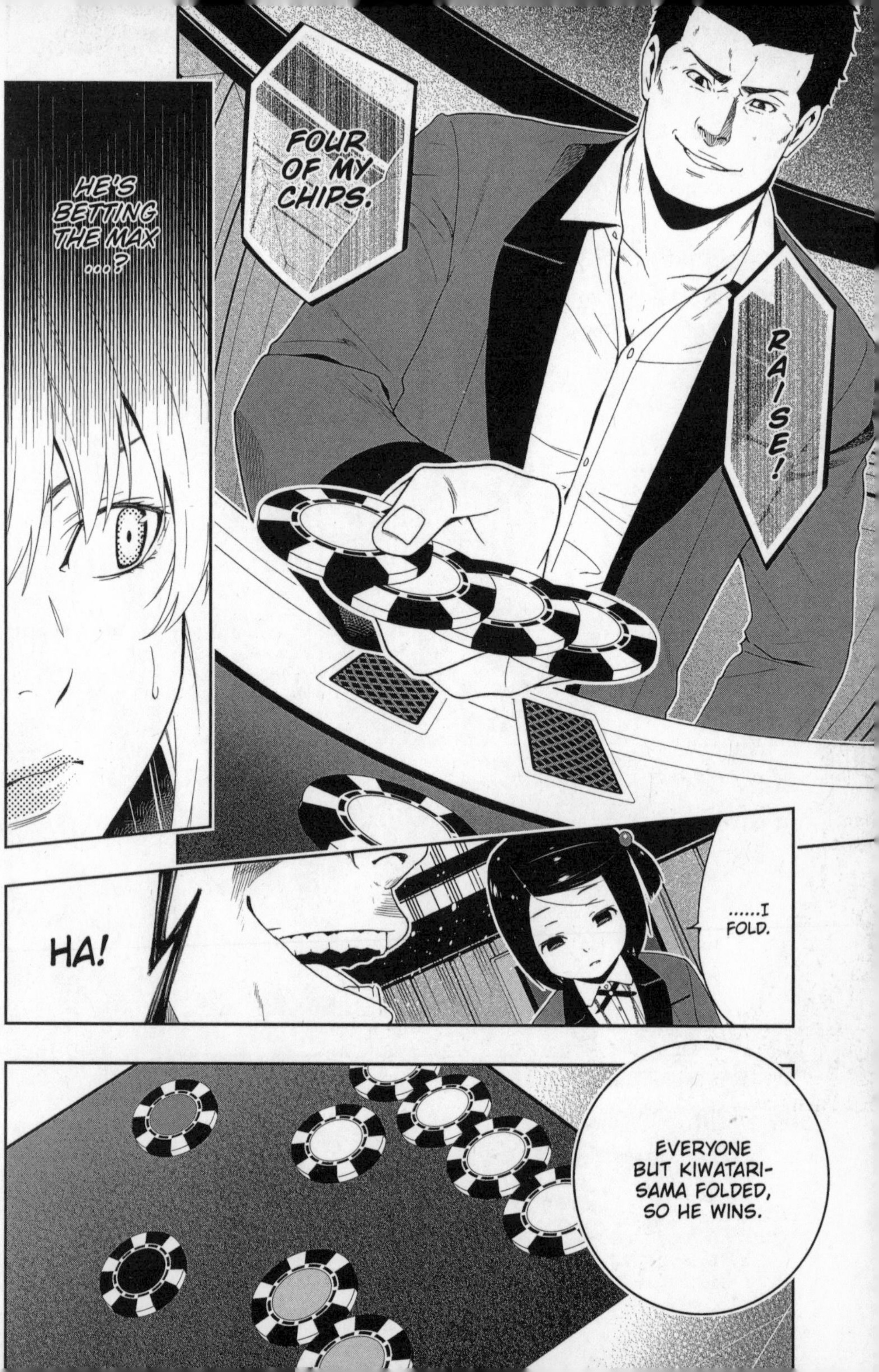
RAISE!
FOUR OF MY CHIPS.
HE'S BETTING THE MAX ...?
......I FOLD.
HA!
EVERYONE BUT KIWATARI-SAMA FOLDED, SO HE WINS.

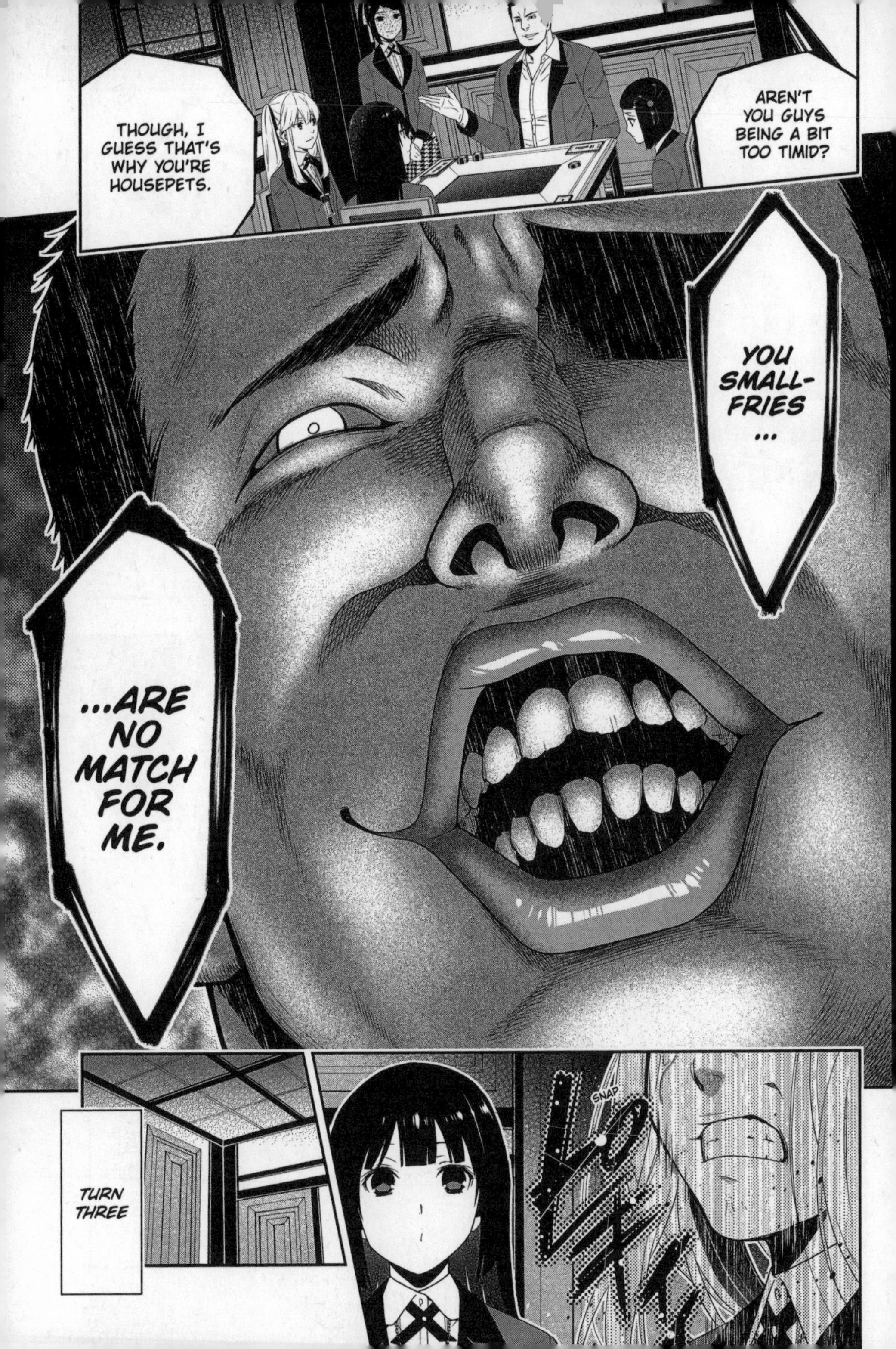
AREN'T YOU GUYS BEING A BIT TOO TIMID?
THOUGH, I GUESS THAT'S WHY YOU'RE HOUSEPETS.
YOU SMALL-FRIES ...
...ARE NO MATCH FOR ME.
SNAP
TURN THREE

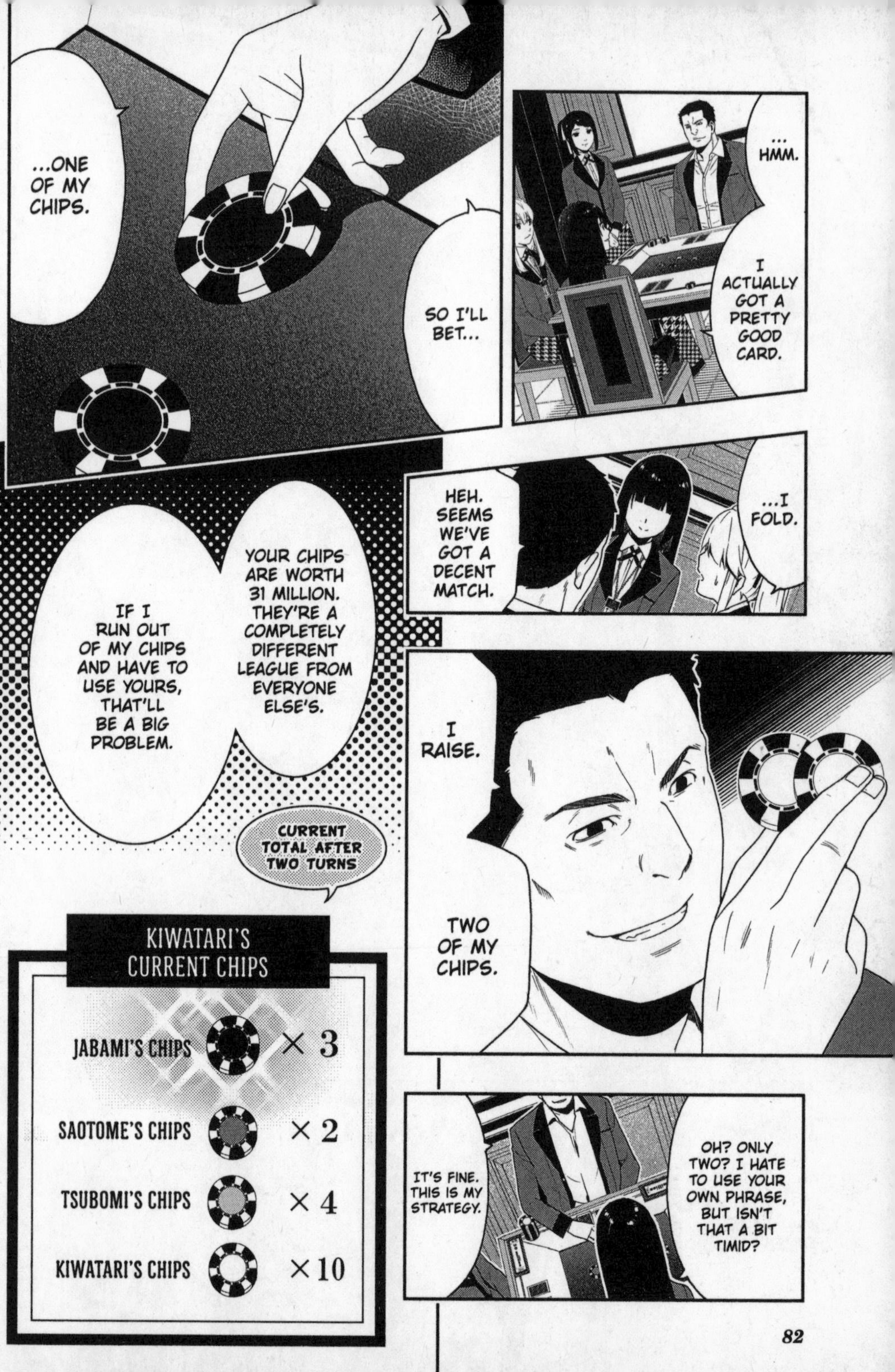
...HMM.
I ACTUALLY GOT A PRETTY GOOD CARD.
SO I'LL BET...
...ONE OF MY CHIPS.
...I FOLD.
HEH. SEEMS WE'VE GOT A DECENT MATCH.
YOUR CHIPS ARE WORTH 31 MILLION. THEY'RE A COMPLETELY DIFFERENT LEAGUE FROM EVERYONE ELSE'S.
IF I RUN OUT OF MY CHIPS AND HAVE TO USE YOURS, THAT'LL BE A BIG PROBLEM.
I RAISE.
TWO OF MY CHIPS.
CURRENT TOTAL AFTER TWO TURNS
KIWATARI'S CURRENT CHIPS
JABAMI'S CHIPS × 3
SAOTOME'S CHIPS × 2
TSUBOMI'S CHIPS × 4
KIWATARI'S CHIPS × 10
OH? ONLY TWO? I HATE TO USE YOUR OWN PHRASE, BUT ISN'T THAT A BIT TIMID?
IT'S FINE. THIS IS MY STRATEGY.

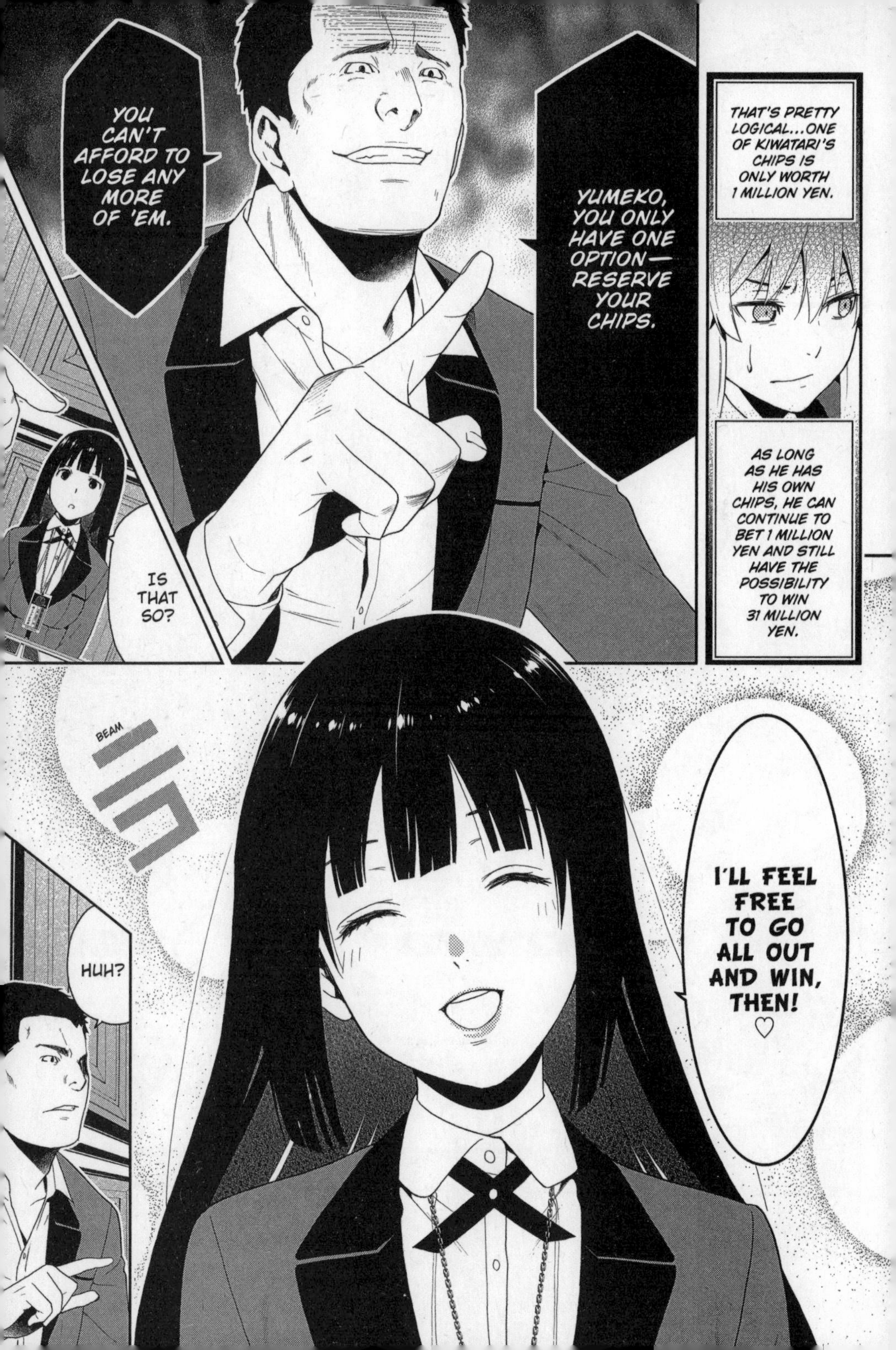
THAT'S PRETTY LOGICAL...ONE OF KIWATARI'S CHIPS IS ONLY WORTH 1 MILLION YEN.
AS LONG AS HE HAS HIS OWN CHIPS, HE CAN CONTINUE TO BET 1 MILLION YEN AND STILL HAVE THE POSSIBILITY TO WIN 31 MILLION YEN.
YUMEKO, YOU ONLY HAVE ONE OPTION—RESERVE YOUR CHIPS.
YOU CAN'T AFFORD TO LOSE ANY MORE OF 'EM.
IS THAT SO?
I'LL FEEL FREE TO GO ALL OUT AND WIN, THEN! ♡
BEAM
HUH?

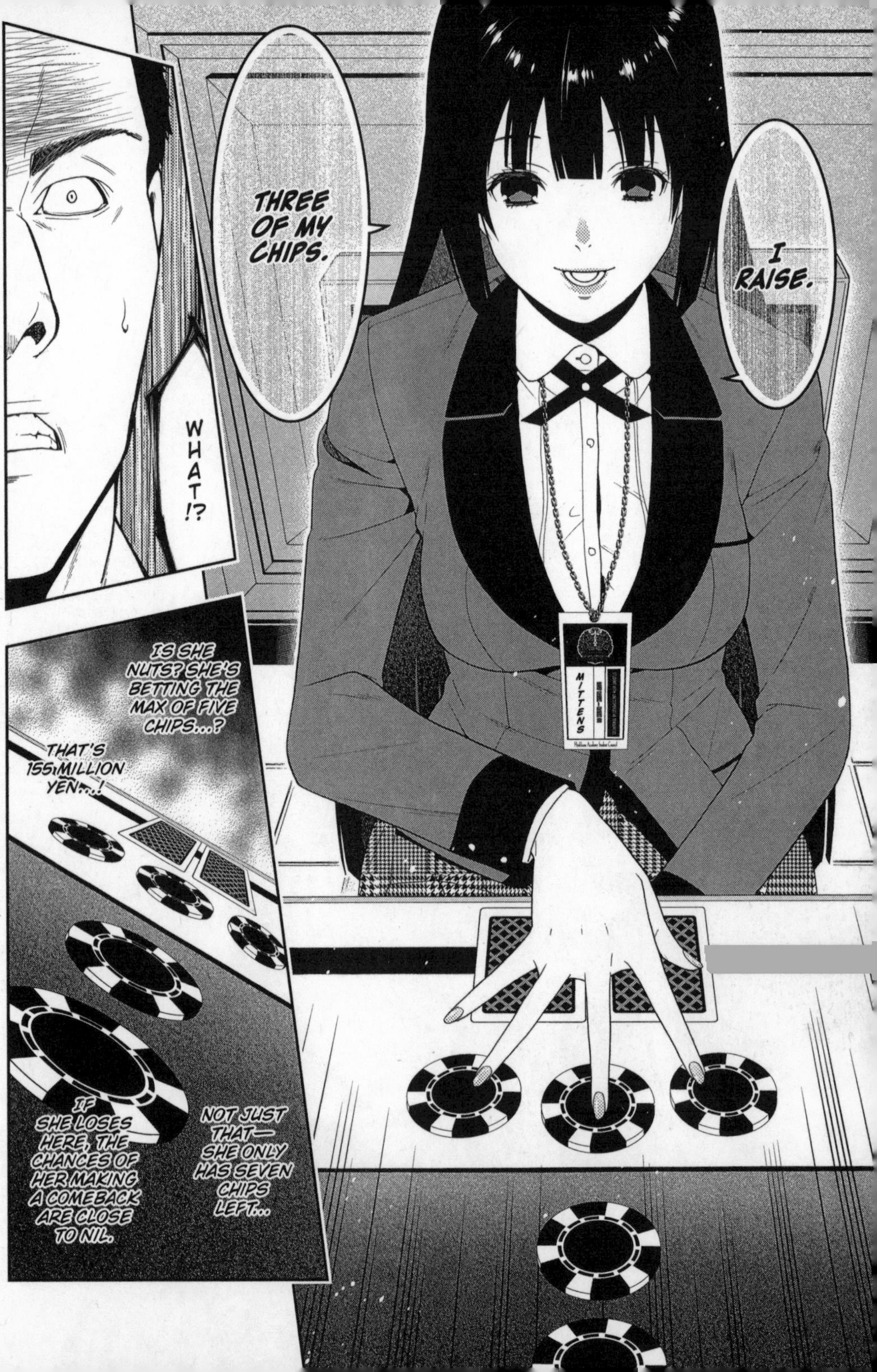
I RAISE.
THREE OF MY CHIPS.
MITTENS
WHAT!?
IS SHE NUTS? SHE'S BETTING THE MAX OF FIVE CHIPS...?
THAT'S 155 MILLION YEN...!
NOT JUST THAT— SHE ONLY HAS SEVEN CHIPS LEFT...
IF SHE LOSES HERE, THE CHANCES OF HER MAKING A COMEBACK ARE CLOSE TO NIL.

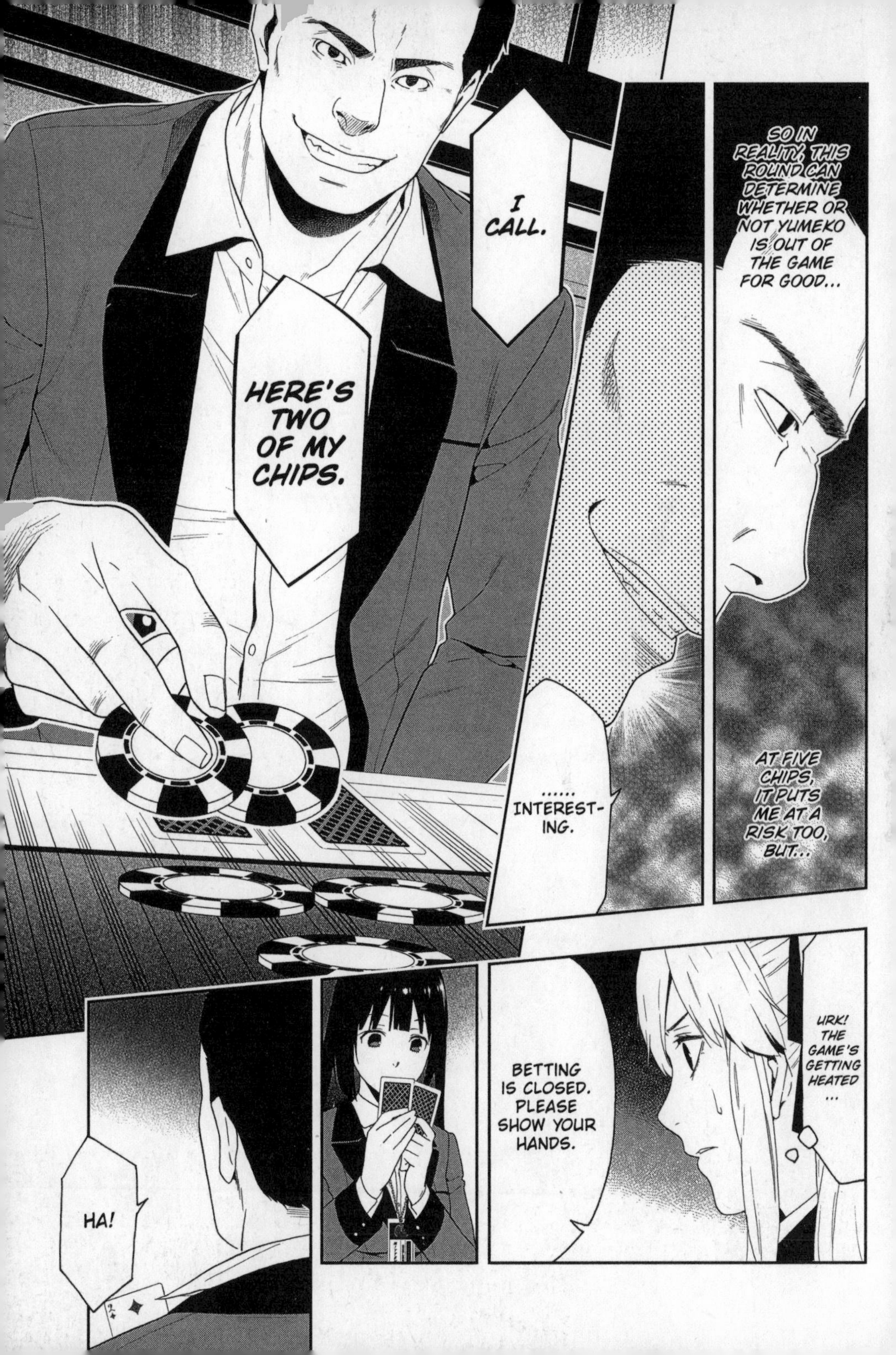
SO IN REALITY, THIS ROUND CAN DETERMINE WHETHER OR NOT YUMEKO IS OUT OF THE GAME FOR GOOD...
AT FIVE CHIPS, IT PUTS ME AT A RISK TOO, BUT...
......INTEREST-ING.
I CALL.
HERE'S TWO OF MY CHIPS.
URK! THE GAME'S GETTING HEATED...
BETTING IS CLOSED. PLEASE SHOW YOUR HANDS.
HA!

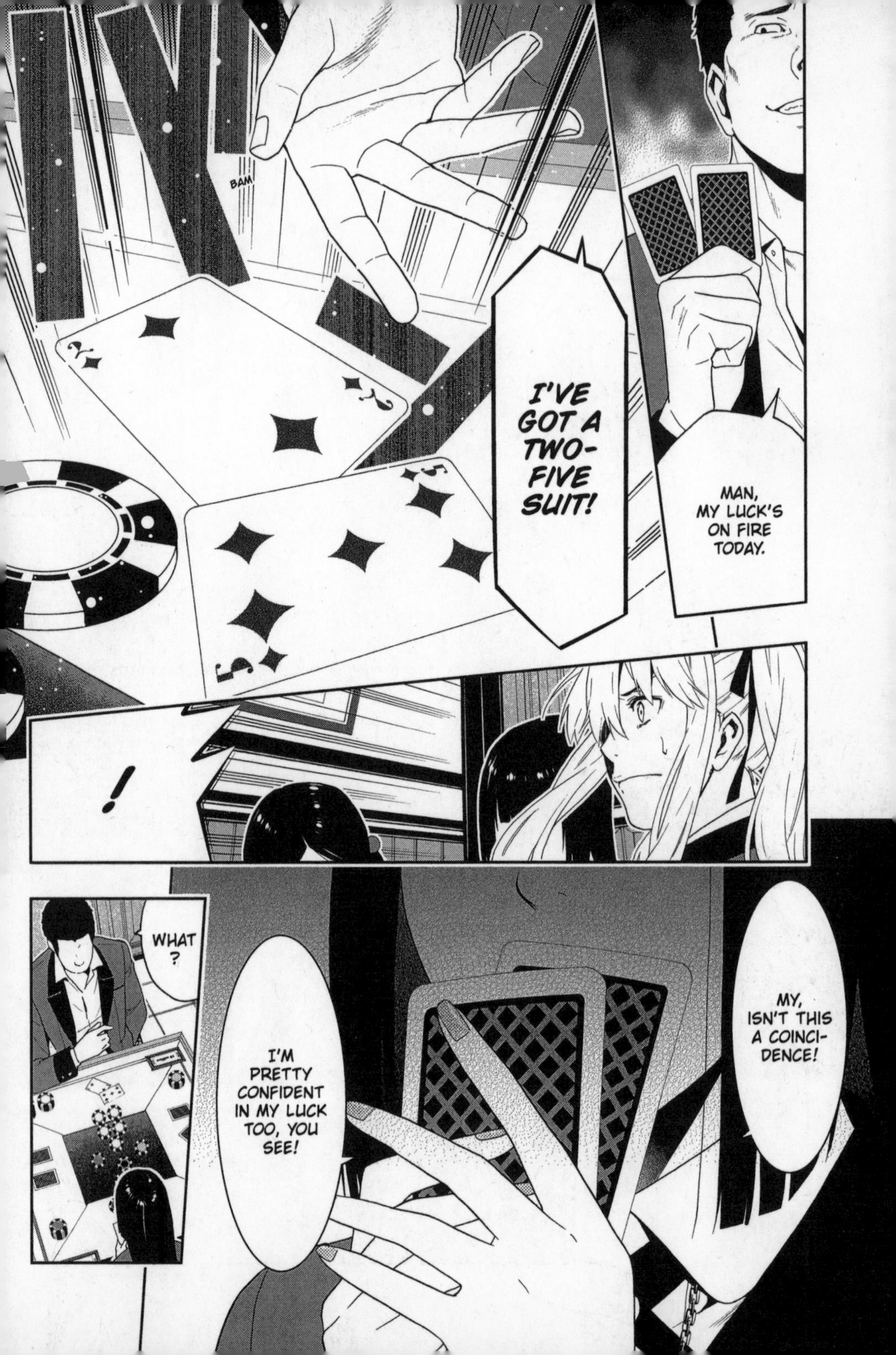
MAN, MY LUCK'S ON FIRE TODAY.
I'VE GOT A TWO-FIVE SUIT!
BAM
!
MY, ISN'T THIS A COINCIDENCE!
I'M PRETTY CONFIDENT IN MY LUCK TOO, YOU SEE!
WHAT?

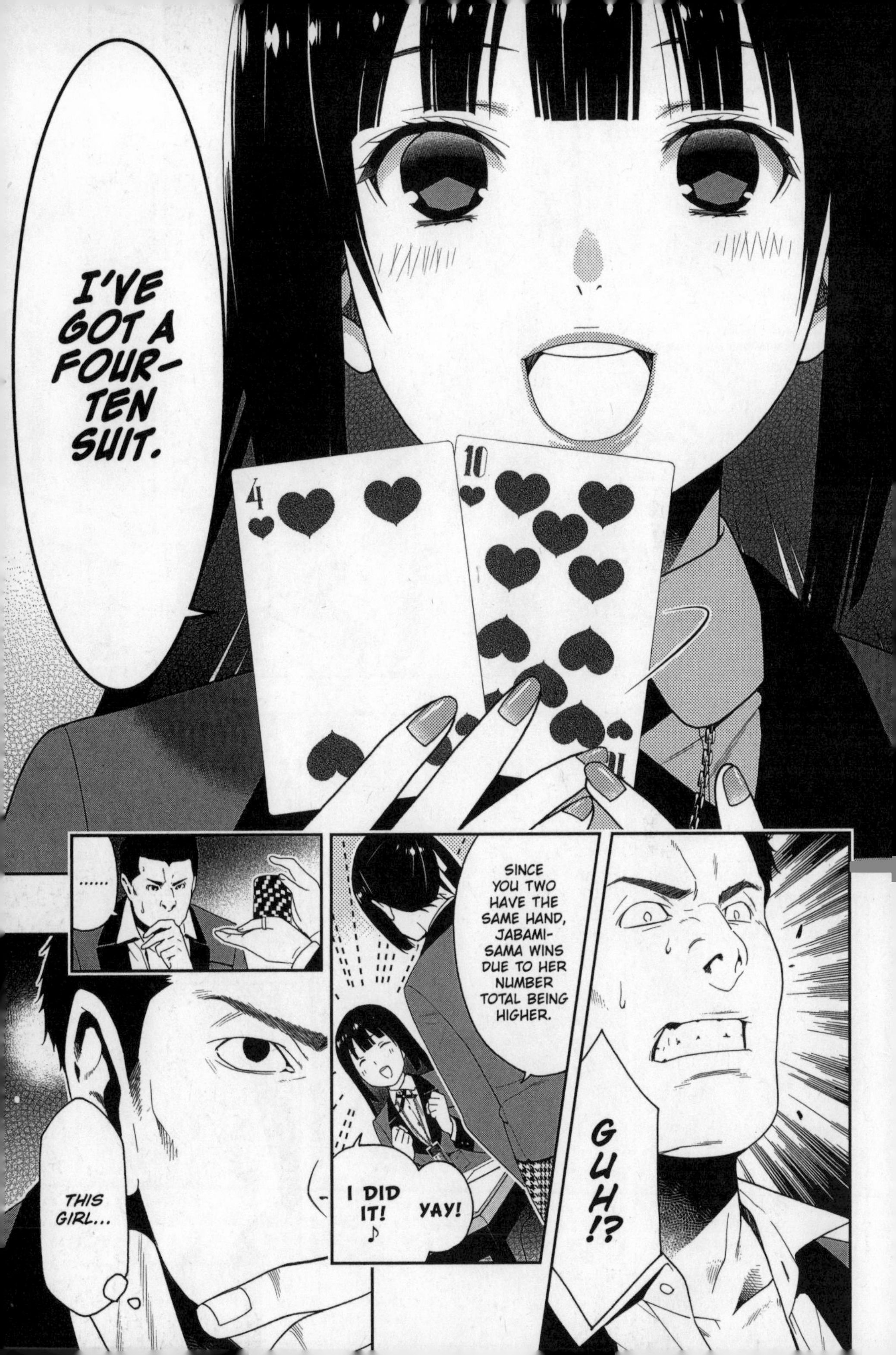
I'VE GOT A FOUR-TEN SUIT.
GUH!?
SINCE YOU TWO HAVE THE SAME HAND, JABAMI-SAMA WINS DUE TO HER NUMBER TOTAL BEING HIGHER.
I DID IT! ♪
YAY!
......
THIS GIRL...

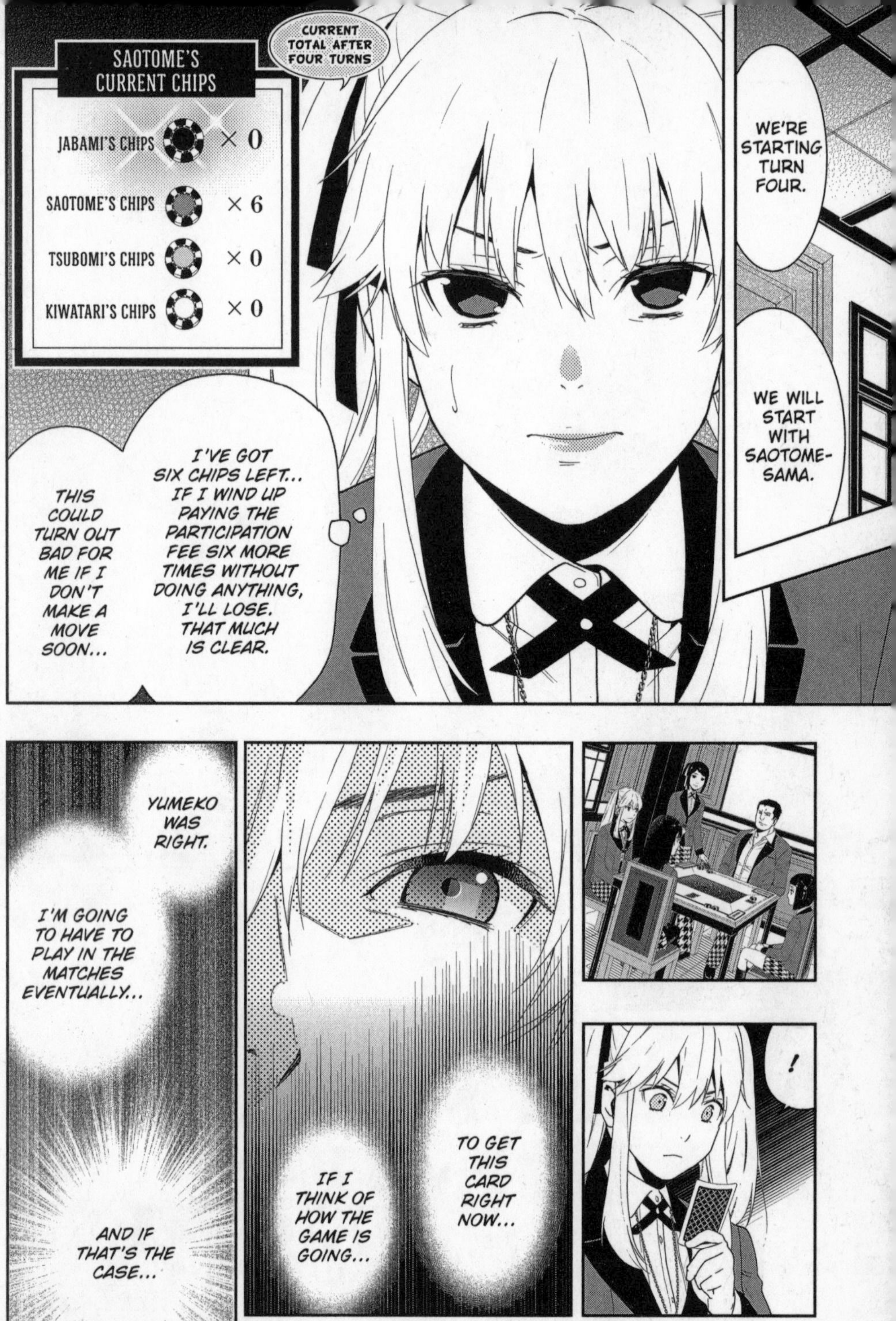
WE'RE STARTING TURN FOUR.
WE WILL START WITH SAOTOME-SAMA.
CURRENT TOTAL AFTER FOUR TURNS
SAOTOME'S CURRENT CHIPS
JABAMI'S CHIPS × 0
SAOTOME'S CHIPS × 6
TSUBOMI'S CHIPS × 0
KIWATARI'S CHIPS × 0
I'VE GOT SIX CHIPS LEFT... IF I WIND UP PAYING THE PARTICIPATION FEE SIX MORE TIMES WITHOUT DOING ANYTHING, I'LL LOSE. THAT MUCH IS CLEAR.
THIS COULD TURN OUT BAD FOR ME IF I DON'T MAKE A MOVE SOON...
!
TO GET THIS CARD RIGHT NOW...
IF I THINK OF HOW THE GAME IS GOING...
YUMEKO WAS RIGHT.
I'M GOING TO HAVE TO PLAY IN THE MATCHES EVENTUALLY...
AND IF THAT'S THE CASE...

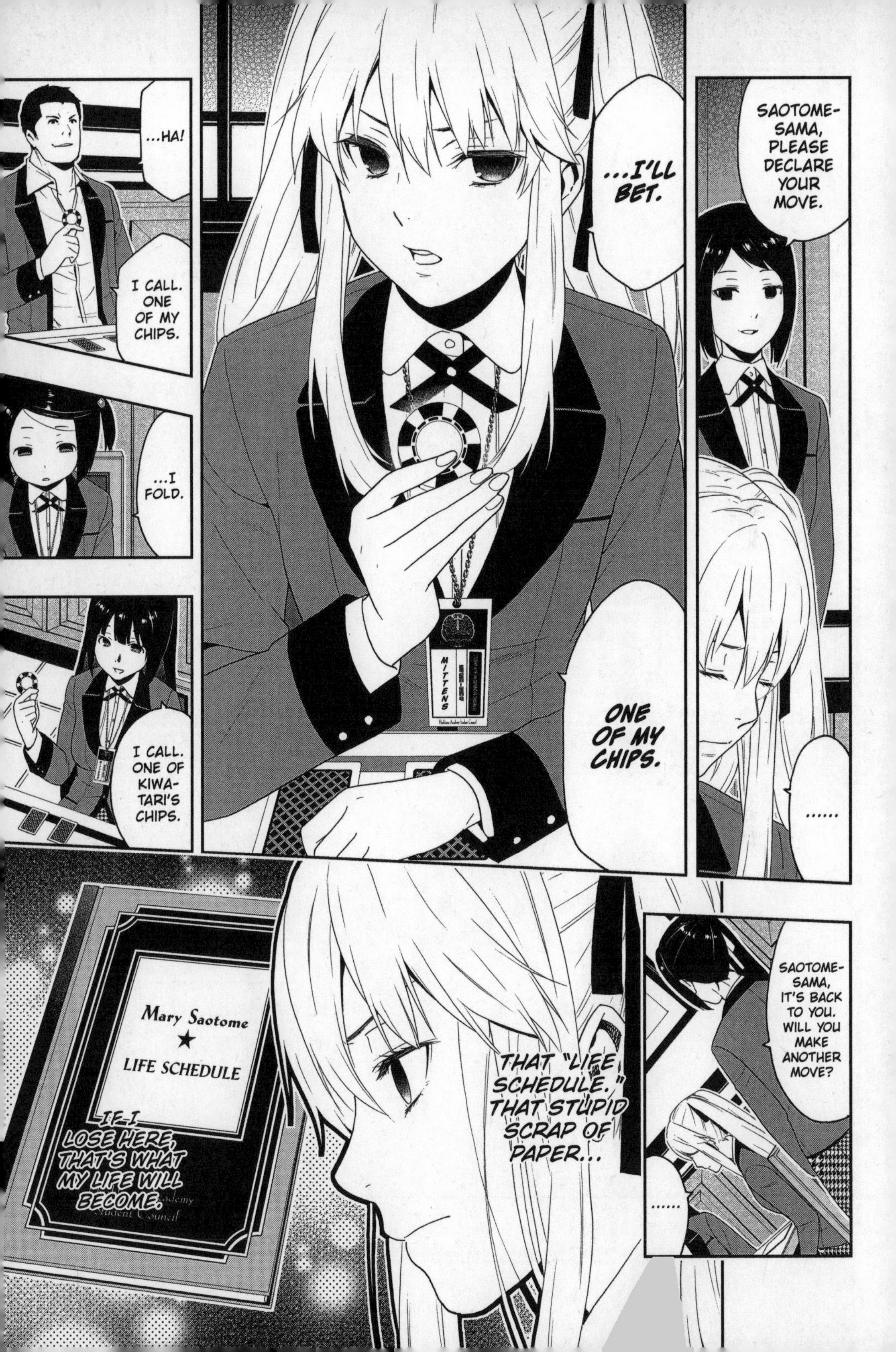
SAOTOME-SAMA, PLEASE DECLARE YOUR MOVE.
......
...I'LL BET.
MITTENS
ONE OF MY CHIPS.
...HA!
I CALL. ONE OF MY CHIPS.
...I FOLD.
I CALL. ONE OF KIWATARI'S CHIPS.
SAOTOME-SAMA, IT'S BACK TO YOU. WILL YOU MAKE ANOTHER MOVE?
......
THAT "LIFE SCHEDULE." THAT STUPID SCRAP OF PAPER...
Mary Saotome
★
LIFE SCHEDULE
IF I LOSE HERE, THAT'S WHAT MY LIFE WILL BECOME.

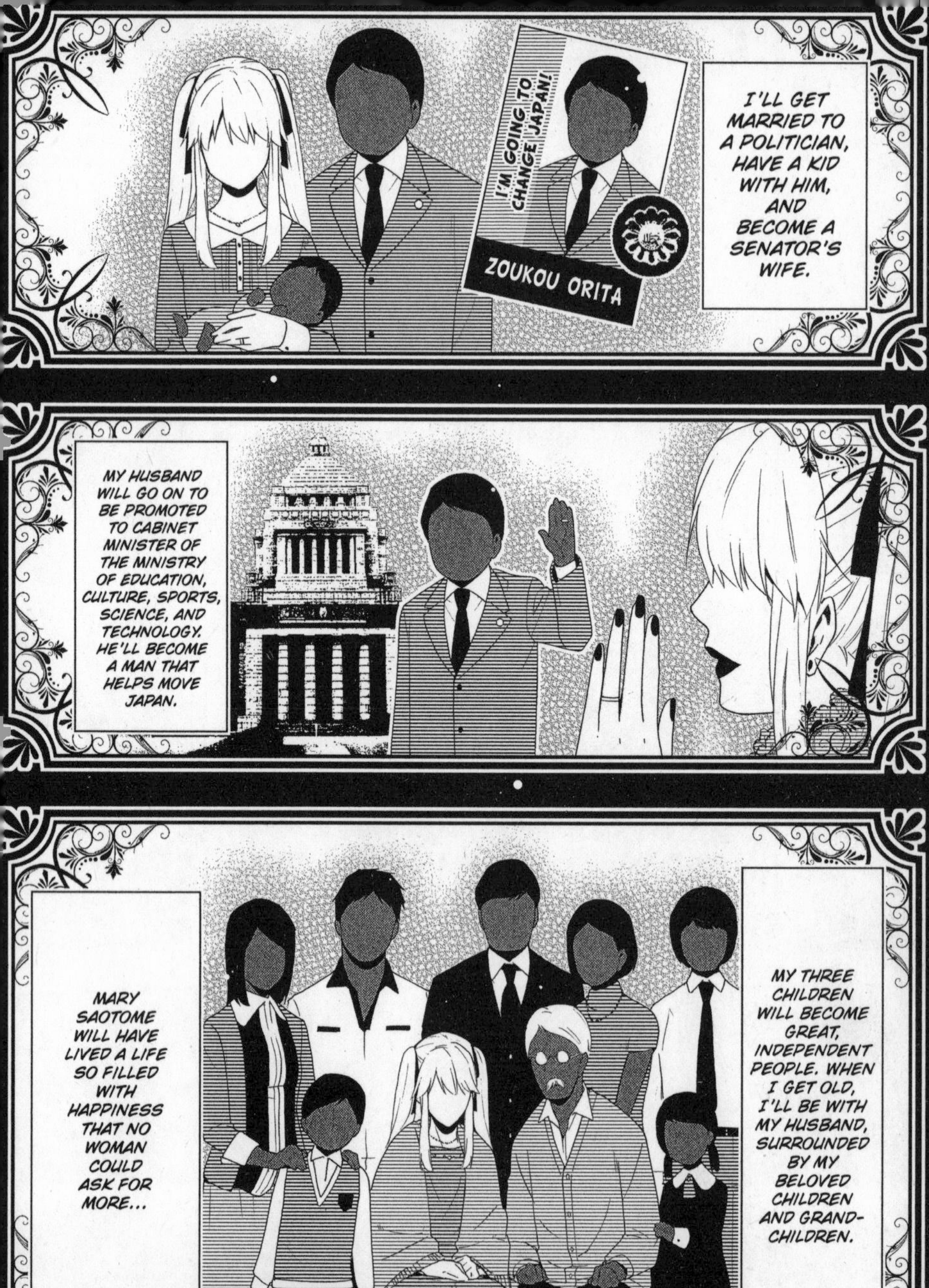
I'LL GET MARRIED TO A POLITICIAN, HAVE A KID WITH HIM, AND BECOME A SENATOR'S WIFE.
I'M GOING TO CHANGE JAPAN!
ZOUKOU ORITA
MY HUSBAND WILL GO ON TO BE PROMOTED TO CABINET MINISTER OF THE MINISTRY OF EDUCATION, CULTURE, SPORTS, SCIENCE, AND TECHNOLOGY. HE'LL BECOME A MAN THAT HELPS MOVE JAPAN.
MY THREE CHILDREN WILL BECOME GREAT, INDEPENDENT PEOPLE. WHEN I GET OLD, I'LL BE WITH MY HUSBAND, SURROUNDED BY MY BELOVED CHILDREN AND GRAND-CHILDREN.
MARY SAOTOME WILL HAVE LIVED A LIFE SO FILLED WITH HAPPINESS THAT NO WOMAN COULD ASK FOR MORE...

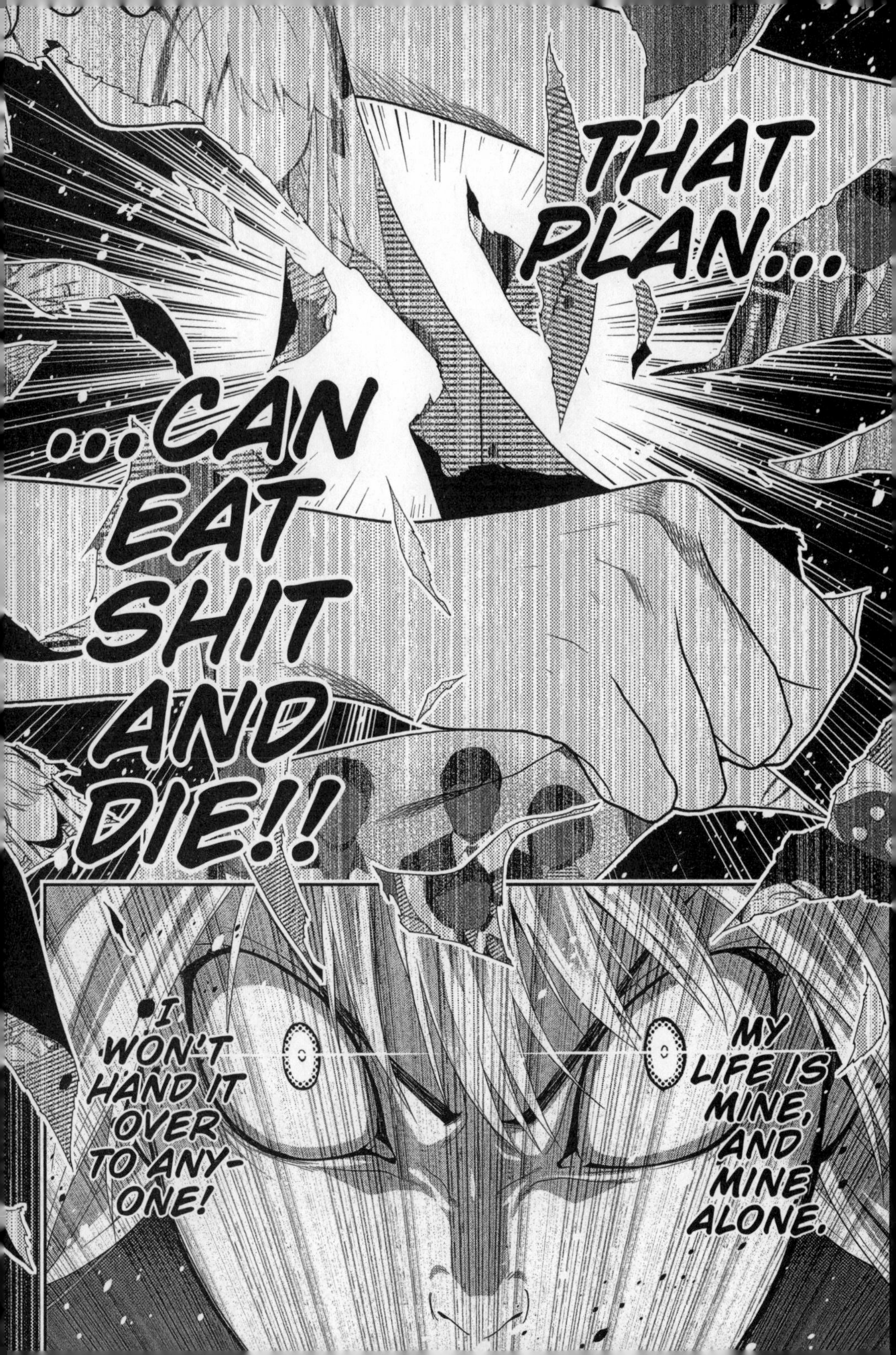
THAT PLAN...
...CAN EAT SHIT AND DIE!!
MY LIFE IS MINE, AND MINE ALONE.
I WON'T HAND IT OVER TO ANYONE!

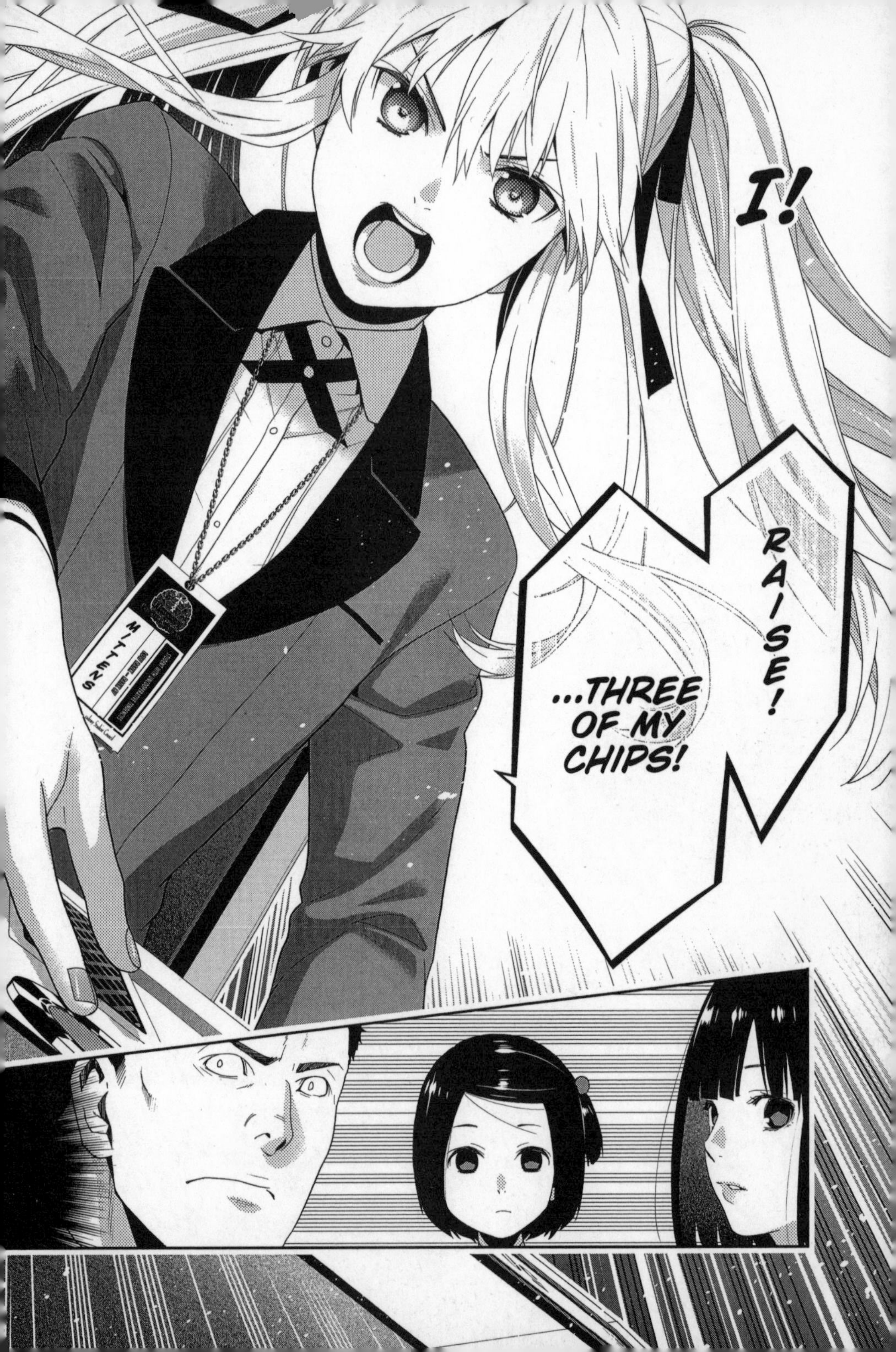
I!
RAISE!
...THREE OF MY CHIPS!

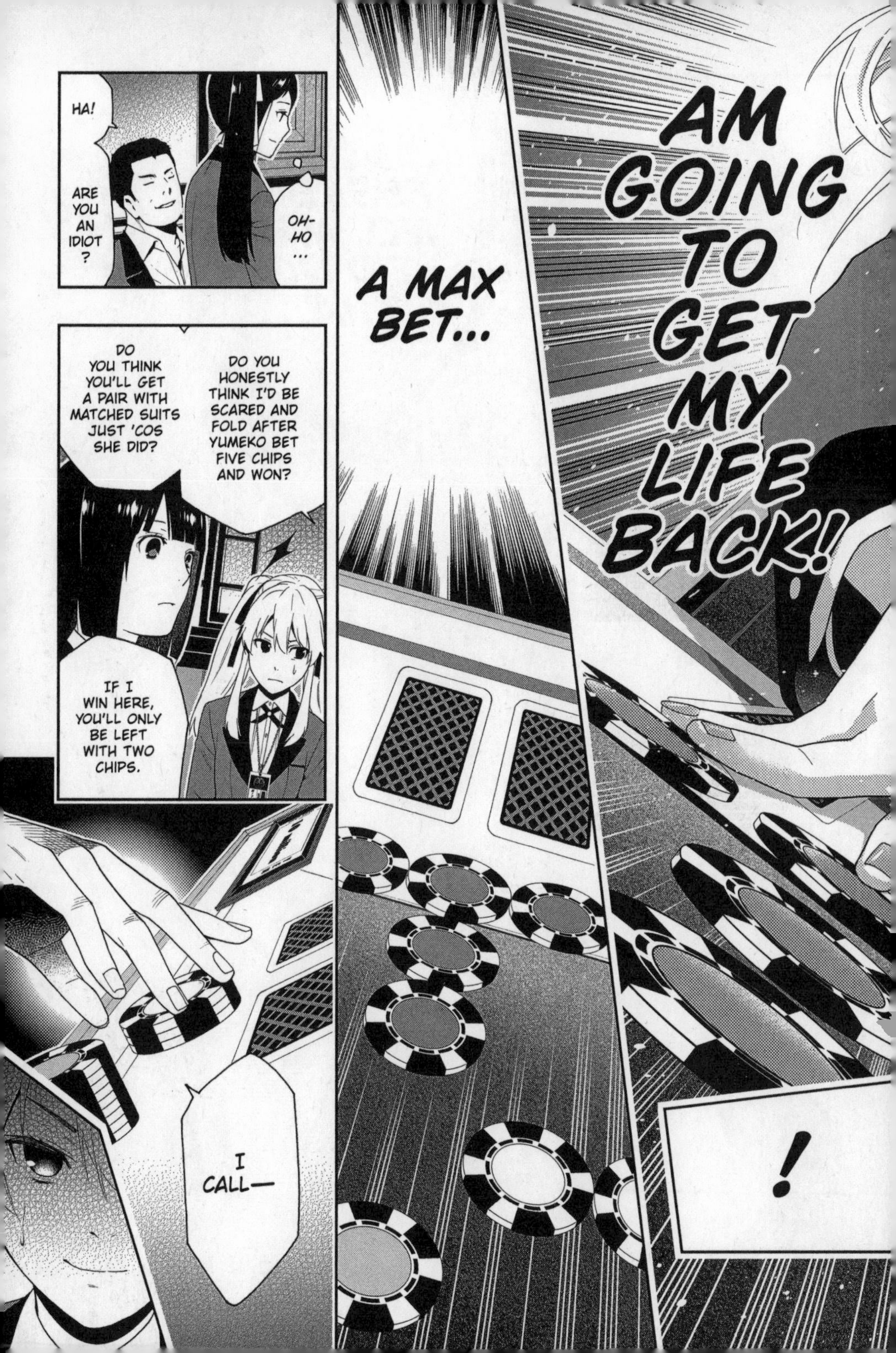
HA!
ARE YOU AN IDIOT?
OH-HO...
DO YOU THINK YOU'LL GET A PAIR WITH MATCHED SUITS JUST 'COS SHE DID?
DO YOU HONESTLY THINK I'D BE SCARED AND FOLD AFTER YUMEKO BET FIVE CHIPS AND WON?
IF I WIN HERE, YOU'LL ONLY BE LEFT WITH TWO CHIPS.
I CALL—
A MAX BET...
AM GOING TO GET MY LIFE BACK!
!

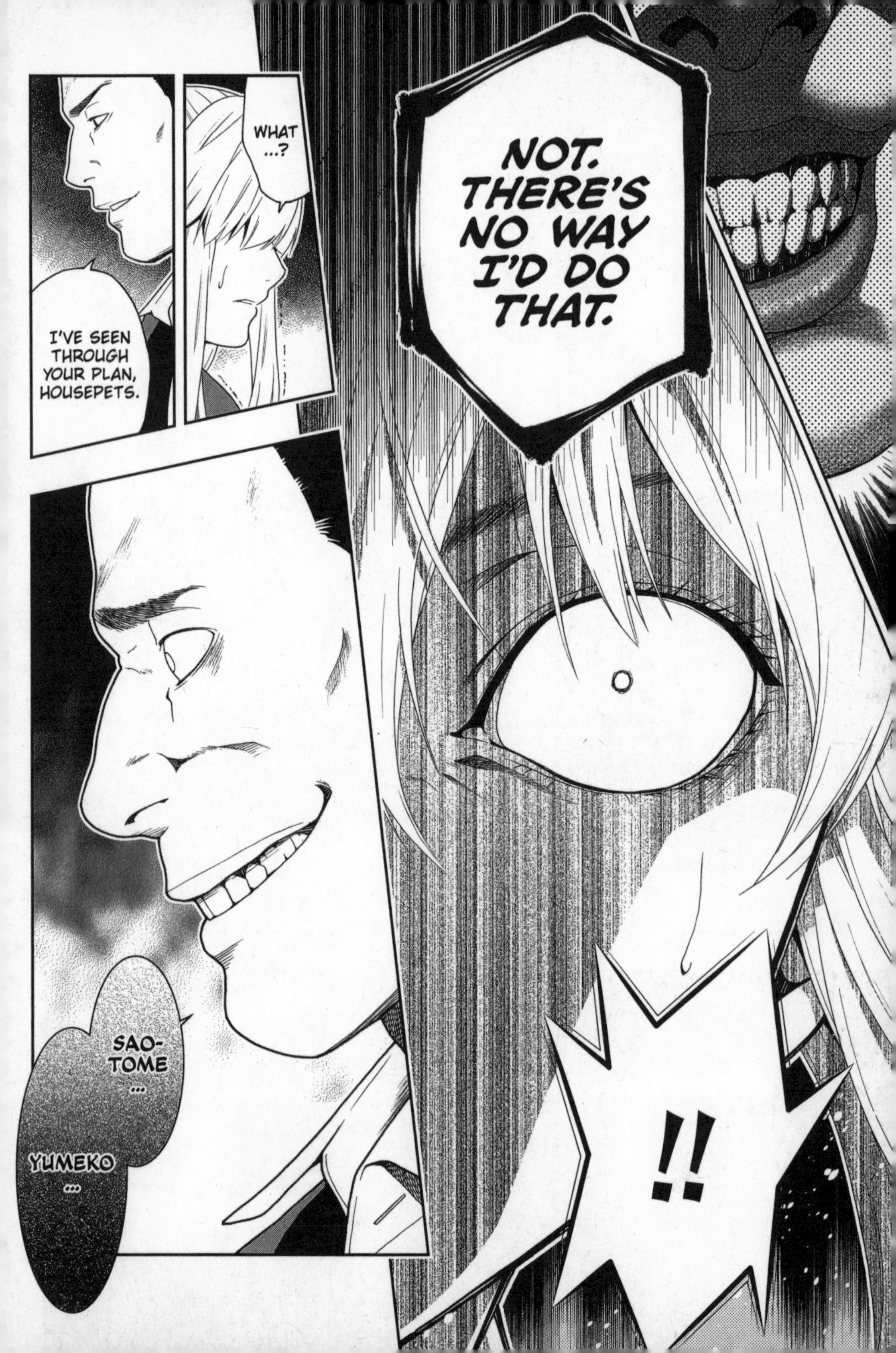
NOT. THERE'S NO WAY I'D DO THAT.
!!
WHAT ...?
I'VE SEEN THROUGH YOUR PLAN, HOUSEPETS.
SAO-TOME ...
YUMEKO ...

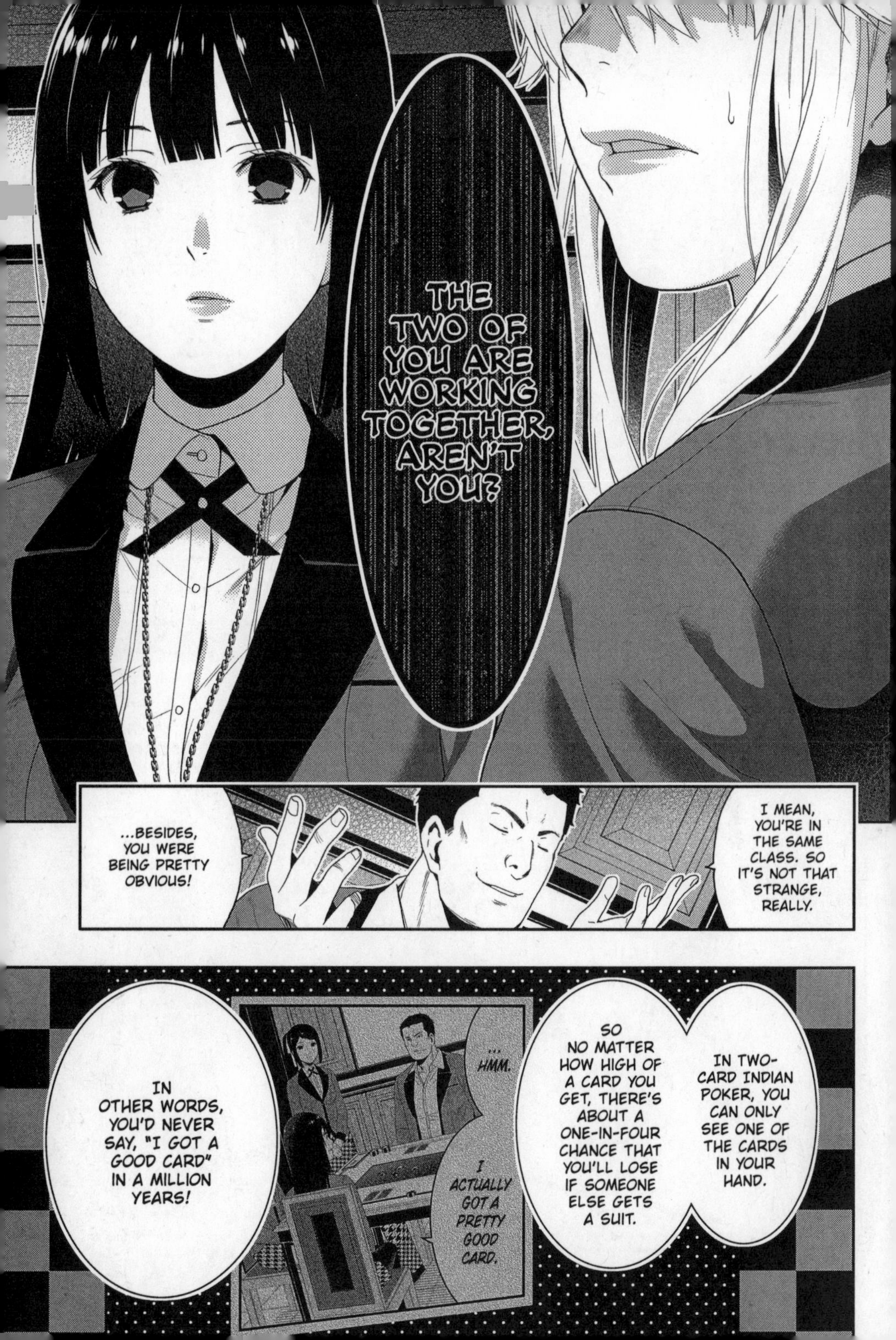
THE TWO OF YOU ARE WORKING TOGETHER, AREN'T YOU?
I MEAN, YOU'RE IN THE SAME CLASS. SO IT'S NOT THAT STRANGE, REALLY.
...BESIDES, YOU WERE BEING PRETTY OBVIOUS!
IN TWO-CARD INDIAN POKER, YOU CAN ONLY SEE ONE OF THE CARDS IN YOUR HAND.
SO NO MATTER HOW HIGH OF A CARD YOU GET, THERE'S ABOUT A ONE-IN-FOUR CHANCE THAT YOU'LL LOSE IF SOMEONE ELSE GETS A SUIT.
...HMM.
I ACTUALLY GOT A PRETTY GOOD CARD.
IN OTHER WORDS, YOU'D NEVER SAY, "I GOT A GOOD CARD" IN A MILLION YEARS!

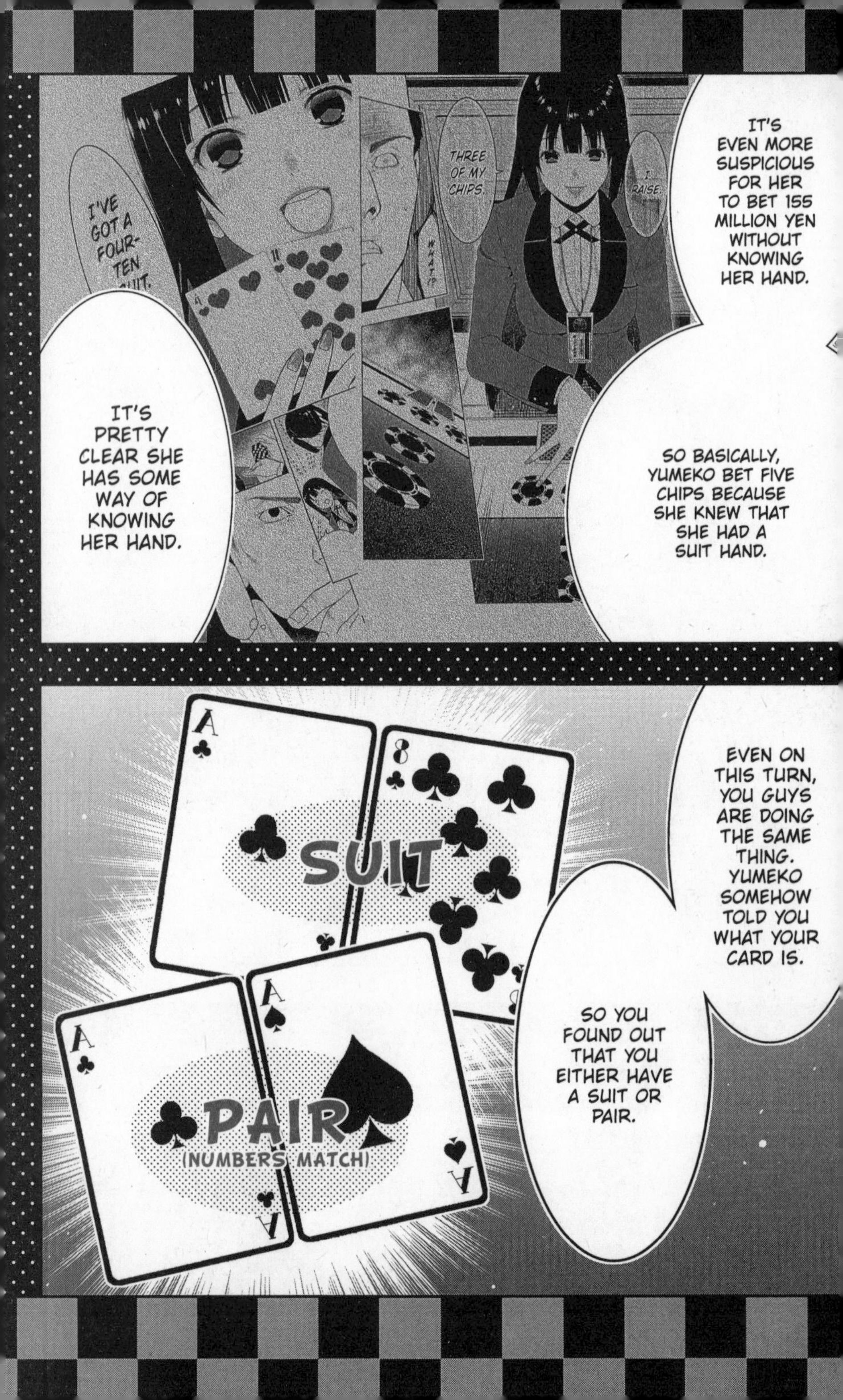
IT'S EVEN MORE SUSPICIOUS FOR HER TO BET 155 MILLION YEN WITHOUT KNOWING HER HAND.
I RAISE.
THREE OF MY CHIPS.
WHAT!?
I'VE GOT A FOUR-TEN
SO BASICALLY, YUMEKO BET FIVE CHIPS BECAUSE SHE KNEW THAT SHE HAD A SUIT HAND.
IT'S PRETTY CLEAR SHE HAS SOME WAY OF KNOWING HER HAND.
EVEN ON THIS TURN, YOU GUYS ARE DOING THE SAME THING. YUMEKO SOMEHOW TOLD YOU WHAT YOUR CARD IS.
SO YOU FOUND OUT THAT YOU EITHER HAVE A SUIT OR PAIR.
SUIT
PAIR
(NUMBERS MATCH)

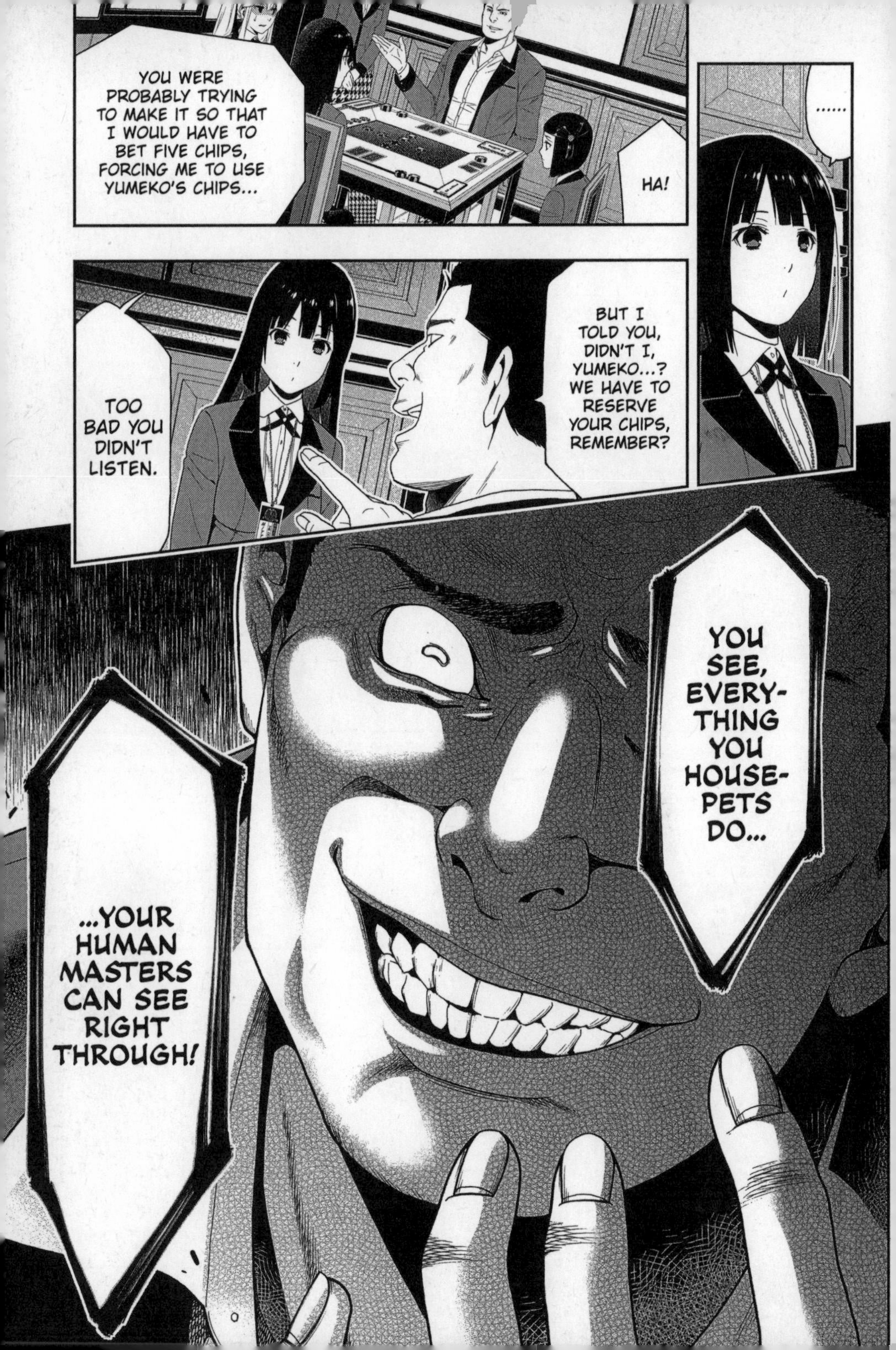
......
HA!
YOU WERE PROBABLY TRYING TO MAKE IT SO THAT I WOULD HAVE TO BET FIVE CHIPS, FORCING ME TO USE YUMEKO'S CHIPS...
BUT I TOLD YOU, DIDN'T I, YUMEKO...? WE HAVE TO RESERVE YOUR CHIPS, REMEMBER?
TOO BAD YOU DIDN'T LISTEN.
YOU SEE, EVERYTHING YOU HOUSEPETS DO...
...YOUR HUMAN MASTERS CAN SEE RIGHT THROUGH!

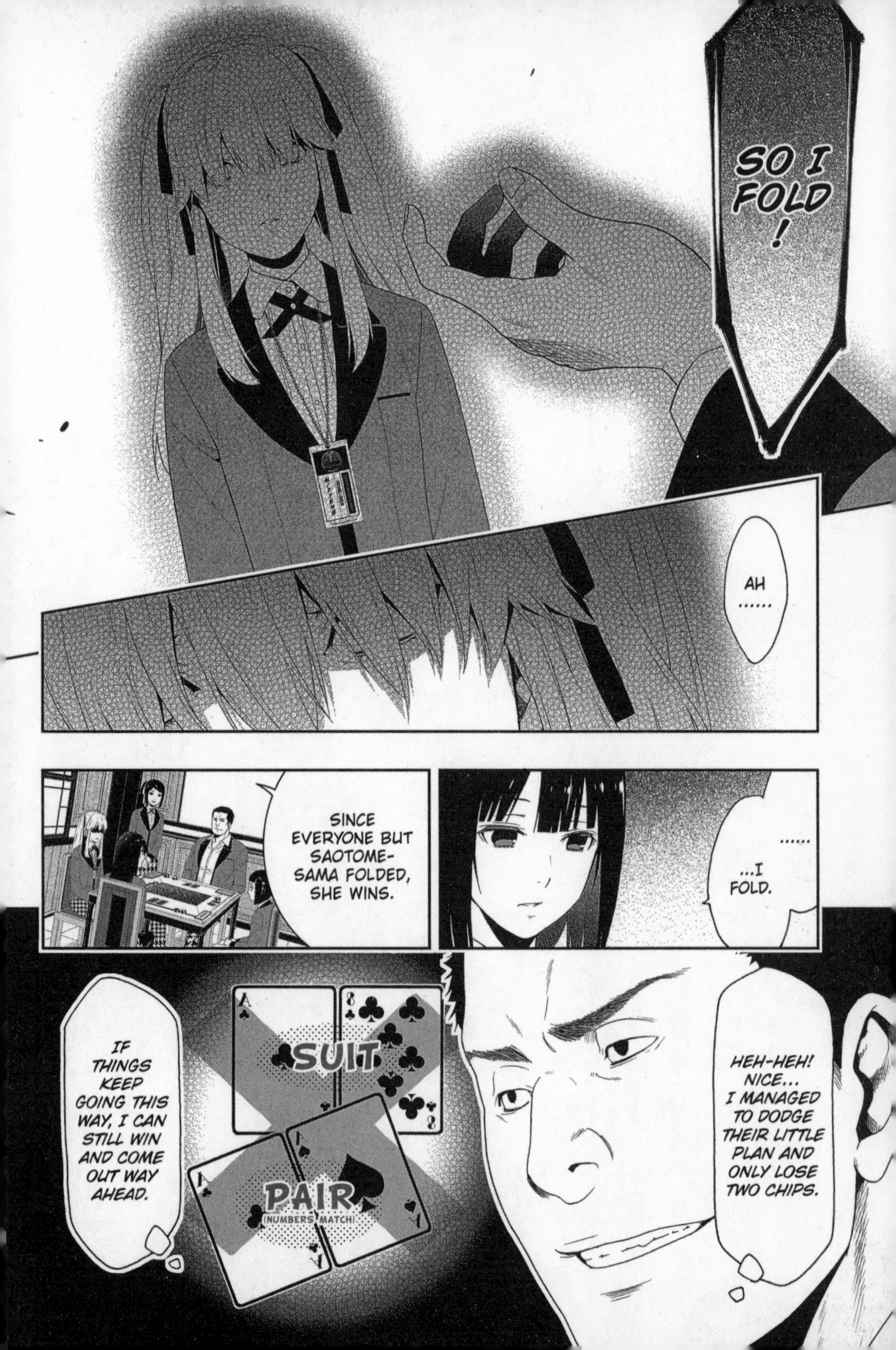
SO I FOLD!
AH ......
......
...I FOLD.
SINCE EVERYONE BUT SAOTOME-SAMA FOLDED, SHE WINS.
HEH-HEH! NICE... I MANAGED TO DODGE THEIR LITTLE PLAN AND ONLY LOSE TWO CHIPS.
SUIT
PAIR
(NUMBERS MATCH)
IF THINGS KEEP GOING THIS WAY, I CAN STILL WIN AND COME OUT WAY AHEAD.

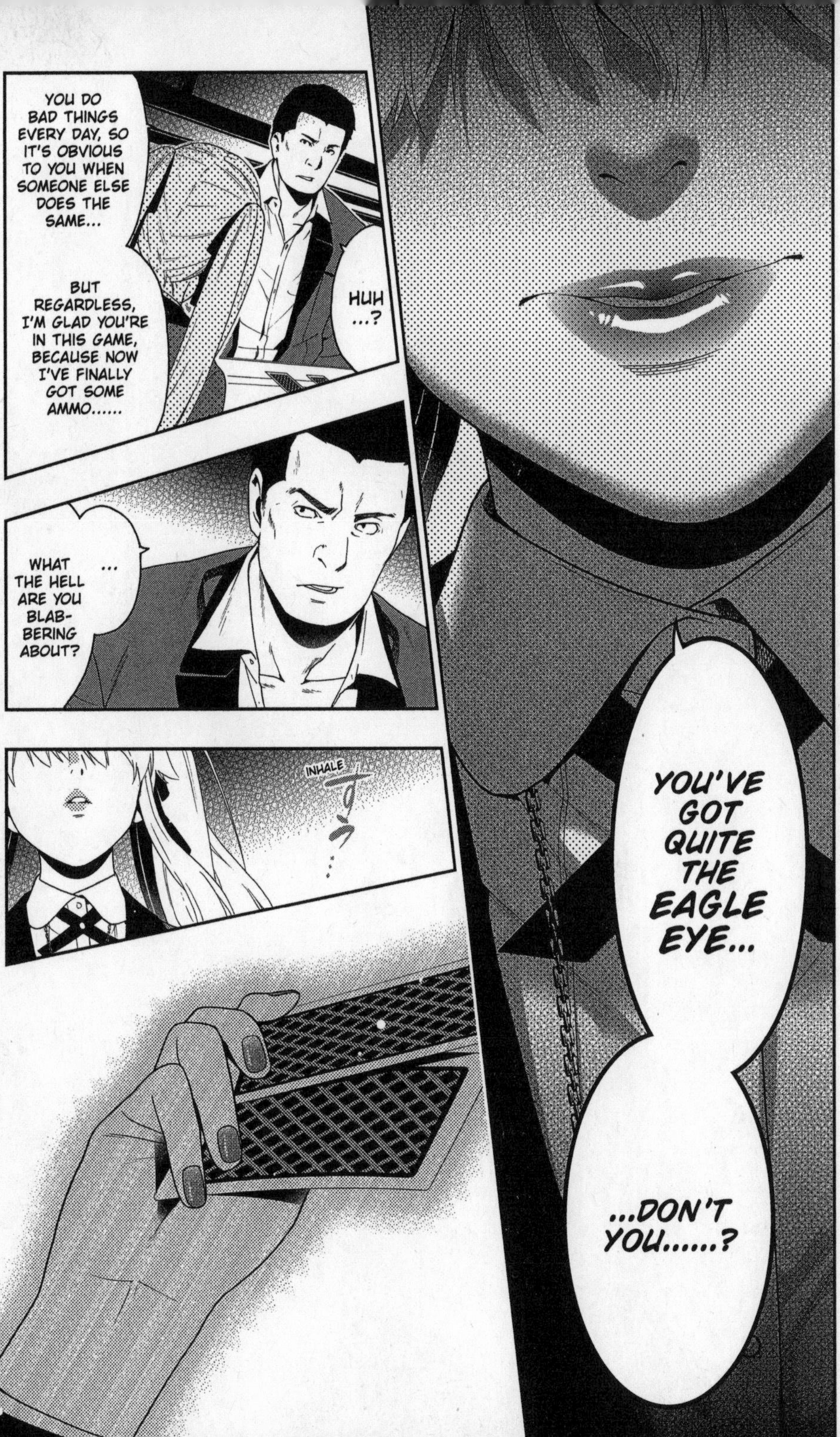
YOU DO BAD THINGS EVERY DAY, SO IT'S OBVIOUS TO YOU WHEN SOMEONE ELSE DOES THE SAME...
BUT REGARDLESS, I'M GLAD YOU'RE IN THIS GAME, BECAUSE NOW I'VE FINALLY GOT SOME AMMO......
HUH ...?
...
WHAT THE HELL ARE YOU BLAB-BERING ABOUT?
INHALE
YOU'VE GOT QUITE THE EAGLE EYE...
...DON'T YOU......?

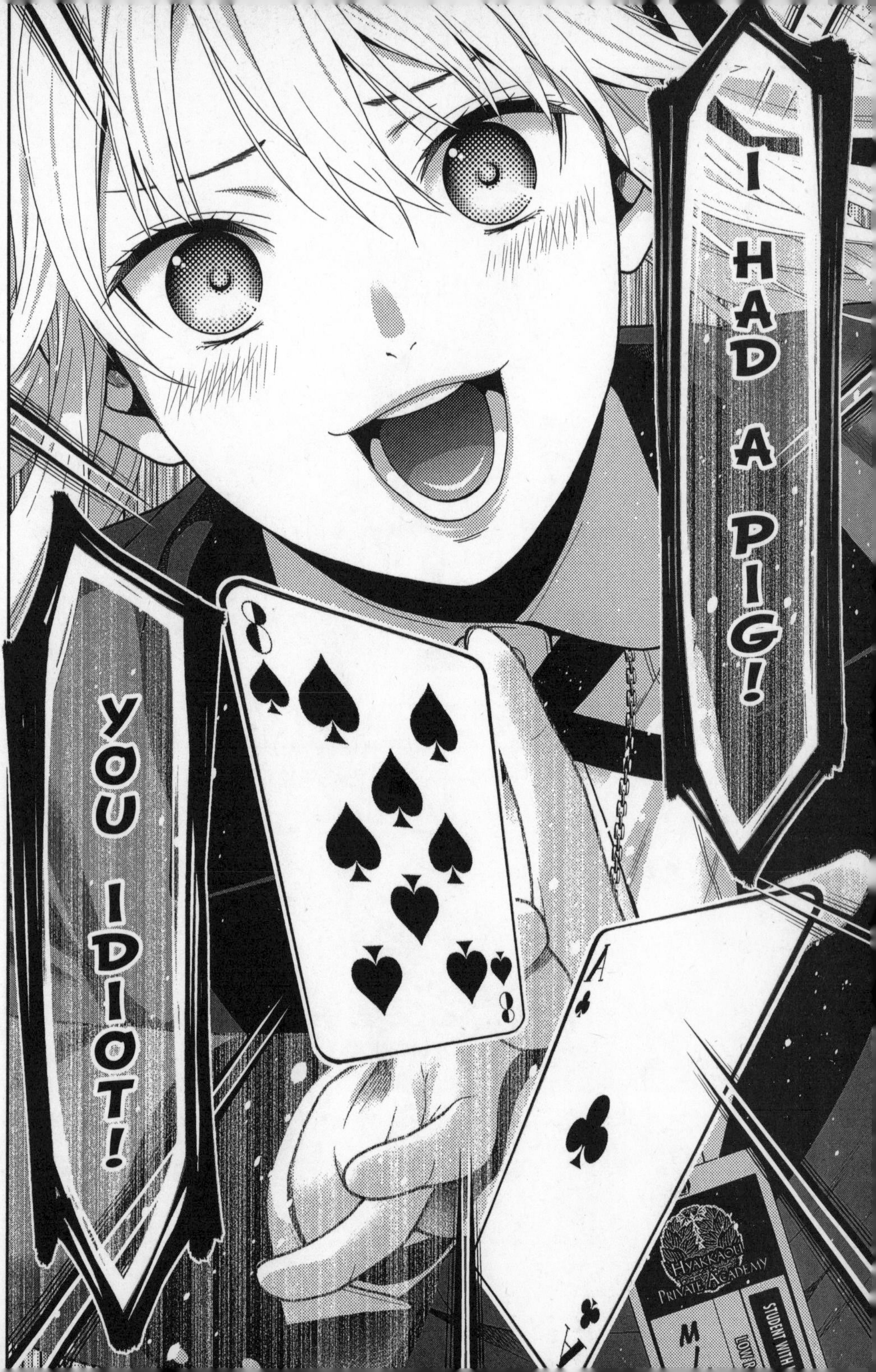
I HAD A PIG!
YOU IDIOT!
HYAKKAOU PRIVATE ACADEMY
STUDENT WITH

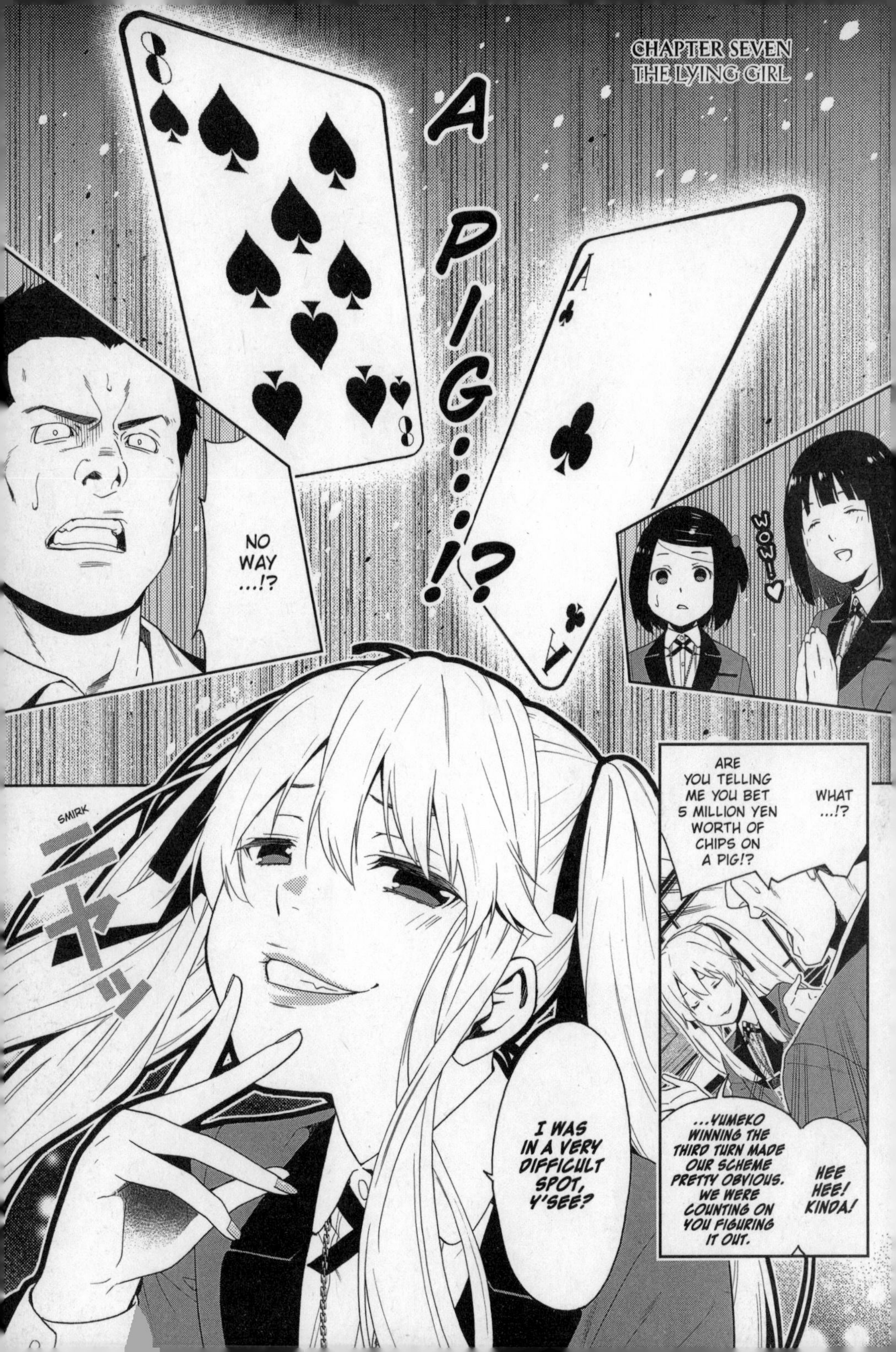
CHAPTER SEVEN
THE LYING GIRL
A PIG...!?
WOW!♥
NO WAY ...!?
WHAT ...!?
ARE YOU TELLING ME YOU BET 5 MILLION YEN WORTH OF CHIPS ON A PIG!?
HEE HEE! KINDA!
...YUMEKO WINNING THE THIRD TURN MADE OUR SCHEME PRETTY OBVIOUS. WE WERE COUNTING ON YOU FIGURING IT OUT.
I WAS IN A VERY DIFFICULT SPOT, Y'SEE?
SMIRK
ニヤッ

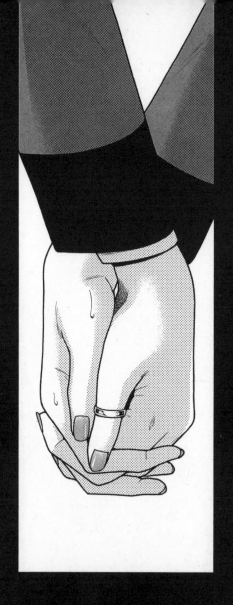

CHAPTER SEVEN
THE LYING GIRL

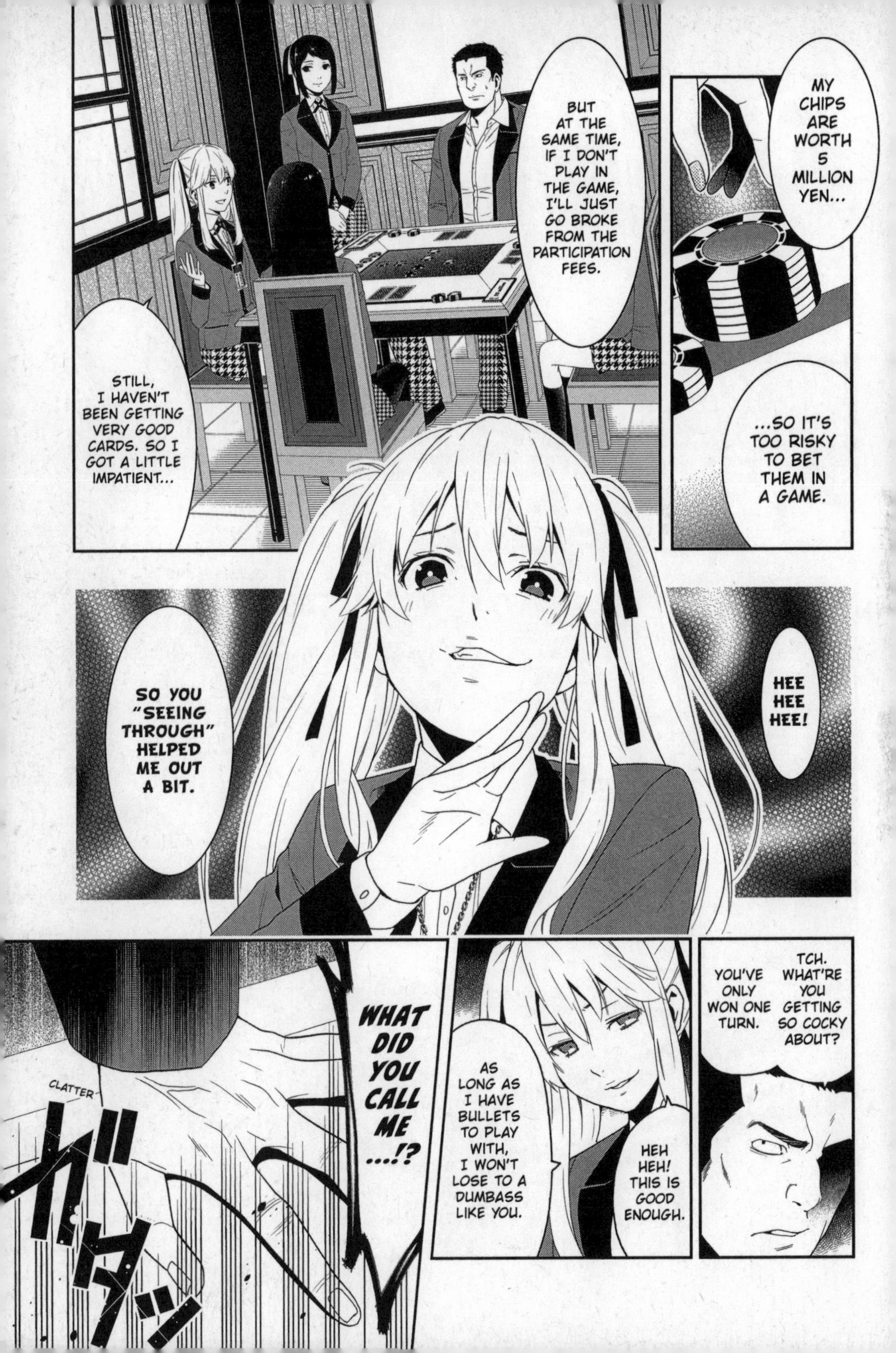
MY CHIPS ARE WORTH 5 MILLION YEN...
...SO IT'S TOO RISKY TO BET THEM IN A GAME.
BUT AT THE SAME TIME, IF I DON'T PLAY IN THE GAME, I'LL JUST GO BROKE FROM THE PARTICIPATION FEES.
STILL, I HAVEN'T BEEN GETTING VERY GOOD CARDS. SO I GOT A LITTLE IMPATIENT...
HEE HEE HEE!
SO YOU "SEEING THROUGH" HELPED ME OUT A BIT.
TCH. WHAT'RE YOU GETTING SO COCKY ABOUT?
YOU'VE ONLY WON ONE TURN.
HEH HEH! THIS IS GOOD ENOUGH.
AS LONG AS I HAVE BULLETS TO PLAY WITH, I WON'T LOSE TO A DUMBASS LIKE YOU.
WHAT DID YOU CALL ME ...!?
CLATTER

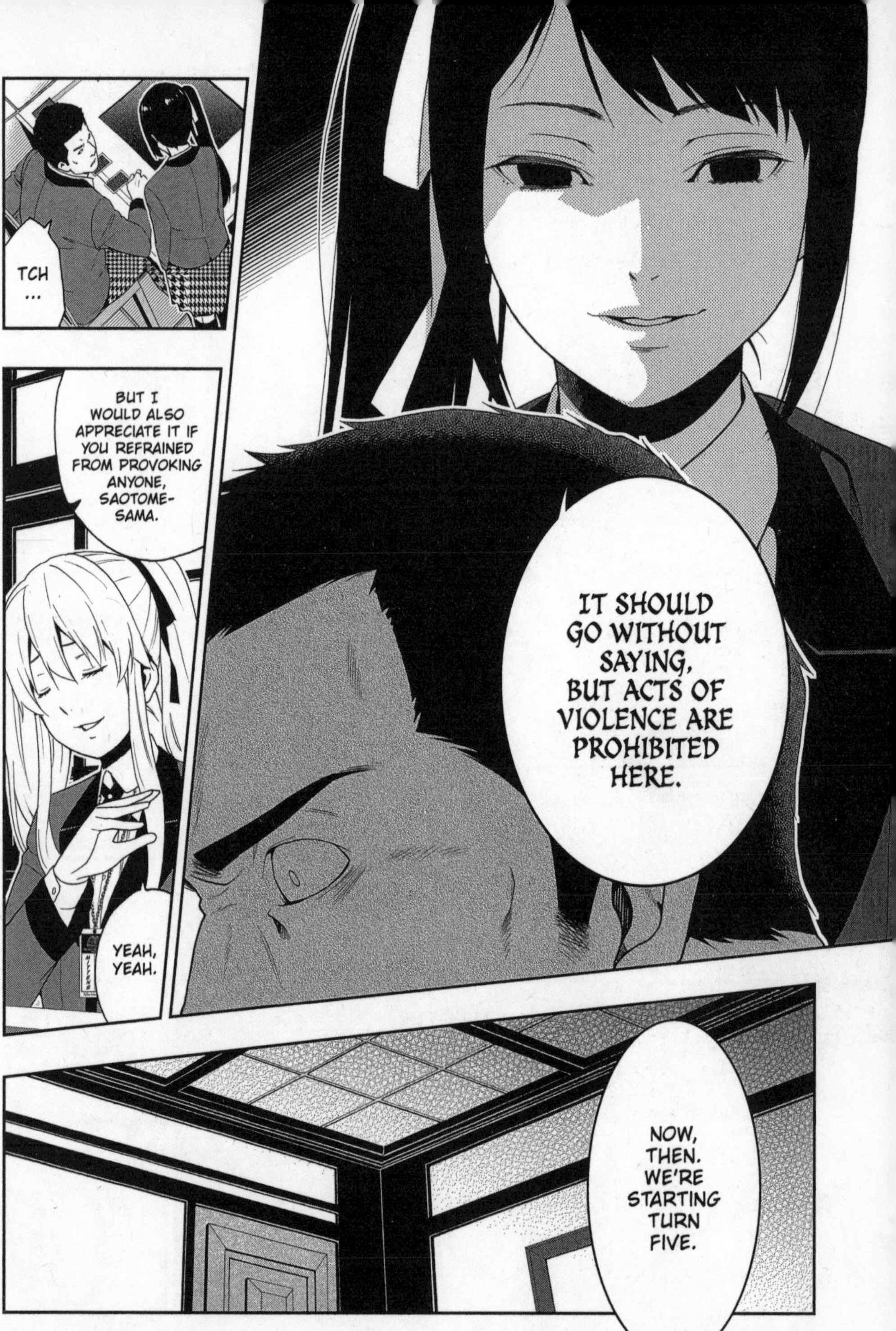
IT SHOULD GO WITHOUT SAYING, BUT ACTS OF VIOLENCE ARE PROHIBITED HERE.
TCH ...
BUT I WOULD ALSO APPRECIATE IT IF YOU REFRAINED FROM PROVOKING ANYONE, SAOTOME-SAMA.
YEAH, YEAH.
NOW, THEN. WE'RE STARTING TURN FIVE.

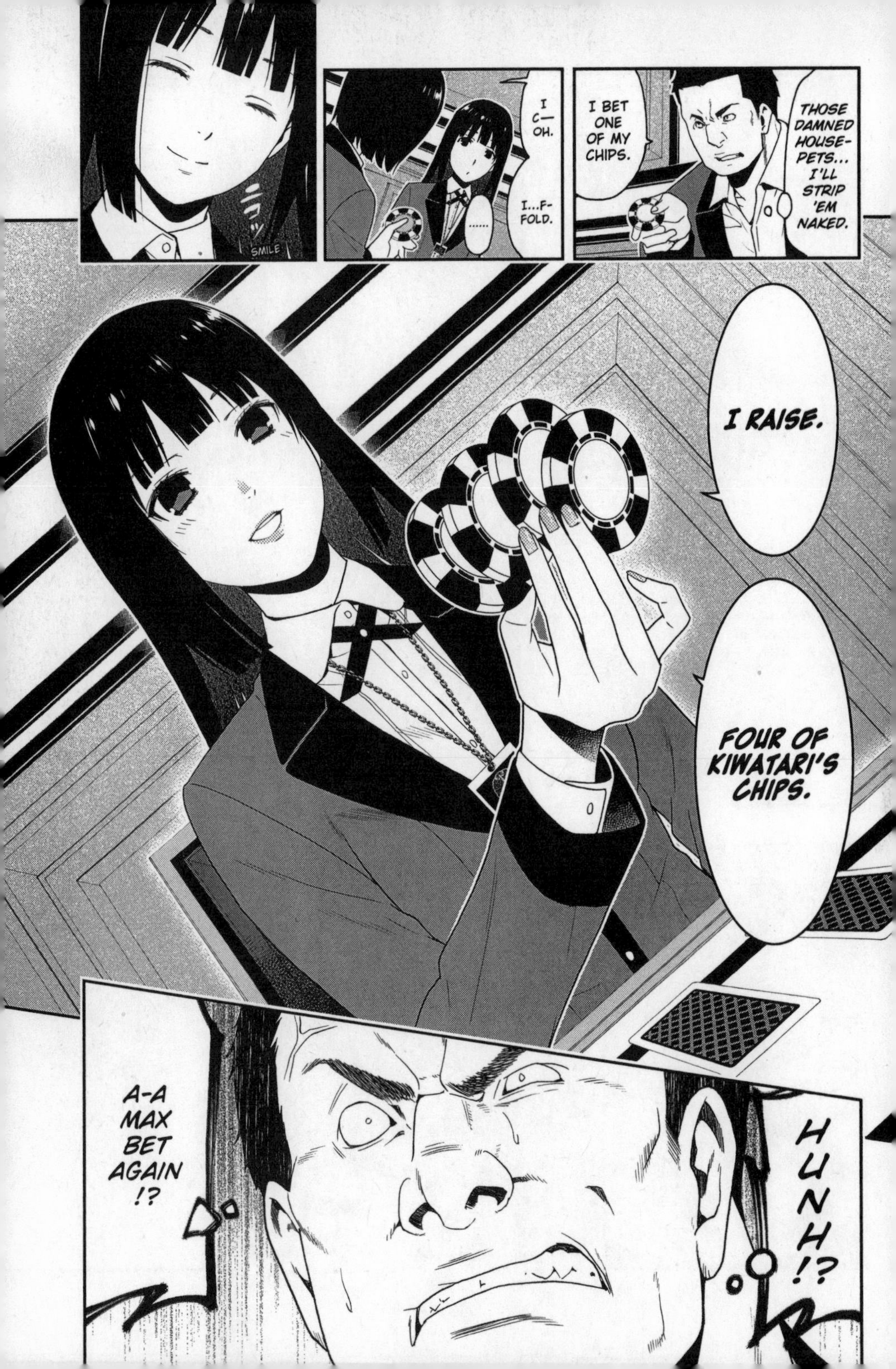
THOSE DAMNED HOUSE-PETS... I'LL STRIP 'EM NAKED.
I BET ONE OF MY CHIPS.
I C— OH.
I...F-FOLD.
......
ニコッ
SMILE
I RAISE.
FOUR OF KIWATARI'S CHIPS.
HUNH!?
A-A MAX BET AGAIN!?

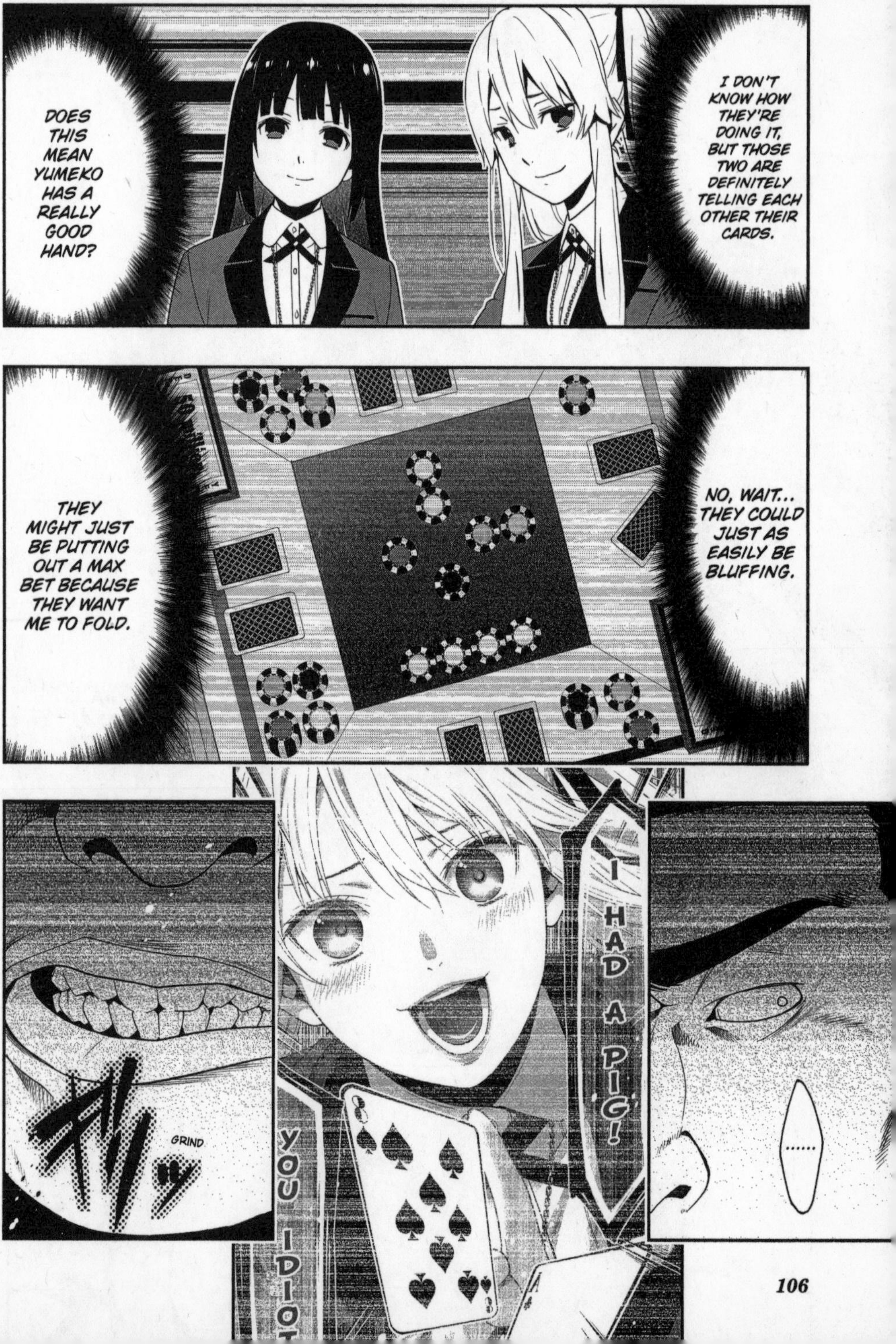
I DON'T KNOW HOW THEY'RE DOING IT, BUT THOSE TWO ARE DEFINITELY TELLING EACH OTHER THEIR CARDS.
DOES THIS MEAN YUMEKO HAS A REALLY GOOD HAND?
NO, WAIT... THEY COULD JUST AS EASILY BE BLUFFING.
THEY MIGHT JUST BE PUTTING OUT A MAX BET BECAUSE THEY WANT ME TO FOLD.
......
I HAD A PIG!
YOU IDIOT
GRIND

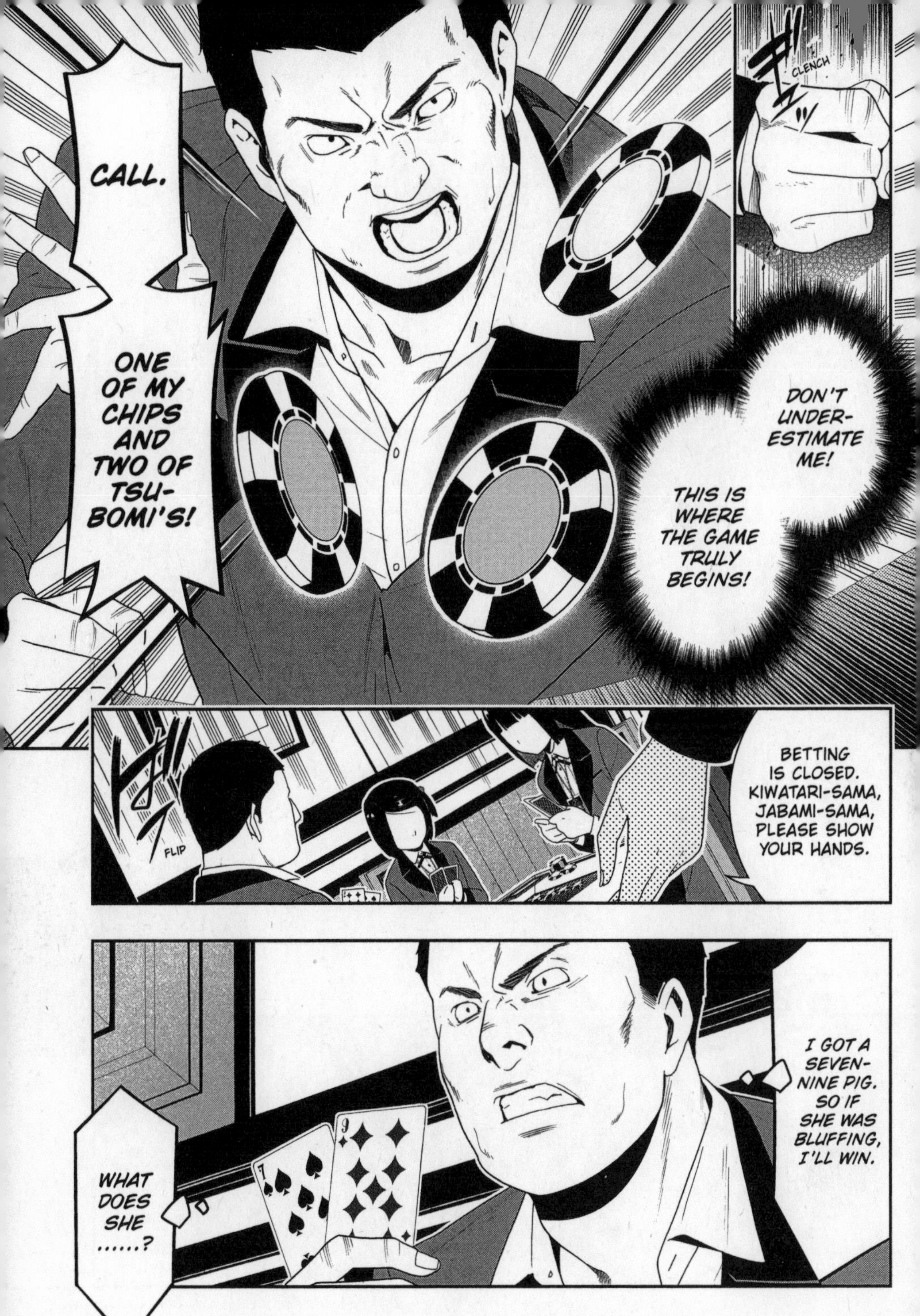
CLENCH
CALL.
ONE OF MY CHIPS AND TWO OF TSU-BOMI'S!
DON'T UNDER-ESTIMATE ME!
THIS IS WHERE THE GAME TRULY BEGINS!
BETTING IS CLOSED. KIWATARI-SAMA, JABAMI-SAMA, PLEASE SHOW YOUR HANDS.
FLIP
I GOT A SEVEN-NINE PIG. SO IF SHE WAS BLUFFING, I'LL WIN.
WHAT DOES SHE ......?

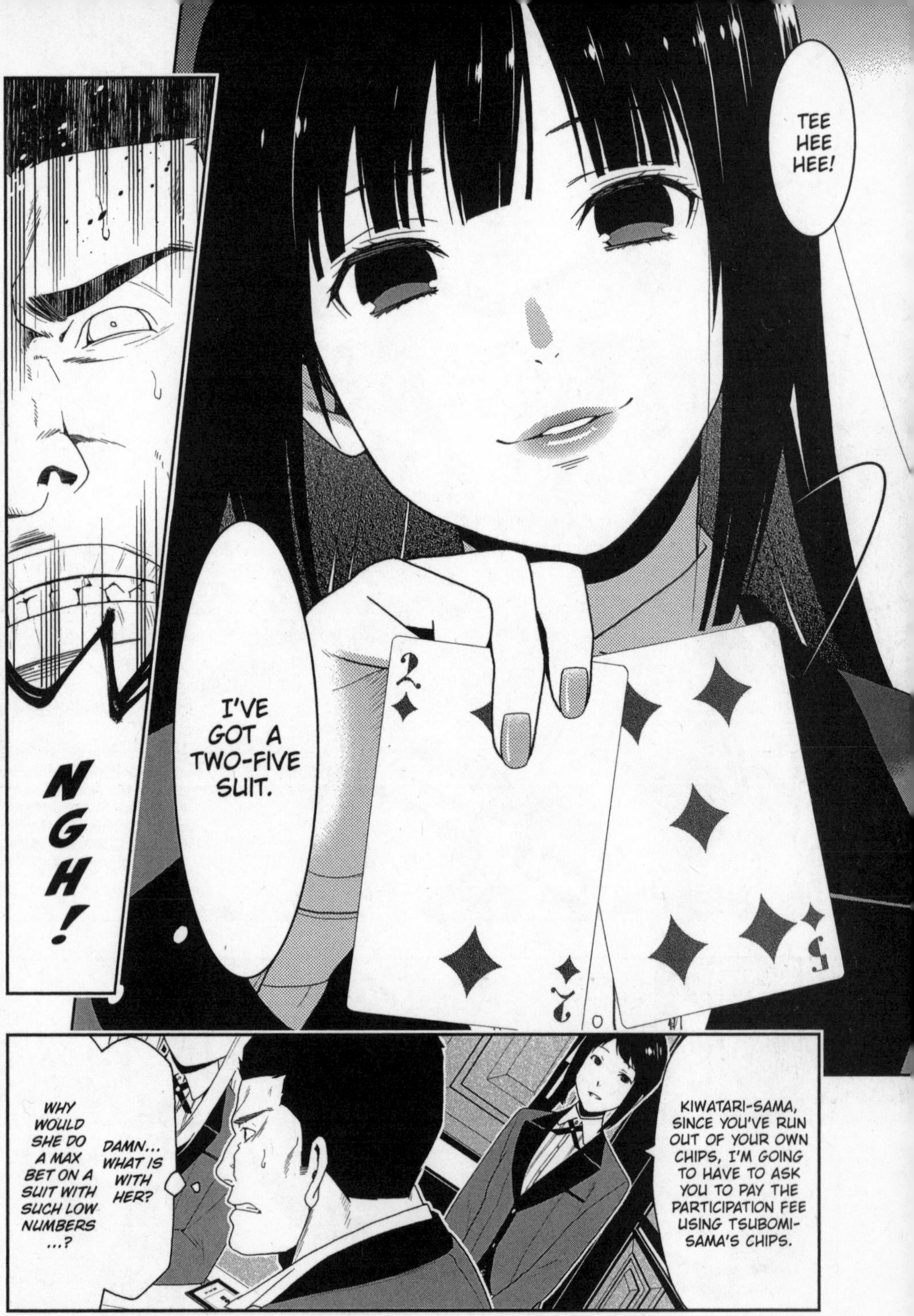
TEE HEE HEE!
I'VE GOT A TWO-FIVE SUIT.
NGH!
KIWATARI-SAMA, SINCE YOU'VE RUN OUT OF YOUR OWN CHIPS, I'M GOING TO HAVE TO ASK YOU TO PAY THE PARTICIPATION FEE USING TSUBOMI-SAMA'S CHIPS.
DAMN... WHAT IS WITH HER?
WHY WOULD SHE DO A MAX BET ON A SUIT WITH SUCH LOW NUMBERS ...?

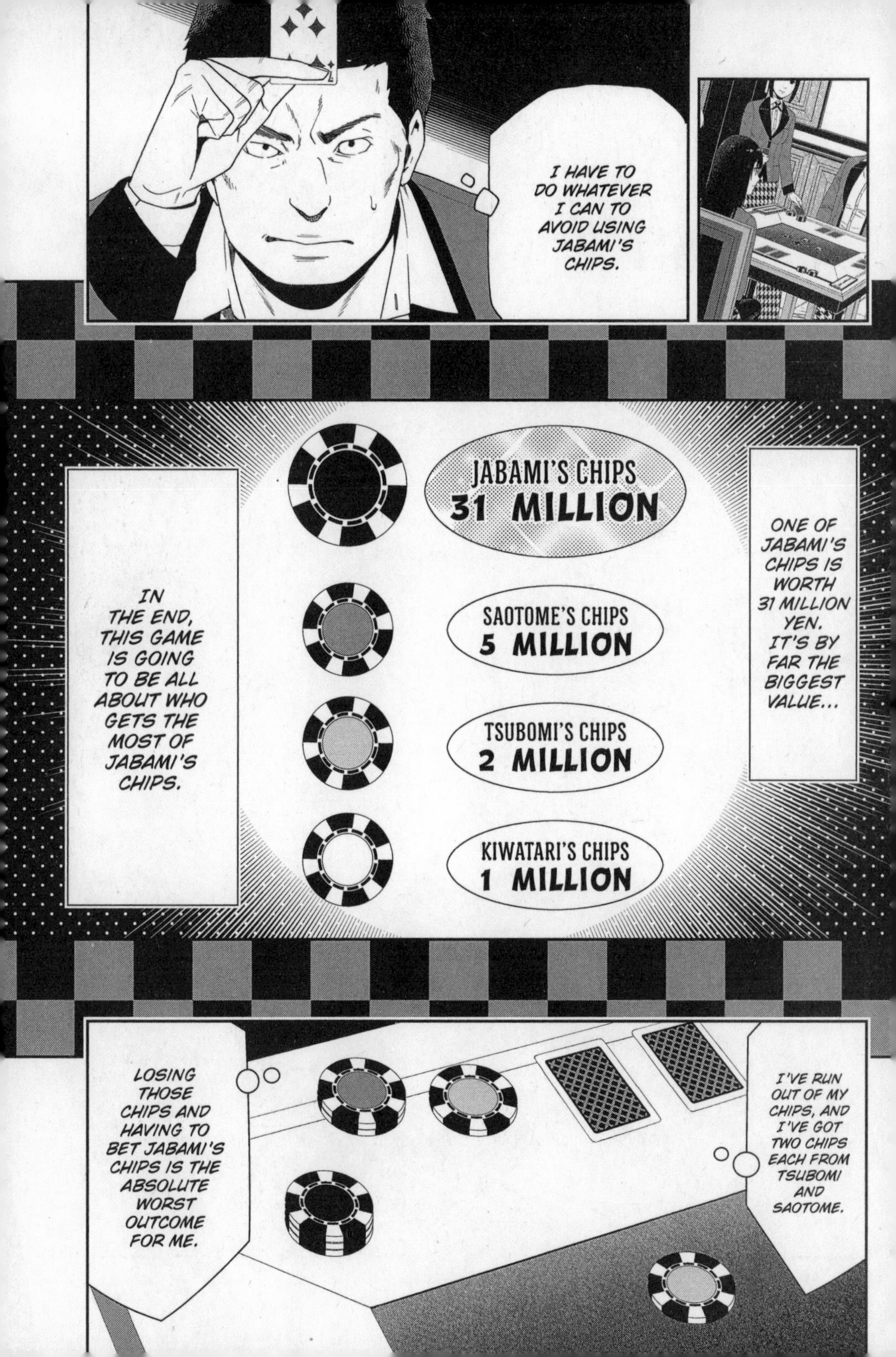

I HAVE TO DO WHATEVER I CAN TO AVOID USING JABAMI'S CHIPS.
ONE OF JABAMI'S CHIPS IS WORTH 31 MILLION YEN. IT'S BY FAR THE BIGGEST VALUE...
JABAMI'S CHIPS 31 MILLION
SAOTOME'S CHIPS 5 MILLION
TSUBOMI'S CHIPS 2 MILLION
KIWATARI'S CHIPS 1 MILLION
IN THE END, THIS GAME IS GOING TO BE ALL ABOUT WHO GETS THE MOST OF JABAMI'S CHIPS.
I'VE RUN OUT OF MY CHIPS, AND I'VE GOT TWO CHIPS EACH FROM TSUBOMI AND SAOTOME.
LOSING THOSE CHIPS AND HAVING TO BET JABAMI'S CHIPS IS THE ABSOLUTE WORST OUTCOME FOR ME.

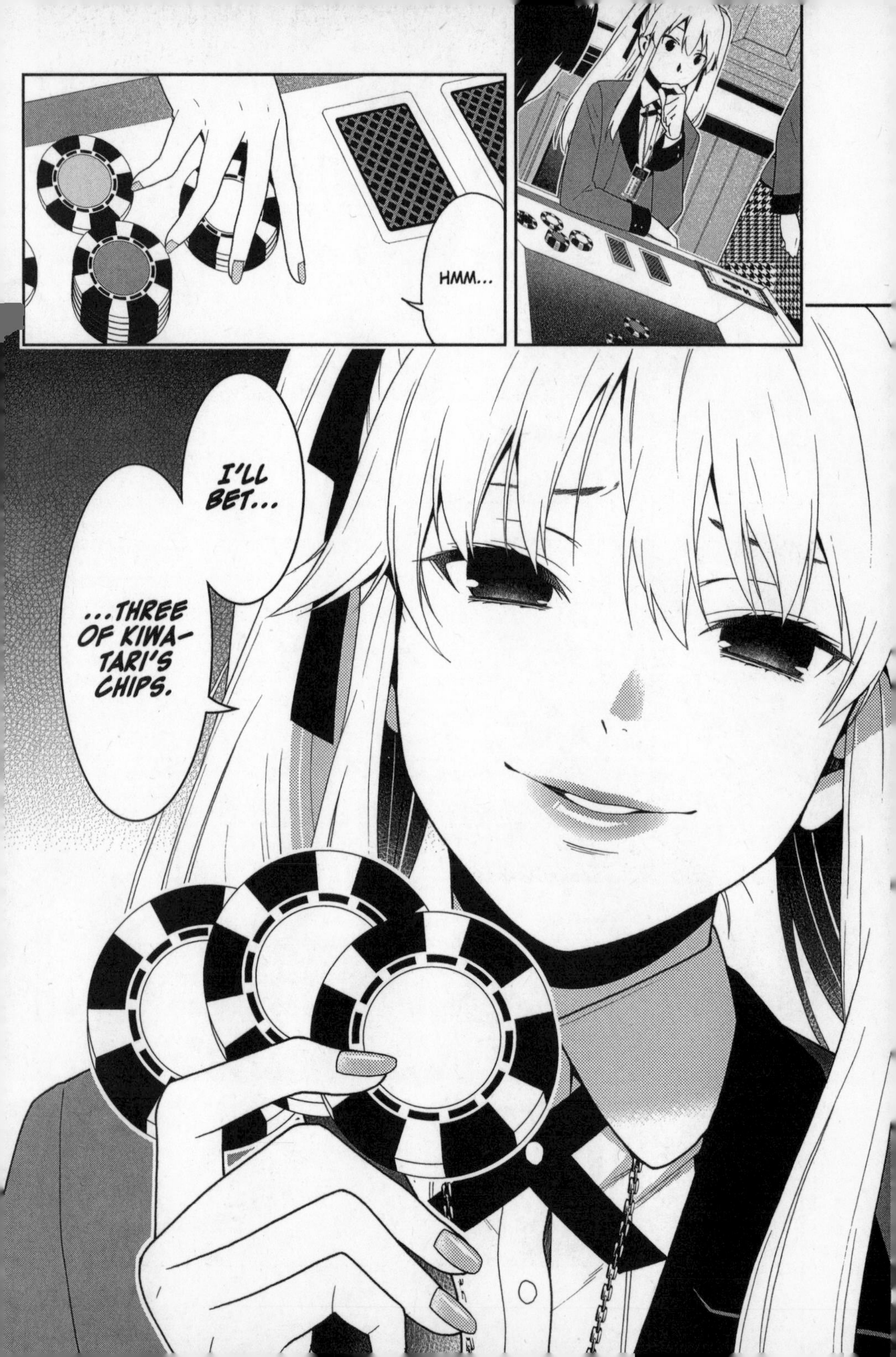
HMM...
I'LL BET...
...THREE OF KIWATARI'S CHIPS.

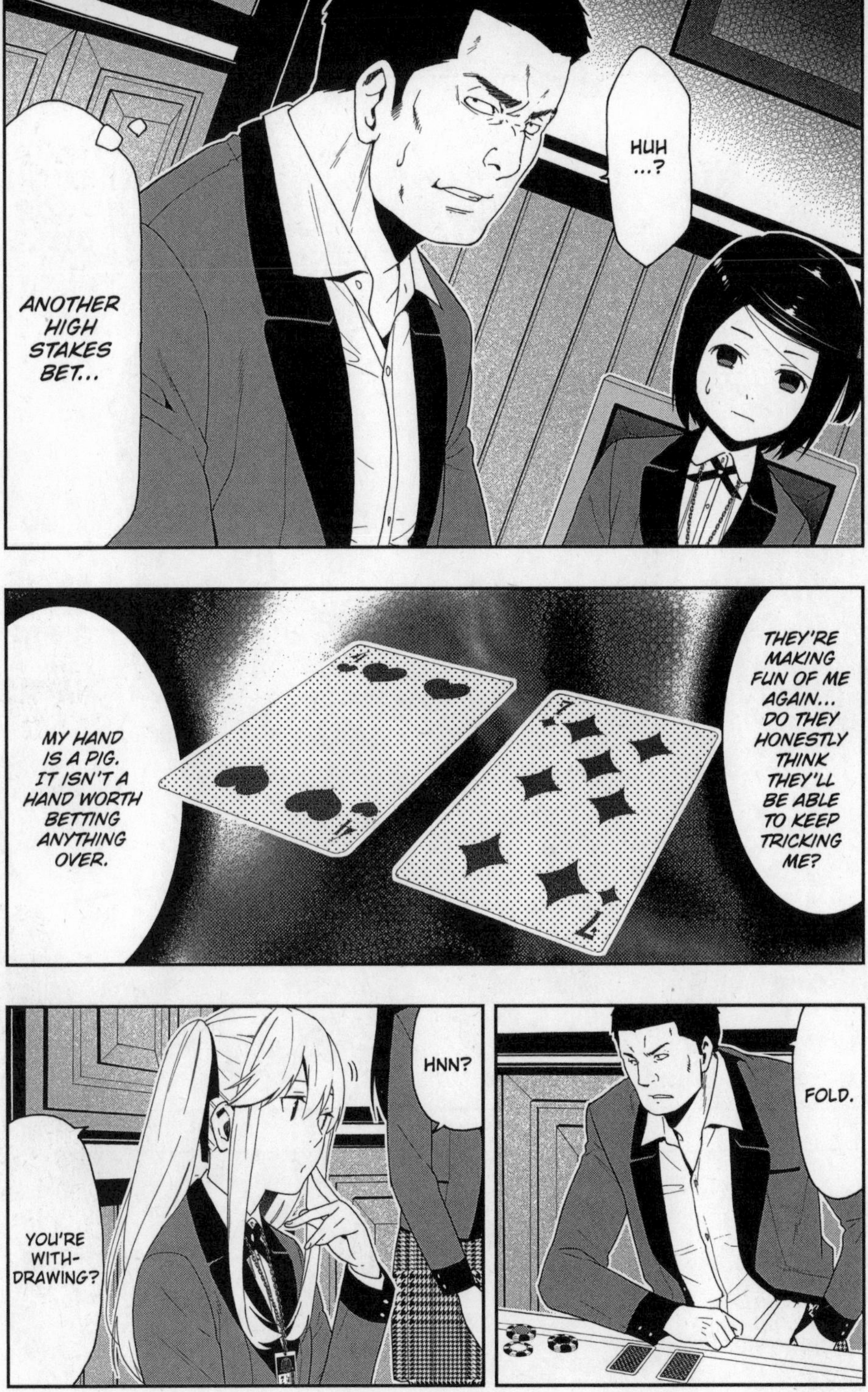
HUH ...?
ANOTHER HIGH STAKES BET...
THEY'RE MAKING FUN OF ME AGAIN... DO THEY HONESTLY THINK THEY'LL BE ABLE TO KEEP TRICKING ME?
MY HAND IS A PIG. IT ISN'T A HAND WORTH BETTING ANYTHING OVER.
FOLD.
HNN?
YOU'RE WITH-DRAWING?

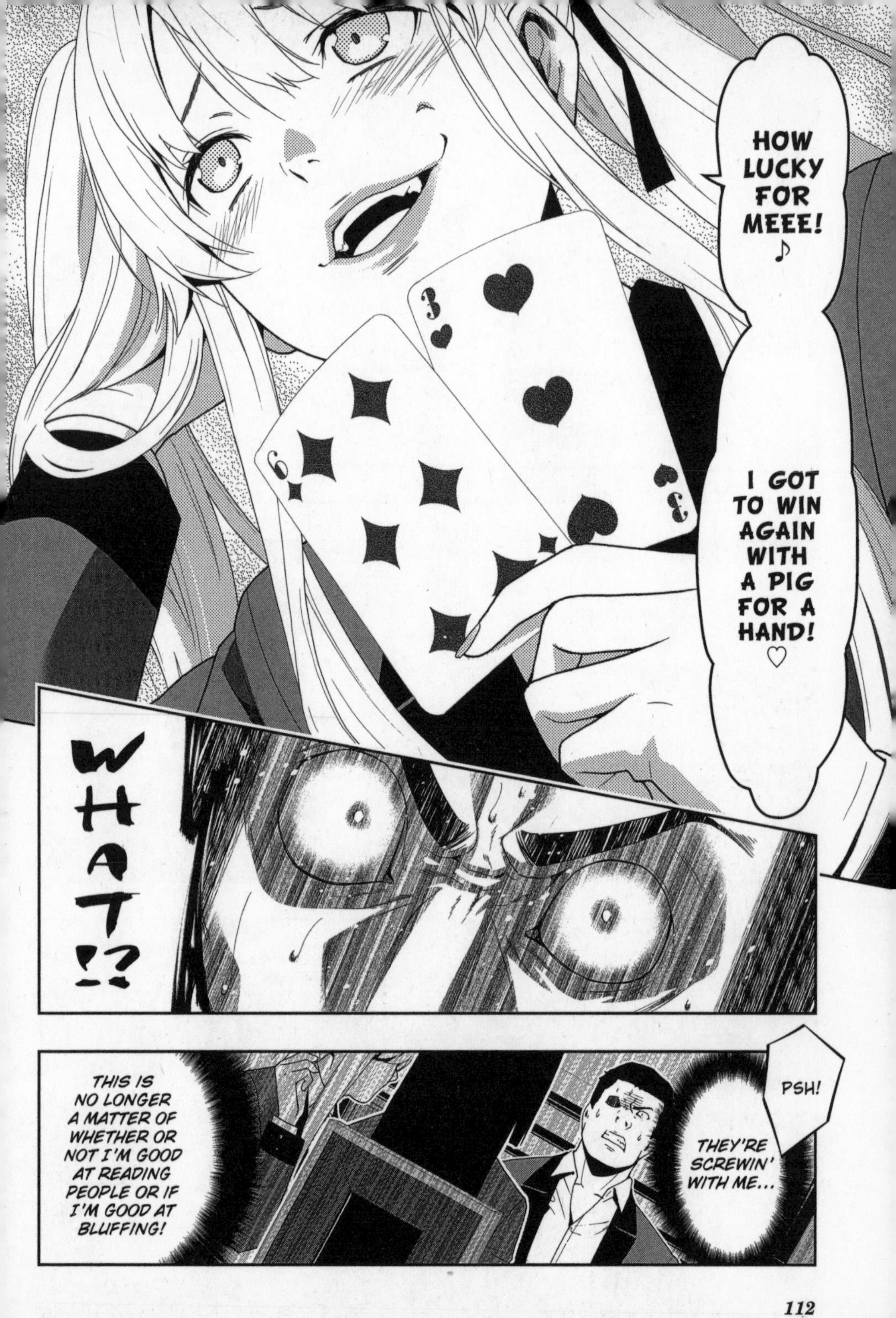
HOW LUCKY FOR MEEE! ♪
I GOT TO WIN AGAIN WITH A PIG FOR A HAND! ♡
WHAT!?
PSH!
THEY'RE SCREWIN' WITH ME...
THIS IS NO LONGER A MATTER OF WHETHER OR NOT I'M GOOD AT READING PEOPLE OR IF I'M GOOD AT BLUFFING!

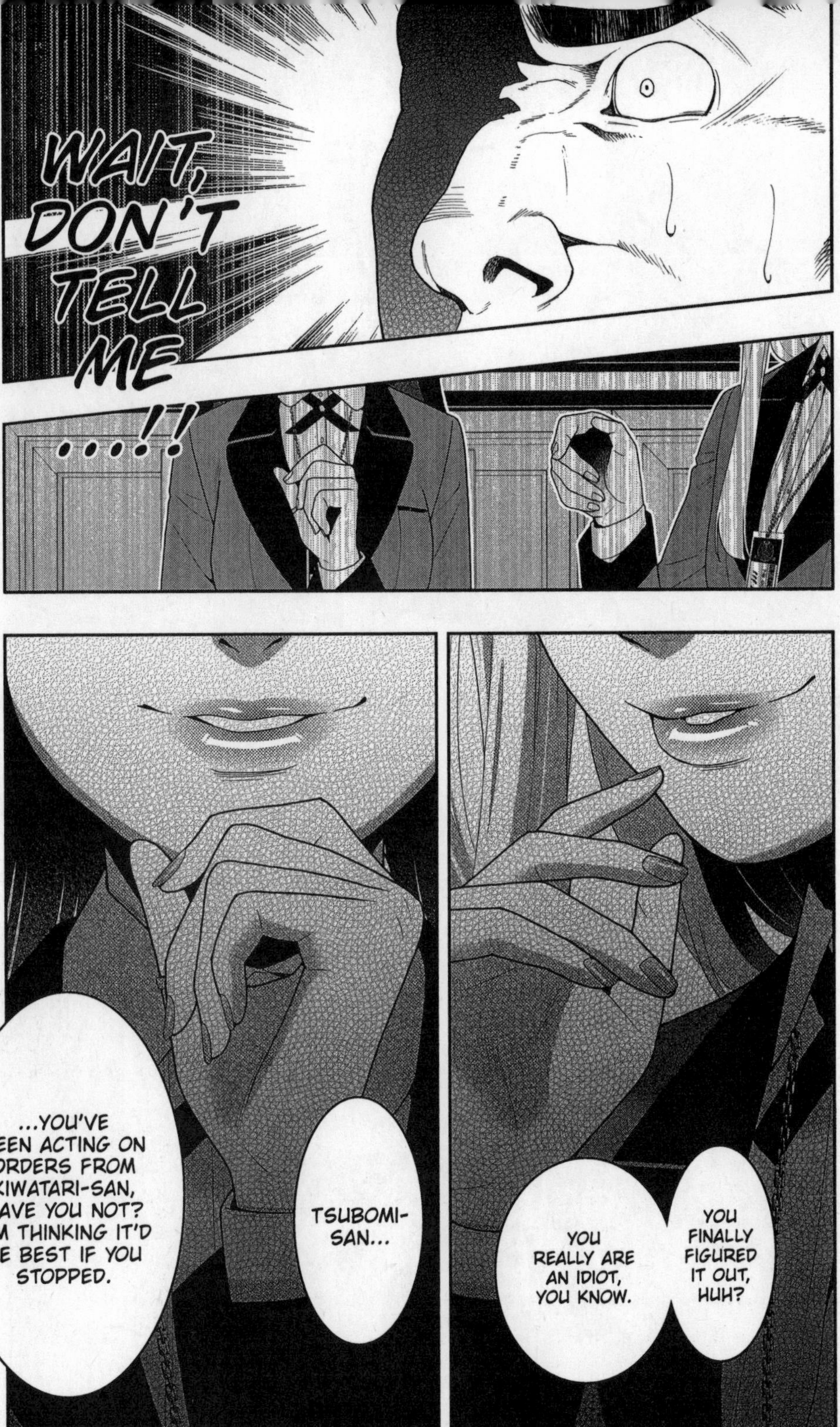
WAIT, DON'T TELL ME
....!!
YOU FINALLY FIGURED IT OUT, HUH?
YOU REALLY ARE AN IDIOT, YOU KNOW.
TSUBOMI-SAN...
...YOU'VE BEEN ACTING ON ORDERS FROM KIWATARI-SAN, HAVE YOU NOT? I'M THINKING IT'D BE BEST IF YOU STOPPED.

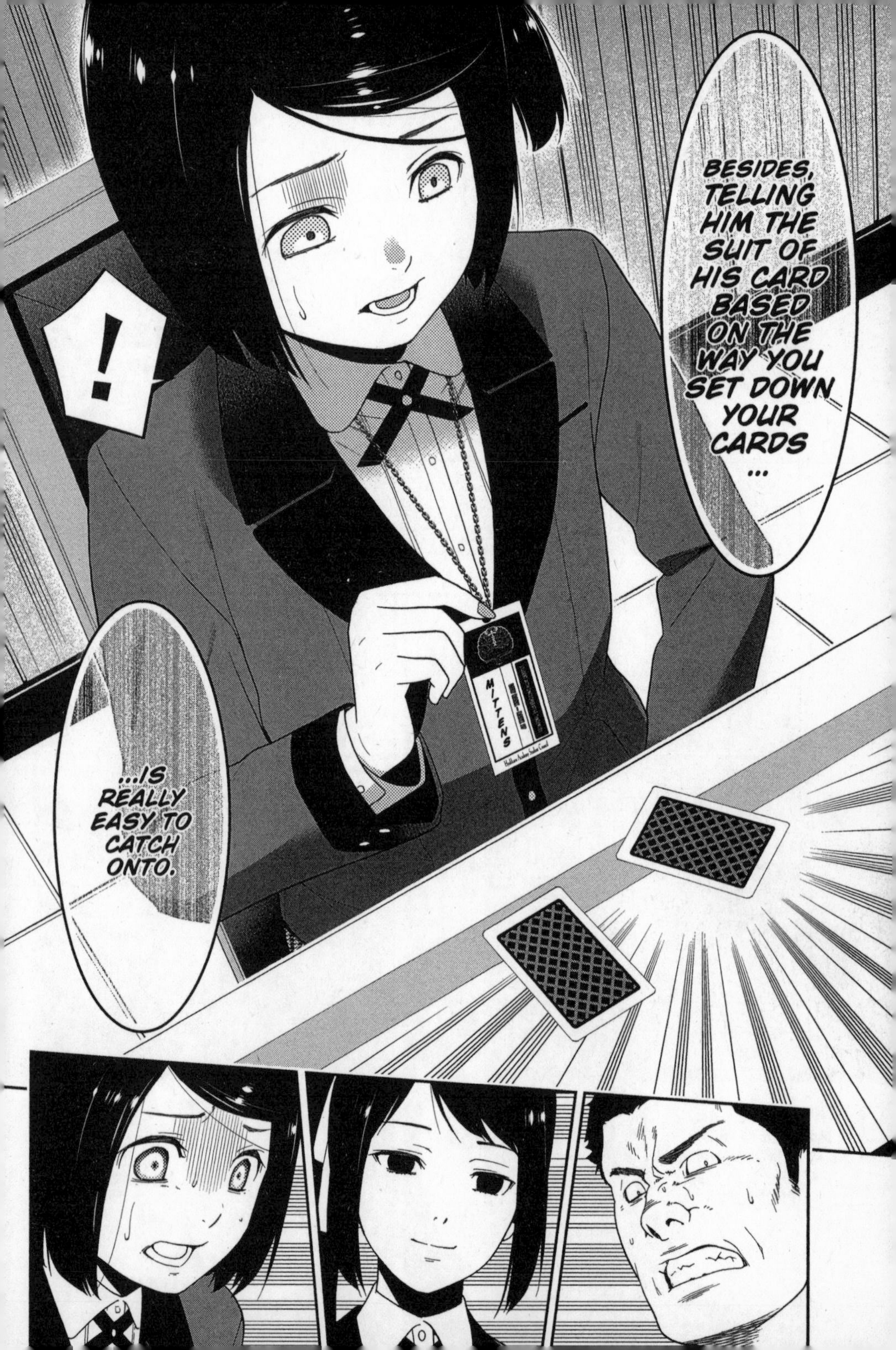
BESIDES, TELLING HIM THE SUIT OF HIS CARD BASED ON THE WAY YOU SET DOWN YOUR CARDS ...
!
...IS REALLY EASY TO CATCH ONTO.
MITTENS

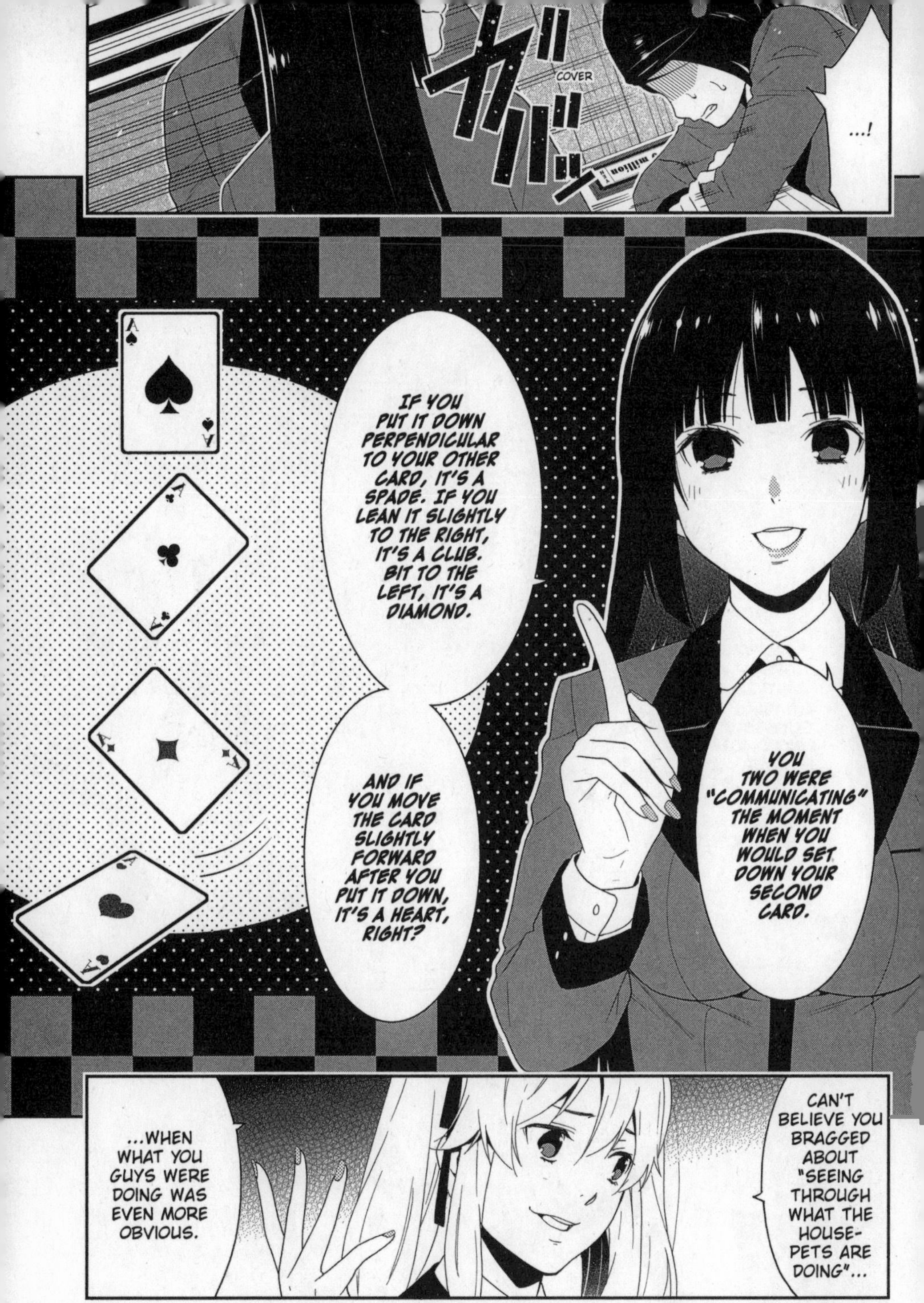
COVER
million
...!
YOU TWO WERE "COMMUNICATING" THE MOMENT WHEN YOU WOULD SET DOWN YOUR SECOND CARD.
IF YOU PUT IT DOWN PERPENDICULAR TO YOUR OTHER CARD, IT'S A SPADE. IF YOU LEAN IT SLIGHTLY TO THE RIGHT, IT'S A CLUB. BIT TO THE LEFT, IT'S A DIAMOND.
AND IF YOU MOVE THE CARD SLIGHTLY FORWARD AFTER YOU PUT IT DOWN, IT'S A HEART, RIGHT?
CAN'T BELIEVE YOU BRAGGED ABOUT "SEEING THROUGH WHAT THE HOUSE-PETS ARE DOING"...
...WHEN WHAT YOU GUYS WERE DOING WAS EVEN MORE OBVIOUS.

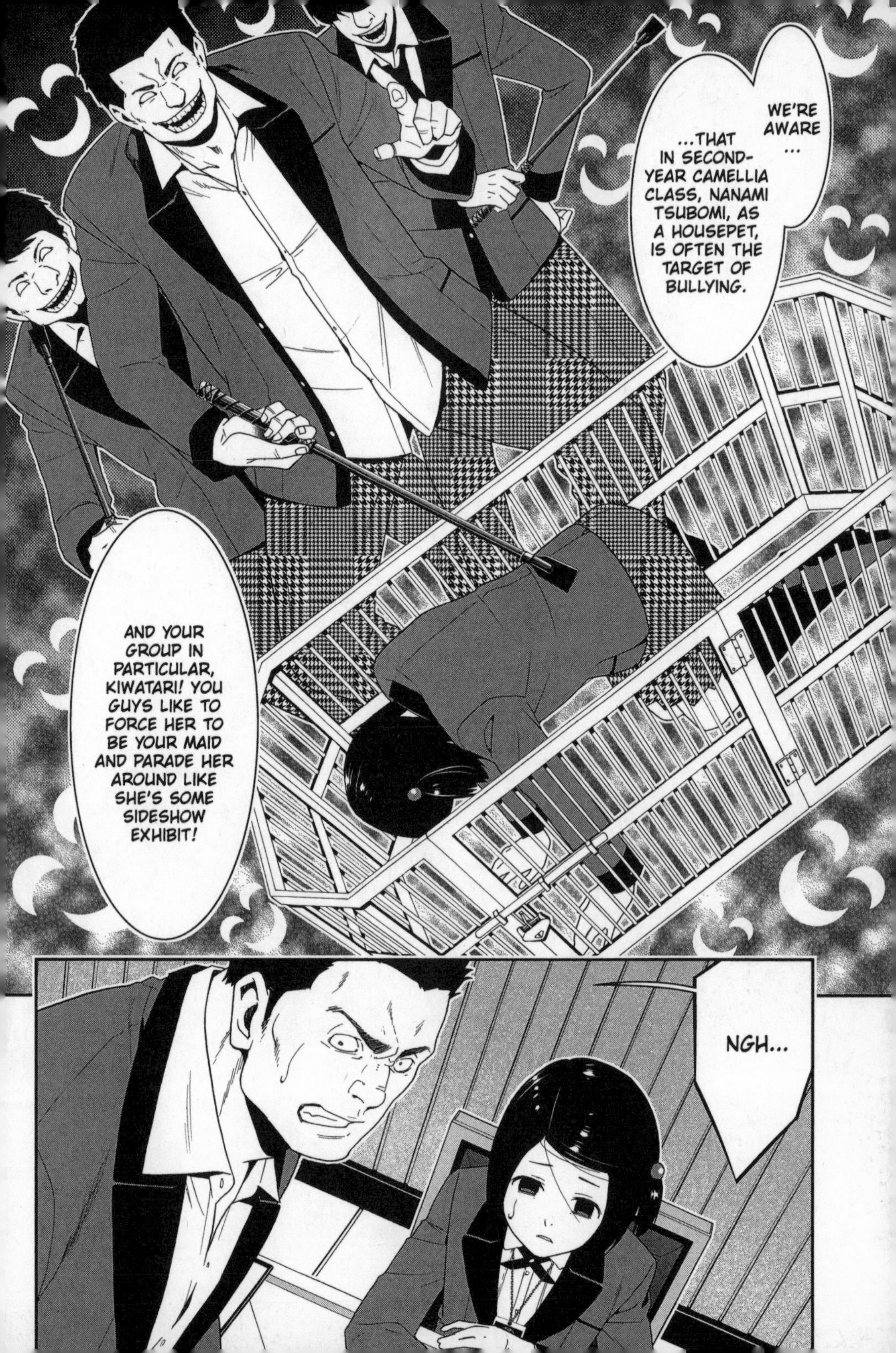
WE'RE AWARE ...
...THAT IN SECOND-YEAR CAMELLIA CLASS, NANAMI TSUBOMI, AS A HOUSEPET, IS OFTEN THE TARGET OF BULLYING.
AND YOUR GROUP IN PARTICULAR, KIWATARI! YOU GUYS LIKE TO FORCE HER TO BE YOUR MAID AND PARADE HER AROUND LIKE SHE'S SOME SIDESHOW EXHIBIT!
NGH...

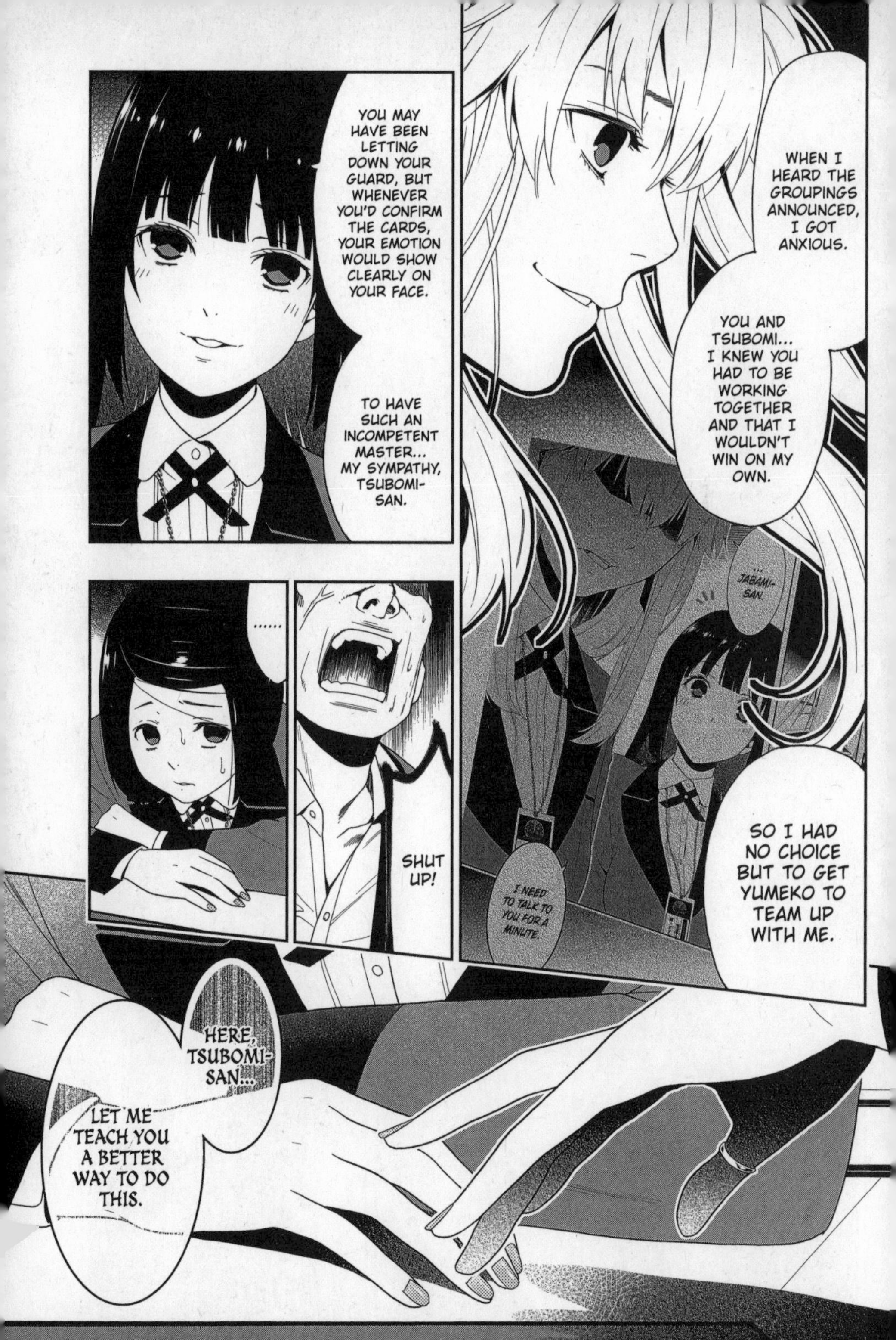
WHEN I HEARD THE GROUPINGS ANNOUNCED, I GOT ANXIOUS.
YOU AND TSUBOMI... I KNEW YOU HAD TO BE WORKING TOGETHER AND THAT I WOULDN'T WIN ON MY OWN.
...JABAMI-SAN.
I NEED TO TALK TO YOU FOR A MINUTE.
SO I HAD NO CHOICE BUT TO GET YUMEKO TO TEAM UP WITH ME.
YOU MAY HAVE BEEN LETTING DOWN YOUR GUARD, BUT WHENEVER YOU'D CONFIRM THE CARDS, YOUR EMOTION WOULD SHOW CLEARLY ON YOUR FACE.
TO HAVE SUCH AN INCOMPETENT MASTER... MY SYMPATHY, TSUBOMI-SAN.
SHUT UP!
......
HERE, TSUBOMI-SAN...
LET ME TEACH YOU A BETTER WAY TO DO THIS.

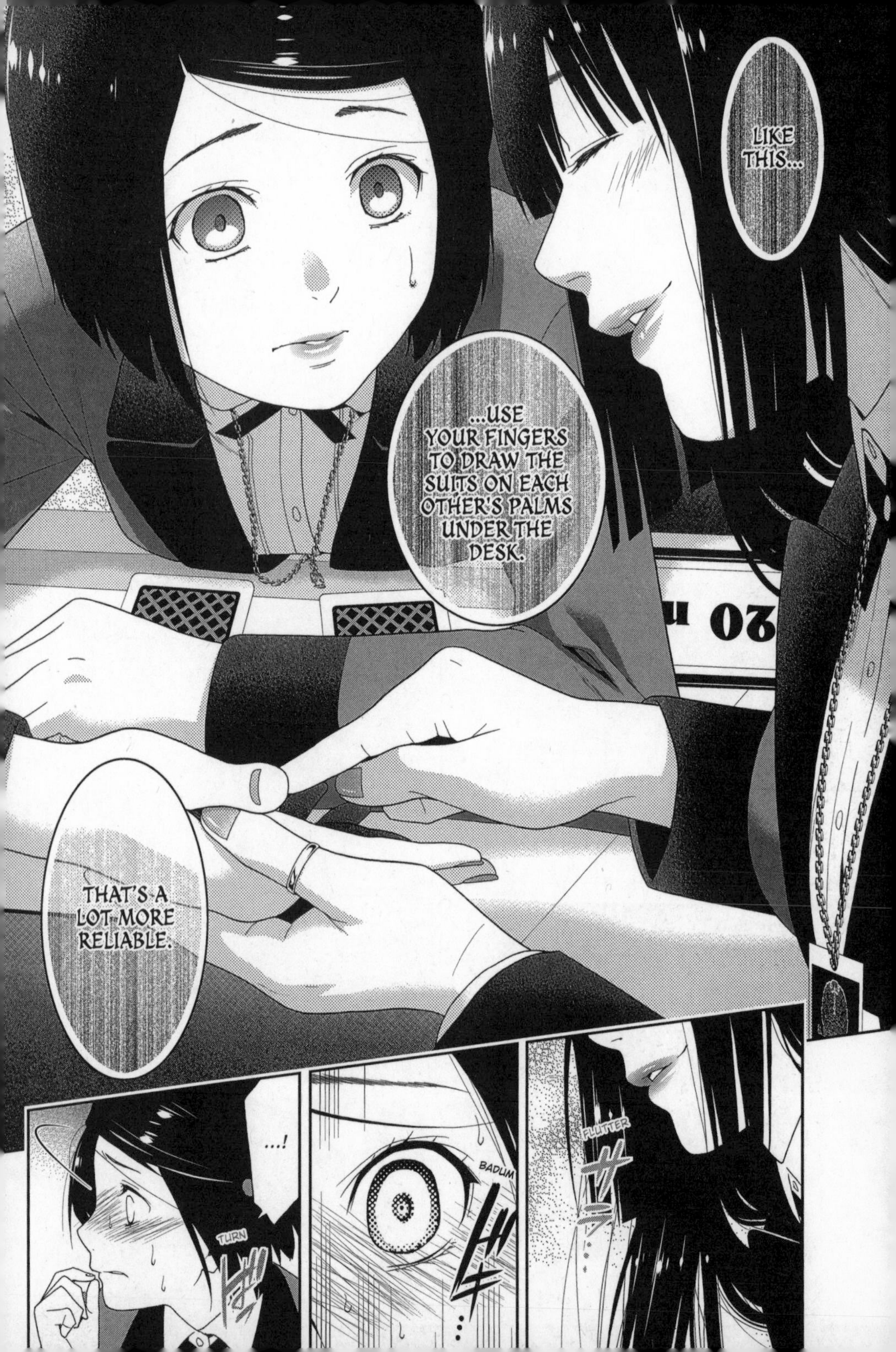
LIKE THIS...
...USE YOUR FINGERS TO DRAW THE SUITS ON EACH OTHER'S PALMS UNDER THE DESK.
THAT'S A LOT MORE RELIABLE.
FLUTTER
BADUM
...!
TURN

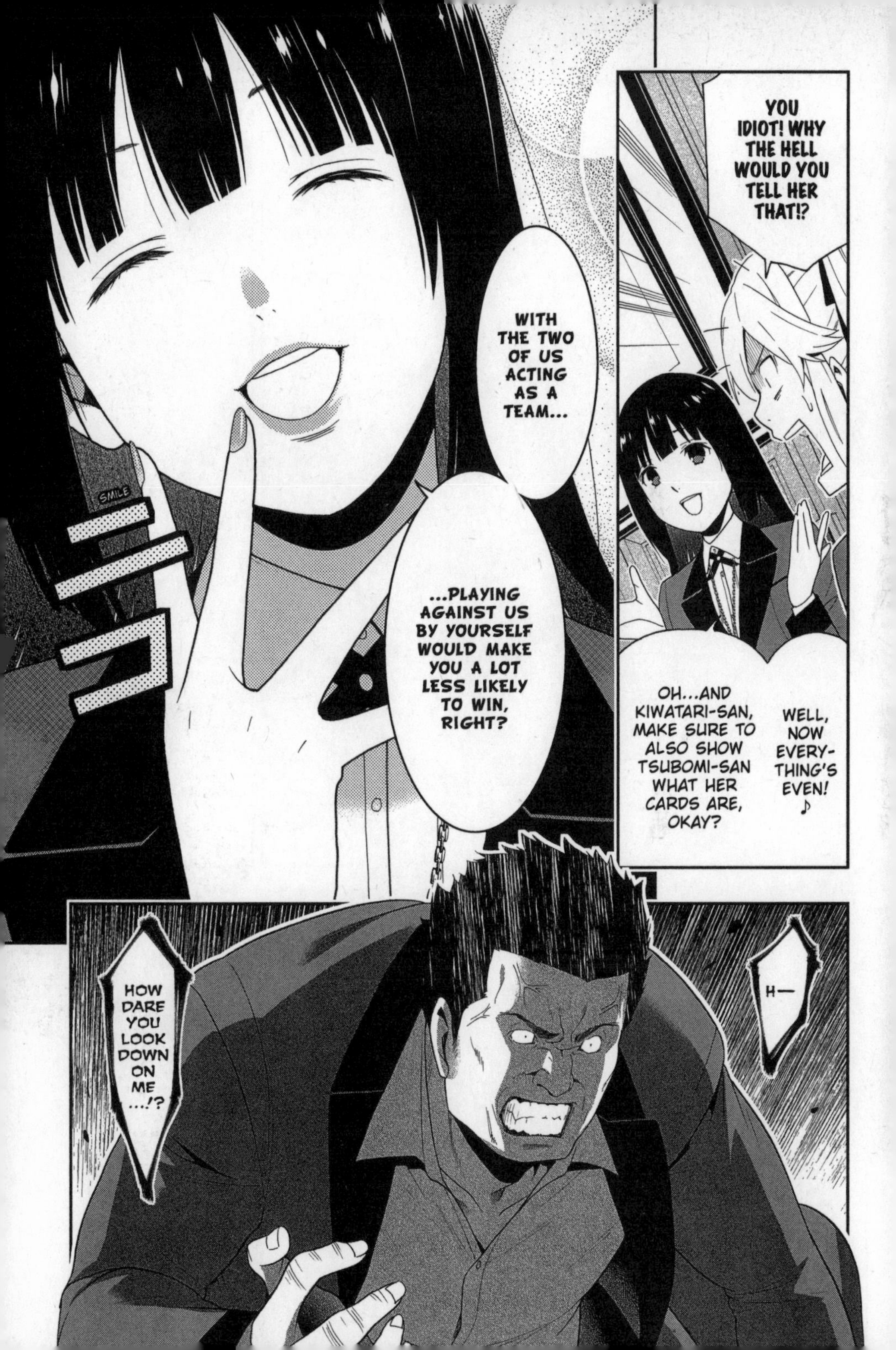
YOU IDIOT! WHY THE HELL WOULD YOU TELL HER THAT!?
WELL, NOW EVERY-THING'S EVEN! ♪
OH...AND KIWATARI-SAN, MAKE SURE TO ALSO SHOW TSUBOMI-SAN WHAT HER CARDS ARE, OKAY?
WITH THE TWO OF US ACTING AS A TEAM...
...PLAYING AGAINST US BY YOURSELF WOULD MAKE YOU A LOT LESS LIKELY TO WIN, RIGHT?
SMILE
H—
HOW DARE YOU LOOK DOWN ON ME ...!?

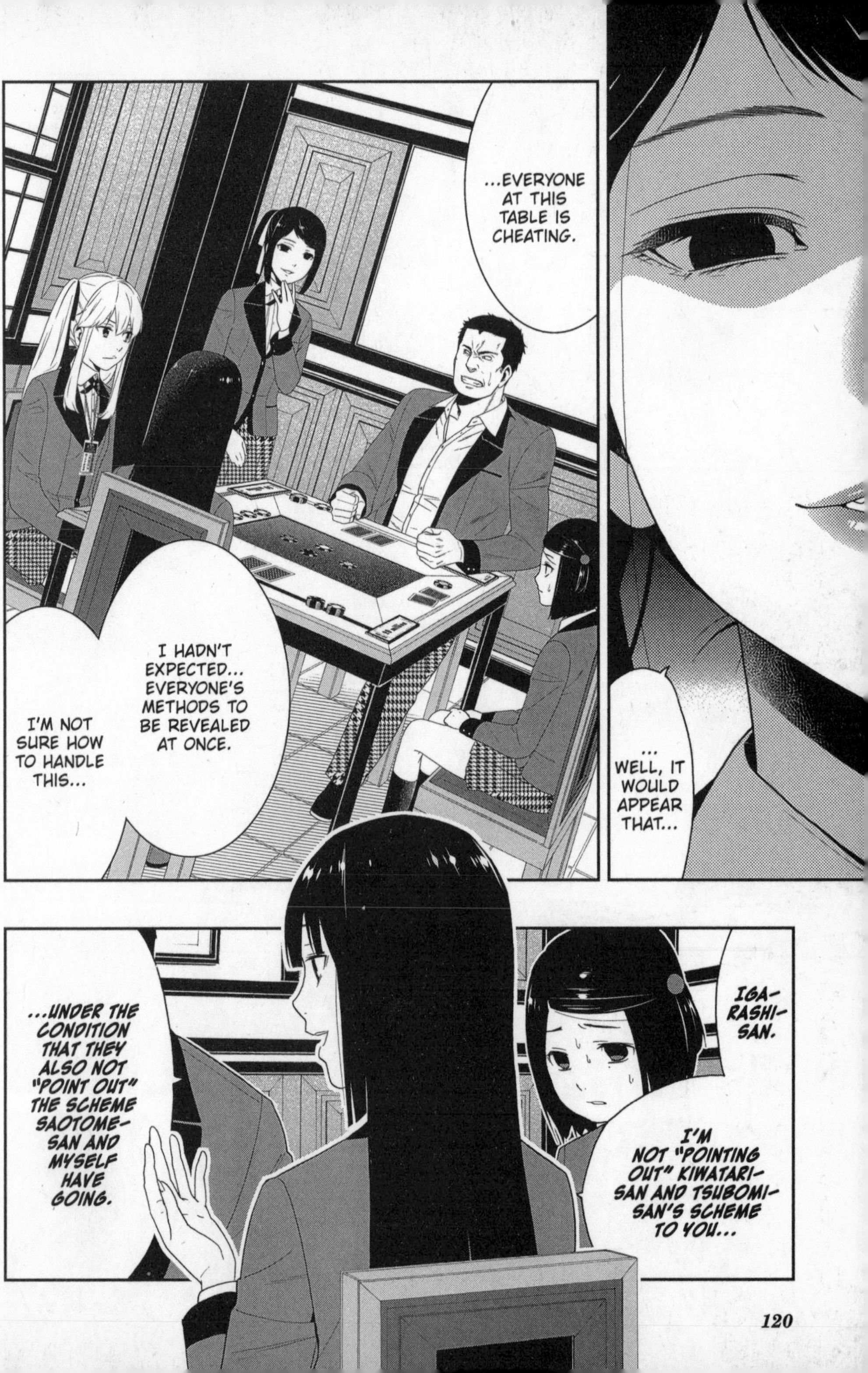
...WELL, IT WOULD APPEAR THAT...
...EVERYONE AT THIS TABLE IS CHEATING.
I HADN'T EXPECTED... EVERYONE'S METHODS TO BE REVEALED AT ONCE.
I'M NOT SURE HOW TO HANDLE THIS...
IGARASHI-SAN.
I'M NOT "POINTING OUT" KIWATARI-SAN AND TSUBOMI-SAN'S SCHEME TO YOU...
...UNDER THE CONDITION THAT THEY ALSO NOT "POINT OUT" THE SCHEME SAOTOME-SAN AND MYSELF HAVE GOING.

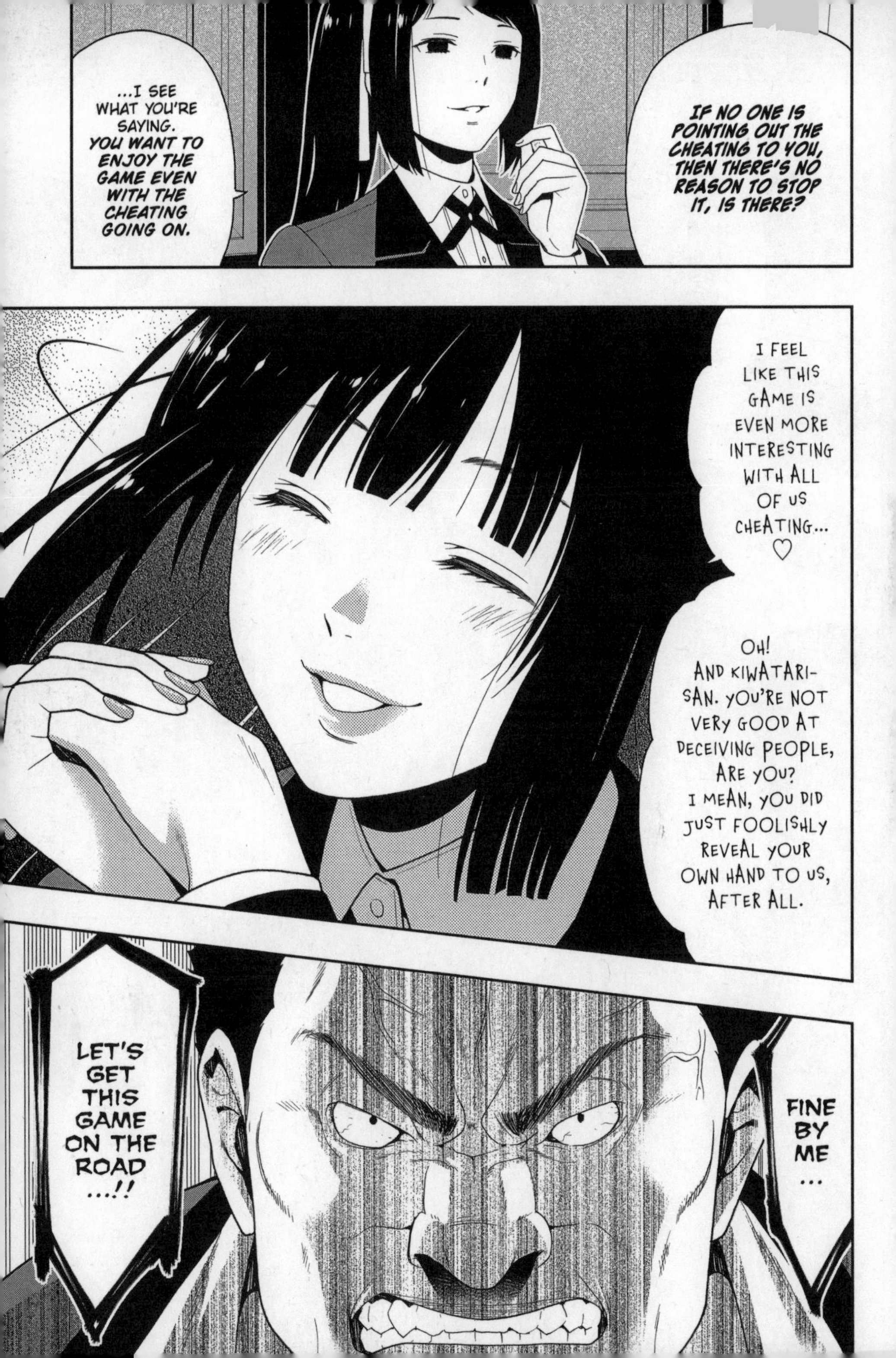
IF NO ONE IS POINTING OUT THE CHEATING TO YOU, THEN THERE'S NO REASON TO STOP IT, IS THERE?
...I SEE WHAT YOU'RE SAYING. YOU WANT TO ENJOY THE GAME EVEN WITH THE CHEATING GOING ON.
I FEEL LIKE THIS GAME IS EVEN MORE INTERESTING WITH ALL OF US CHEATING... ♡
OH! AND KIWATARI-SAN. YOU'RE NOT VERY GOOD AT DECEIVING PEOPLE, ARE YOU? I MEAN, YOU DID JUST FOOLISHLY REVEAL YOUR OWN HAND TO US, AFTER ALL.
FINE BY ME...
LET'S GET THIS GAME ON THE ROAD...!!

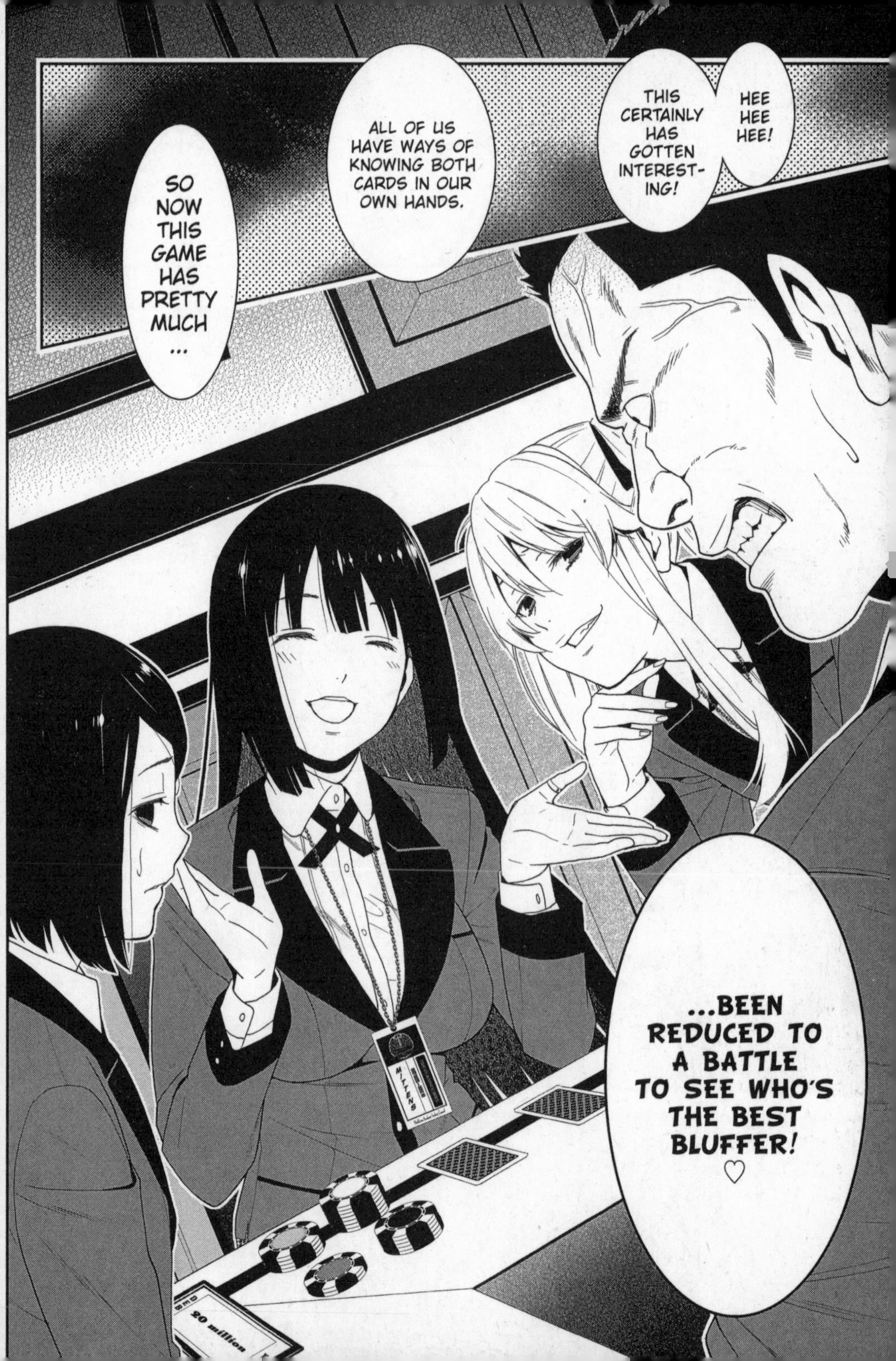
HEE HEE HEE!
THIS CERTAINLY HAS GOTTEN INTEREST-ING!
ALL OF US HAVE WAYS OF KNOWING BOTH CARDS IN OUR OWN HANDS.
SO NOW THIS GAME HAS PRETTY MUCH ...
...BEEN REDUCED TO A BATTLE TO SEE WHO'S THE BEST BLUFFER! ♡
MITTENS
20 million

KAKEGURUI

— Compulsive Gambler —

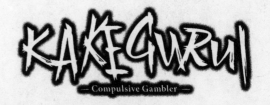

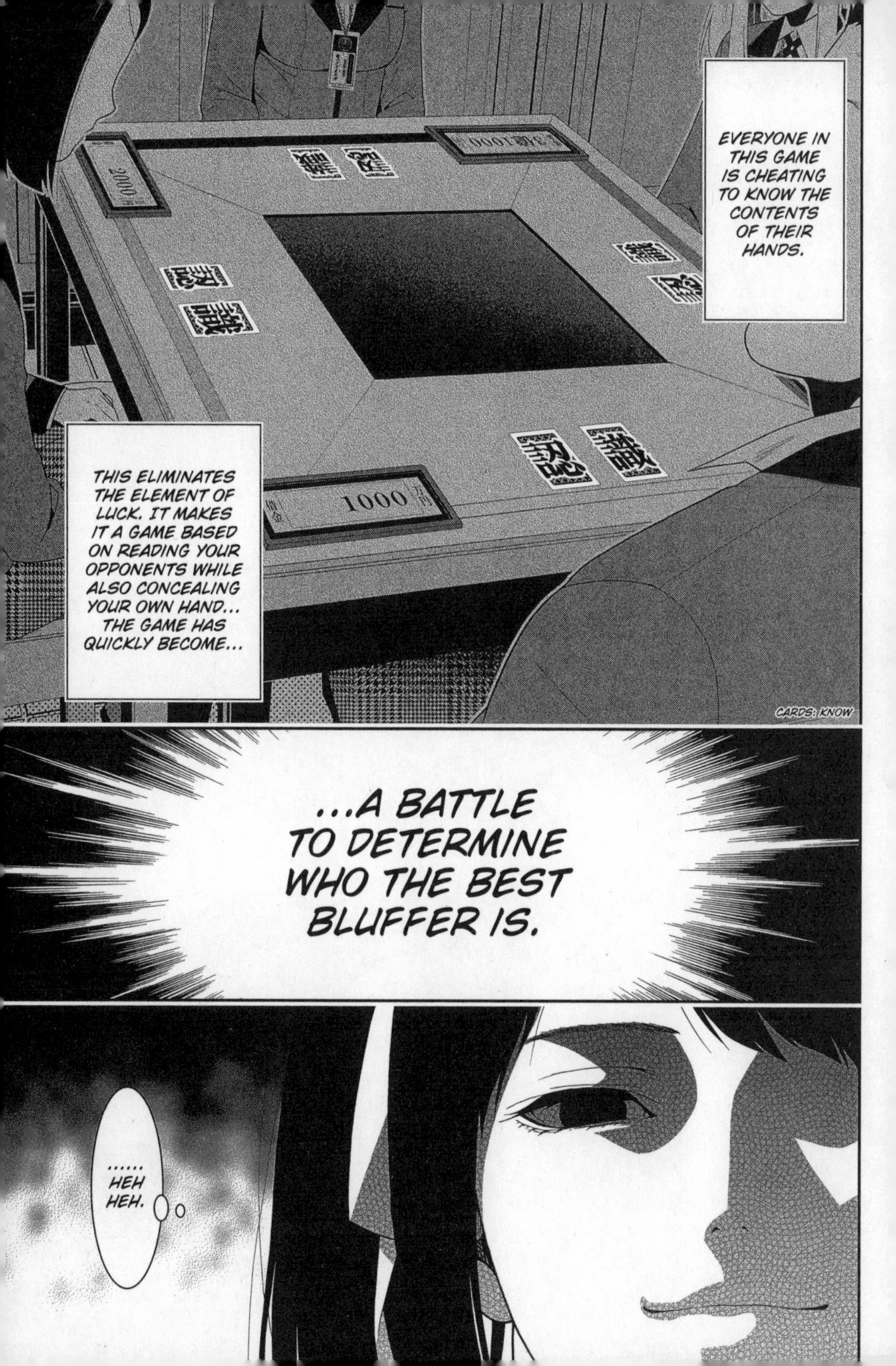
EVERYONE IN THIS GAME IS CHEATING TO KNOW THE CONTENTS OF THEIR HANDS.
1000
2000
1000
THIS ELIMINATES THE ELEMENT OF LUCK. IT MAKES IT A GAME BASED ON READING YOUR OPPONENTS WHILE ALSO CONCEALING YOUR OWN HAND... THE GAME HAS QUICKLY BECOME...
CARDS: KNOW
...A BATTLE TO DETERMINE WHO THE BEST BLUFFER IS.
...... HEH HEH.

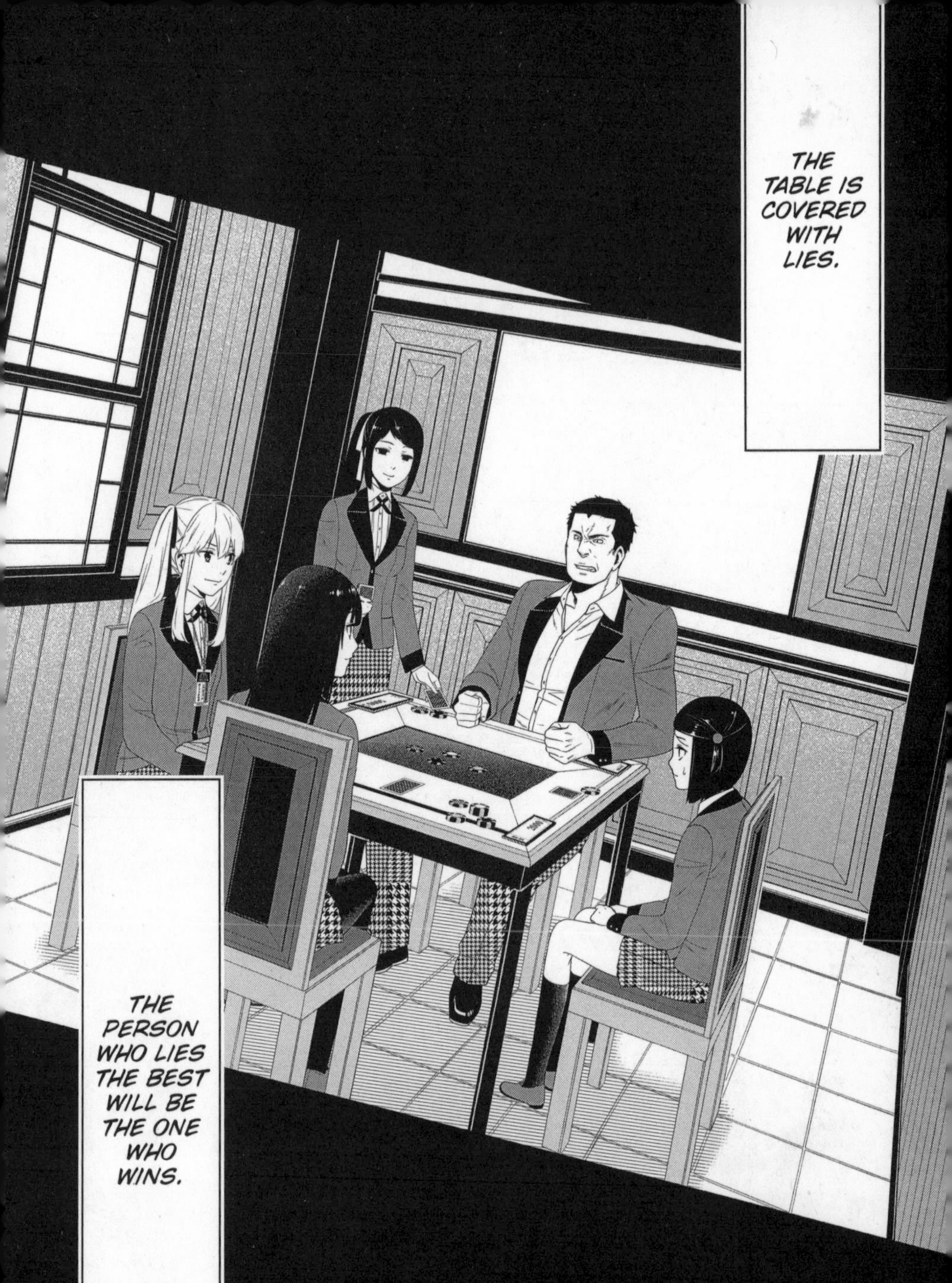
THE TABLE IS COVERED WITH LIES.
THE PERSON WHO LIES THE BEST WILL BE THE ONE WHO WINS.

CHAPTER EIGHT
THE GIRL IS HUMAN AGAIN

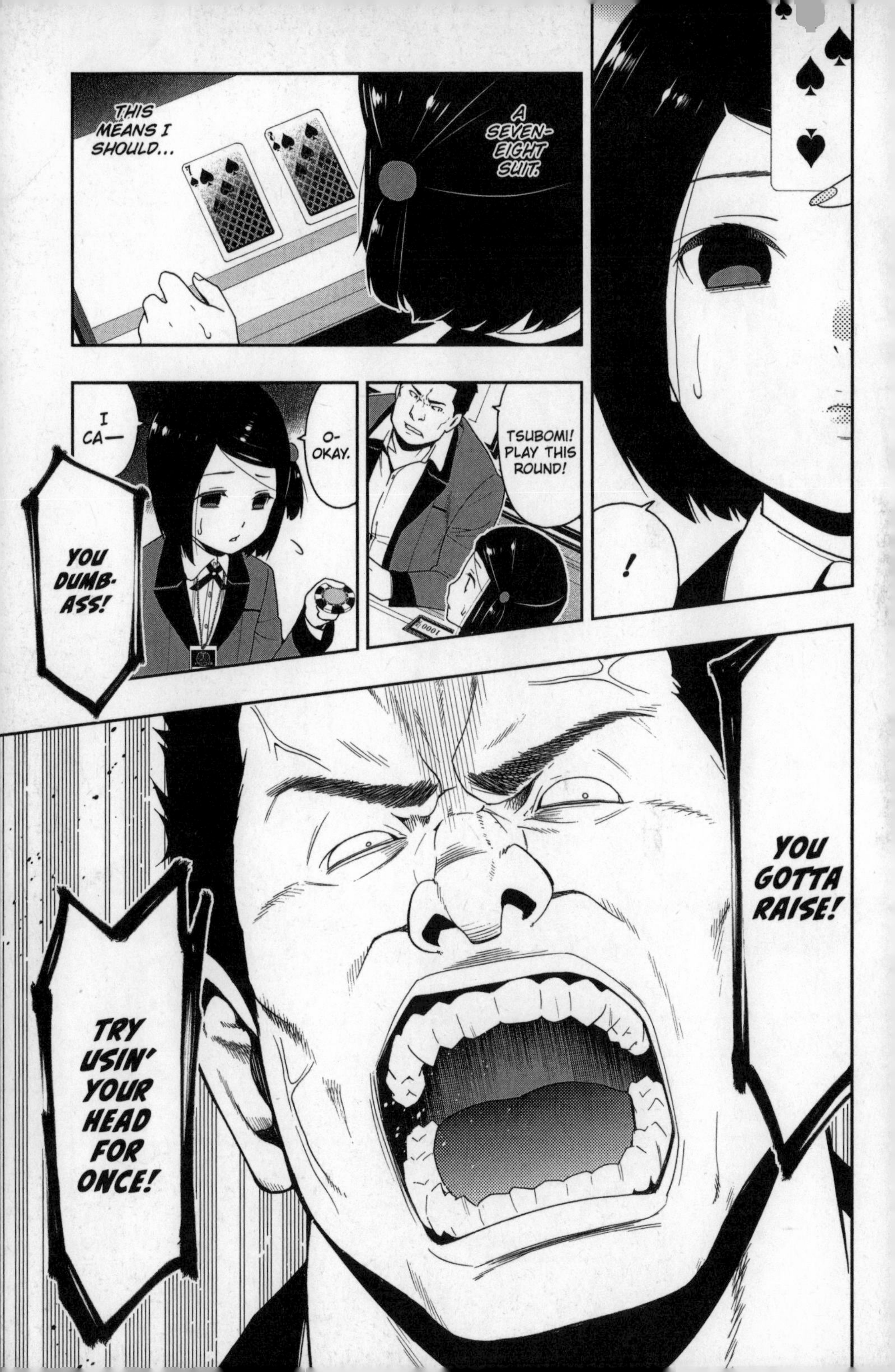

!
A SEVEN-EIGHT SUIT.
THIS MEANS I SHOULD...
TSUBOMI! PLAY THIS ROUND!
O-OKAY.
I CA—
YOU DUMB-ASS!
YOU GOTTA RAISE!
TRY USIN' YOUR HEAD FOR ONCE!

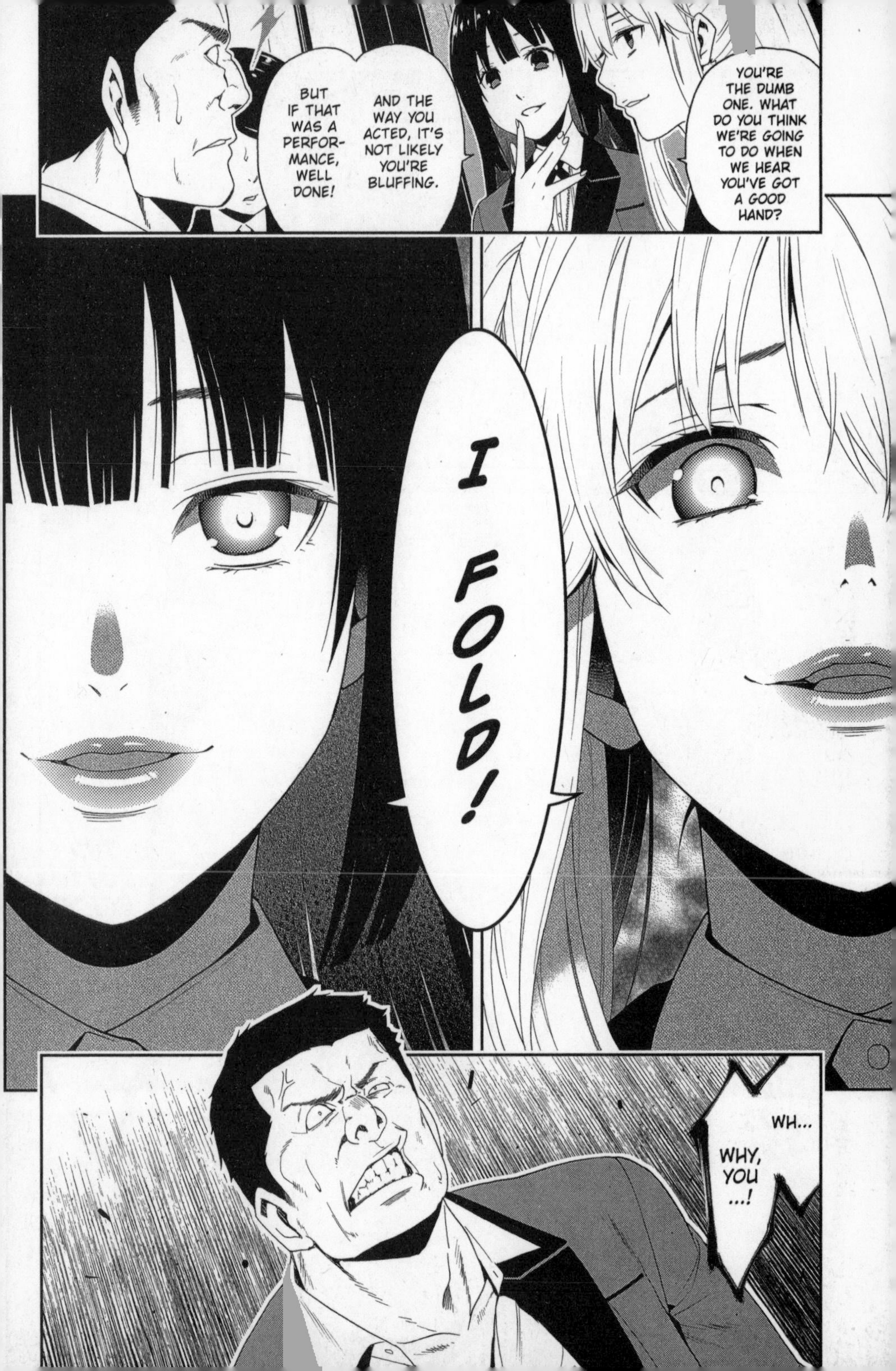
YOU'RE THE DUMB ONE. WHAT DO YOU THINK WE'RE GOING TO DO WHEN WE HEAR YOU'VE GOT A GOOD HAND?
AND THE WAY YOU ACTED, IT'S NOT LIKELY YOU'RE BLUFFING.
BUT IF THAT WAS A PERFOR-MANCE, WELL DONE!
I FOLD!
WH...
WHY, YOU ...!

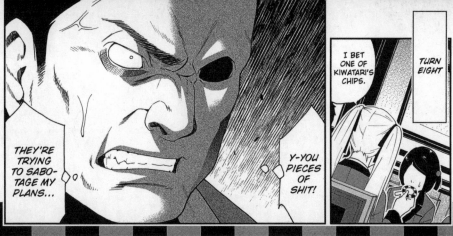

TURN EIGHT
I BET ONE OF KIWATARI'S CHIPS.

Y-YOU PIECES OF SHIT!
THEY'RE TRYING TO SABOTAGE MY PLANS...

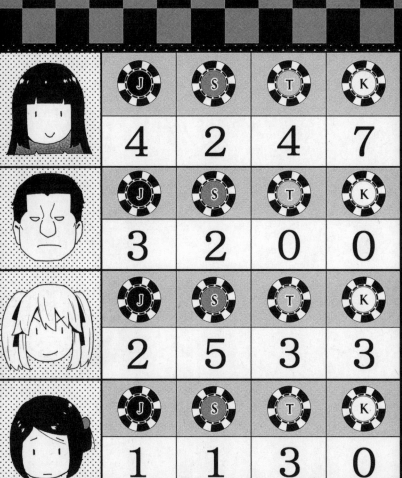

THE CURRENT CHIP TOTALS

	J	S	T	K
	4	2	4	7
	3	2	0	0
	2	5	3	3
	1	1	3	0

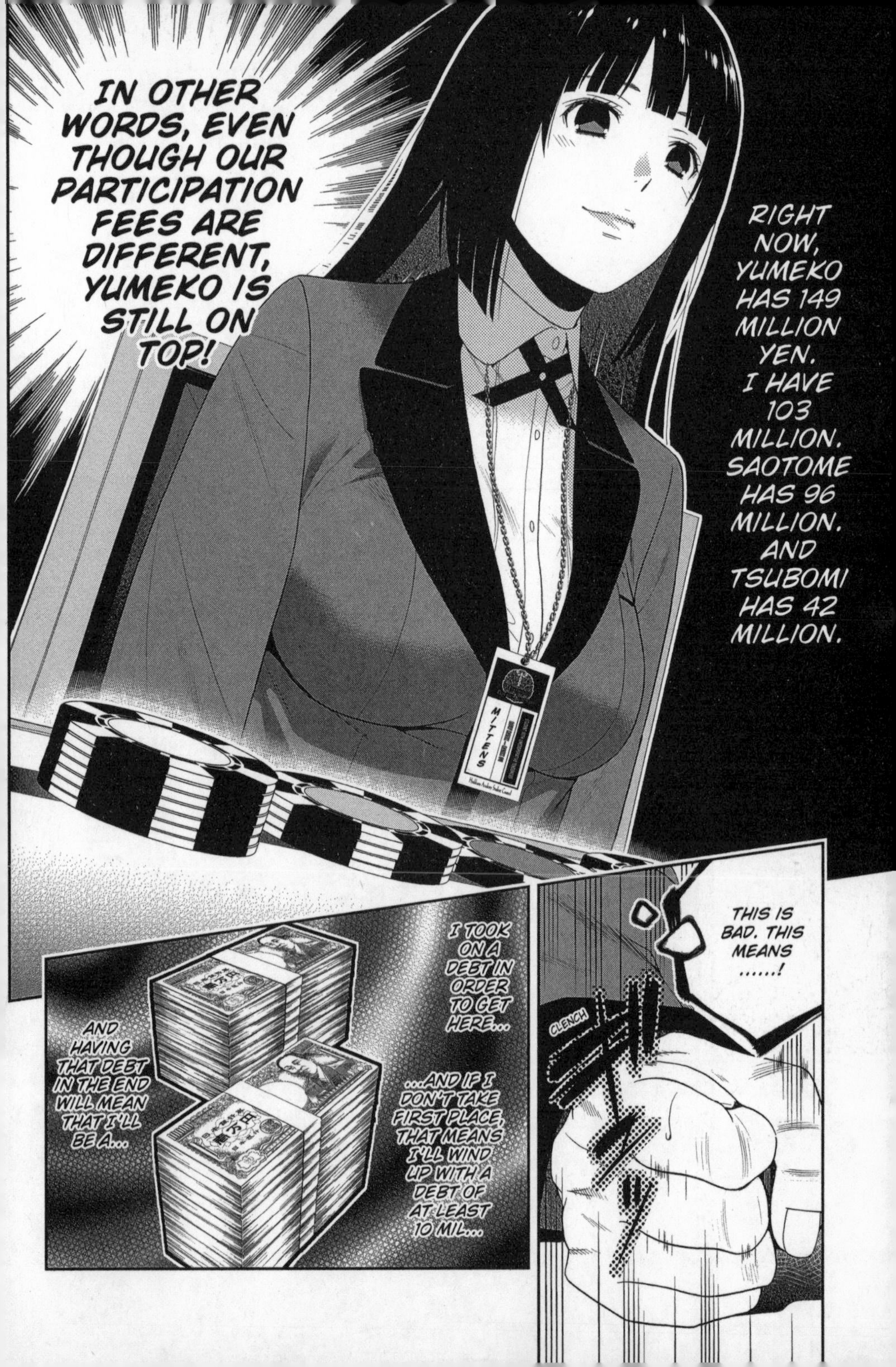
RIGHT NOW, YUMEKO HAS 149 MILLION YEN. I HAVE 103 MILLION. SAOTOME HAS 96 MILLION. AND TSUBOMI HAS 42 MILLION.
IN OTHER WORDS, EVEN THOUGH OUR PARTICIPATION FEES ARE DIFFERENT, YUMEKO IS STILL ON TOP!
MITTENS
THIS IS BAD. THIS MEANS ......!
CLENCH
I TOOK ON A DEBT IN ORDER TO GET HERE...
...AND IF I DON'T TAKE FIRST PLACE, THAT MEANS I'LL WIND UP WITH A DEBT OF AT LEAST 10 MIL...
AND HAVING THAT DEBT IN THE END WILL MEAN THAT I'LL BE A...

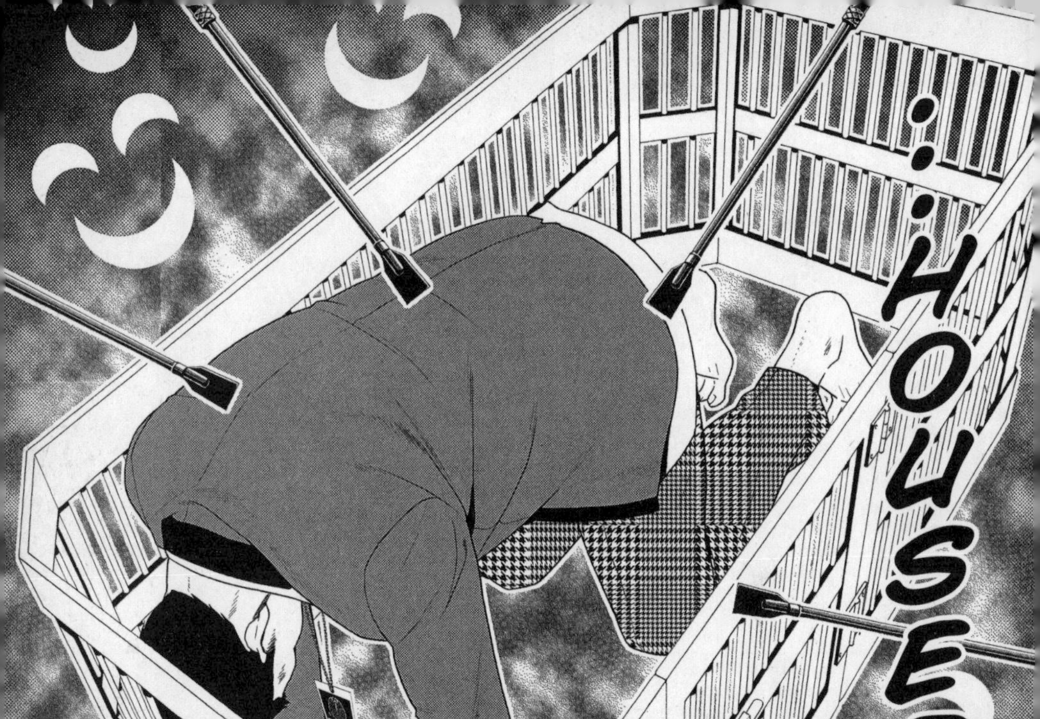
HOUSEPET!!

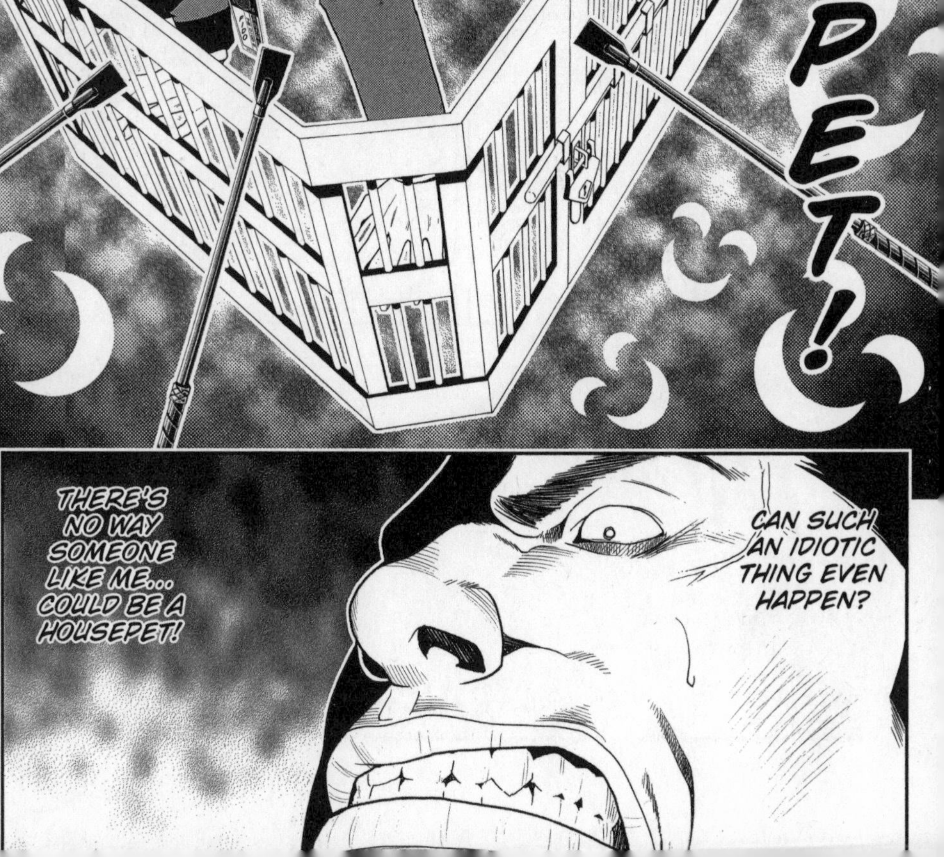
CAN SUCH AN IDIOTIC THING EVEN HAPPEN?
THERE'S NO WAY SOMEONE LIKE ME... COULD BE A HOUSEPET!

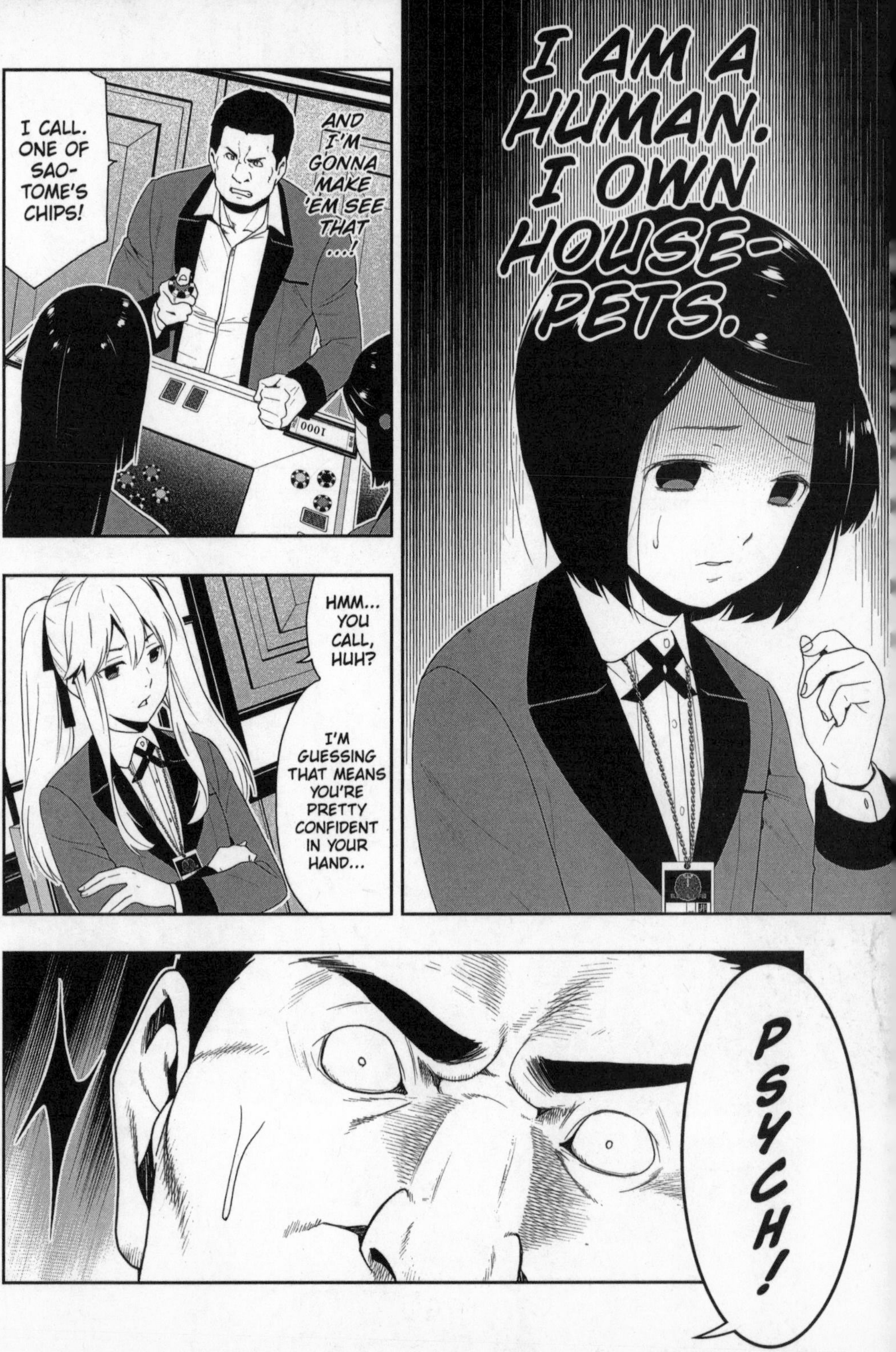
I AM A HUMAN. I OWN HOUSE-PETS.
AND I'M GONNA MAKE 'EM SEE THAT ...!
I CALL. ONE OF SAO-TOME'S CHIPS!
HMM... YOU CALL, HUH?
I'M GUESSING THAT MEANS YOU'RE PRETTY CONFIDENT IN YOUR HAND...
PSYCH!

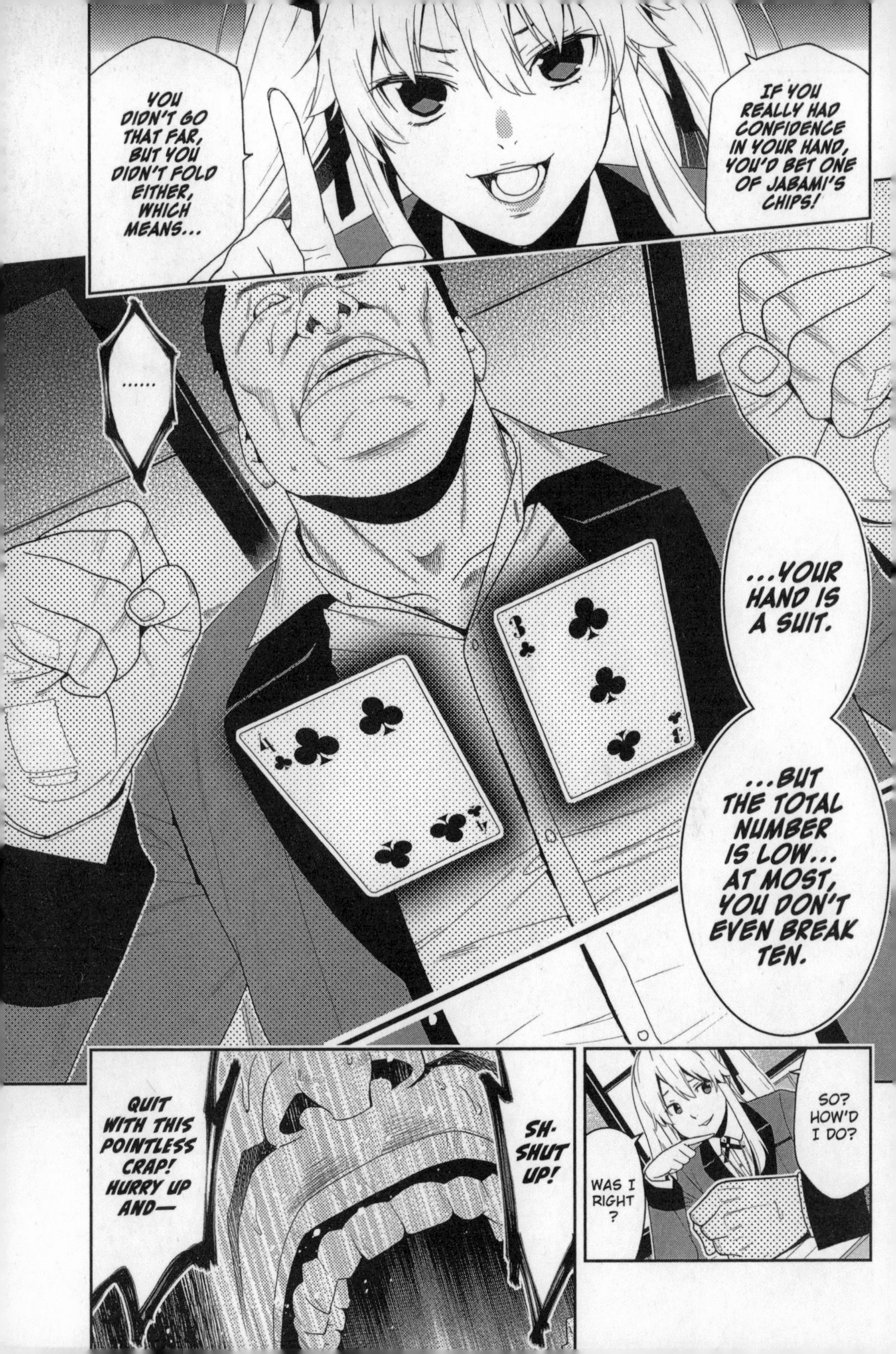
IF YOU REALLY HAD CONFIDENCE IN YOUR HAND, YOU'D BET ONE OF JABAMI'S CHIPS!
YOU DIDN'T GO THAT FAR, BUT YOU DIDN'T FOLD EITHER, WHICH MEANS...
...YOUR HAND IS A SUIT.
...BUT THE TOTAL NUMBER IS LOW... AT MOST, YOU DON'T EVEN BREAK TEN.
......
SO? HOW'D I DO?
WAS I RIGHT?
SH-SHUT UP!
QUIT WITH THIS POINTLESS CRAP! HURRY UP AND—

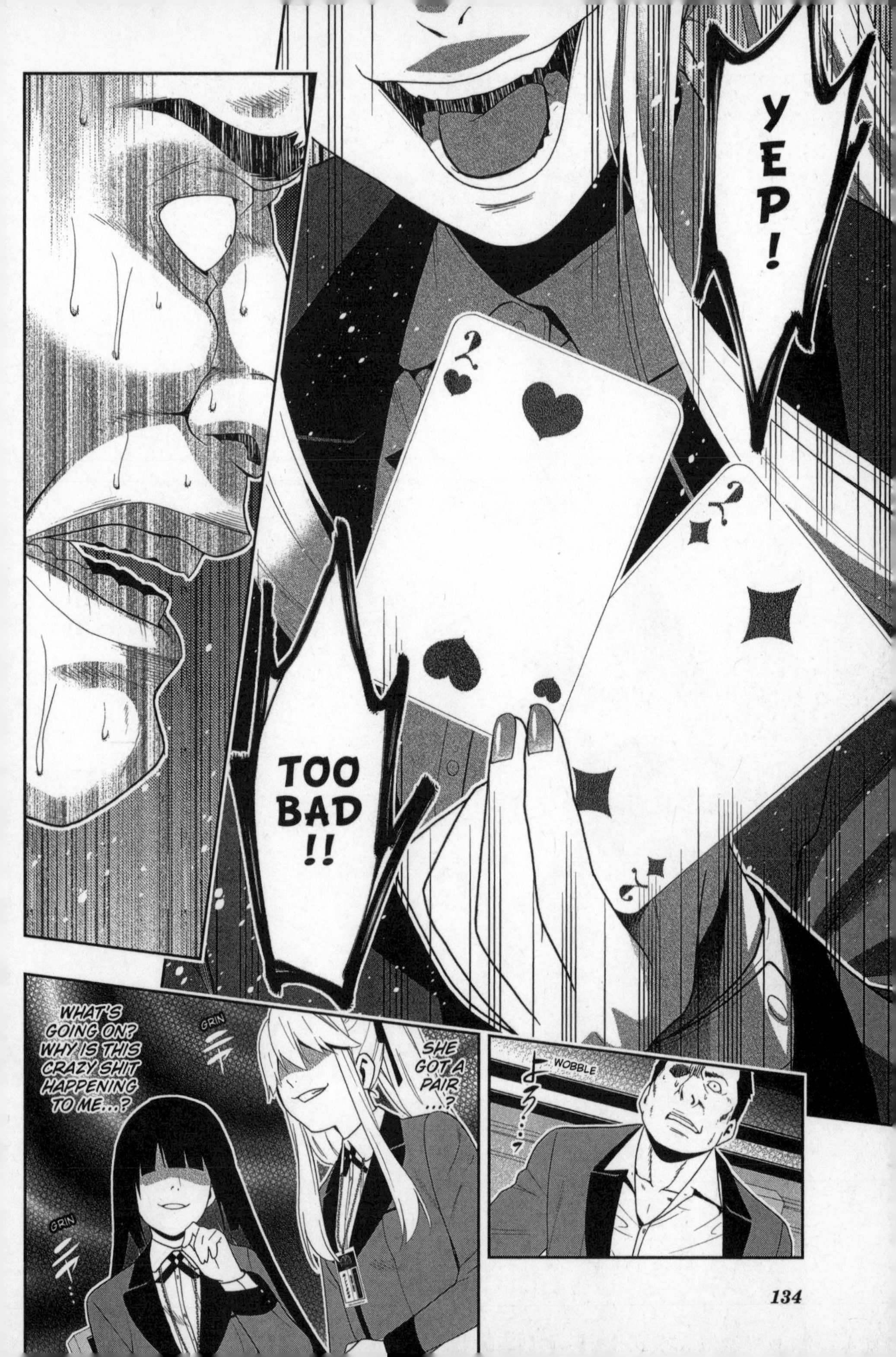
YEP!
TOO BAD!!
WOBBLE
SHE GOT A PAIR...?
GRIN
WHAT'S GOING ON? WHY IS THIS CRAZY SHIT HAPPENING TO ME...?
GRIN

TURN NINE

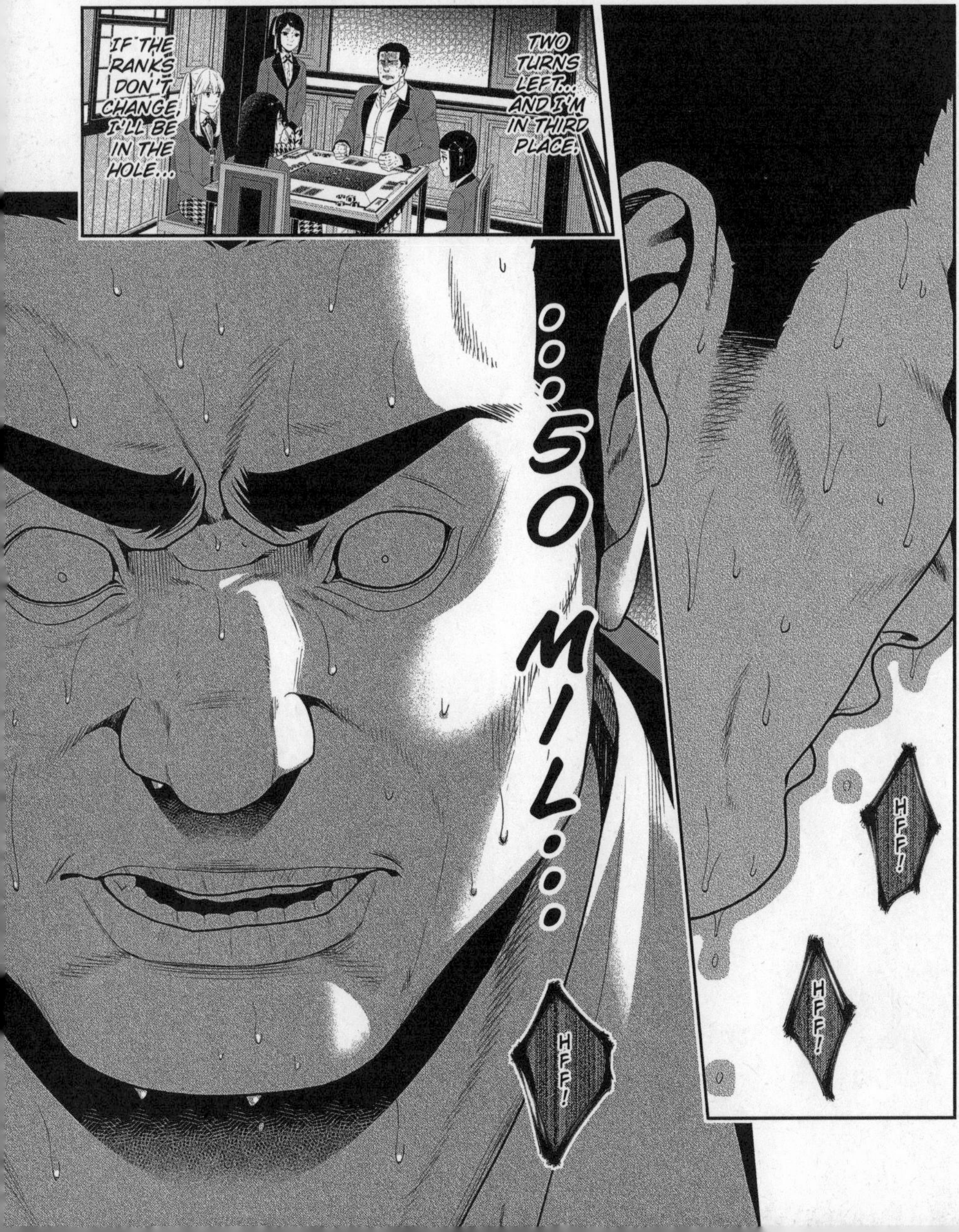
TWO TURNS LEFT... AND I'M IN THIRD PLACE.
IF THE RANKS DON'T CHANGE, I'LL BE IN THE HOLE...
...50 MIL...
HFF!
HFF!
HFF!

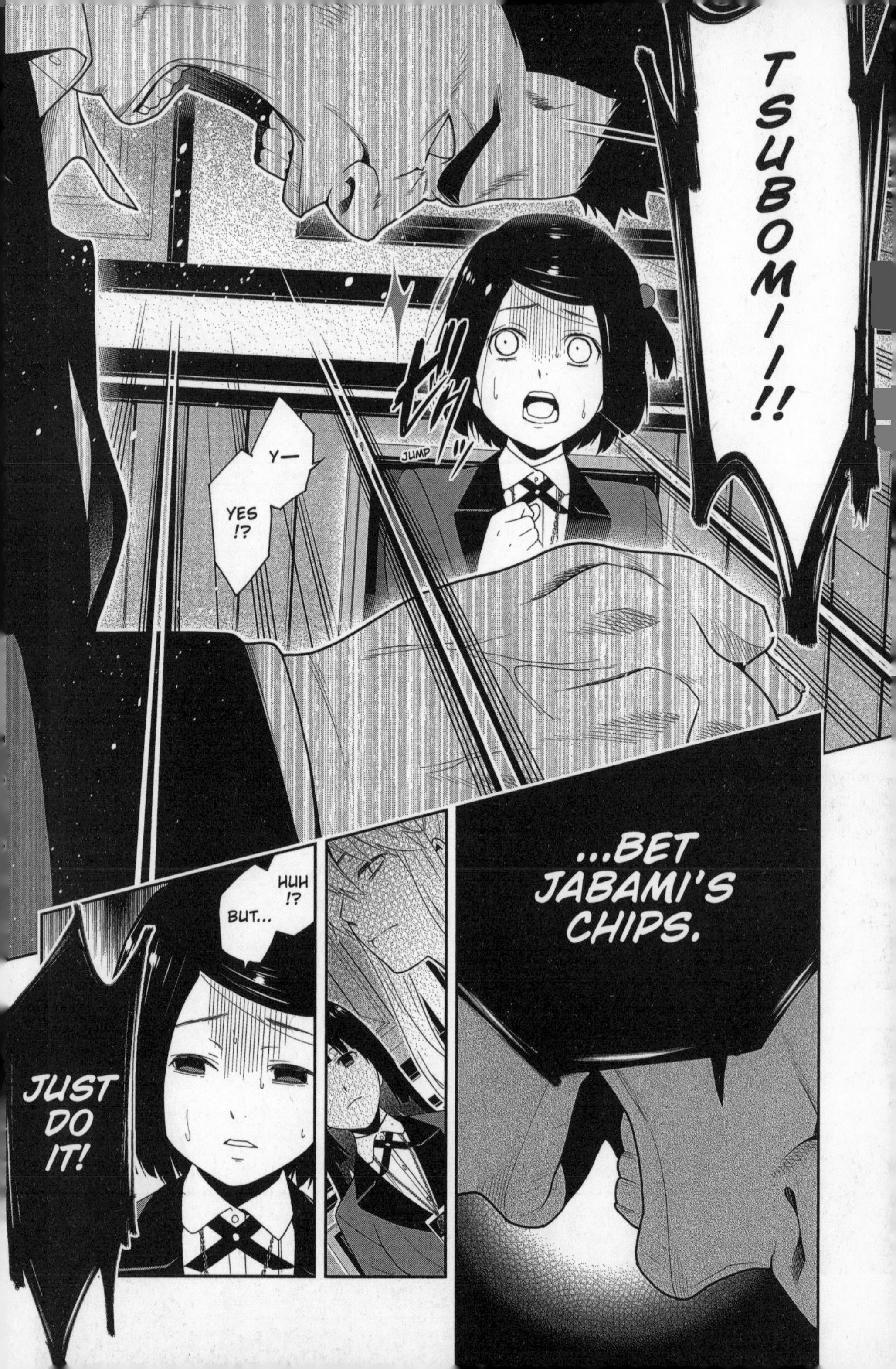
TSUBOMI!!
JUMP
Y— YES!?
...BET JABAMI'S CHIPS.
HUH!? BUT...
JUST DO IT!

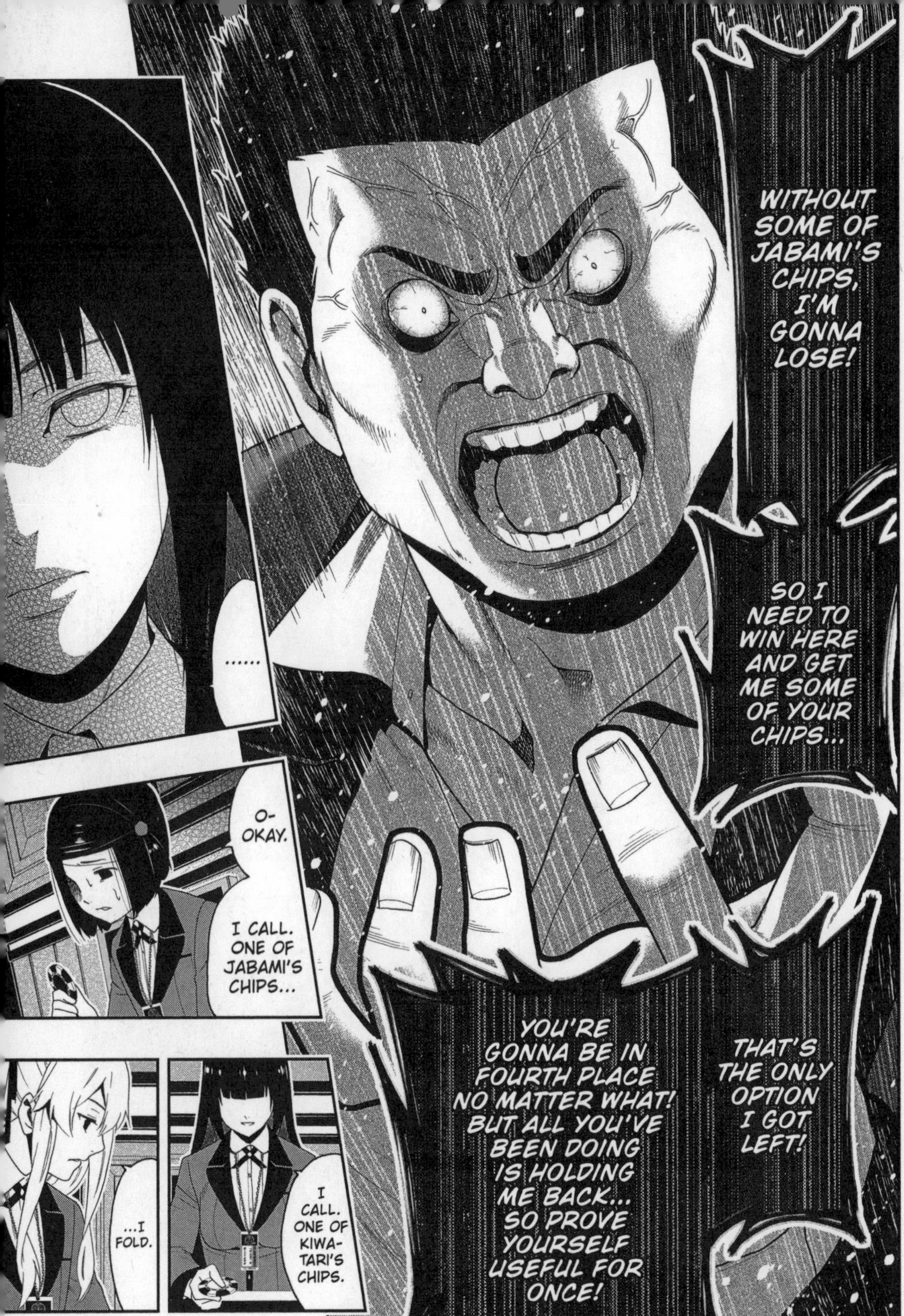
WITHOUT SOME OF JABAMI'S CHIPS, I'M GONNA LOSE!
SO I NEED TO WIN HERE AND GET ME SOME OF YOUR CHIPS...
THAT'S THE ONLY OPTION I GOT LEFT!
YOU'RE GONNA BE IN FOURTH PLACE NO MATTER WHAT! BUT ALL YOU'VE BEEN DOING IS HOLDING ME BACK... SO PROVE YOURSELF USEFUL FOR ONCE!
......
O-OKAY.
I CALL. ONE OF JABAMI'S CHIPS...
I CALL. ONE OF KIWATARI'S CHIPS.
...I FOLD.

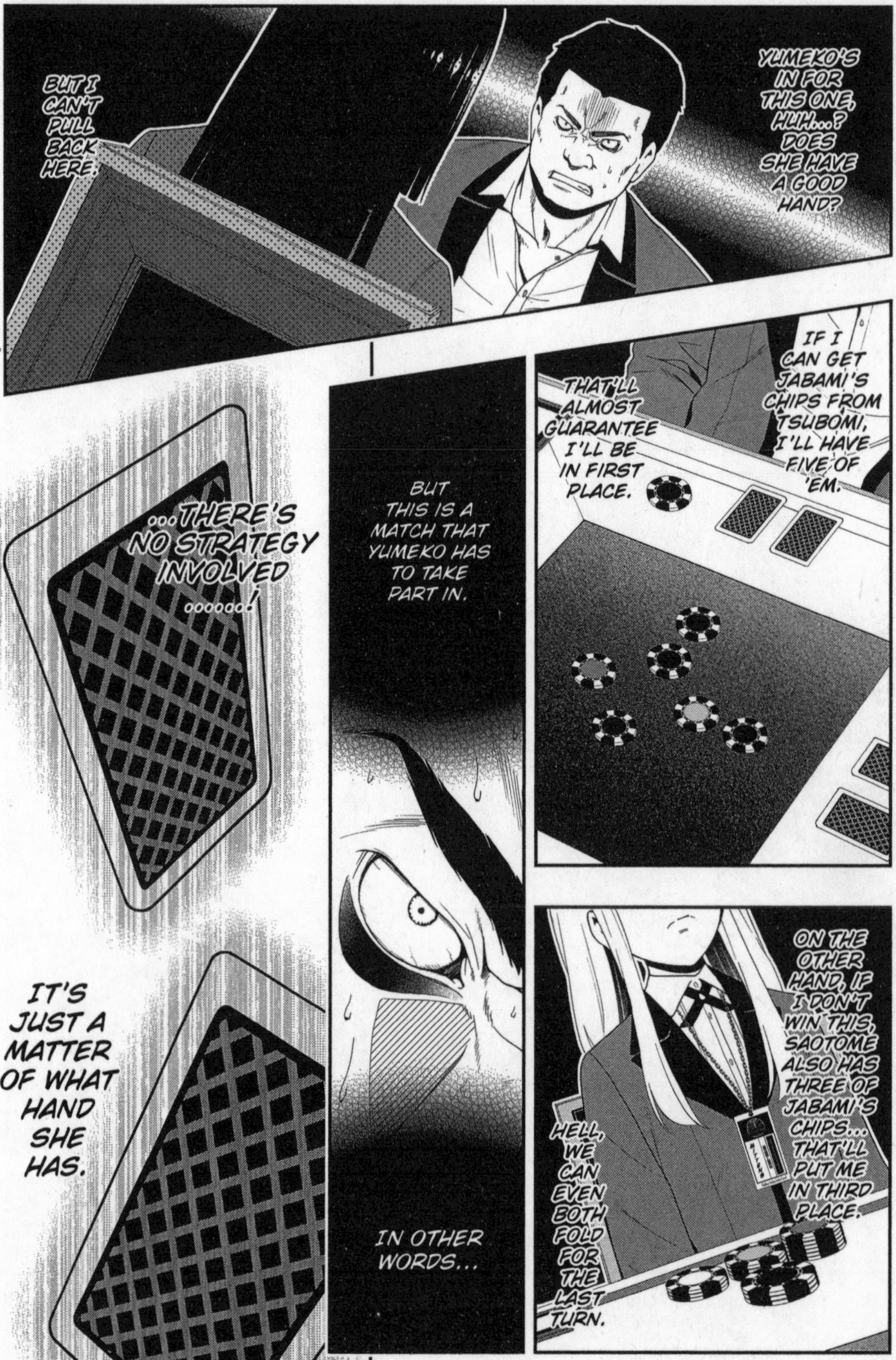

YUMEKO'S IN FOR THIS ONE, HUH...? DOES SHE HAVE A GOOD HAND?
BUT I CAN'T PULL BACK HERE.
IF I CAN GET JABAMI'S CHIPS FROM TSUBOMI, I'LL HAVE FIVE OF 'EM.
THAT'LL ALMOST GUARANTEE I'LL BE IN FIRST PLACE.
ON THE OTHER HAND, IF I DON'T WIN THIS, SAOTOME ALSO HAS THREE OF JABAMI'S CHIPS... THAT'LL PUT ME IN THIRD PLACE.
HELL, WE CAN EVEN BOTH FOLD FOR THE LAST TURN.
BUT THIS IS A MATCH THAT YUMEKO HAS TO TAKE PART IN.
IN OTHER WORDS...
...THERE'S NO STRATEGY INVOLVED.......!
IT'S JUST A MATTER OF WHAT HAND SHE HAS.

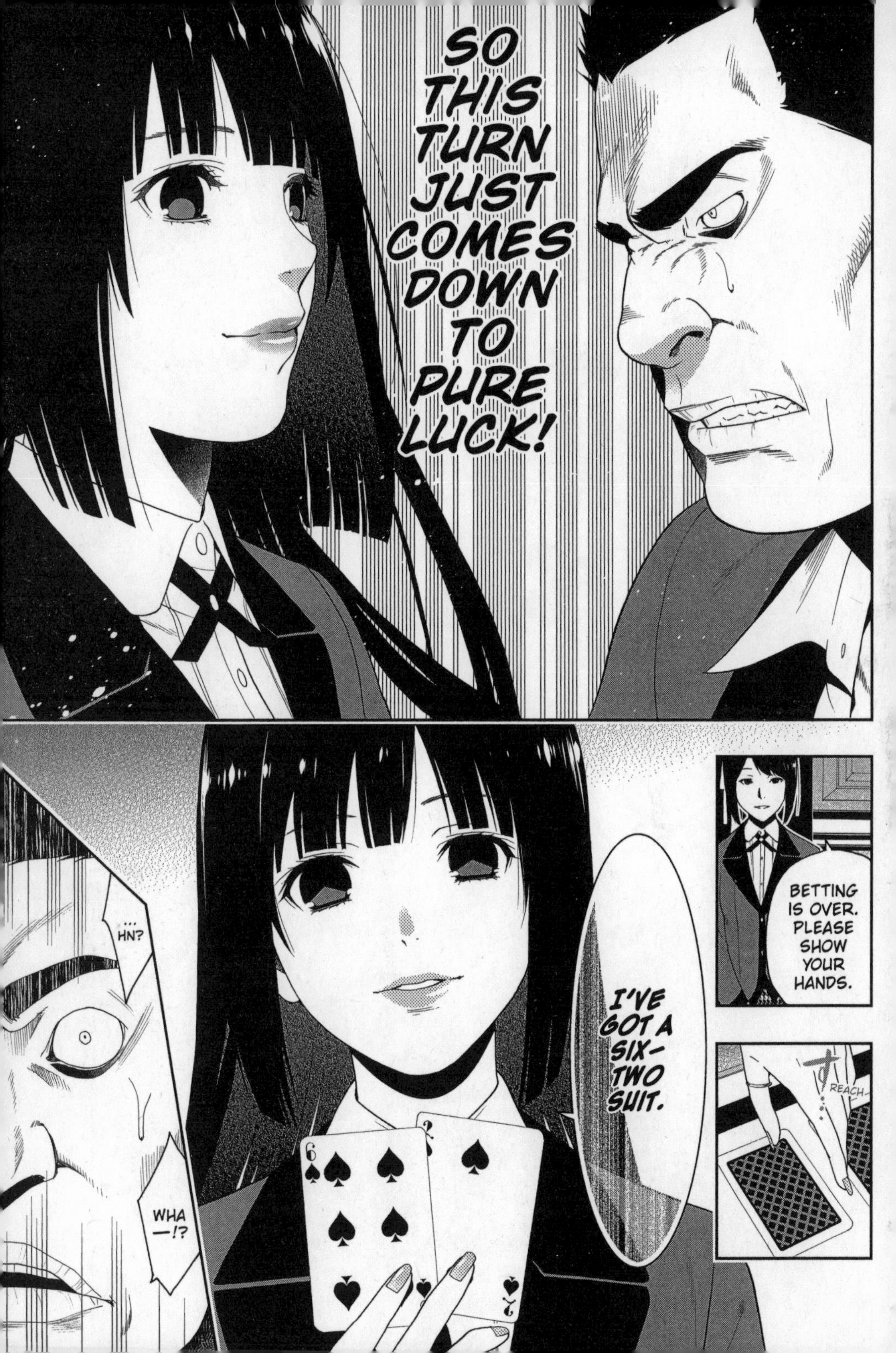
SO THIS TURN JUST COMES DOWN TO PURE LUCK!
BETTING IS OVER. PLEASE SHOW YOUR HANDS.
す
REACH
I'VE GOT A SIX-TWO SUIT.
... HN?
WHA—!?

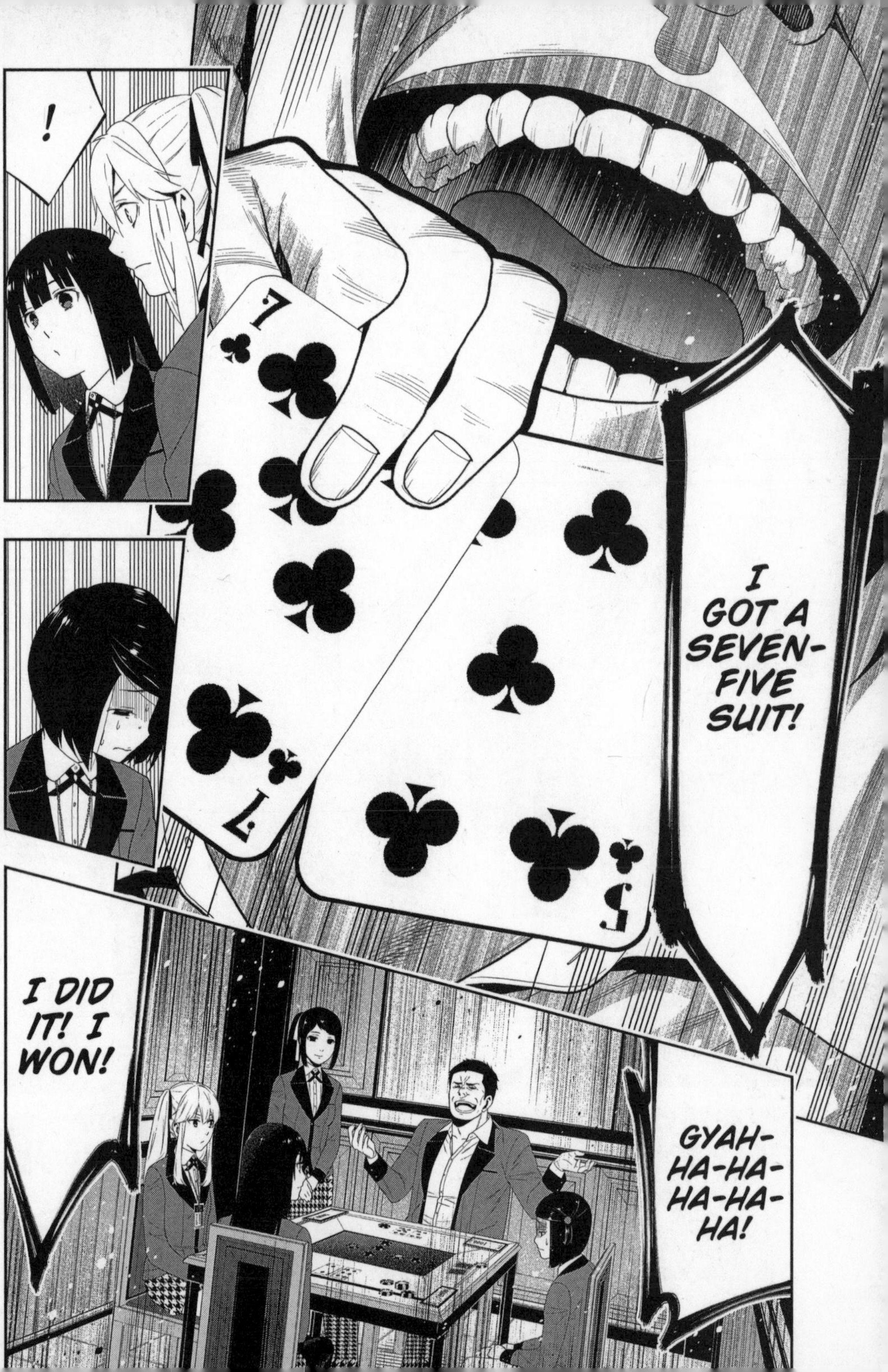

I GOT A SEVEN-FIVE SUIT!
!
GYAH-HA-HA-HA-HA-HA!
I DID IT! I WON!

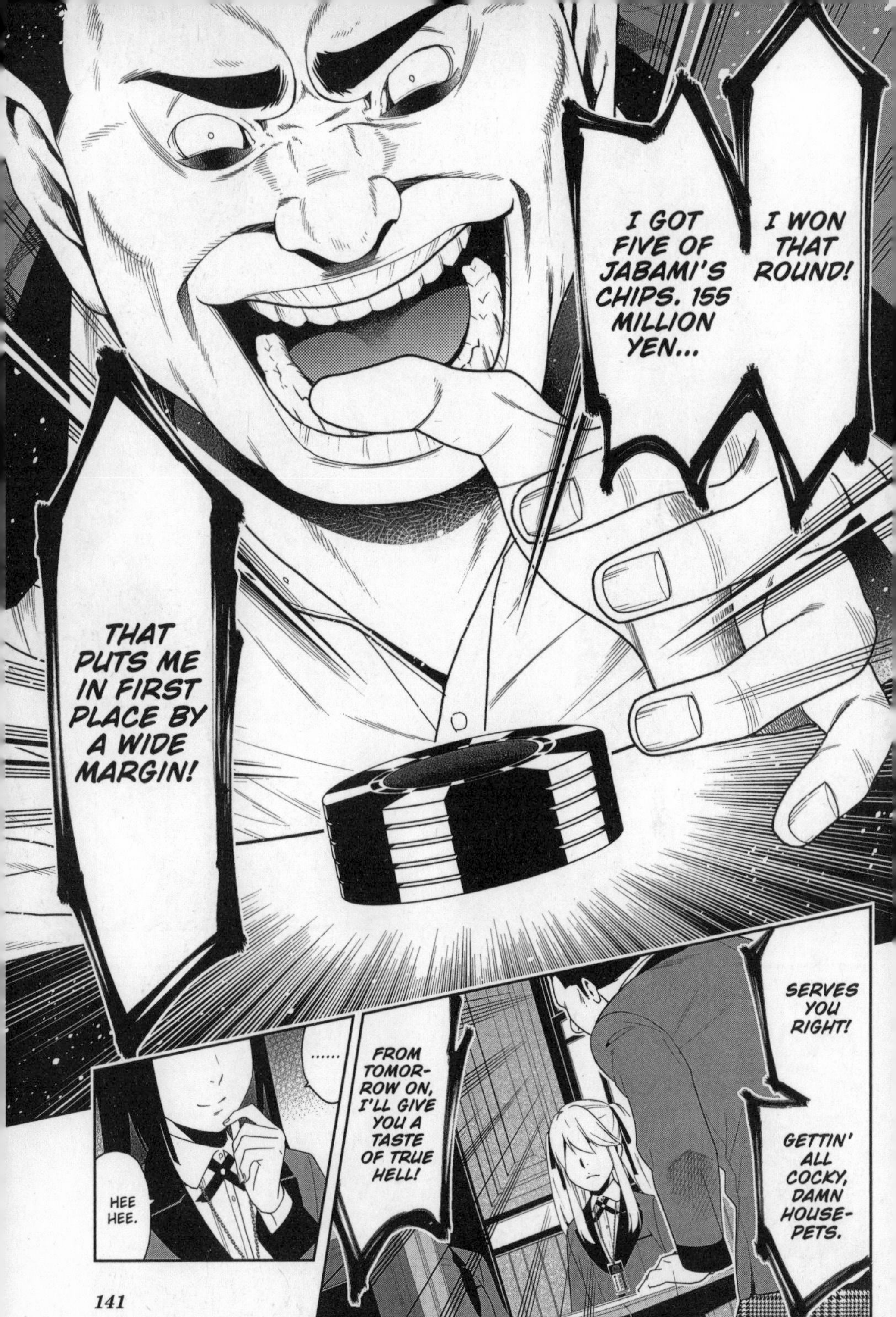
I WON THAT ROUND!
I GOT FIVE OF JABAMI'S CHIPS. 155 MILLION YEN...
THAT PUTS ME IN FIRST PLACE BY A WIDE MARGIN!
SERVES YOU RIGHT!
GETTIN' ALL COCKY, DAMN HOUSE-PETS.
FROM TOMOR-ROW ON, I'LL GIVE YOU A TASTE OF TRUE HELL!
......
HEE HEE.

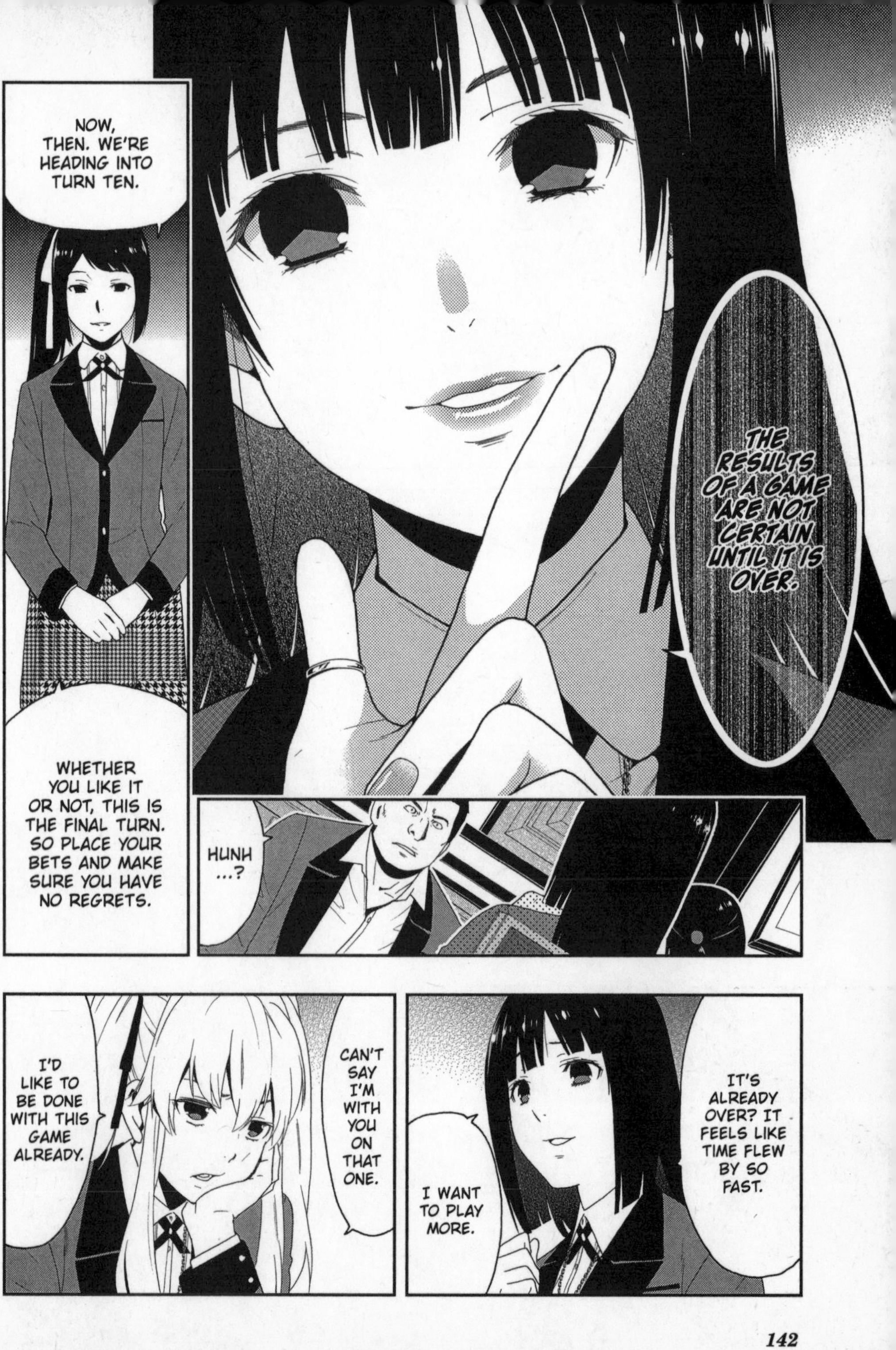
THE RESULTS OF A GAME ARE NOT CERTAIN UNTIL IT IS OVER.
HUNH ...?
NOW, THEN. WE'RE HEADING INTO TURN TEN.
WHETHER YOU LIKE IT OR NOT, THIS IS THE FINAL TURN. SO PLACE YOUR BETS AND MAKE SURE YOU HAVE NO REGRETS.
IT'S ALREADY OVER? IT FEELS LIKE TIME FLEW BY SO FAST.
I WANT TO PLAY MORE.
CAN'T SAY I'M WITH YOU ON THAT ONE.
I'D LIKE TO BE DONE WITH THIS GAME ALREADY.

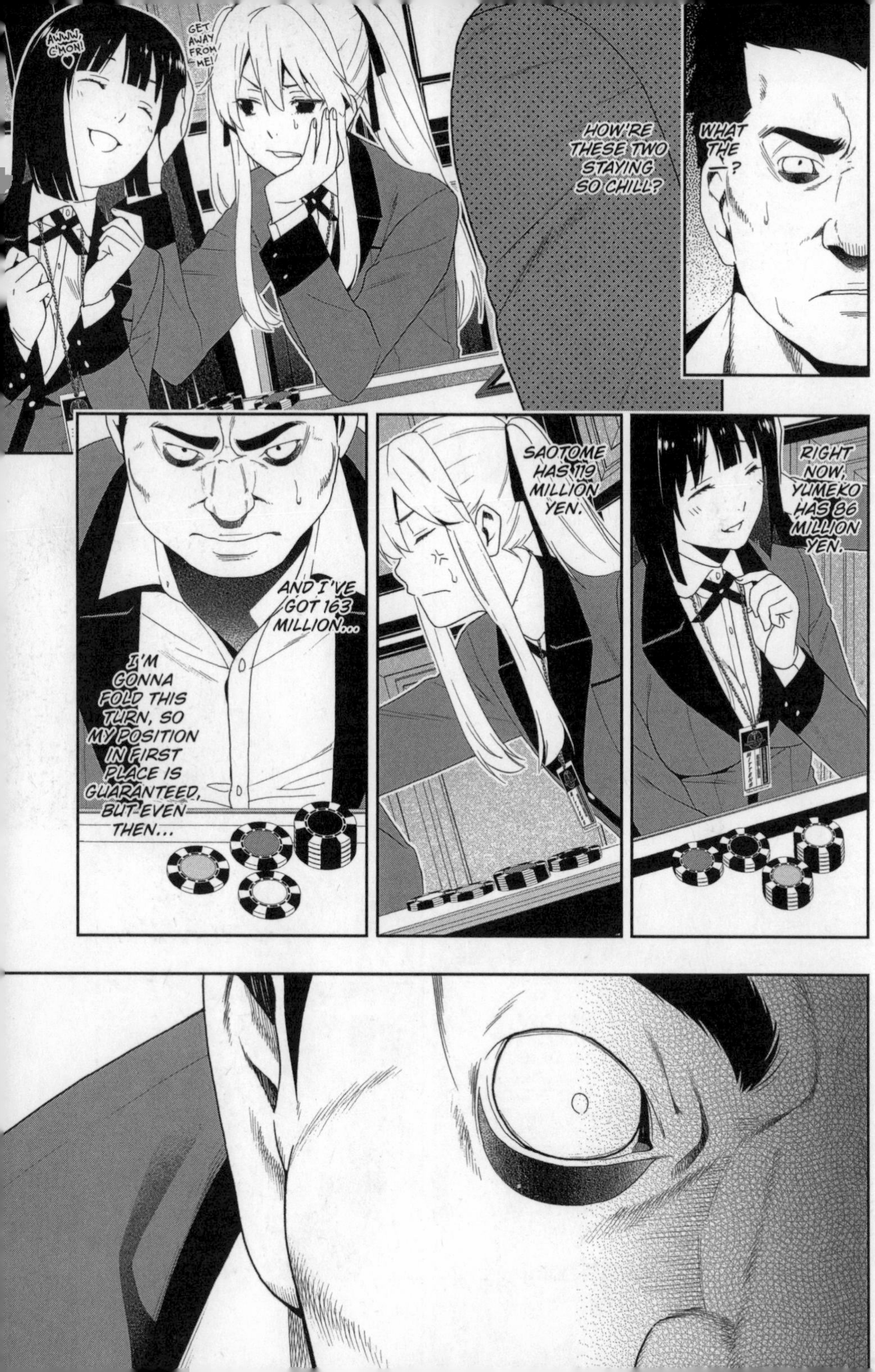
WHAT THE —?
HOW'RE THESE TWO STAYING SO CHILL?
GET AWAY FROM ME!
AWWW, C'MON! ♥
RIGHT NOW, YUMEKO HAS 86 MILLION YEN.
SAOTOME HAS 119 MILLION YEN.
AND I'VE GOT 163 MILLION...
I'M GONNA FOLD THIS TURN, SO MY POSITION IN FIRST PLACE IS GUARANTEED, BUT EVEN THEN...

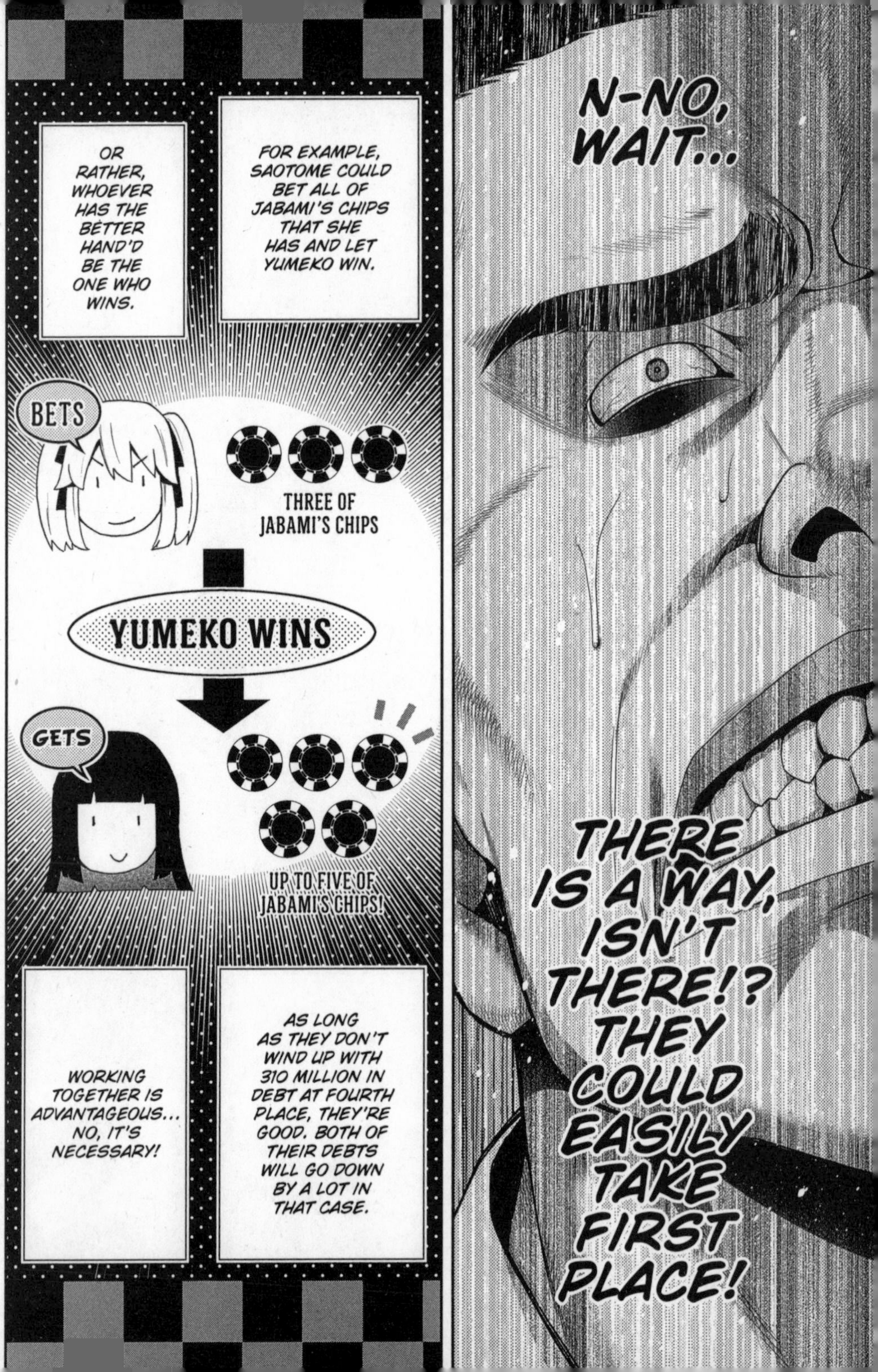

N-NO, WAIT...
THERE IS A WAY, ISN'T THERE!? THEY COULD EASILY TAKE FIRST PLACE!
FOR EXAMPLE, SAOTOME COULD BET ALL OF JABAMI'S CHIPS THAT SHE HAS AND LET YUMEKO WIN.
OR RATHER, WHOEVER HAS THE BETTER HAND'D BE THE ONE WHO WINS.
BETS
THREE OF JABAMI'S CHIPS
YUMEKO WINS
GETS
UP TO FIVE OF JABAMI'S CHIPS!
AS LONG AS THEY DON'T WIND UP WITH 310 MILLION IN DEBT AT FOURTH PLACE, THEY'RE GOOD. BOTH OF THEIR DEBTS WILL GO DOWN BY A LOT IN THAT CASE.
WORKING TOGETHER IS ADVANTAGEOUS... NO, IT'S NECESSARY!

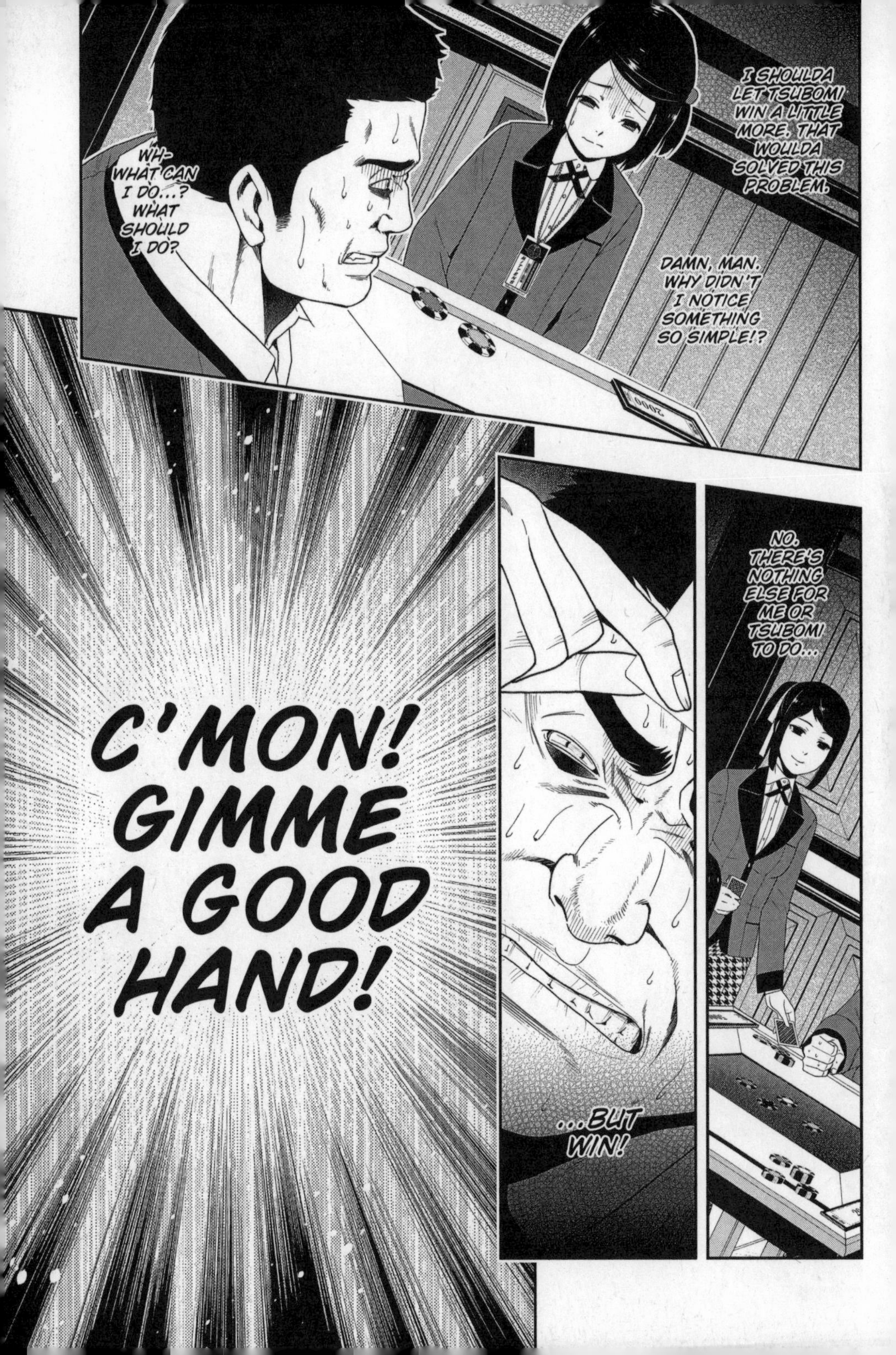
I SHOULDA LET TSUBOMI WIN A LITTLE MORE. THAT WOULDA SOLVED THIS PROBLEM.
WH- WHAT CAN I DO...? WHAT SHOULD I DO?
DAMN, MAN. WHY DIDN'T I NOTICE SOMETHING SO SIMPLE!?
NO. THERE'S NOTHING ELSE FOR ME OR TSUBOMI TO DO...
...BUT WIN!
C'MON! GIMME A GOOD HAND!

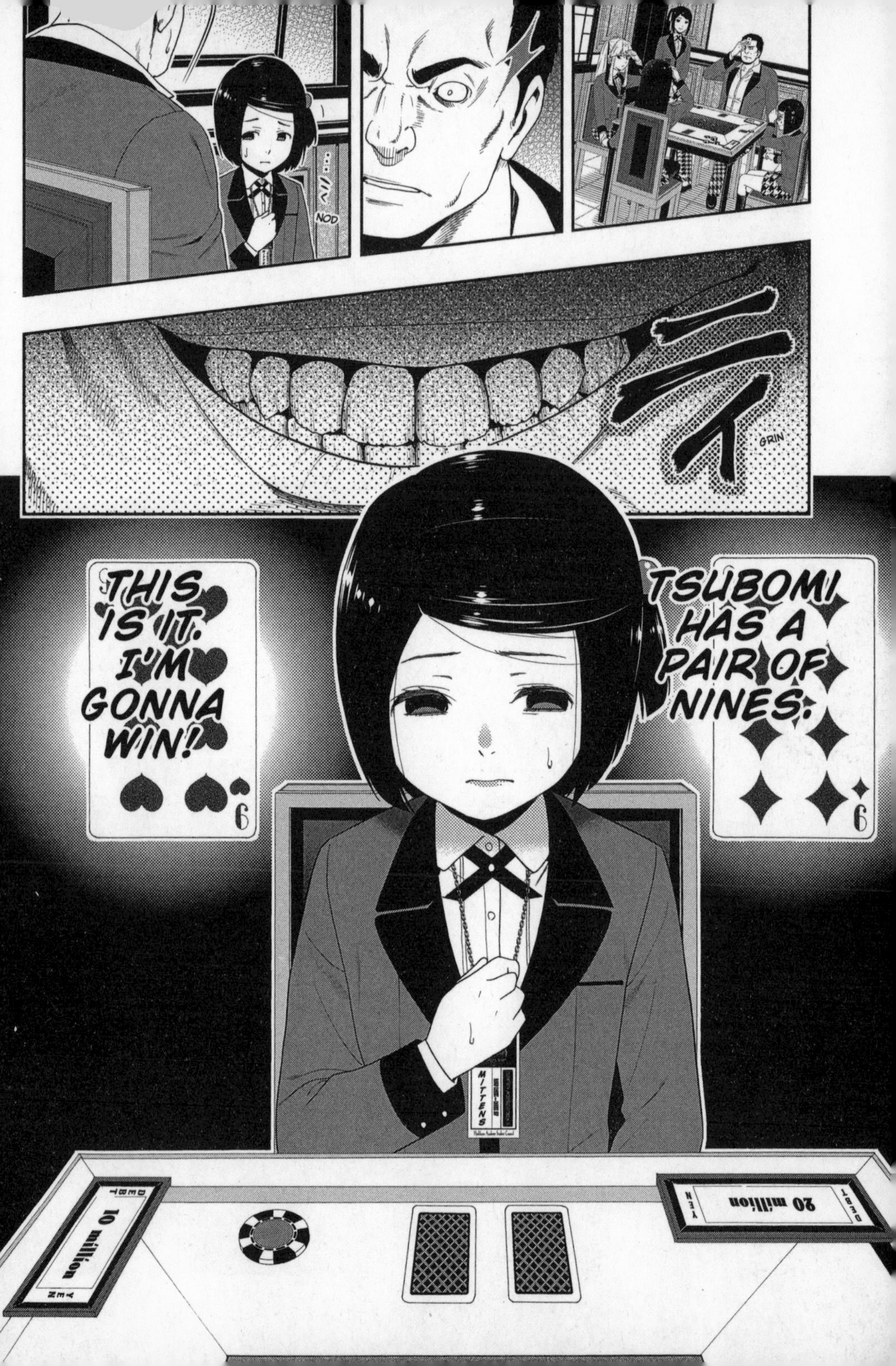
NOD
GRIN
TSUBOMI HAS A PAIR OF NINES.
THIS IS IT. I'M GONNA WIN!
DEBT 10 million YEN
DEBT 20 million YEN

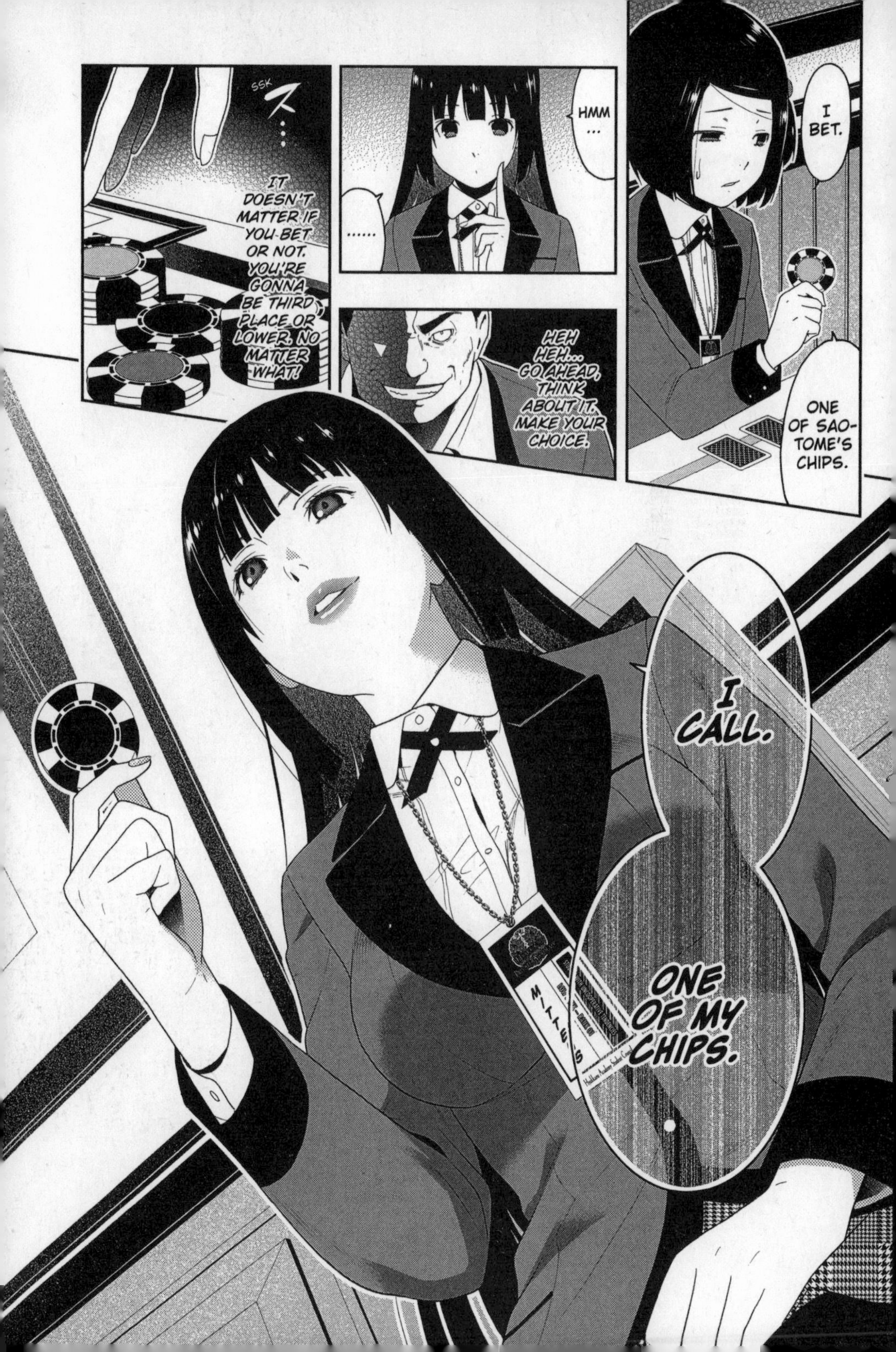
I BET.
ONE OF SAOTOME'S CHIPS.
HMM...
......
HEH HEH... GO AHEAD, THINK ABOUT IT. MAKE YOUR CHOICE.
SSK
ス...
IT DOESN'T MATTER IF YOU BET OR NOT. YOU'RE GONNA BE THIRD PLACE OR LOWER, NO MATTER WHAT!
I CALL.
ONE OF MY CHIPS.

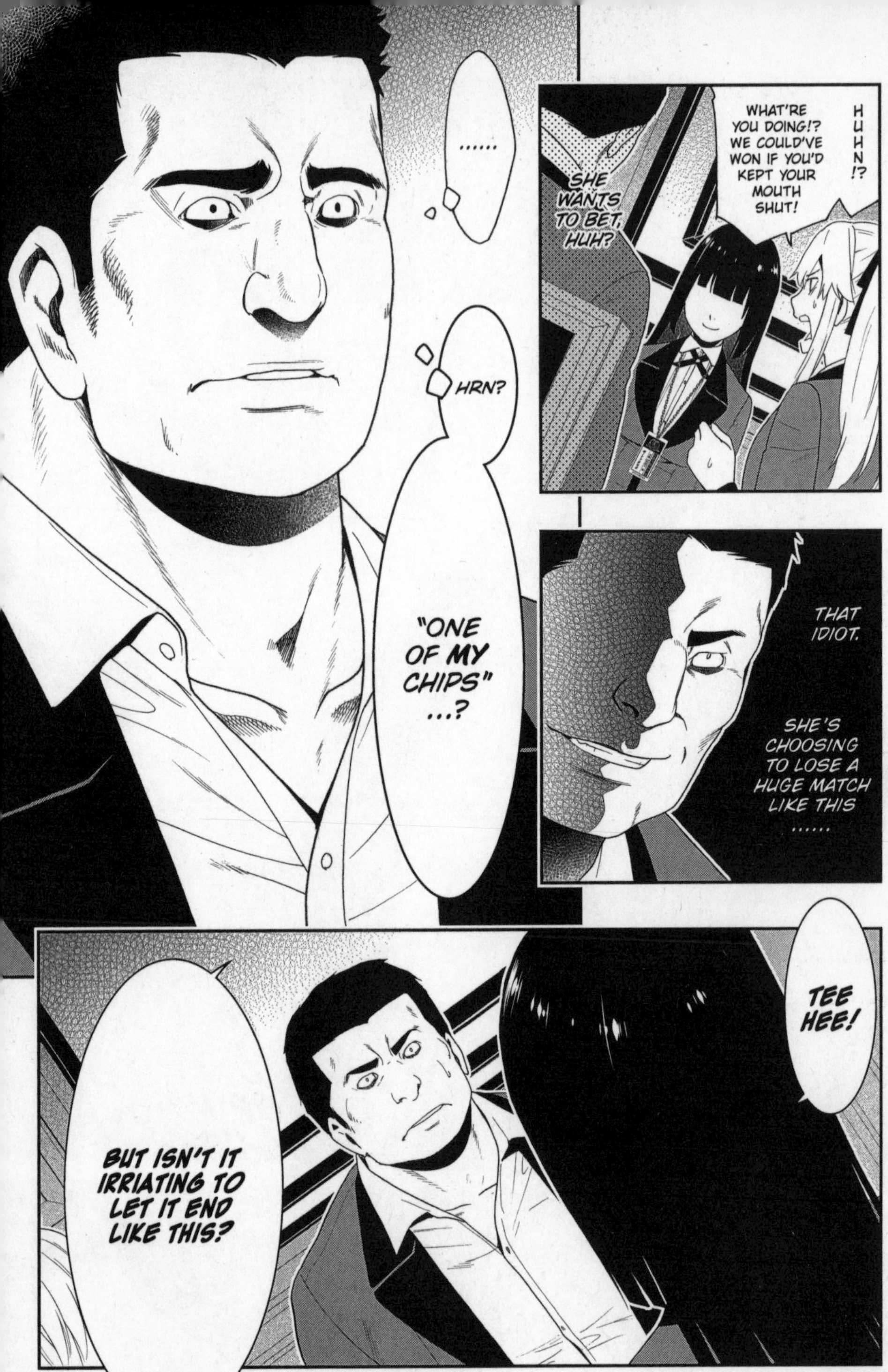
HUHN!?
WHAT'RE YOU DOING!? WE COULD'VE WON IF YOU'D KEPT YOUR MOUTH SHUT!
SHE WANTS TO BET, HUH?
THAT IDIOT.
SHE'S CHOOSING TO LOSE A HUGE MATCH LIKE THIS......
......
HRN?
"ONE OF MY CHIPS"...?
TEE HEE!
BUT ISN'T IT IRRIATING TO LET IT END LIKE THIS?

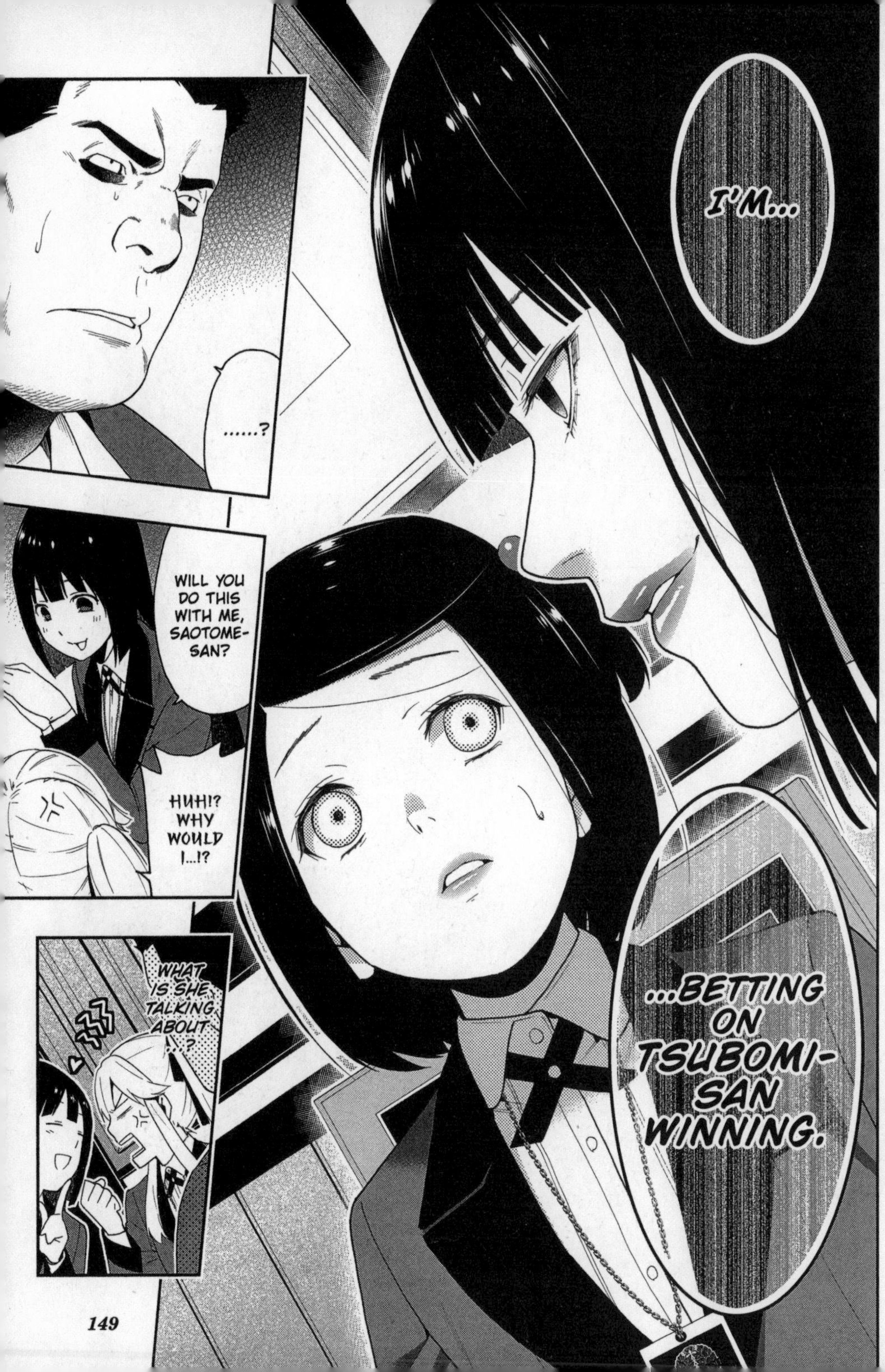
I'M...
...BETTING ON TSUBOMI-SAN WINNING.
......?
WILL YOU DO THIS WITH ME, SAOTOME-SAN?
HUH!? WHY WOULD I...!?
WHAT IS SHE TALKING ABOUT...?

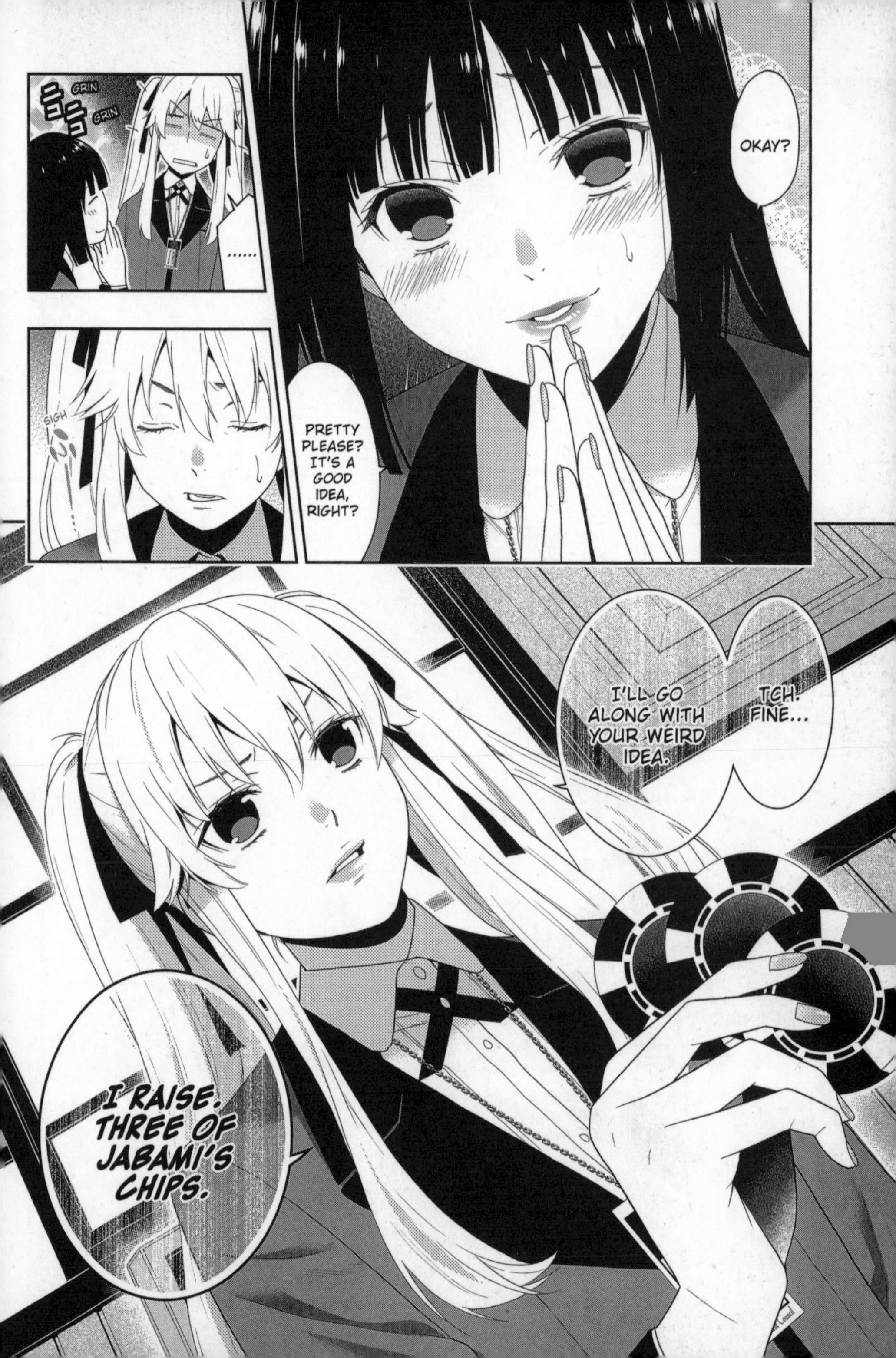
OKAY?
PRETTY PLEASE? IT'S A GOOD IDEA, RIGHT?
GRIN GRIN
......
SIGH
TCH. FINE...
I'LL GO ALONG WITH YOUR WEIRD IDEA.
I RAISE. THREE OF JABAMI'S CHIPS.

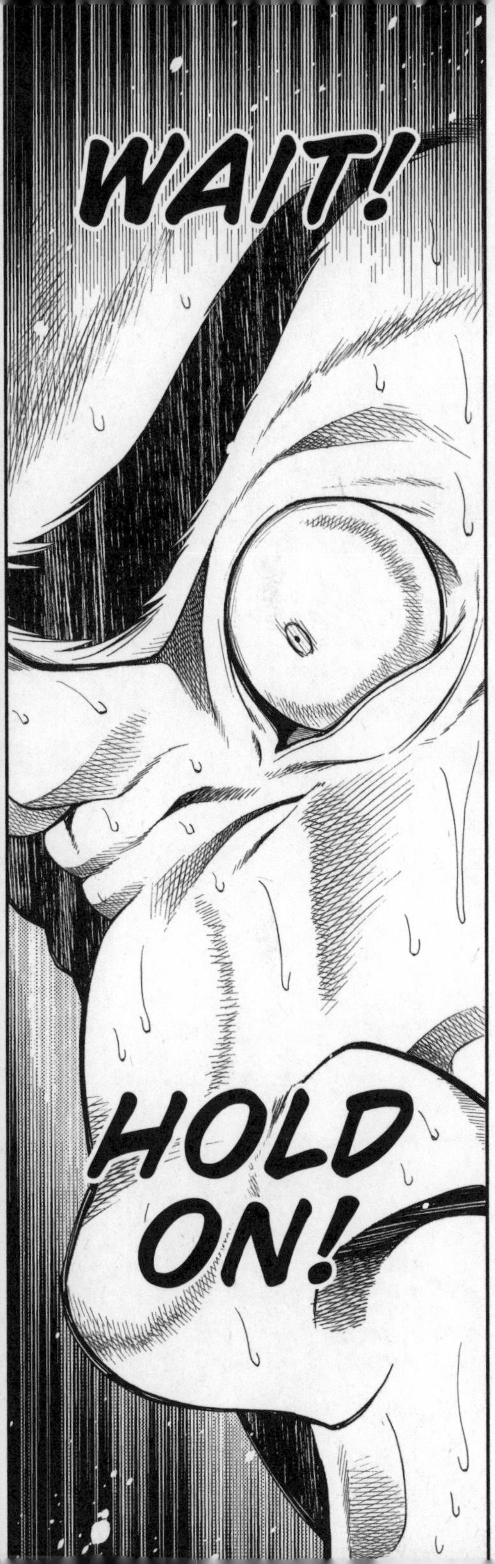
WAIT!
HOLD ON!
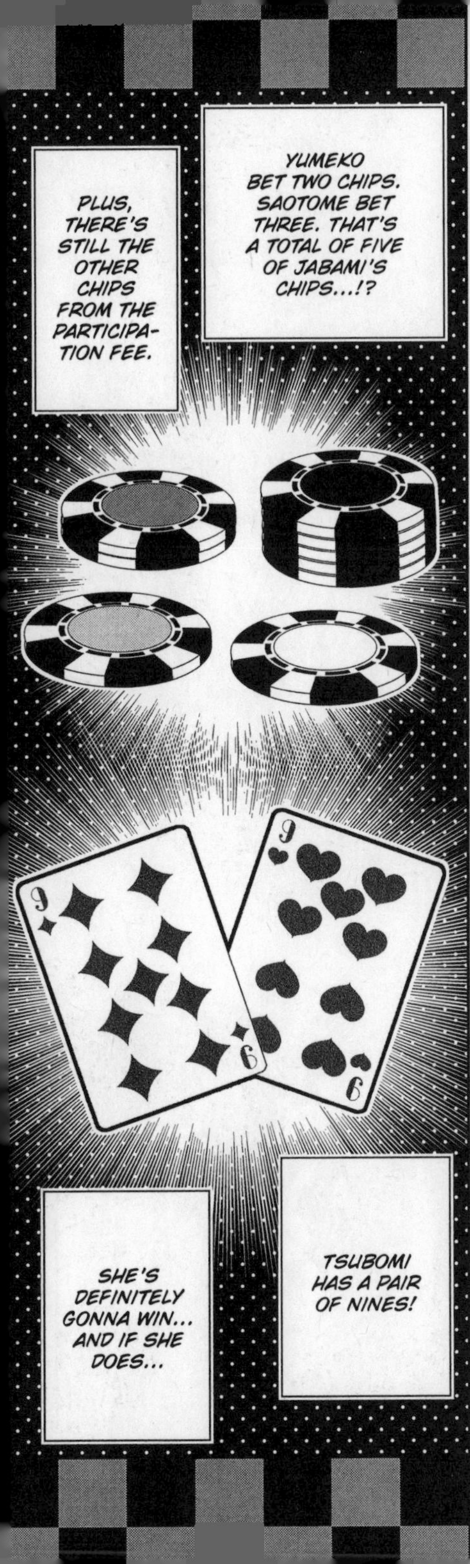
YUMEKO BET TWO CHIPS. SAOTOME BET THREE. THAT'S A TOTAL OF FIVE OF JABAMI'S CHIPS...!?
PLUS, THERE'S STILL THE OTHER CHIPS FROM THE PARTICIPATION FEE.
TSUBOMI HAS A PAIR OF NINES!
SHE'S DEFINITELY GONNA WIN... AND IF SHE DOES...

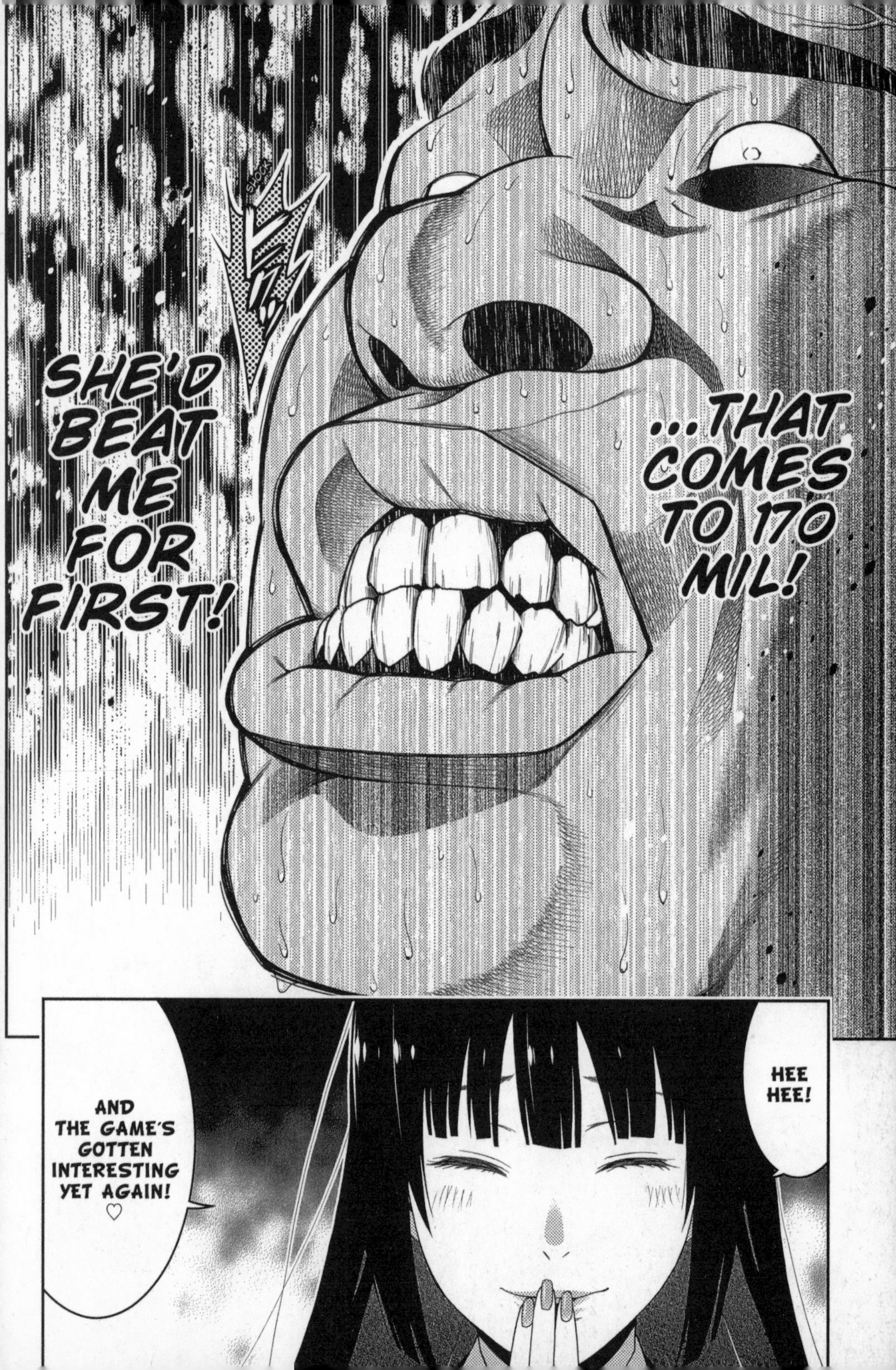
...THAT COMES TO 170 MIL!
SHOCK
SHE'D BEAT ME FOR FIRST!
HEE HEE!
AND THE GAME'S GOTTEN INTERESTING YET AGAIN! ♡

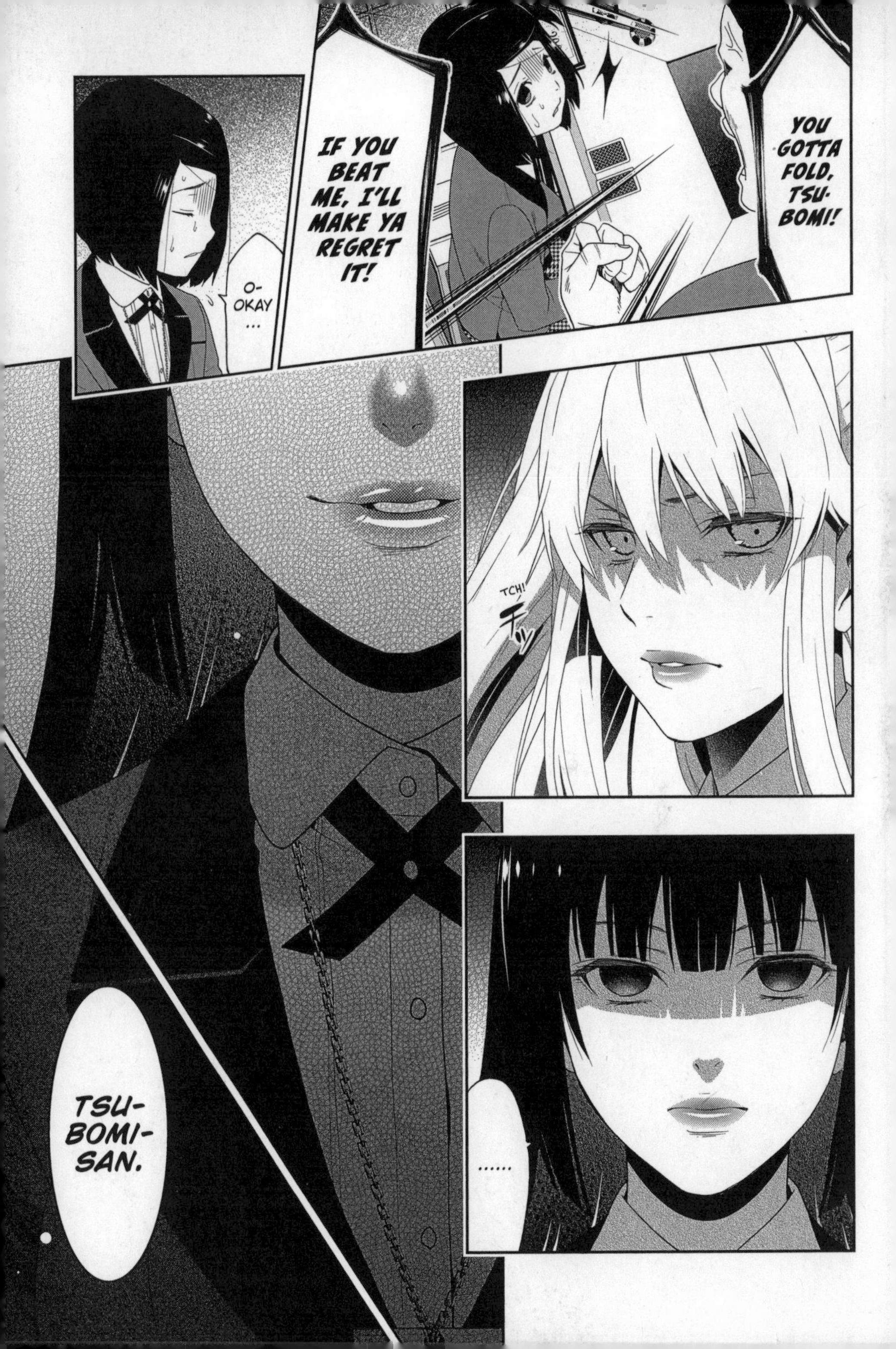
YOU GOTTA FOLD, TSU-BOMI!
IF YOU BEAT ME, I'LL MAKE YA REGRET IT!
O-OKAY ...
TCH!
チッ
......
TSU-BOMI-SAN.

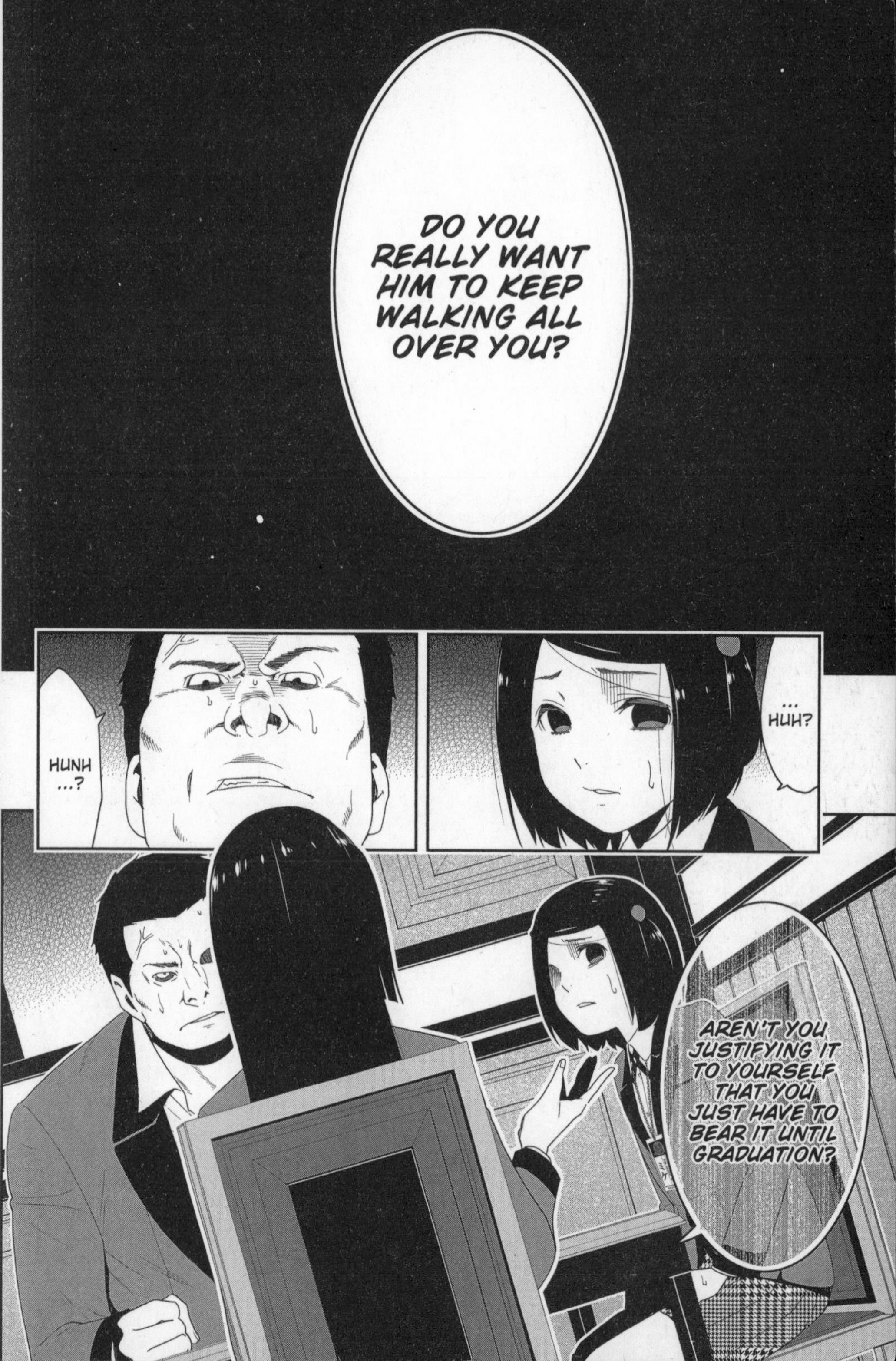
DO YOU REALLY WANT HIM TO KEEP WALKING ALL OVER YOU?
...HUH?
HUNH ...?
AREN'T YOU JUSTIFYING IT TO YOURSELF THAT YOU JUST HAVE TO BEAR IT UNTIL GRADUATION?

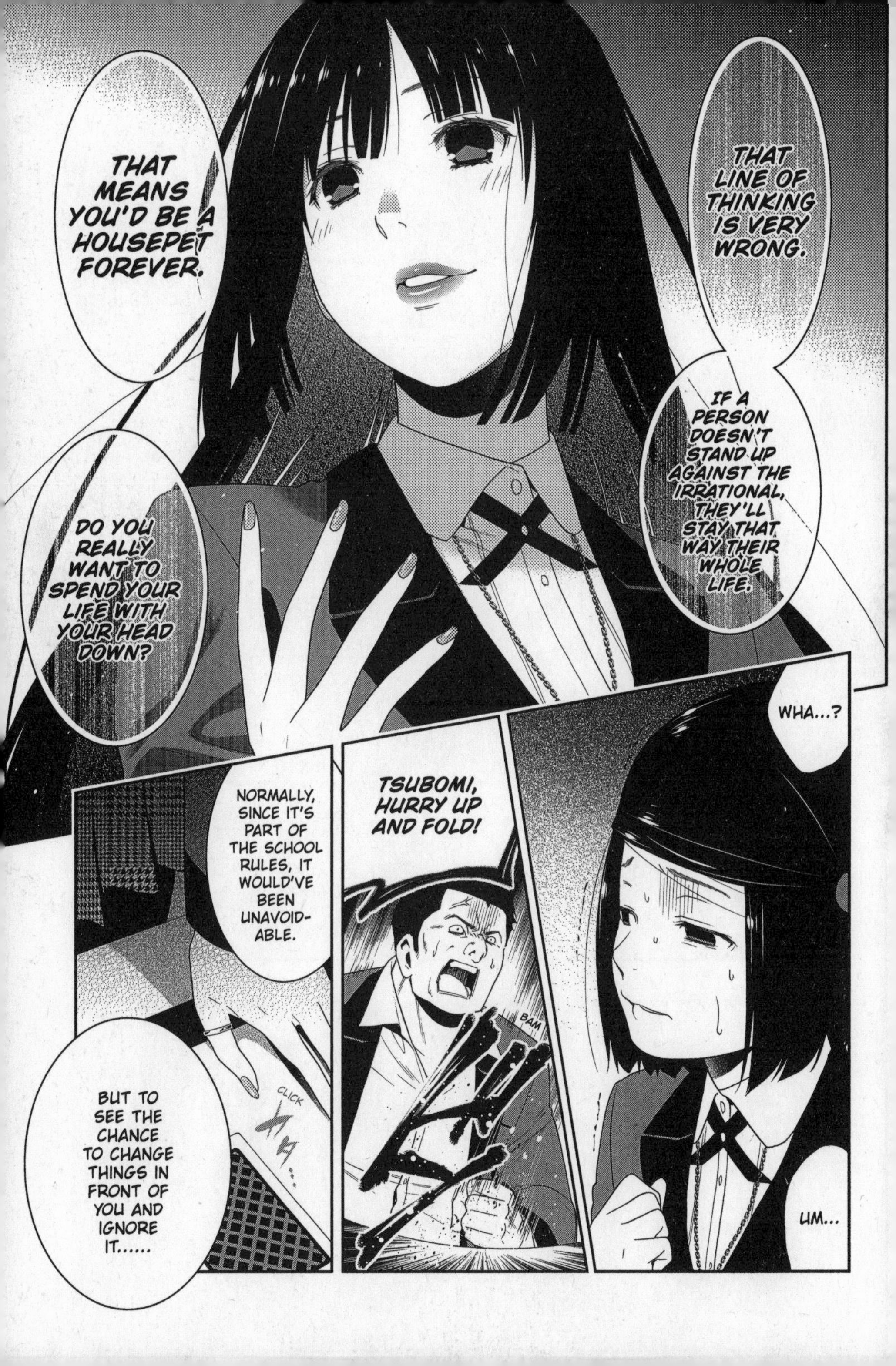
THAT LINE OF THINKING IS VERY WRONG.
IF A PERSON DOESN'T STAND UP AGAINST THE IRRATIONAL, THEY'LL STAY THAT WAY THEIR WHOLE LIFE.
THAT MEANS YOU'D BE A HOUSEPET FOREVER.
DO YOU REALLY WANT TO SPEND YOUR LIFE WITH YOUR HEAD DOWN?
WHA...?
UM...
TSUBOMI, HURRY UP AND FOLD!
BAM
NORMALLY, SINCE IT'S PART OF THE SCHOOL RULES, IT WOULD'VE BEEN UNAVOIDABLE.
CLICK
BUT TO SEE THE CHANCE TO CHANGE THINGS IN FRONT OF YOU AND IGNORE IT......

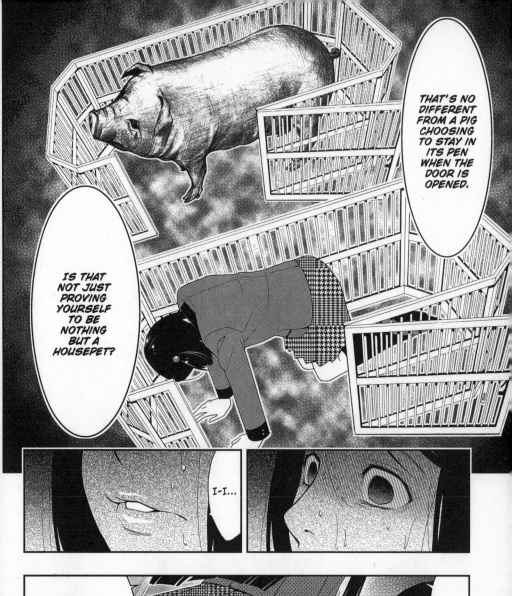

THAT'S NO DIFFERENT FROM A PIG CHOOSING TO STAY IN ITS PEN WHEN THE DOOR IS OPENED.

IS THAT NOT JUST PROVING YOURSELF TO BE NOTHING BUT A HOUSEPET?

I-I...

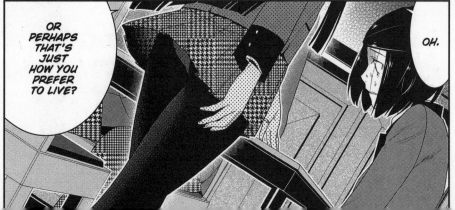

OR PERHAPS THAT'S JUST HOW YOU PREFER TO LIVE?

OH.

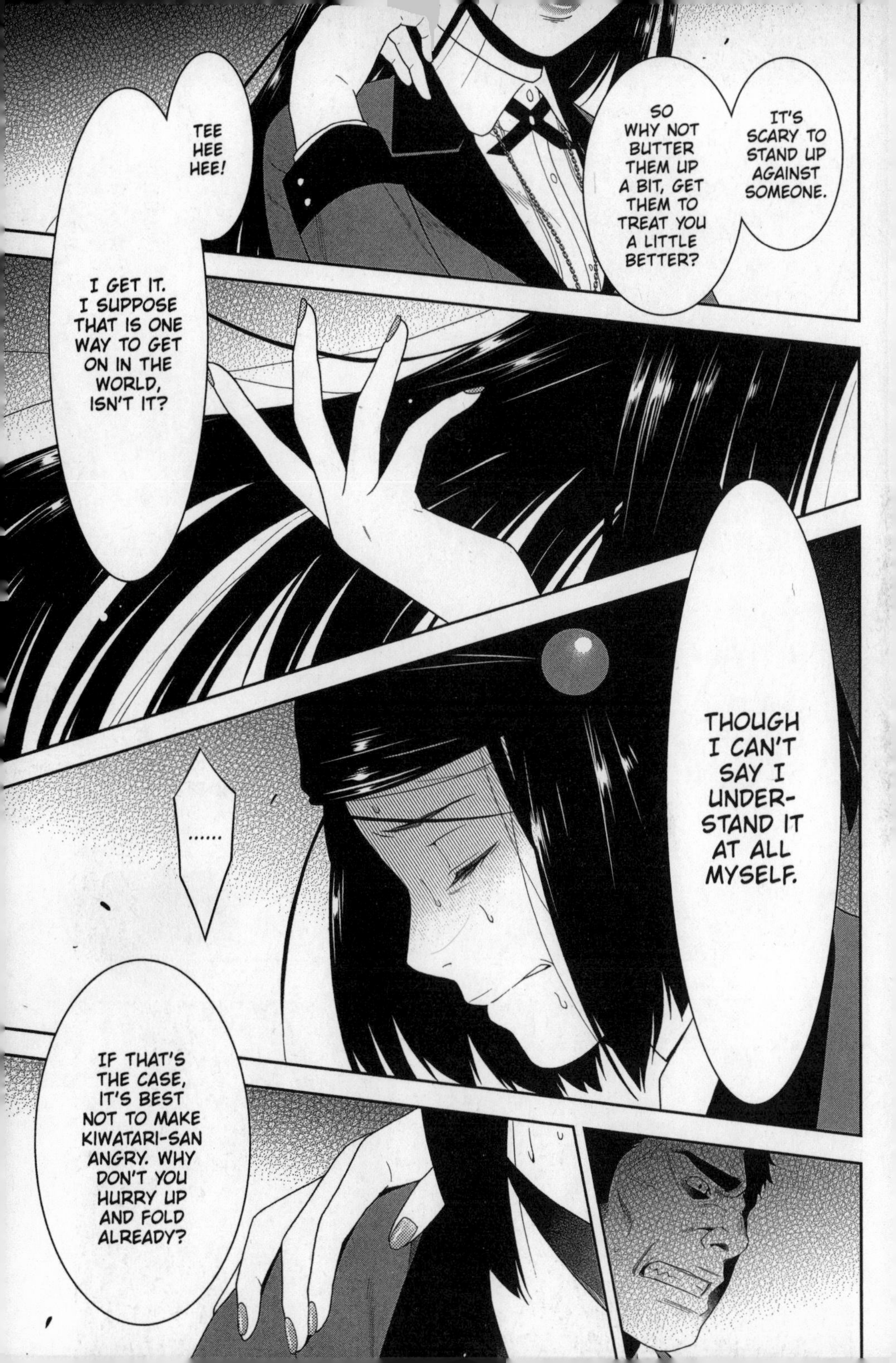
IT'S SCARY TO STAND UP AGAINST SOMEONE.
SO WHY NOT BUTTER THEM UP A BIT, GET THEM TO TREAT YOU A LITTLE BETTER?
TEE HEE HEE!
I GET IT. I SUPPOSE THAT IS ONE WAY TO GET ON IN THE WORLD, ISN'T IT?
THOUGH I CAN'T SAY I UNDER-STAND IT AT ALL MYSELF.
......
IF THAT'S THE CASE, IT'S BEST NOT TO MAKE KIWATARI-SAN ANGRY. WHY DON'T YOU HURRY UP AND FOLD ALREADY?

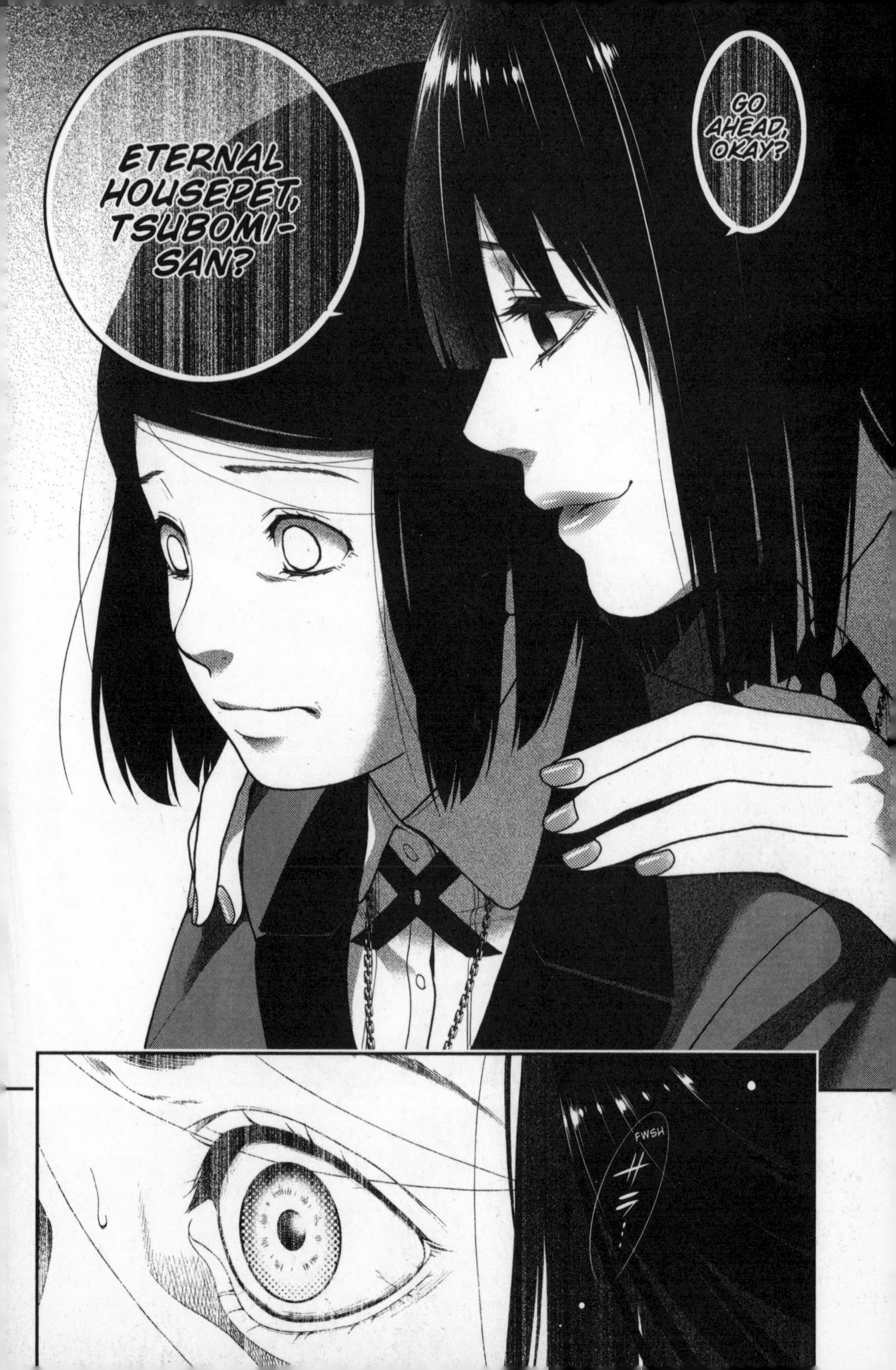
GO AHEAD, OKAY?
ETERNAL HOUSEPET, TSUBOMI-SAN?
FWSH

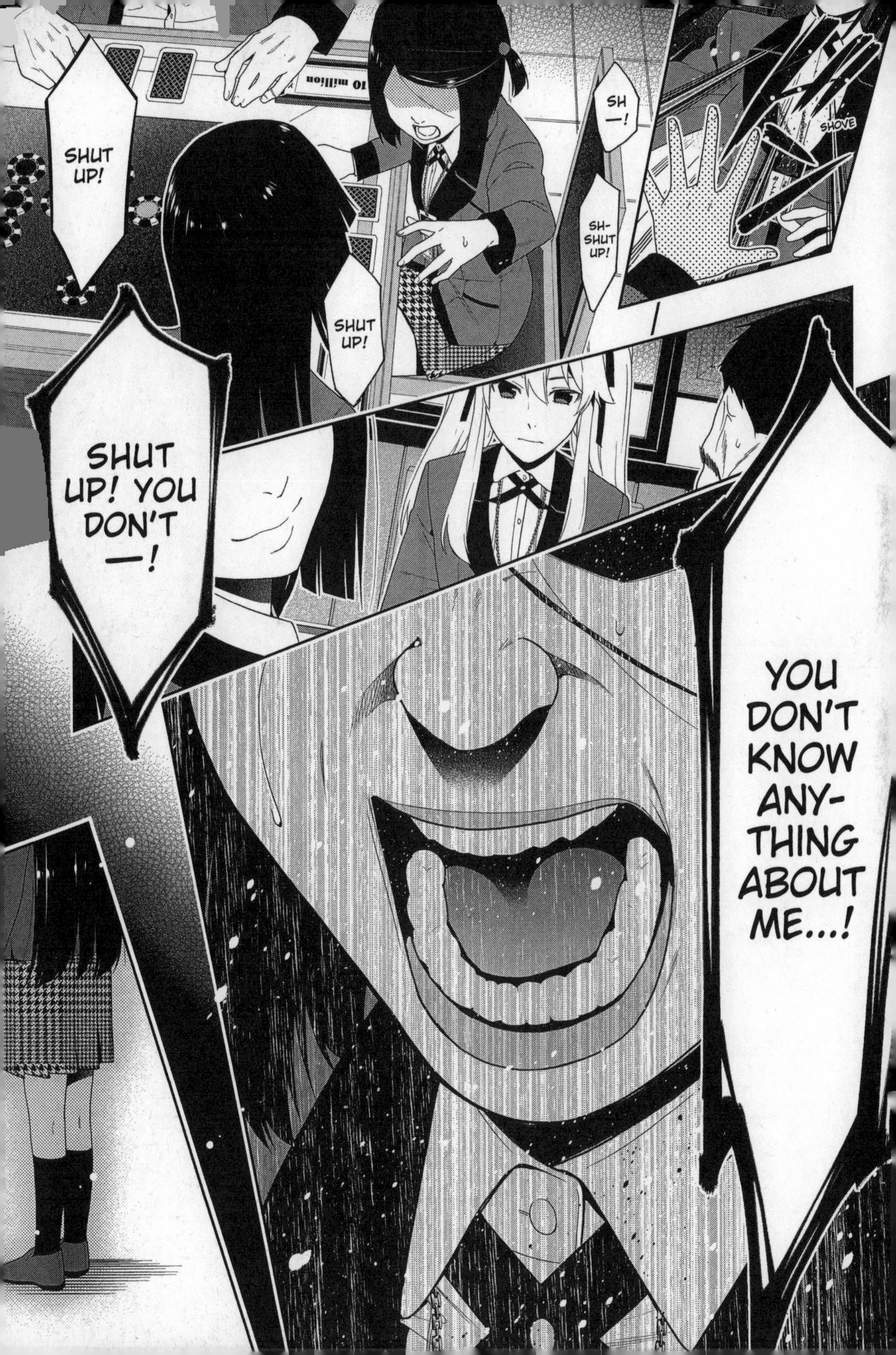
SH—!
SHOVE
SH-SHUT UP!
SHUT UP!
SHUT UP!
SHUT UP! YOU DON'T—!
YOU DON'T KNOW ANYTHING ABOUT ME...!

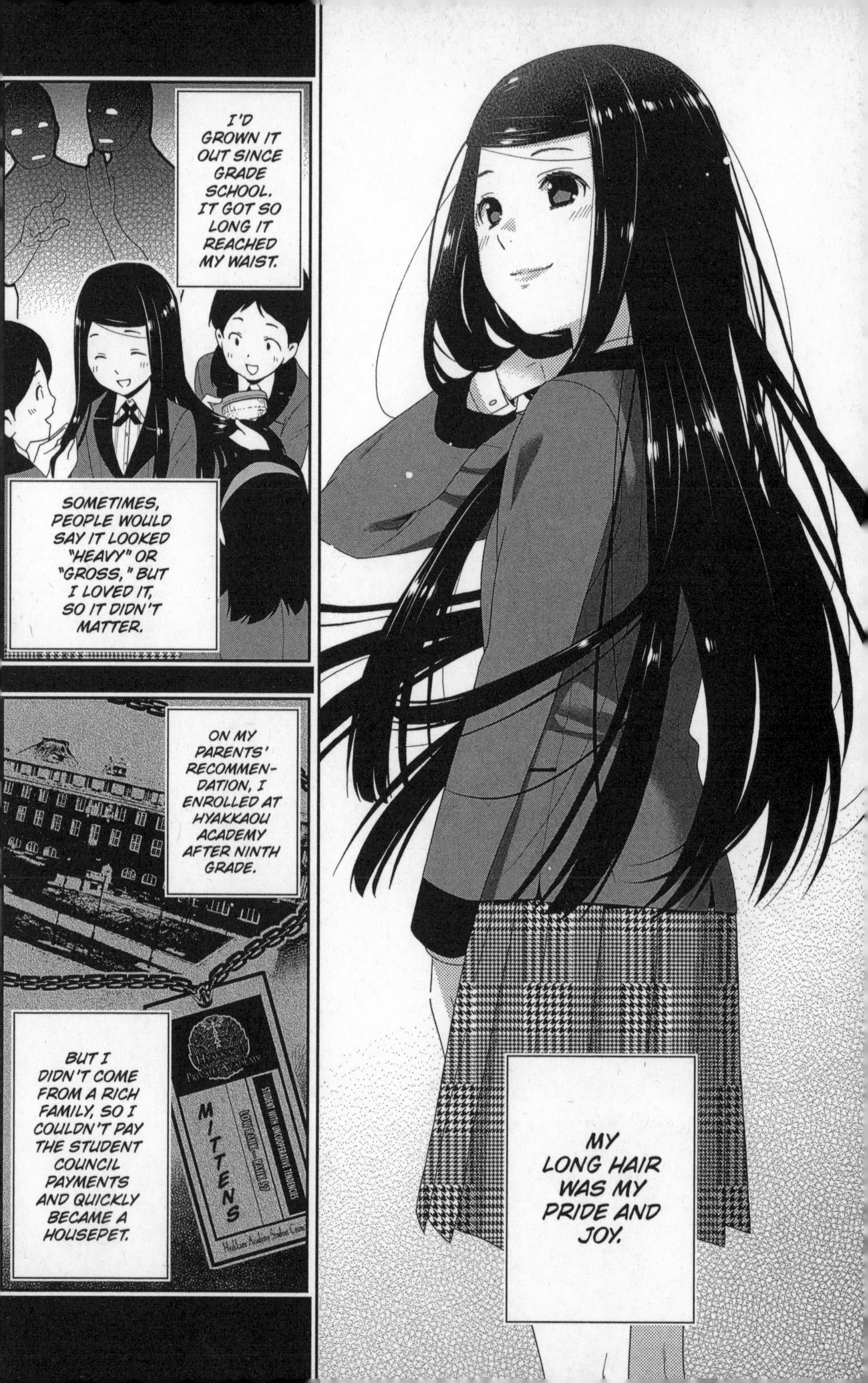
MY LONG HAIR WAS MY PRIDE AND JOY.
I'D GROWN IT OUT SINCE GRADE SCHOOL. IT GOT SO LONG IT REACHED MY WAIST.
SOMETIMES, PEOPLE WOULD SAY IT LOOKED "HEAVY" OR "GROSS," BUT I LOVED IT, SO IT DIDN'T MATTER.
ON MY PARENTS' RECOMMENDATION, I ENROLLED AT HYAKKAOU ACADEMY AFTER NINTH GRADE.
BUT I DIDN'T COME FROM A RICH FAMILY, SO I COULDN'T PAY THE STUDENT COUNCIL PAYMENTS AND QUICKLY BECAME A HOUSEPET.
STUDENT WITH UNCOOPERATIVE TENDENCIES
MITTENS

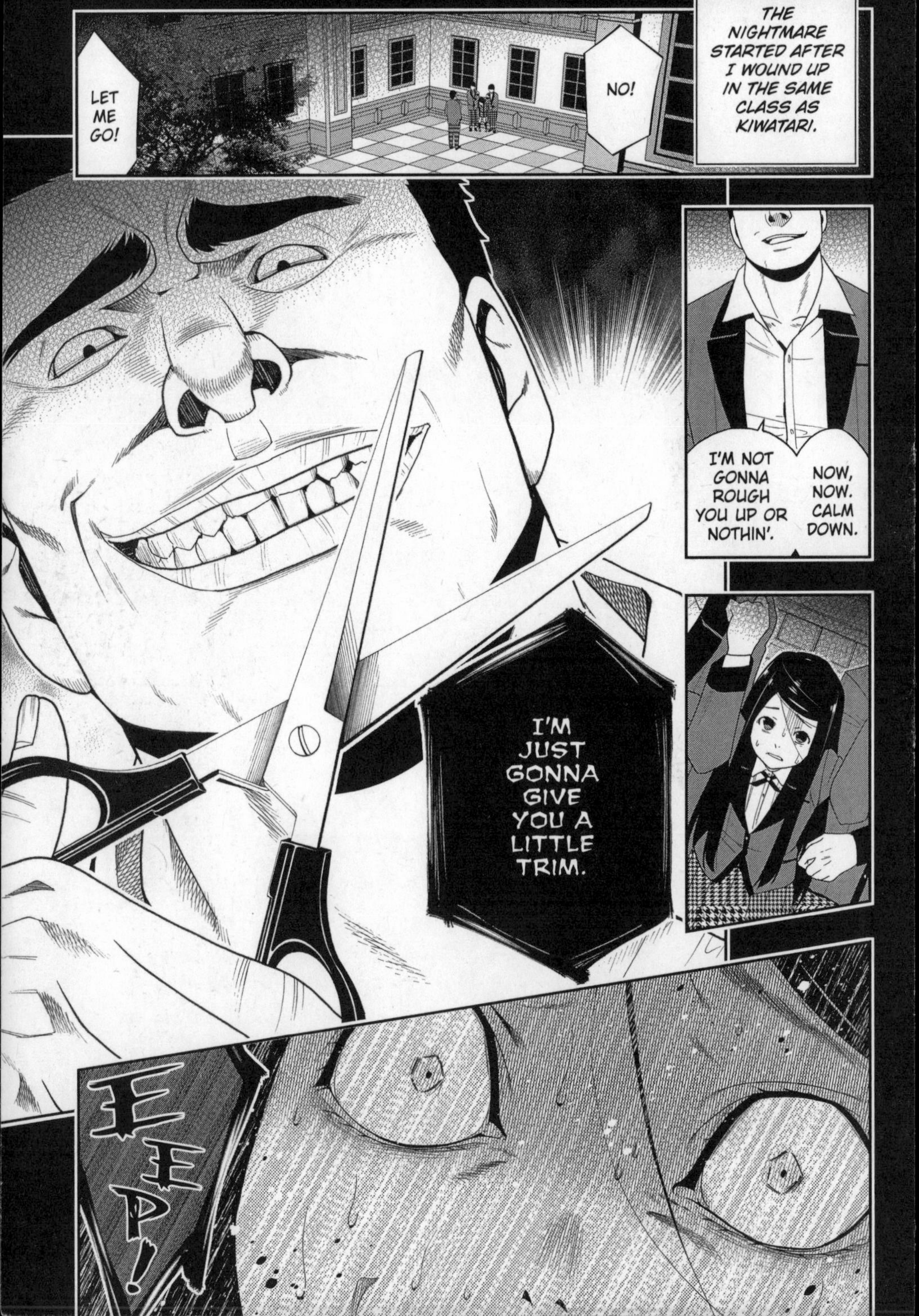
THE NIGHTMARE STARTED AFTER I WOUND UP IN THE SAME CLASS AS KIWATARI.
NO!
LET ME GO!
NOW, NOW. CALM DOWN.
I'M NOT GONNA ROUGH YOU UP OR NOTHIN'.
I'M JUST GONNA GIVE YOU A LITTLE TRIM.
EEEP!

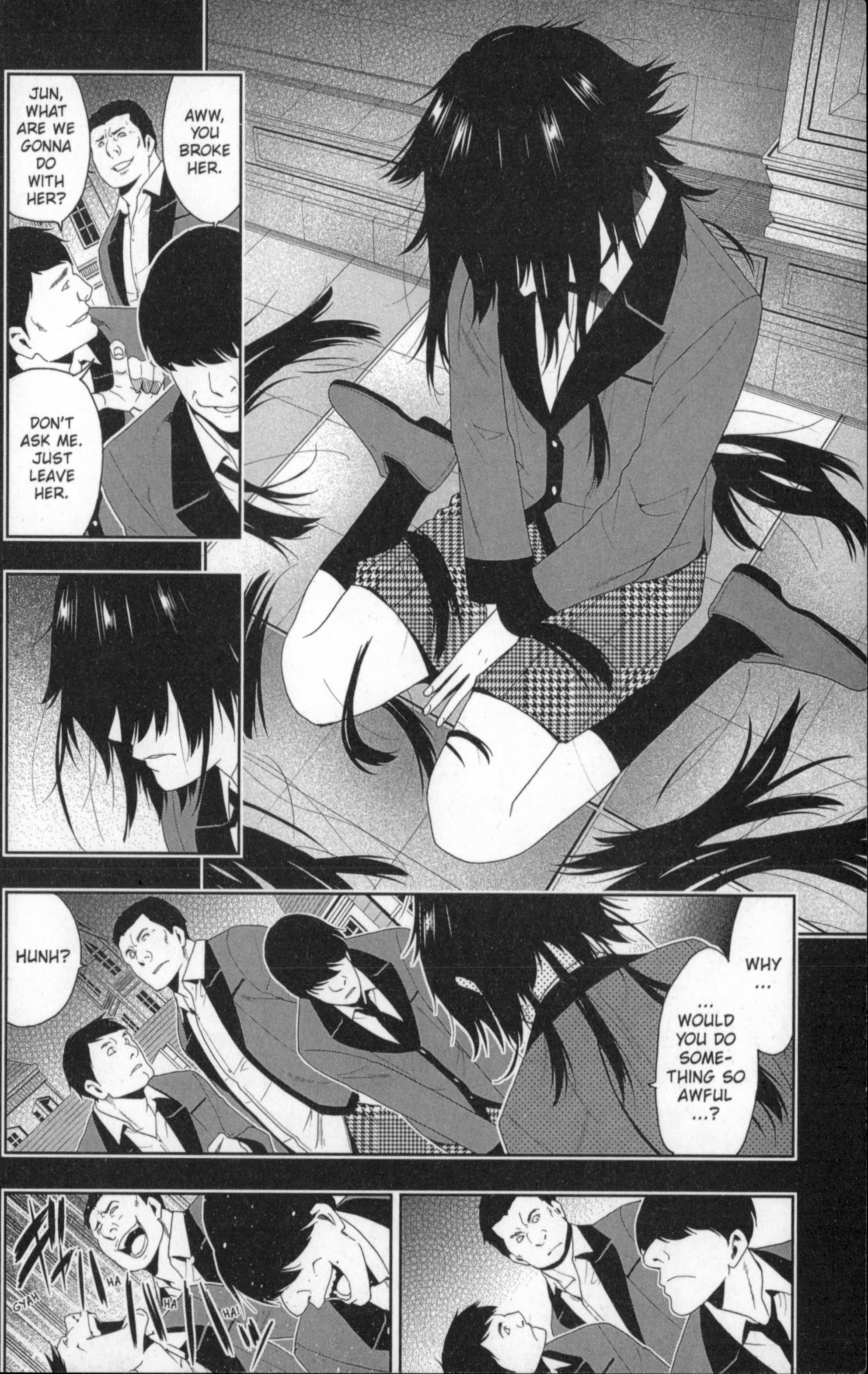
AWW, YOU BROKE HER.
JUN, WHAT ARE WE GONNA DO WITH HER?
DON'T ASK ME. JUST LEAVE HER.
WHY ... ... WOULD YOU DO SOME-THING SO AWFUL ...?
HUNH?
HA HA HA!
GYAH

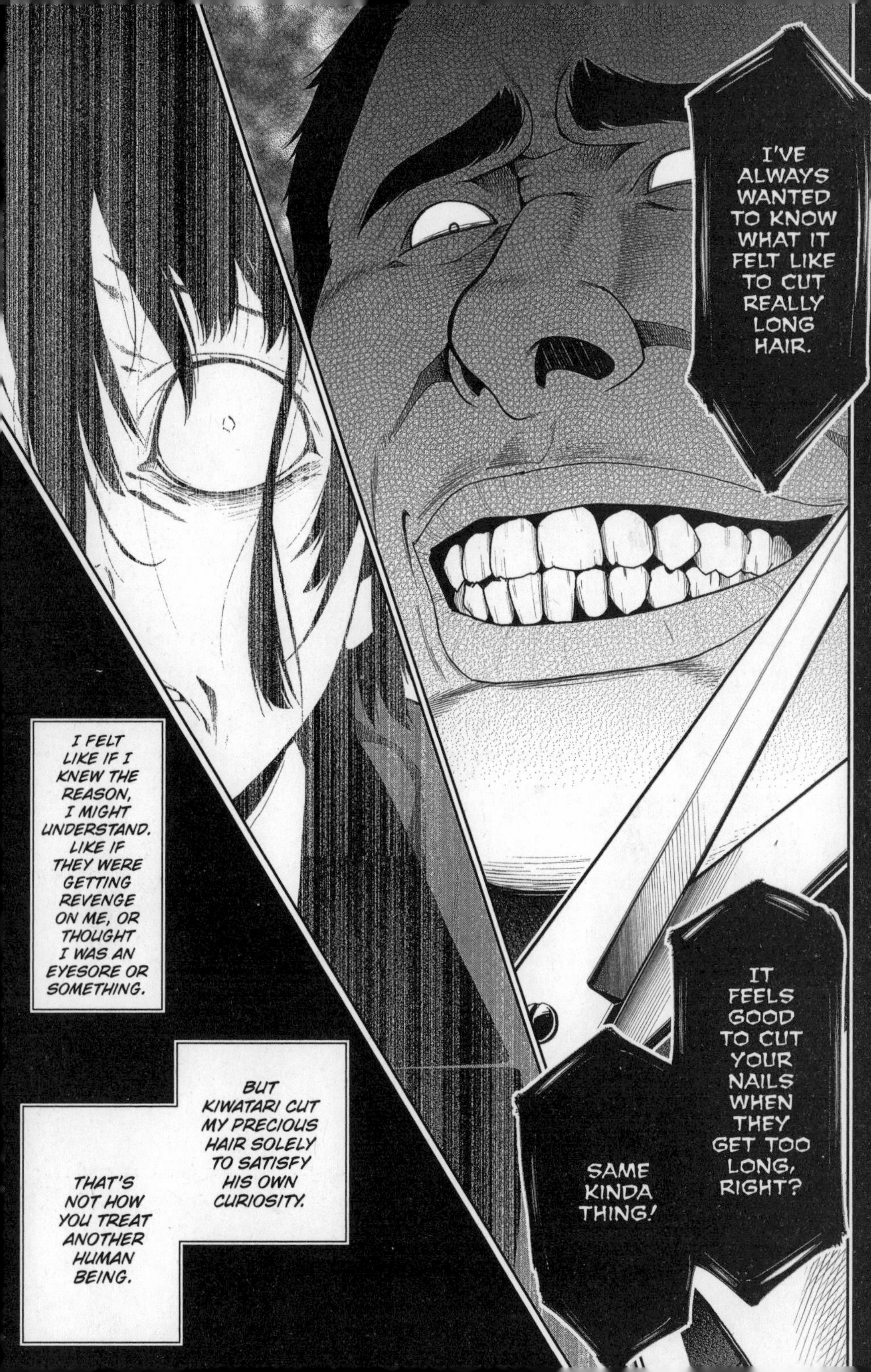
I'VE ALWAYS WANTED TO KNOW WHAT IT FELT LIKE TO CUT REALLY LONG HAIR.
IT FEELS GOOD TO CUT YOUR NAILS WHEN THEY GET TOO LONG, RIGHT?
SAME KINDA THING!
I FELT LIKE IF I KNEW THE REASON, I MIGHT UNDERSTAND. LIKE IF THEY WERE GETTING REVENGE ON ME, OR THOUGHT I WAS AN EYESORE OR SOMETHING.
BUT KIWATARI CUT MY PRECIOUS HAIR SOLELY TO SATISFY HIS OWN CURIOSITY.
THAT'S NOT HOW YOU TREAT ANOTHER HUMAN BEING.

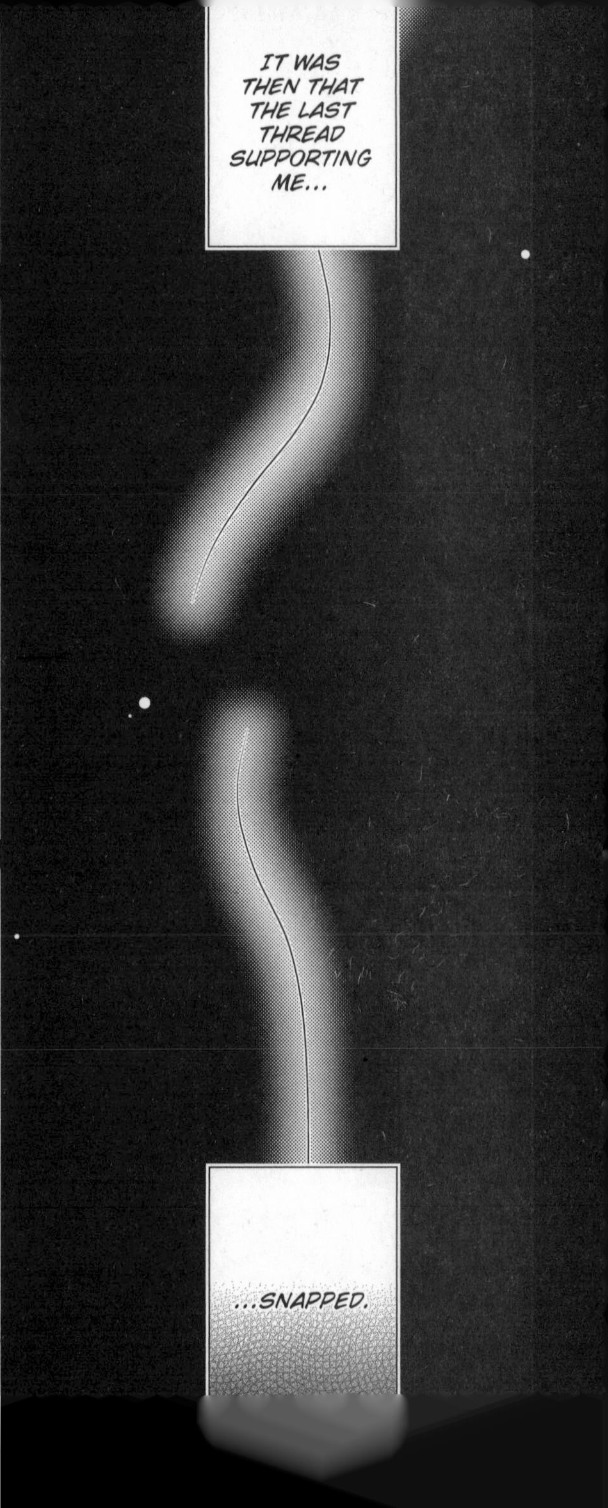
IT WAS THEN THAT THE LAST THREAD SUPPORTING ME...
...SNAPPED.

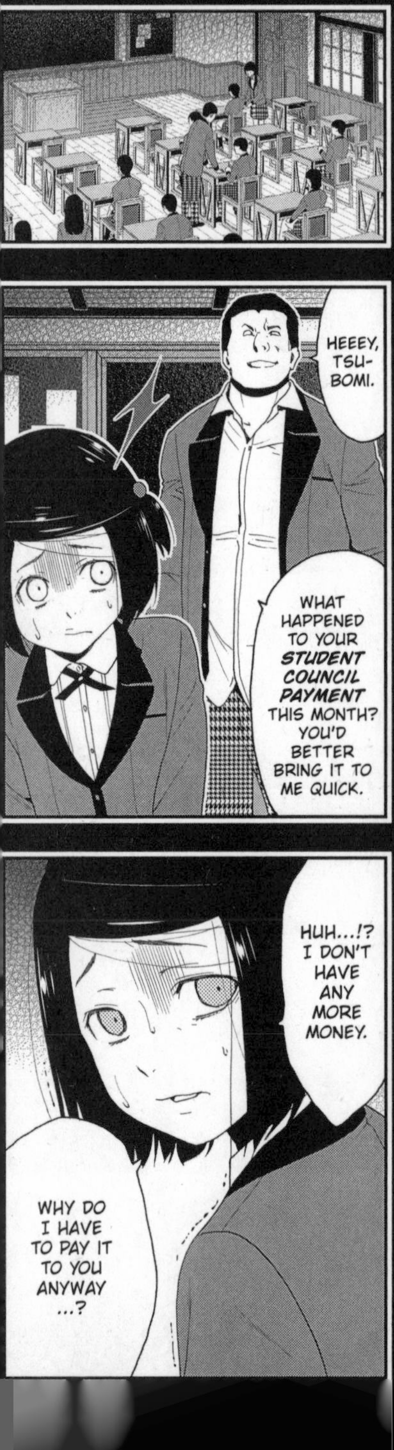
HEEEY, TSU-BOMI.
WHAT HAPPENED TO YOUR STUDENT COUNCIL PAYMENT THIS MONTH? YOU'D BETTER BRING IT TO ME QUICK.
HUH...!? I DON'T HAVE ANY MORE MONEY.
WHY DO I HAVE TO PAY IT TO YOU ANYWAY ...?

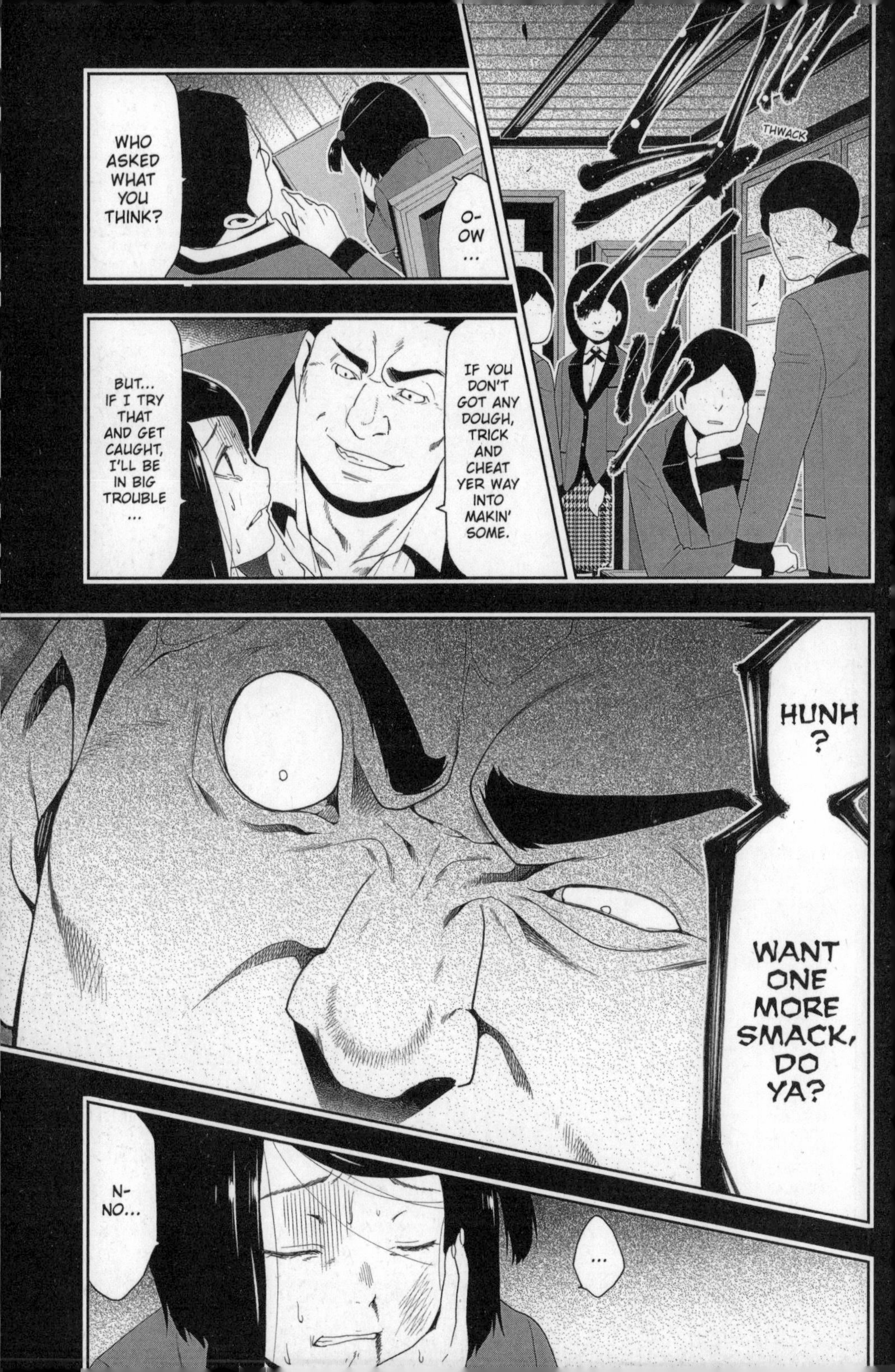
THWACK
O-OW...
WHO ASKED WHAT YOU THINK?
IF YOU DON'T GOT ANY DOUGH, TRICK AND CHEAT YER WAY INTO MAKIN' SOME.
BUT... IF I TRY THAT AND GET CAUGHT, I'LL BE IN BIG TROUBLE...
HUNH?
WANT ONE MORE SMACK, DO YA?
...
N-NO...

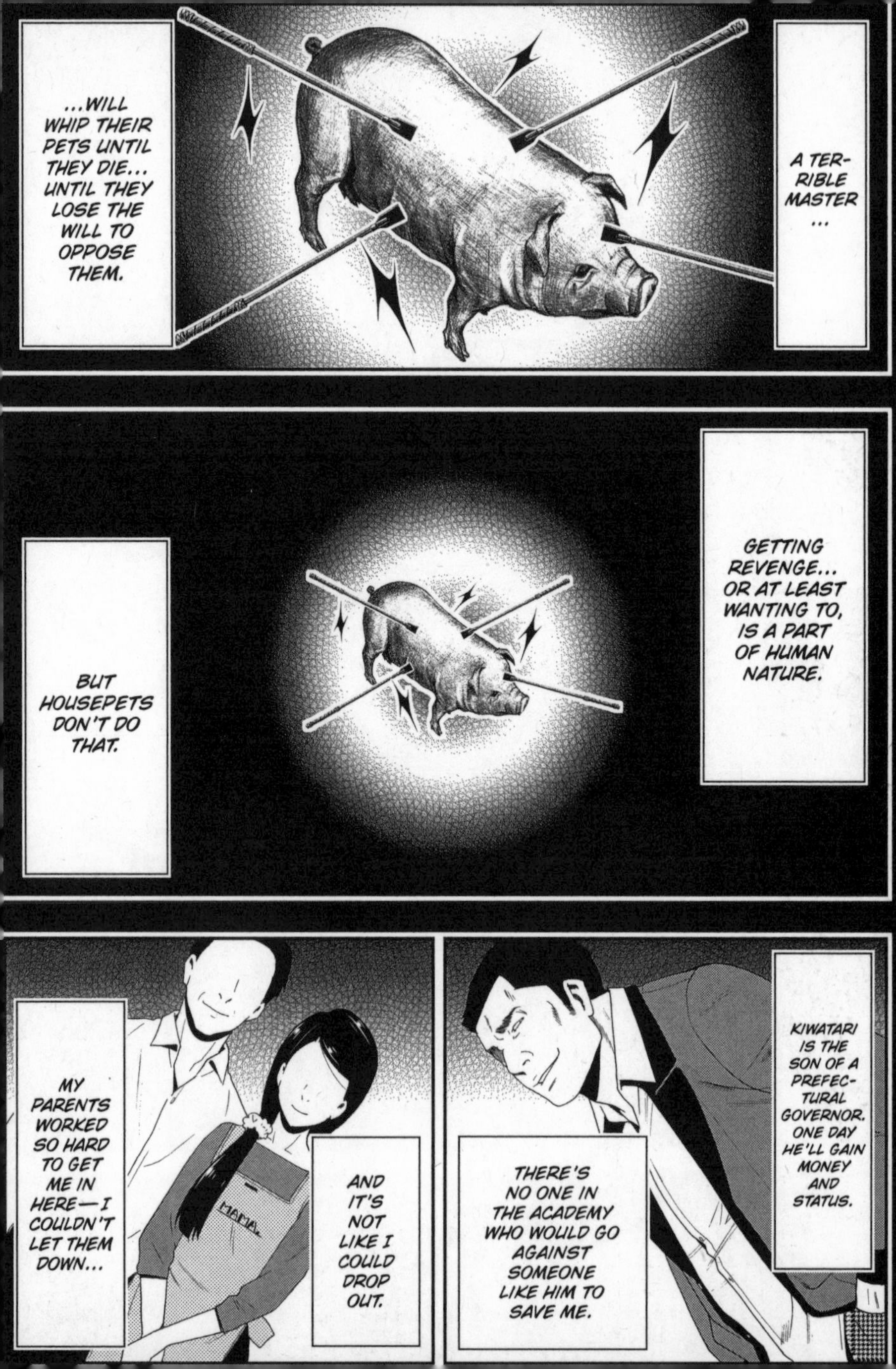
A TERRIBLE MASTER...
...WILL WHIP THEIR PETS UNTIL THEY DIE... UNTIL THEY LOSE THE WILL TO OPPOSE THEM.
GETTING REVENGE... OR AT LEAST WANTING TO, IS A PART OF HUMAN NATURE.
BUT HOUSEPETS DON'T DO THAT.
KIWATARI IS THE SON OF A PREFECTURAL GOVERNOR. ONE DAY HE'LL GAIN MONEY AND STATUS.
THERE'S NO ONE IN THE ACADEMY WHO WOULD GO AGAINST SOMEONE LIKE HIM TO SAVE ME.
MY PARENTS WORKED SO HARD TO GET ME IN HERE—I COULDN'T LET THEM DOWN...
MAMA
AND IT'S NOT LIKE I COULD DROP OUT.

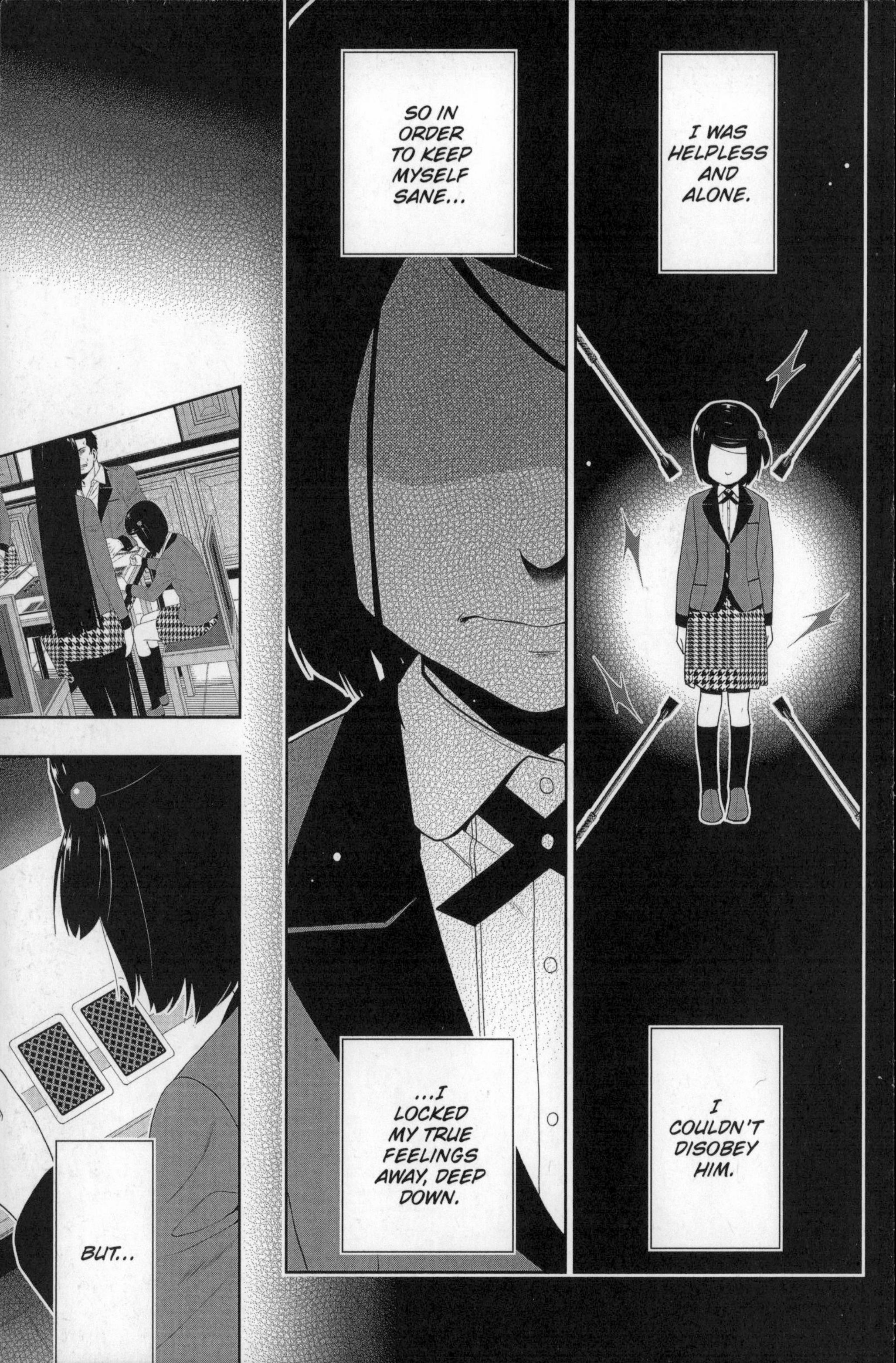
I WAS HELPLESS AND ALONE.
I COULDN'T DISOBEY HIM.
SO IN ORDER TO KEEP MYSELF SANE...
...I LOCKED MY TRUE FEELINGS AWAY, DEEP DOWN.
BUT...

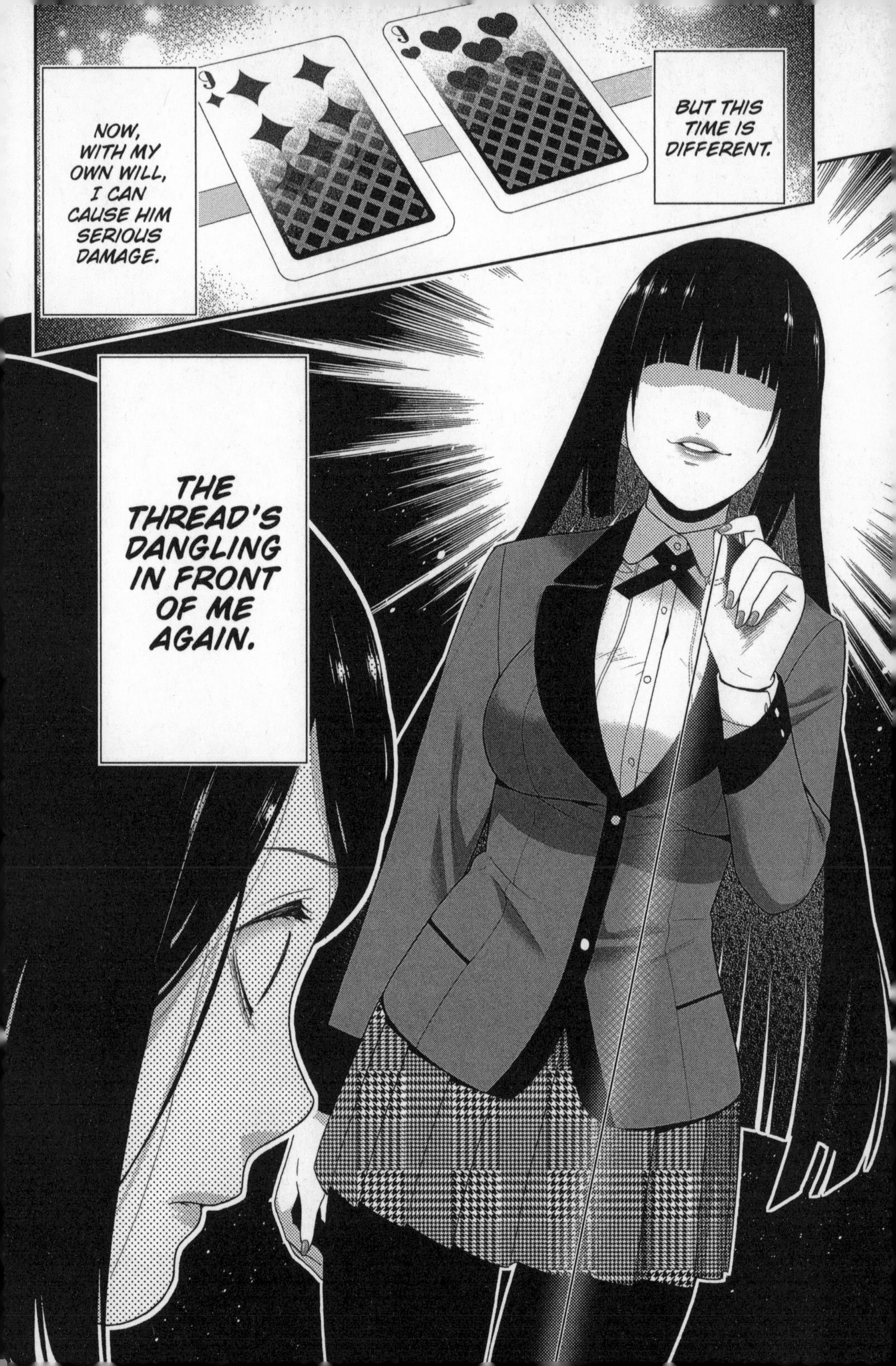
BUT THIS TIME IS DIFFERENT.
NOW, WITH MY OWN WILL, I CAN CAUSE HIM SERIOUS DAMAGE.
THE THREAD'S DANGLING IN FRONT OF ME AGAIN.

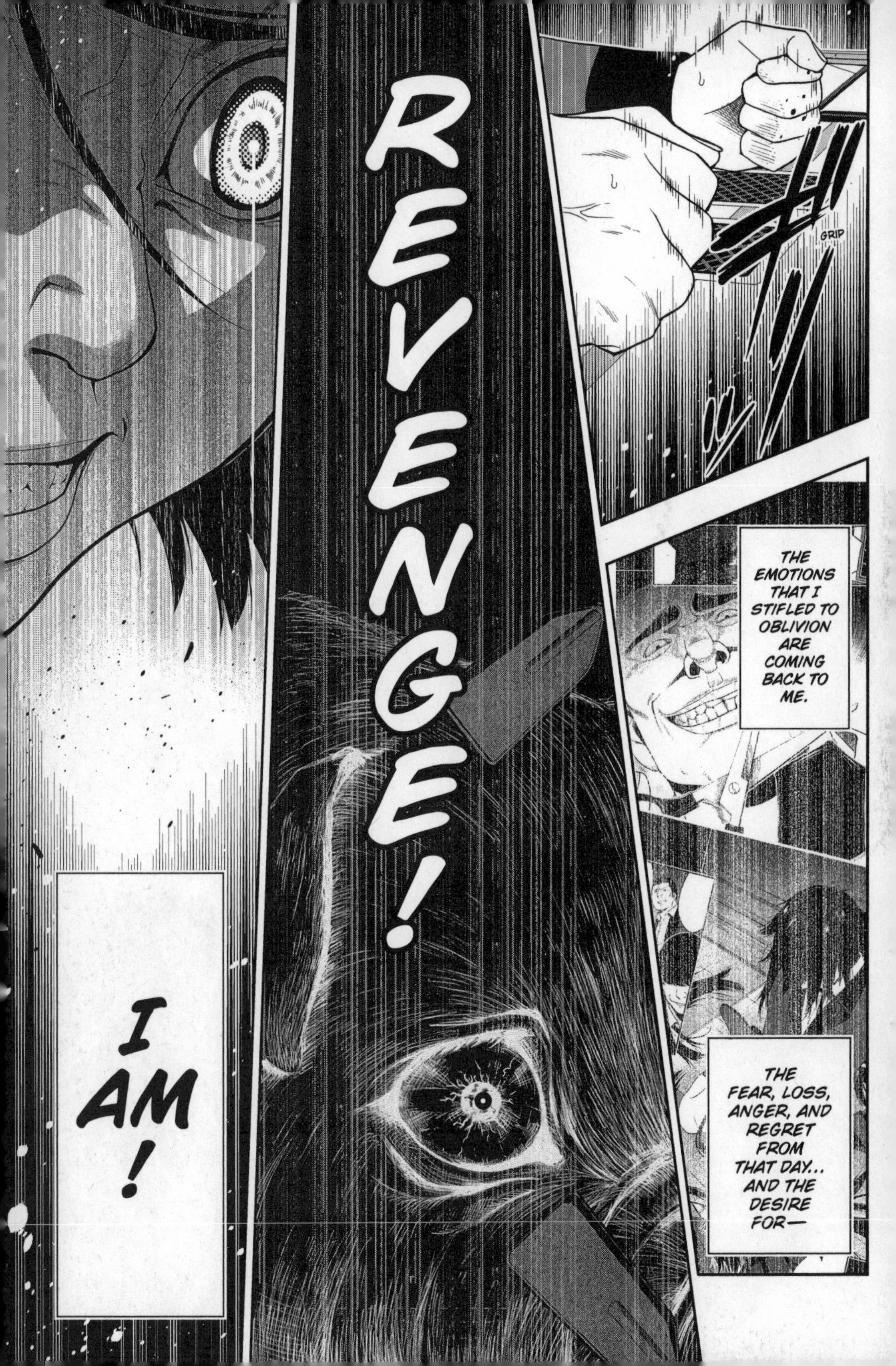
GRIP
THE EMOTIONS THAT I STIFLED TO OBLIVION ARE COMING BACK TO ME.
THE FEAR, LOSS, ANGER, AND REGRET FROM THAT DAY... AND THE DESIRE FOR—
REVENGE!
I AM!

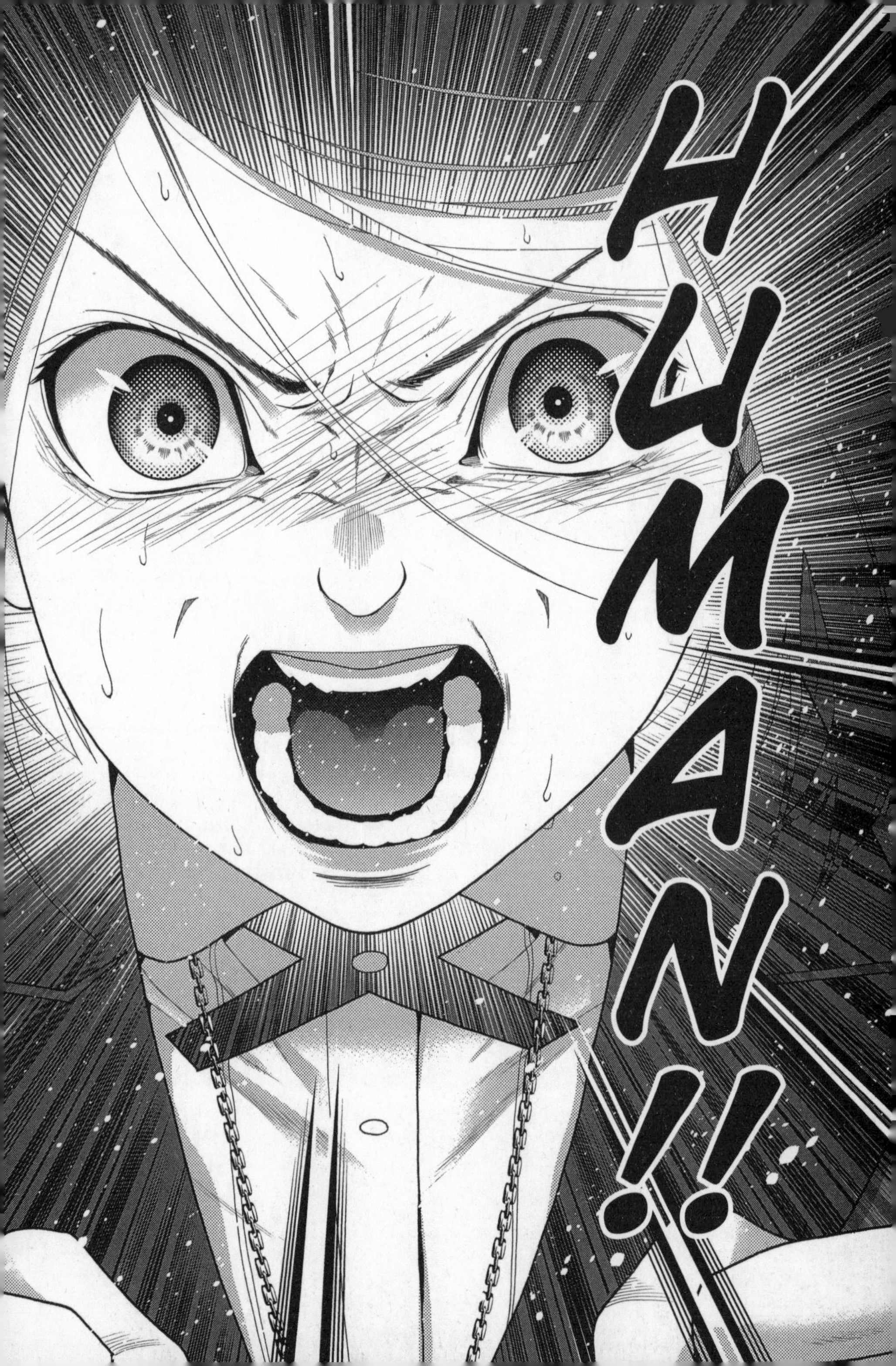
HUMAN!!

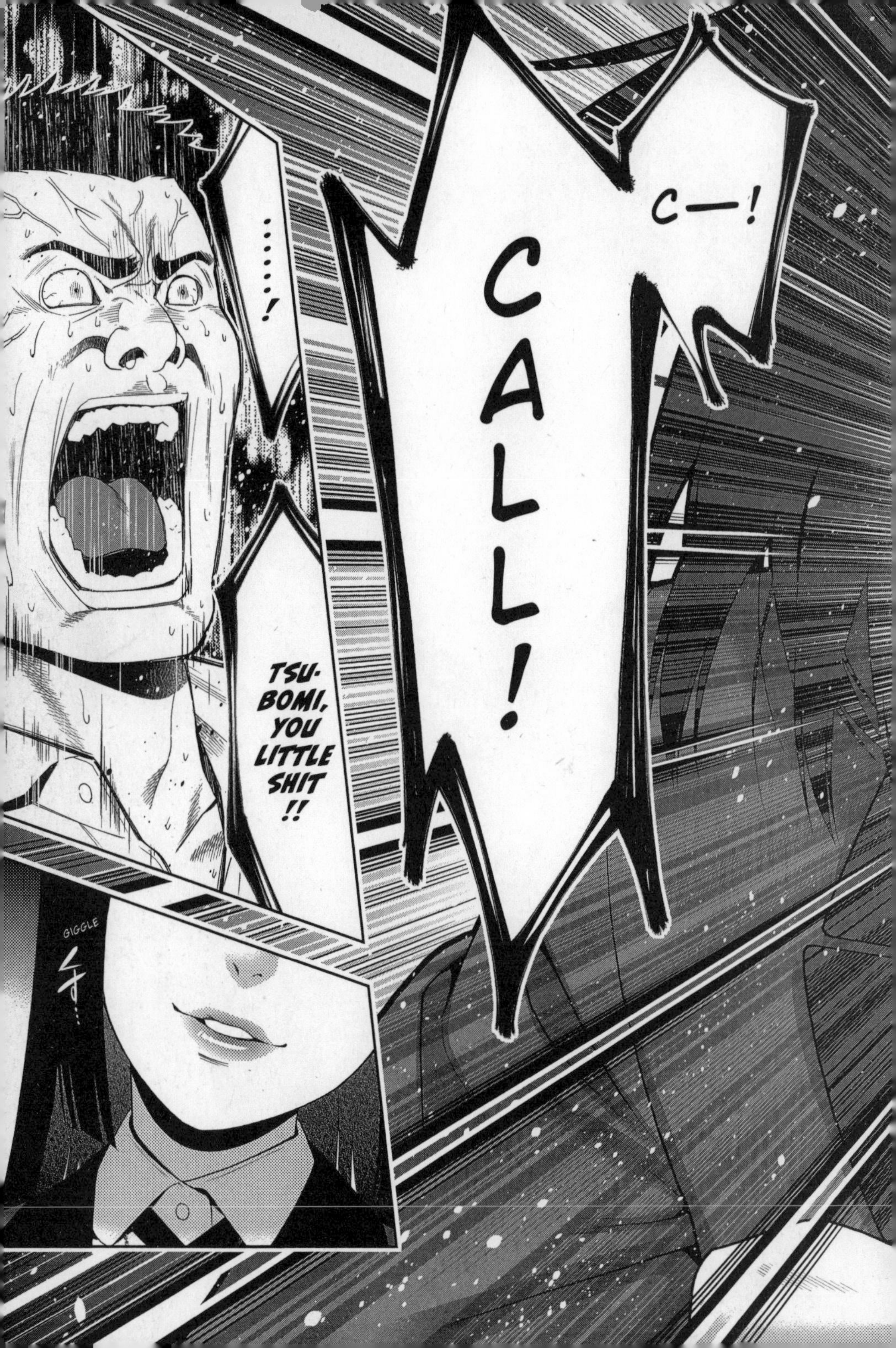
C—!
CALL!
......!
TSU-BOMI, YOU LITTLE SHIT!!
GIGGLE
くす…

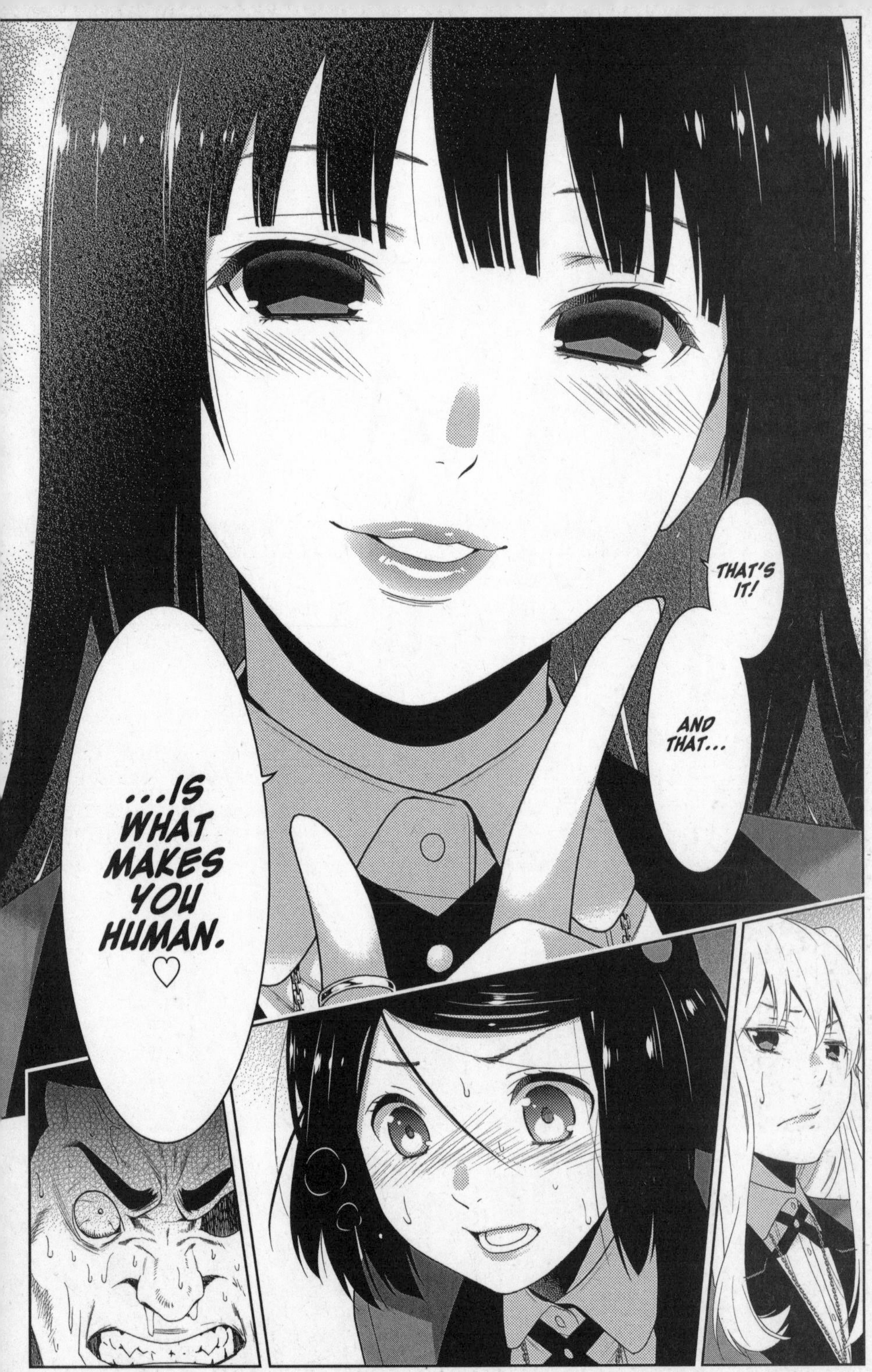
THAT'S IT!
AND THAT...
...IS WHAT MAKES YOU HUMAN. ♡

KAKEGURUI

— Compulsive Gambler —

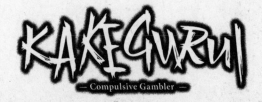

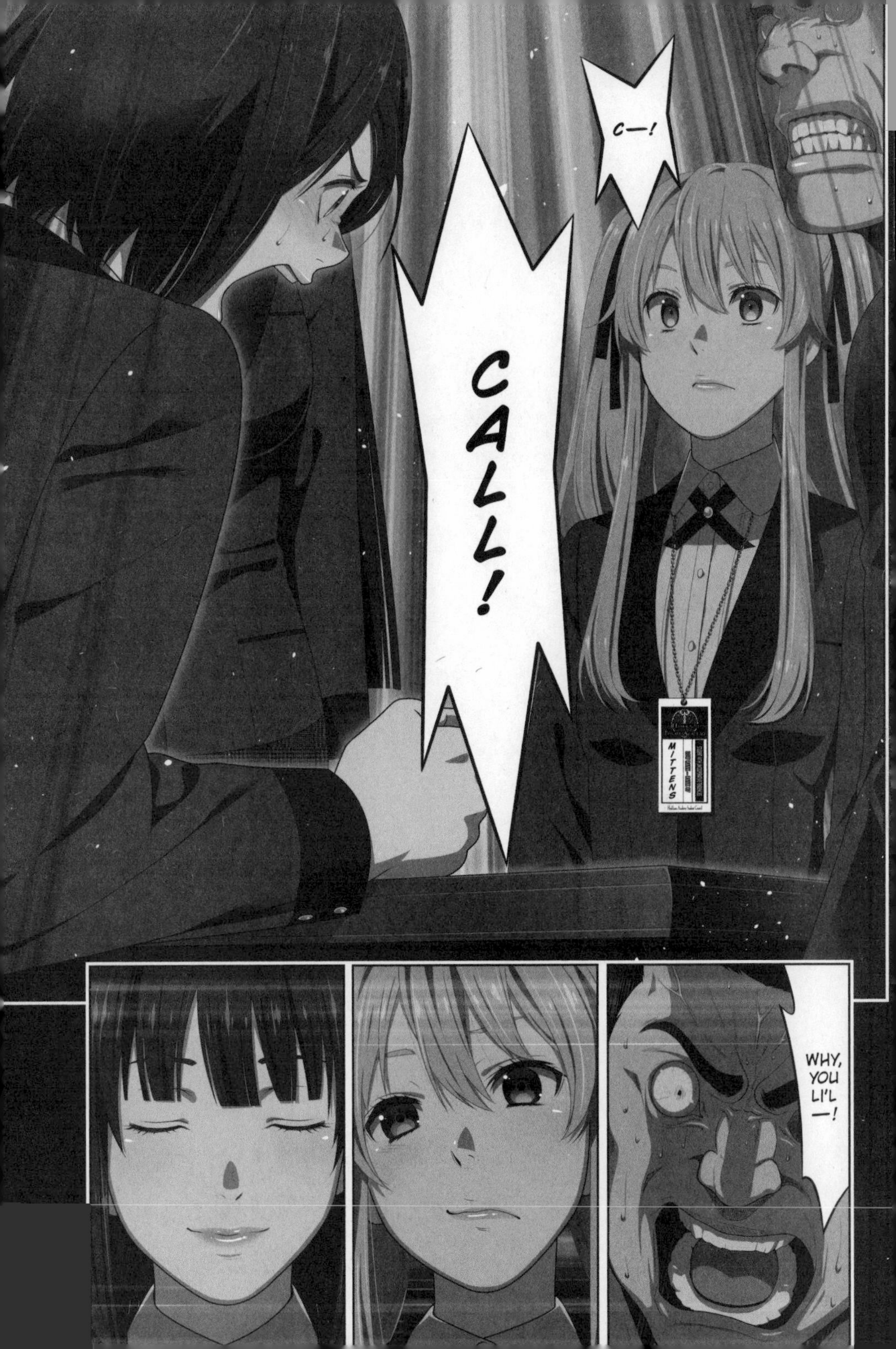
C—!
CALL!
MITTENS
WHY, YOU LI'L —!

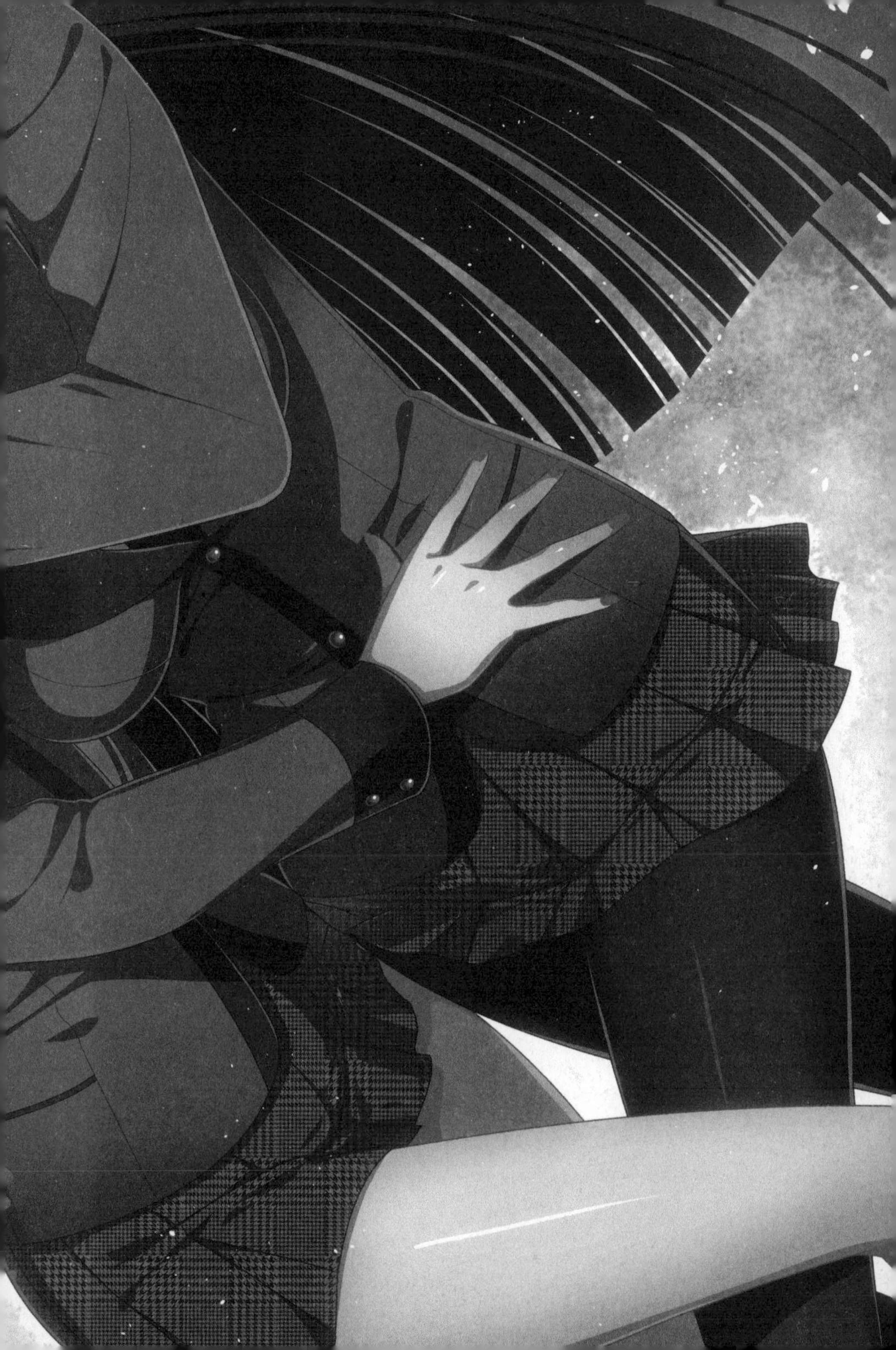

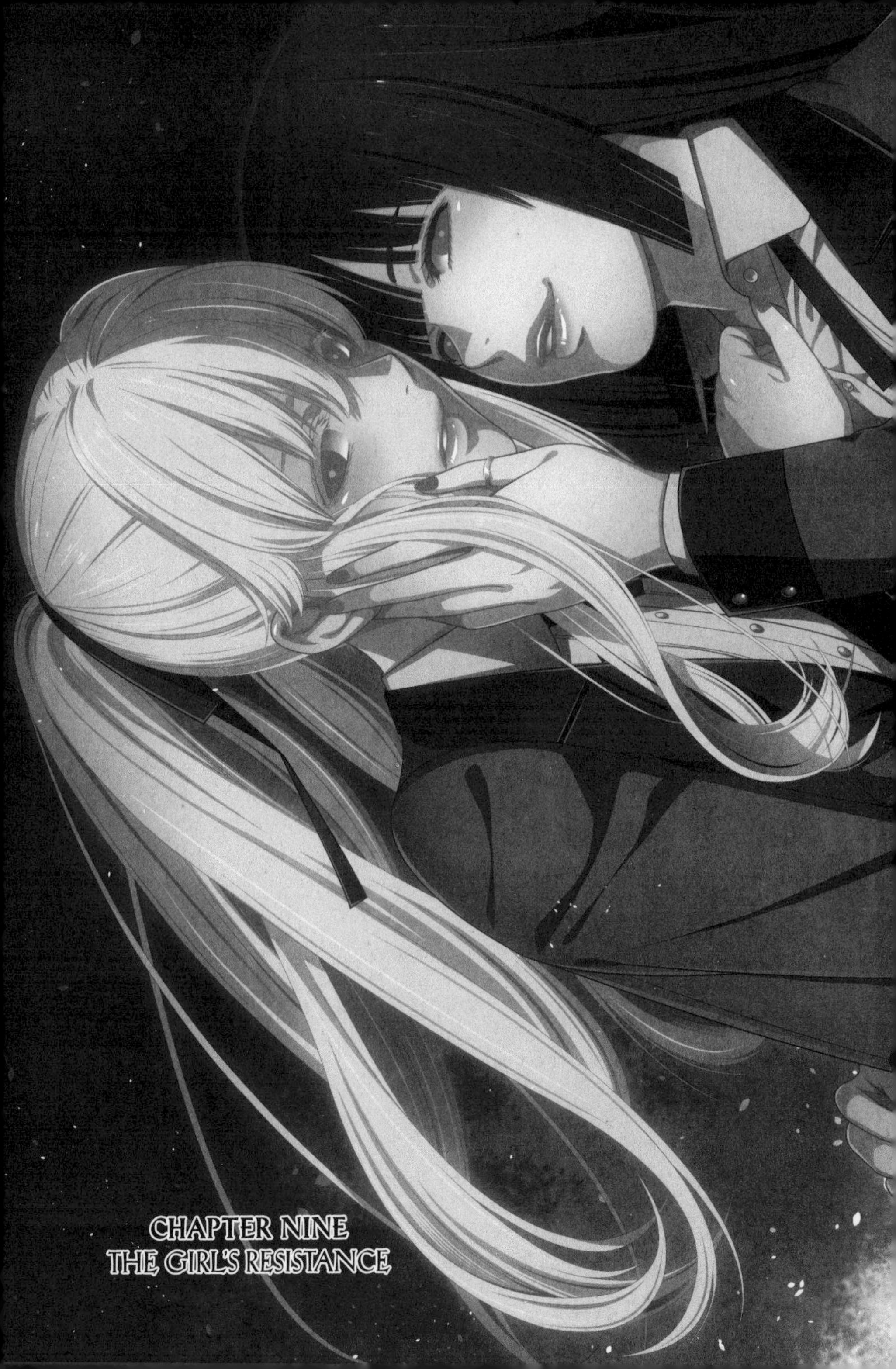
CHAPTER NINE
THE GIRL'S RESISTANCE

KAKEGURUI
— Compulsive Gambler —

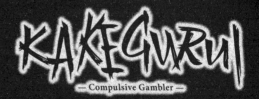

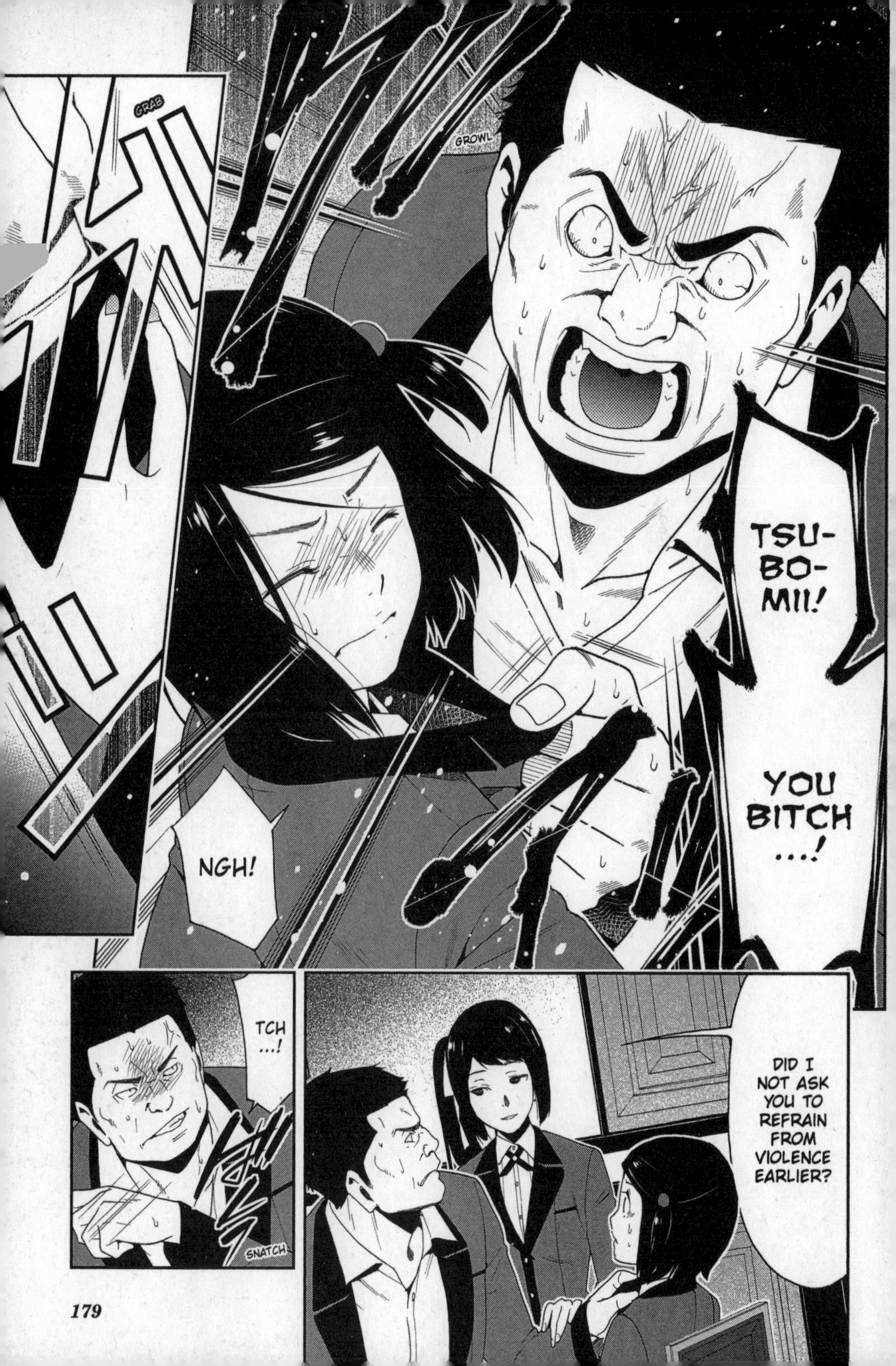
GROWL
TSU-BO-MII!
YOU BITCH...!
NGH!
GRAB
DID I NOT ASK YOU TO REFRAIN FROM VIOLENCE EARLIER?
TCH...!
SNATCH

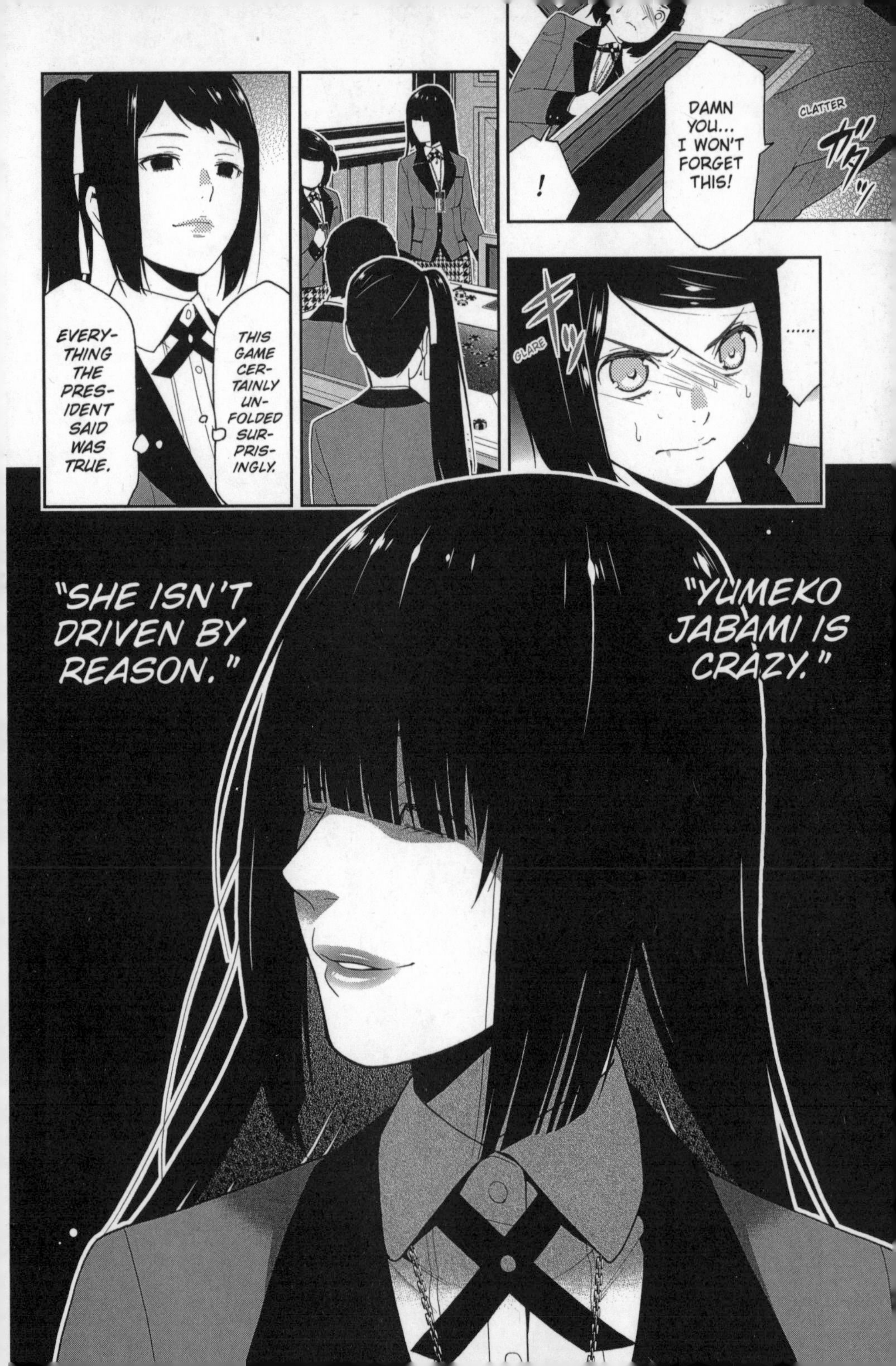
CLATTER
DAMN YOU... I WON'T FORGET THIS!
!
GLARE
......
THIS GAME CERTAINLY UNFOLDED SURPRISINGLY.
EVERYTHING THE PRESIDENT SAID WAS TRUE.
"YUMEKO JABAMI IS CRAZY."
"SHE ISN'T DRIVEN BY REASON."

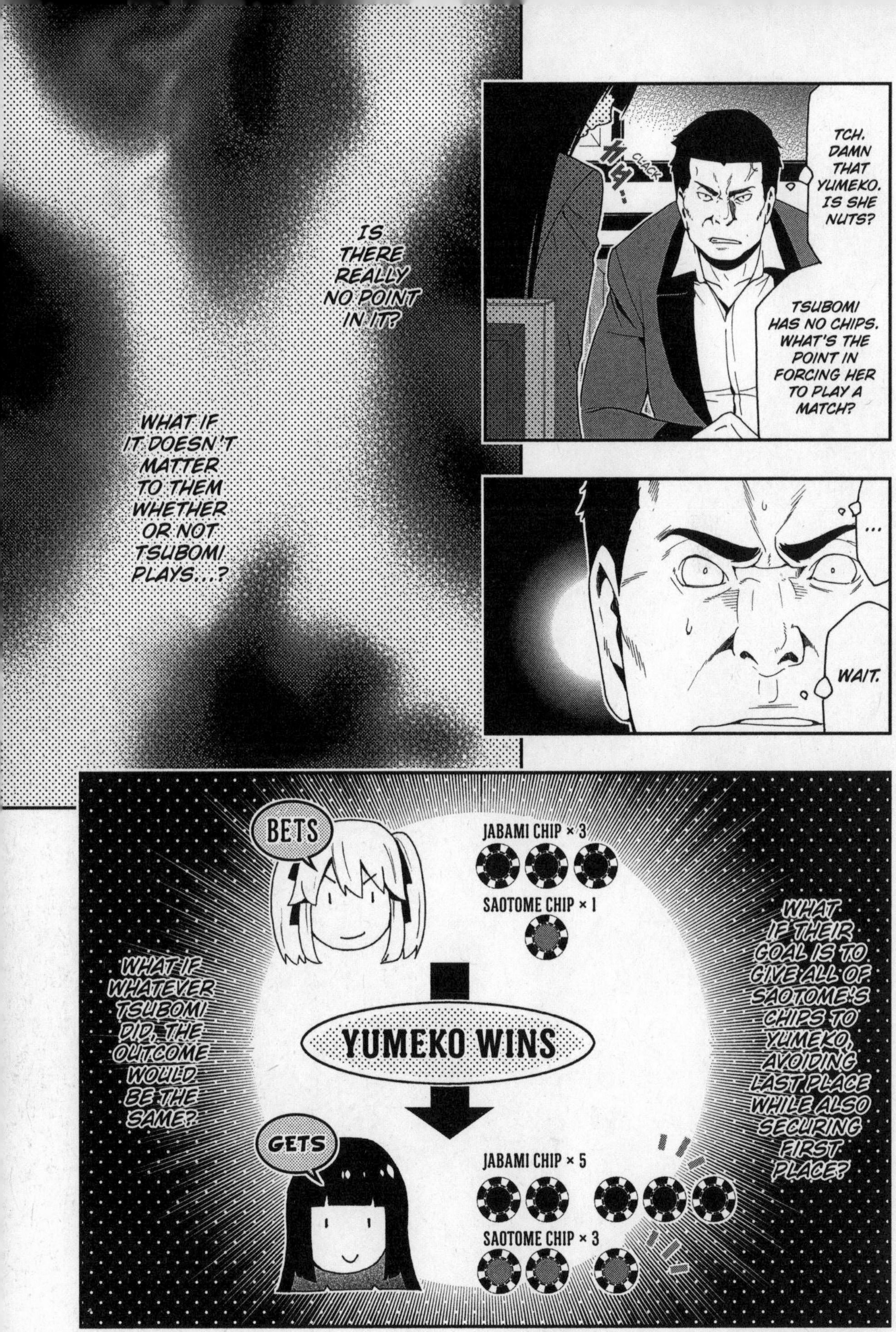
CLACK
TCH. DAMN THAT YUMEKO. IS SHE NUTS?
TSUBOMI HAS NO CHIPS. WHAT'S THE POINT IN FORCING HER TO PLAY A MATCH?
...
WAIT.
IS THERE REALLY NO POINT IN IT?
WHAT IF IT DOESN'T MATTER TO THEM WHETHER OR NOT TSUBOMI PLAYS...?
WHAT IF THEIR GOAL IS TO GIVE ALL OF SAOTOME'S CHIPS TO YUMEKO, AVOIDING LAST PLACE WHILE ALSO SECURING FIRST PLACE?
BETS
JABAMI CHIP × 3
SAOTOME CHIP × 1
YUMEKO WINS
GETS
JABAMI CHIP × 5
SAOTOME CHIP × 3
WHAT IF WHATEVER TSUBOMI DID, THE OUTCOME WOULD BE THE SAME?

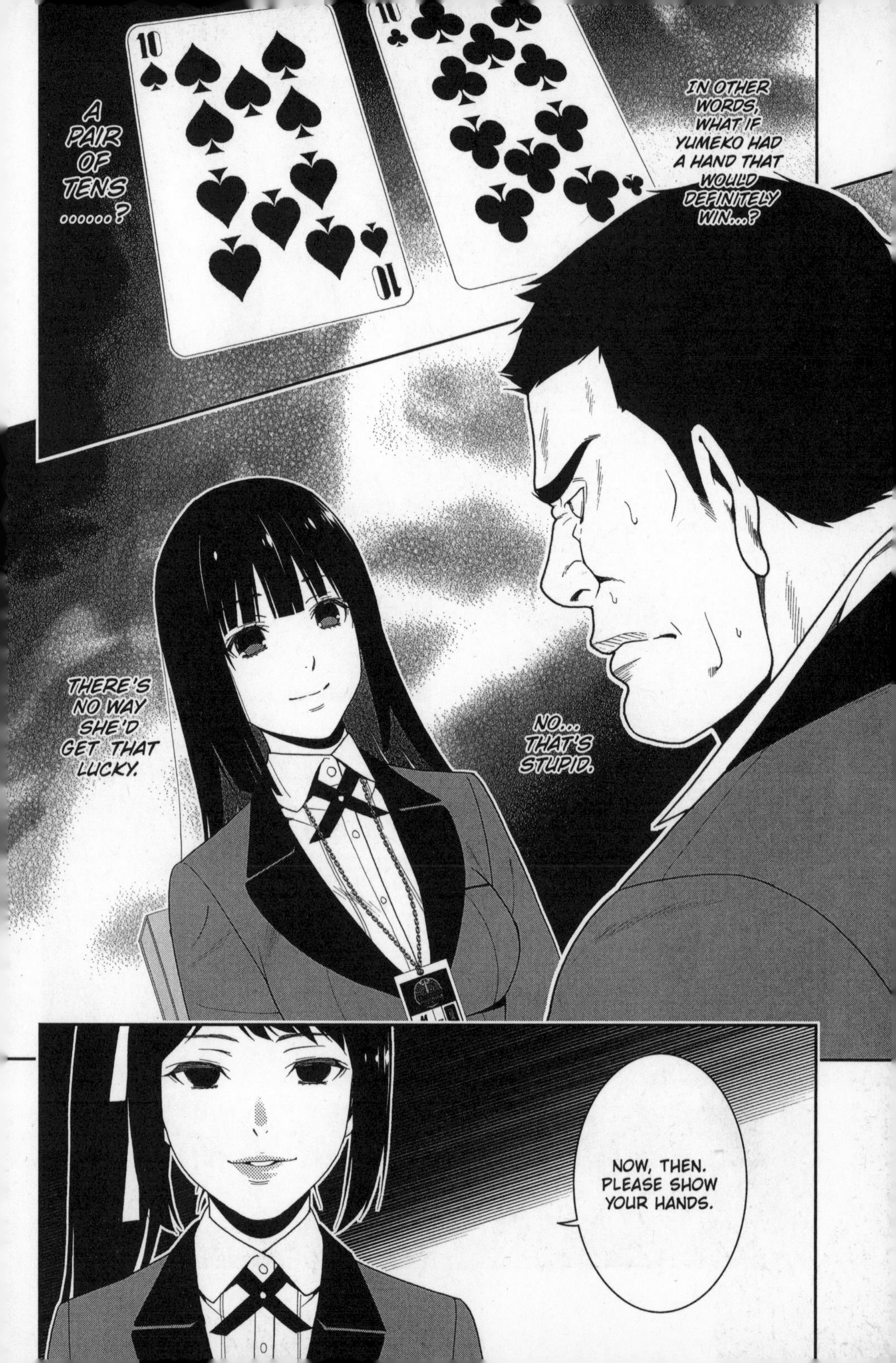
IN OTHER WORDS, WHAT IF YUMEKO HAD A HAND THAT WOULD DEFINITELY WIN...?
A PAIR OF TENS ......?
NO... THAT'S STUPID.
THERE'S NO WAY SHE'D GET THAT LUCKY.
NOW, THEN. PLEASE SHOW YOUR HANDS.

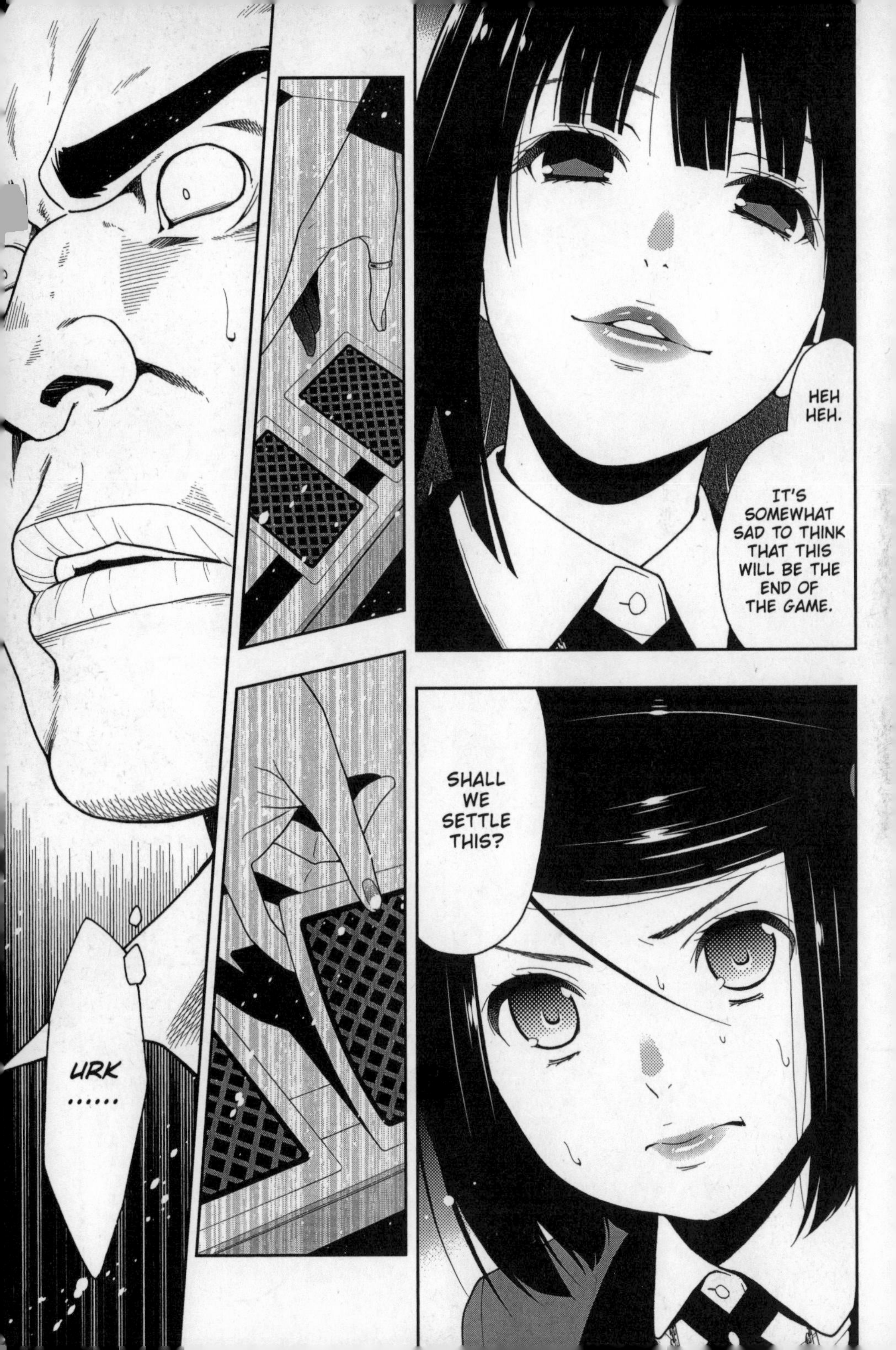
HEH HEH.
IT'S SOMEWHAT SAD TO THINK THAT THIS WILL BE THE END OF THE GAME.
SHALL WE SETTLE THIS?
URK ......

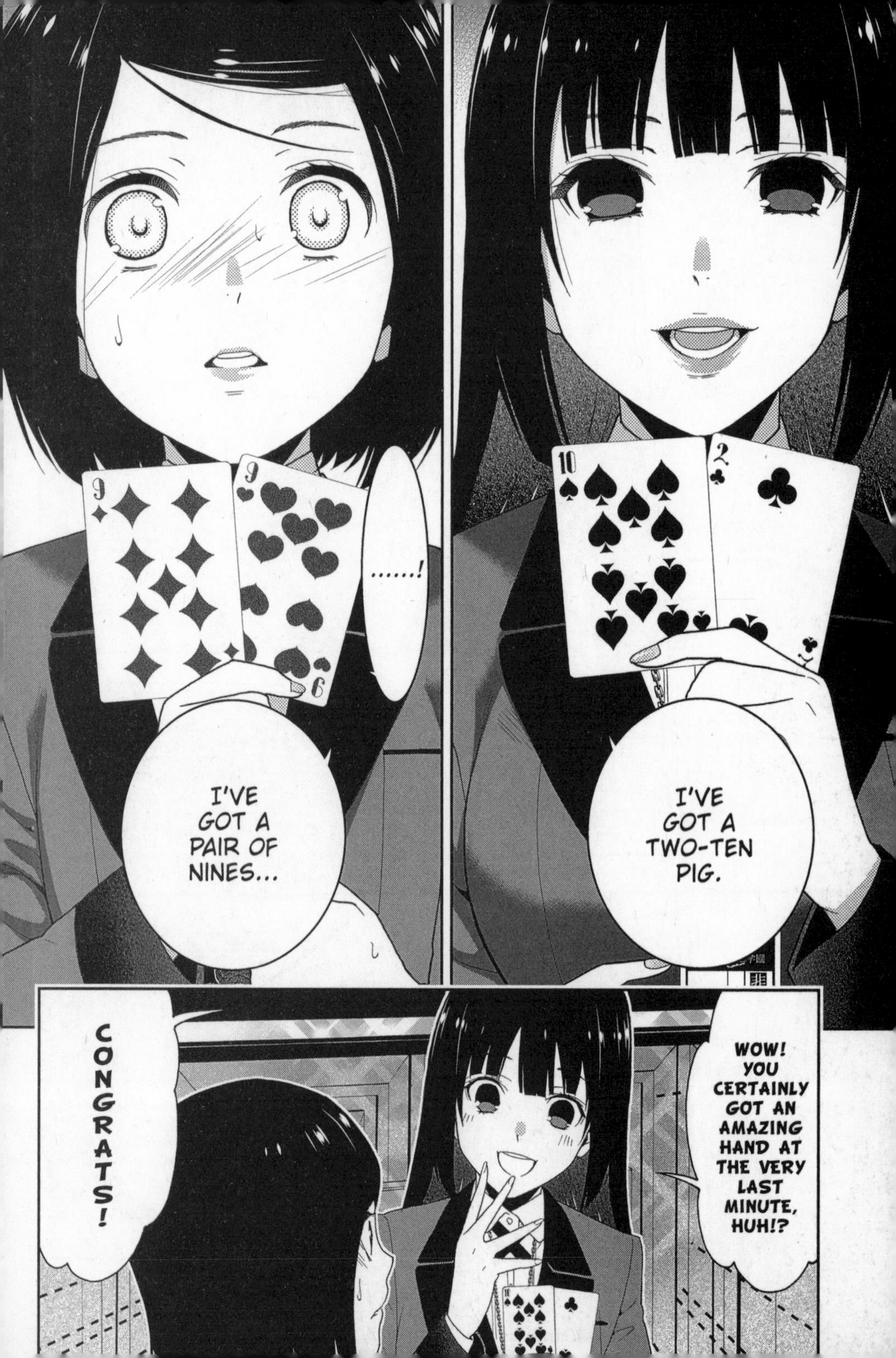
I'VE GOT A TWO-TEN PIG.
......!
I'VE GOT A PAIR OF NINES...
WOW! YOU CERTAINLY GOT AN AMAZING HAND AT THE VERY LAST MINUTE, HUH!?
CONGRATS!

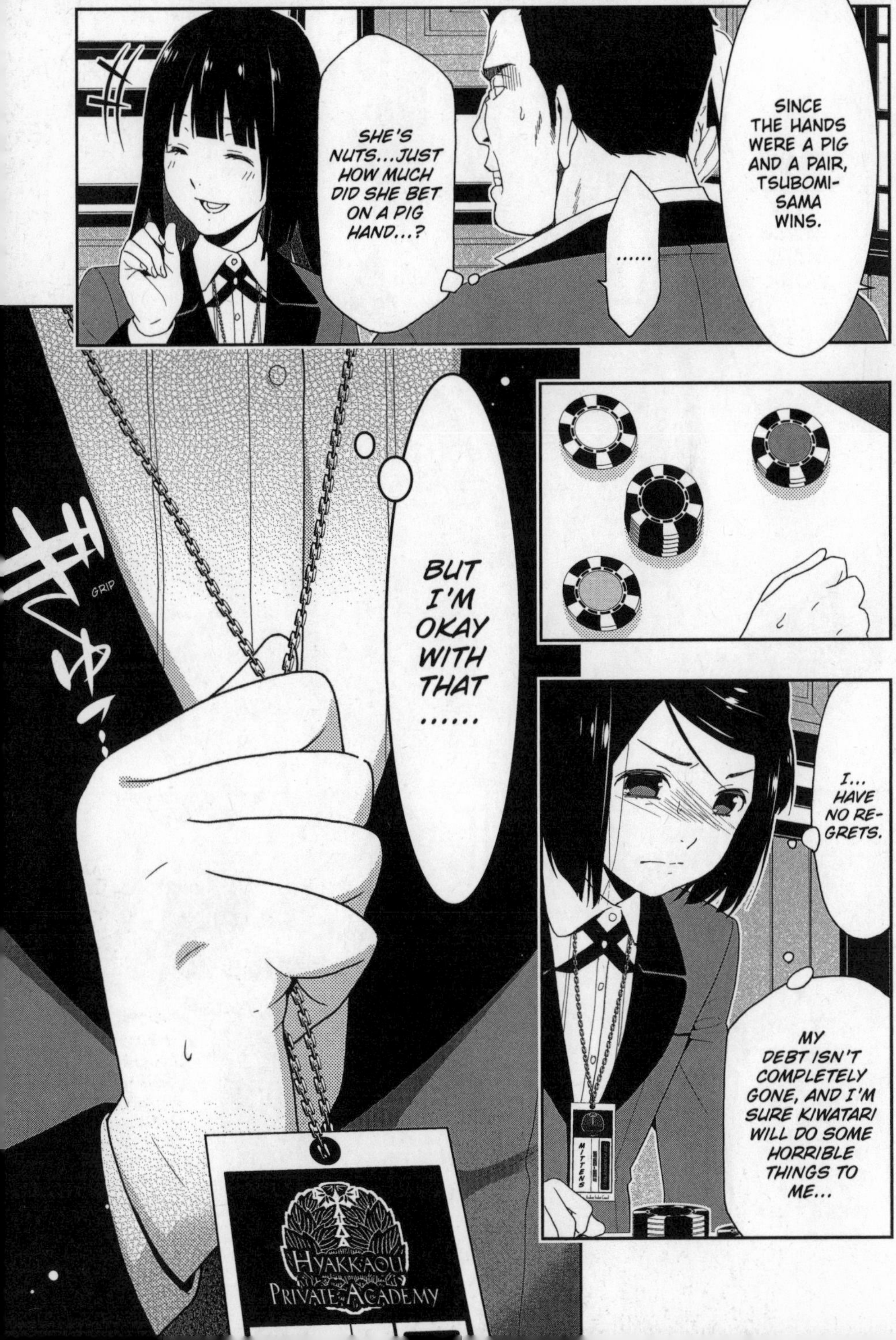
SINCE THE HANDS WERE A PIG AND A PAIR, TSUBOMI-SAMA WINS.
......
SHE'S NUTS...JUST HOW MUCH DID SHE BET ON A PIG HAND...?
I... HAVE NO RE-GRETS.
MY DEBT ISN'T COMPLETELY GONE, AND I'M SURE KIWATARI WILL DO SOME HORRIBLE THINGS TO ME...
BUT I'M OKAY WITH THAT......
GRIP
HYAKKAOU PRIVATE ACADEMY

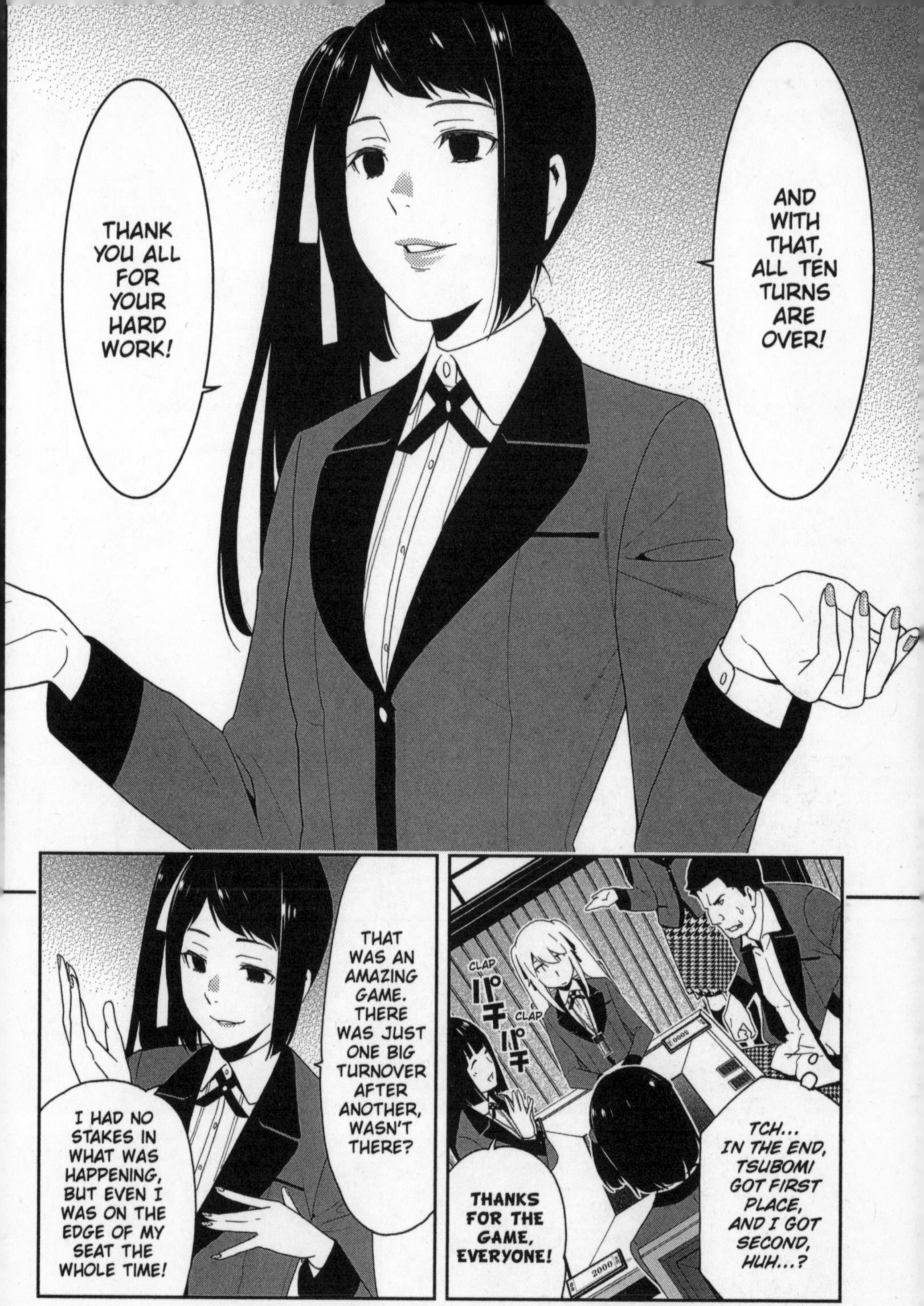
AND WITH THAT, ALL TEN TURNS ARE OVER!
THANK YOU ALL FOR YOUR HARD WORK!
TCH... IN THE END, TSUBOMI GOT FIRST PLACE, AND I GOT SECOND, HUH...?
CLAP パチ
CLAP パチ
THANKS FOR THE GAME, EVERYONE!
THAT WAS AN AMAZING GAME. THERE WAS JUST ONE BIG TURNOVER AFTER ANOTHER, WASN'T THERE?
I HAD NO STAKES IN WHAT WAS HAPPENING, BUT EVEN I WAS ON THE EDGE OF MY SEAT THE WHOLE TIME!

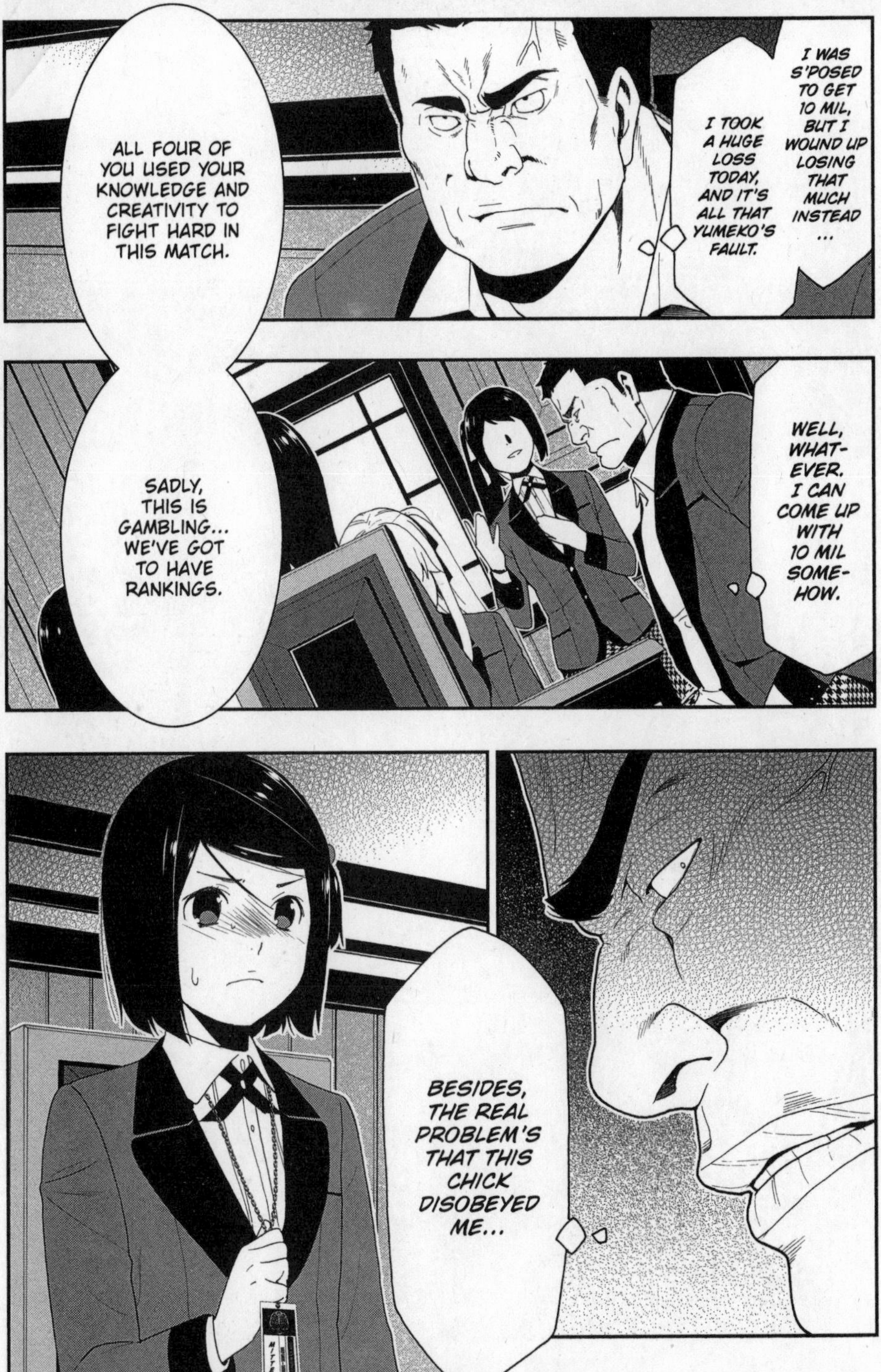
I WAS S'POSED TO GET 10 MIL, BUT I WOUND UP LOSING THAT MUCH INSTEAD...
I TOOK A HUGE LOSS TODAY, AND IT'S ALL THAT YUMEKO'S FAULT.
ALL FOUR OF YOU USED YOUR KNOWLEDGE AND CREATIVITY TO FIGHT HARD IN THIS MATCH.
WELL, WHATEVER. I CAN COME UP WITH 10 MIL SOMEHOW.
SADLY, THIS IS GAMBLING... WE'VE GOT TO HAVE RANKINGS.
BESIDES, THE REAL PROBLEM'S THAT THIS CHICK DISOBEYED ME...

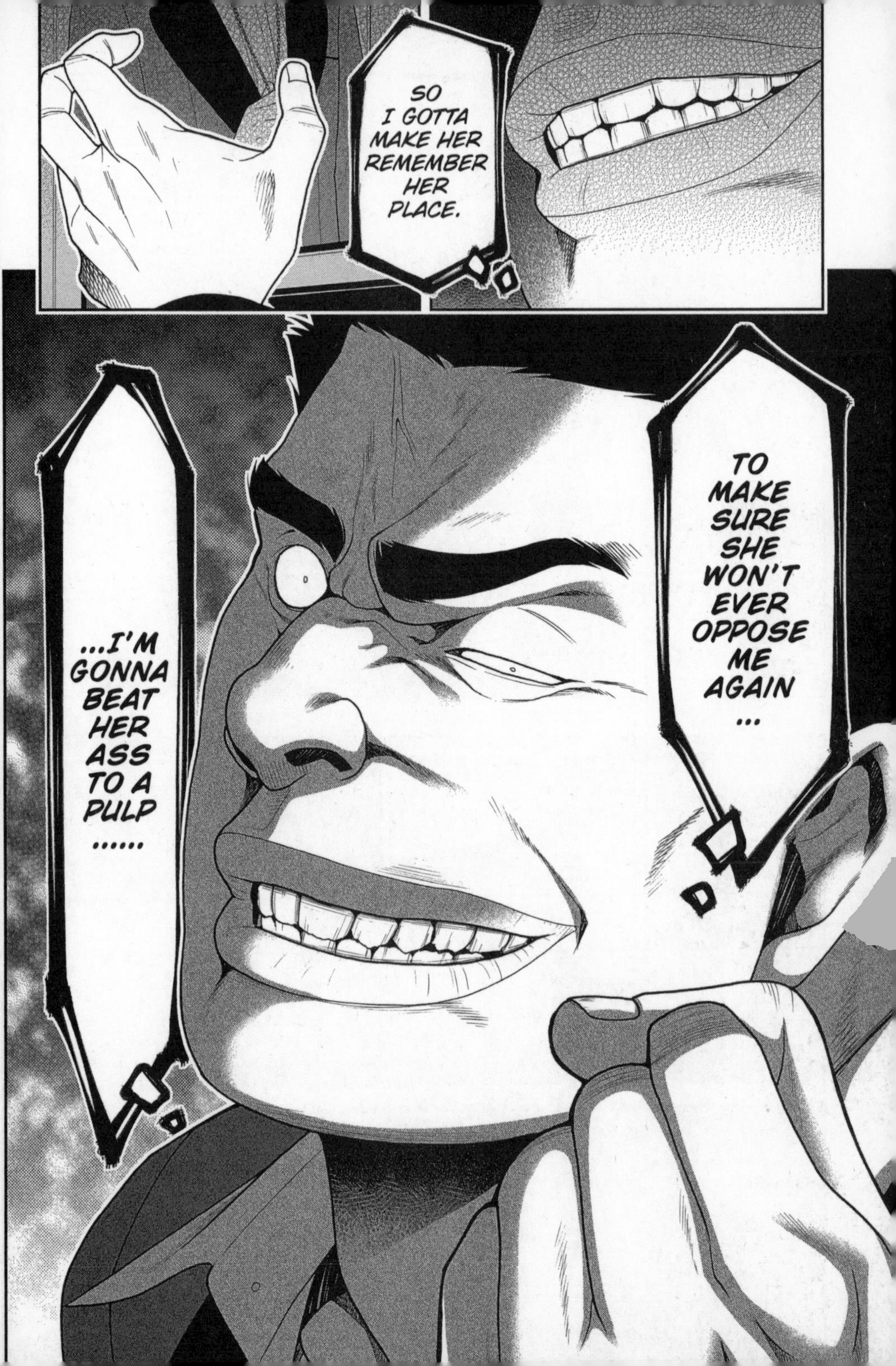
SO I GOTTA MAKE HER REMEMBER HER PLACE.
TO MAKE SURE SHE WON'T EVER OPPOSE ME AGAIN ...
...I'M GONNA BEAT HER ASS TO A PULP ......

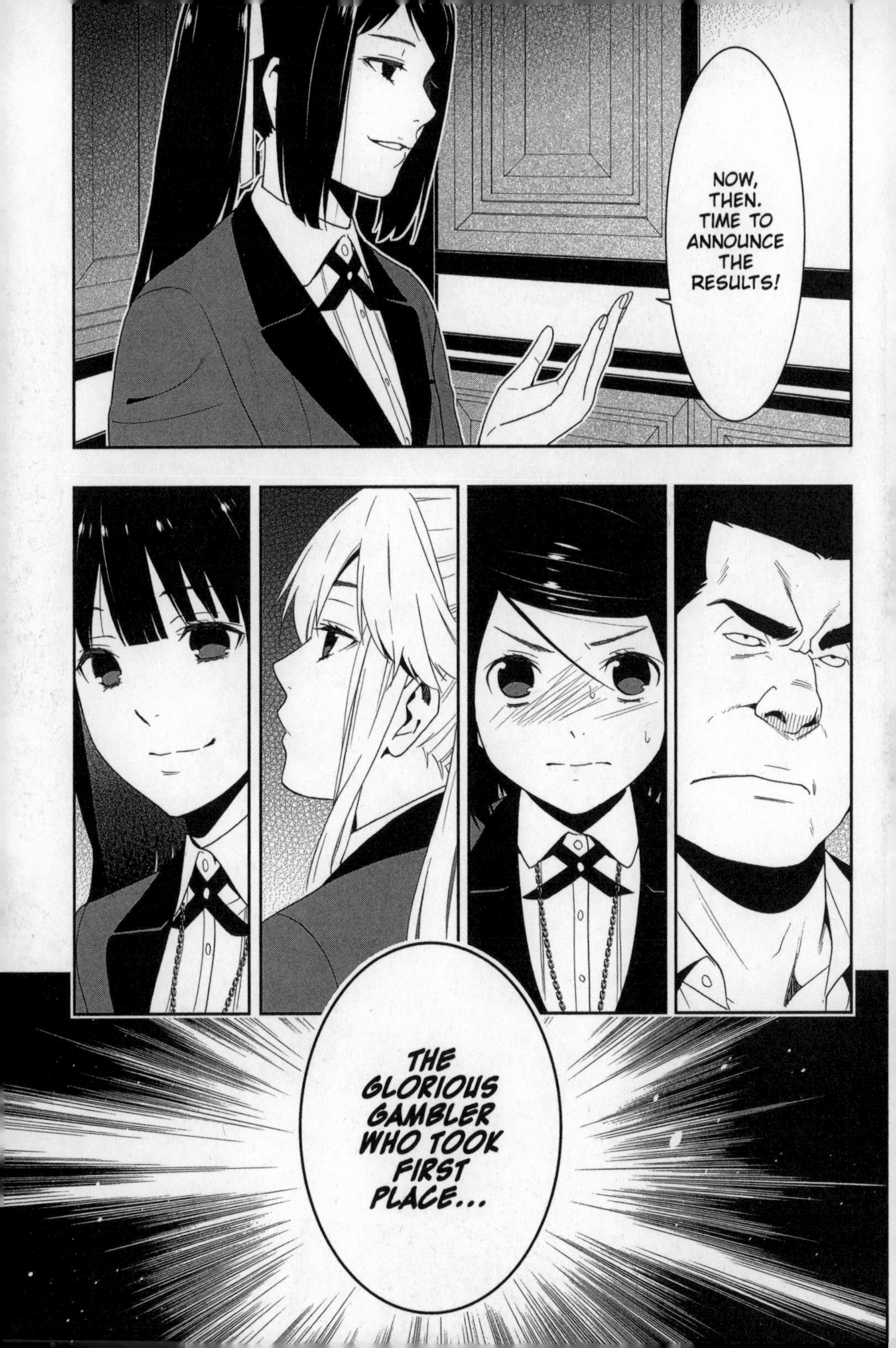
NOW, THEN. TIME TO ANNOUNCE THE RESULTS!
THE GLORIOUS GAMBLER WHO TOOK FIRST PLACE...

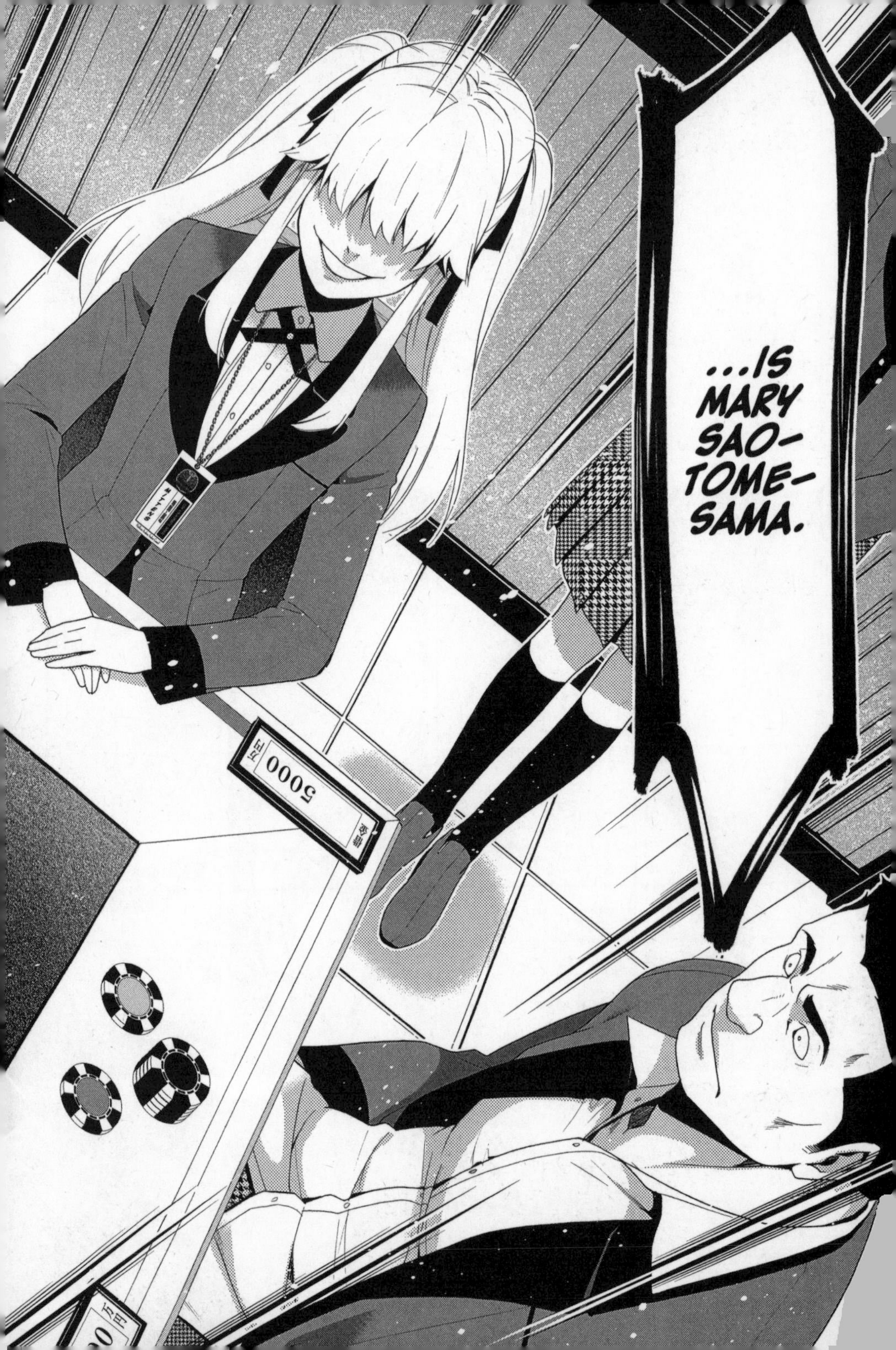
...IS MARY SAO-TOME-SAMA.

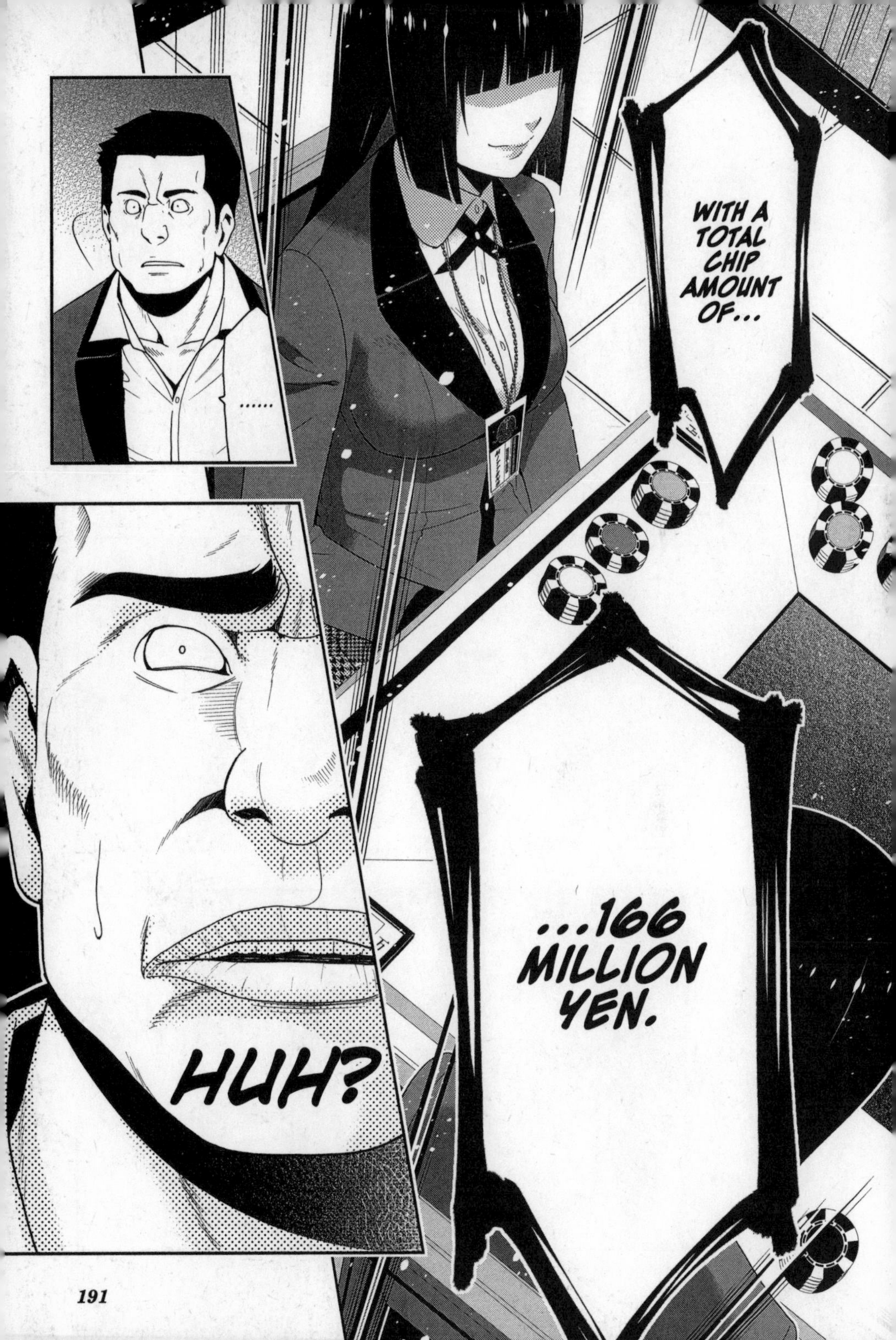
WITH A TOTAL CHIP AMOUNT OF...
......
...166 MILLION YEN.
HUH?

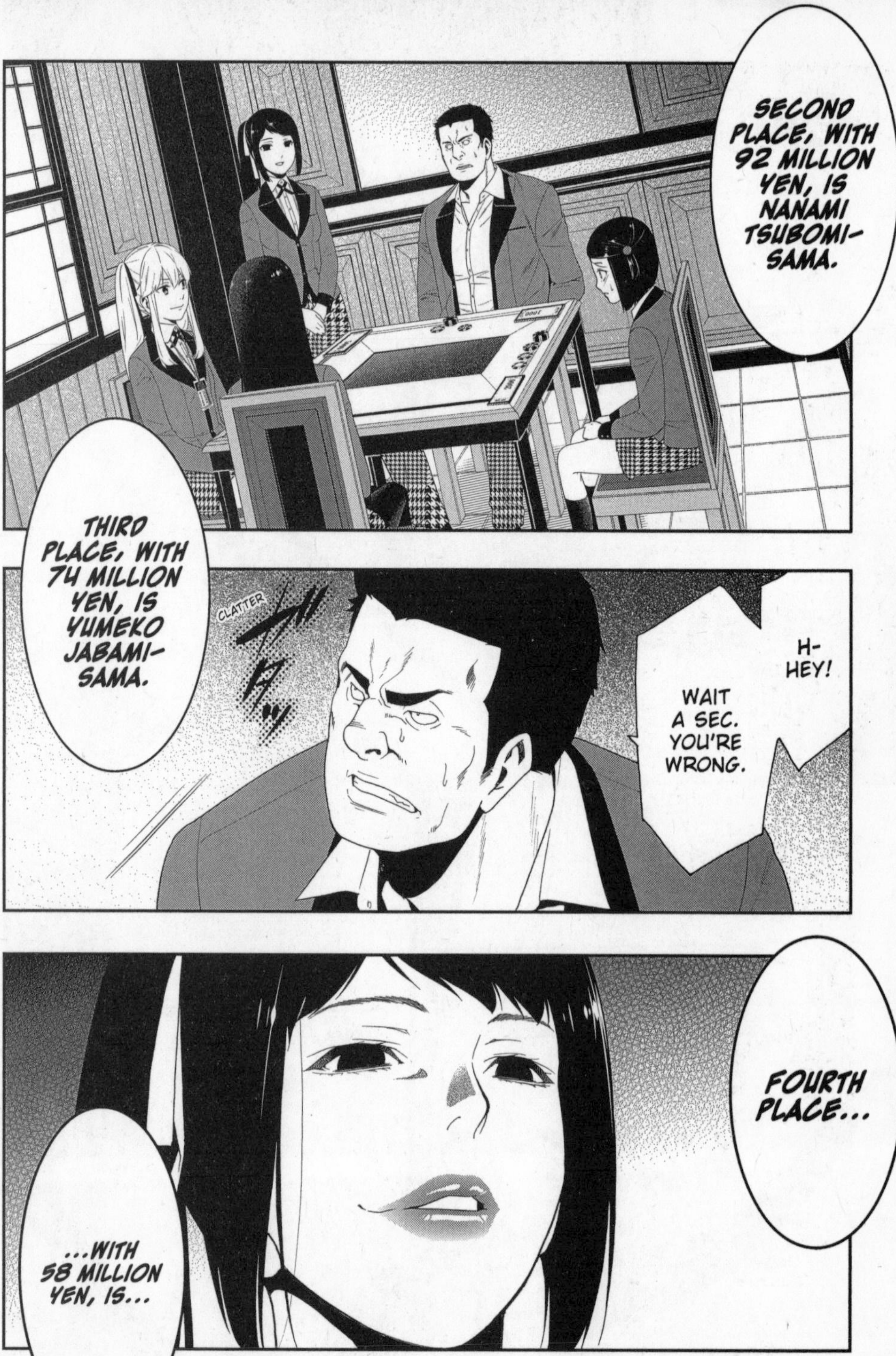
SECOND PLACE, WITH 92 MILLION YEN, IS NANAMI TSUBOMI-SAMA.
THIRD PLACE, WITH 74 MILLION YEN, IS YUMEKO JABAMI-SAMA.
CLATTER
H-HEY!
WAIT A SEC. YOU'RE WRONG.
FOURTH PLACE...
...WITH 58 MILLION YEN, IS...

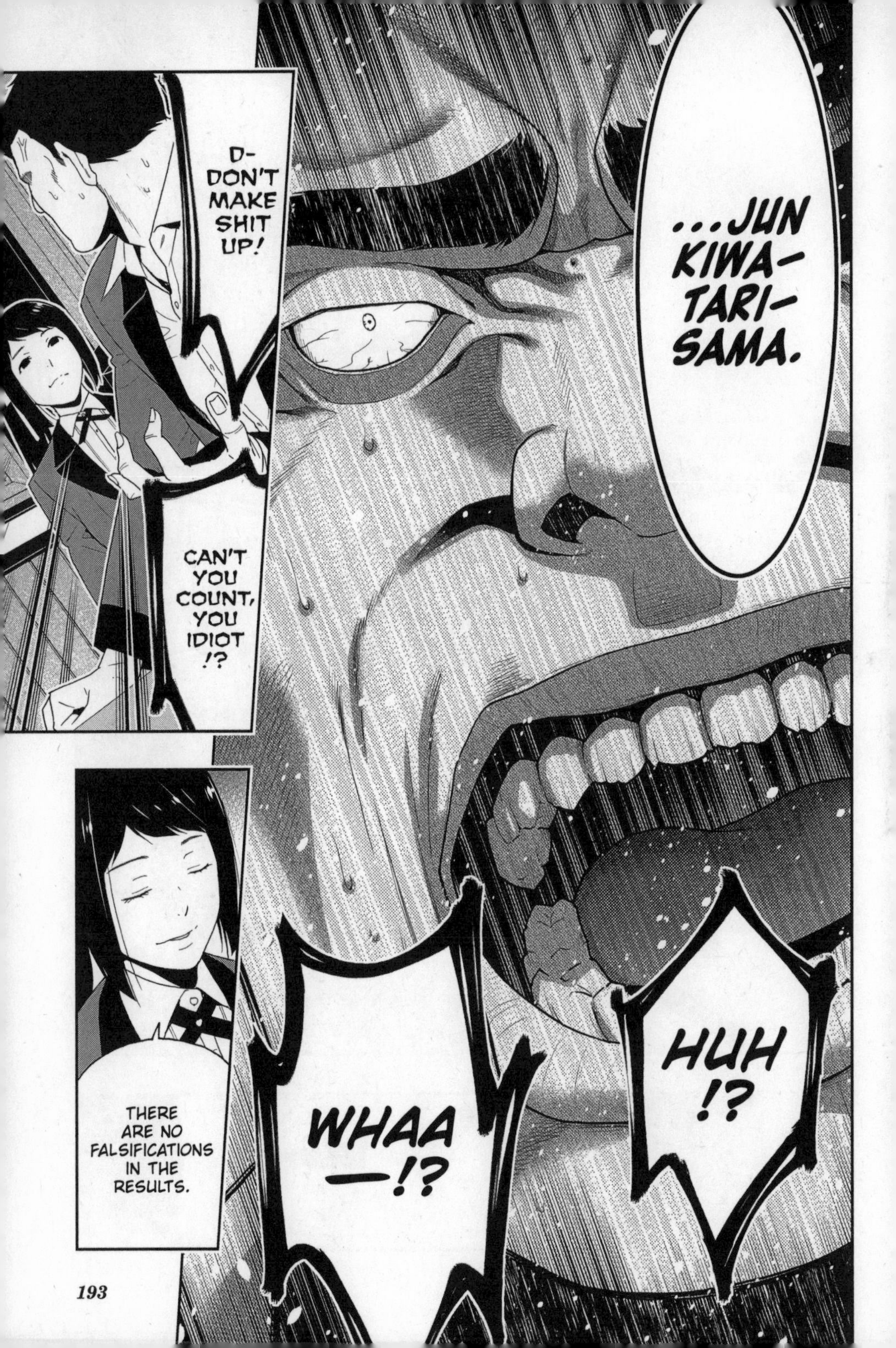

...JUN KIWATARI-SAMA.
HUH!?
WHAA—!?
D-DON'T MAKE SHIT UP!
CAN'T YOU COUNT, YOU IDIOT!?
THERE ARE NO FALSIFICATIONS IN THE RESULTS.

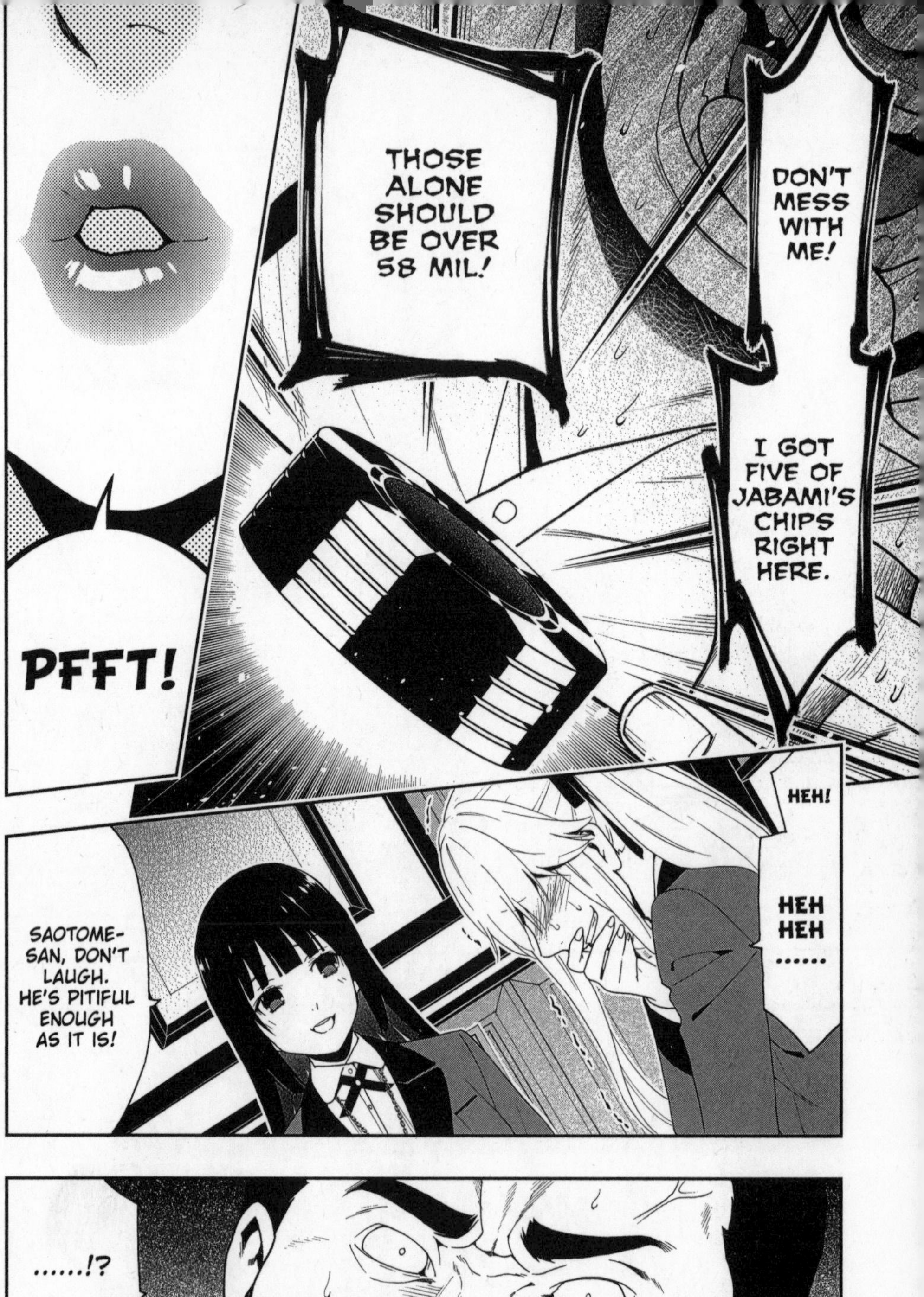
DON'T MESS WITH ME!
I GOT FIVE OF JABAMI'S CHIPS RIGHT HERE.
THOSE ALONE SHOULD BE OVER 58 MIL!
PFFT!
HEH!
HEH HEH ......
SAOTOME-SAN, DON'T LAUGH. HE'S PITIFUL ENOUGH AS IT IS!
......!?

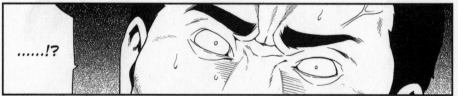

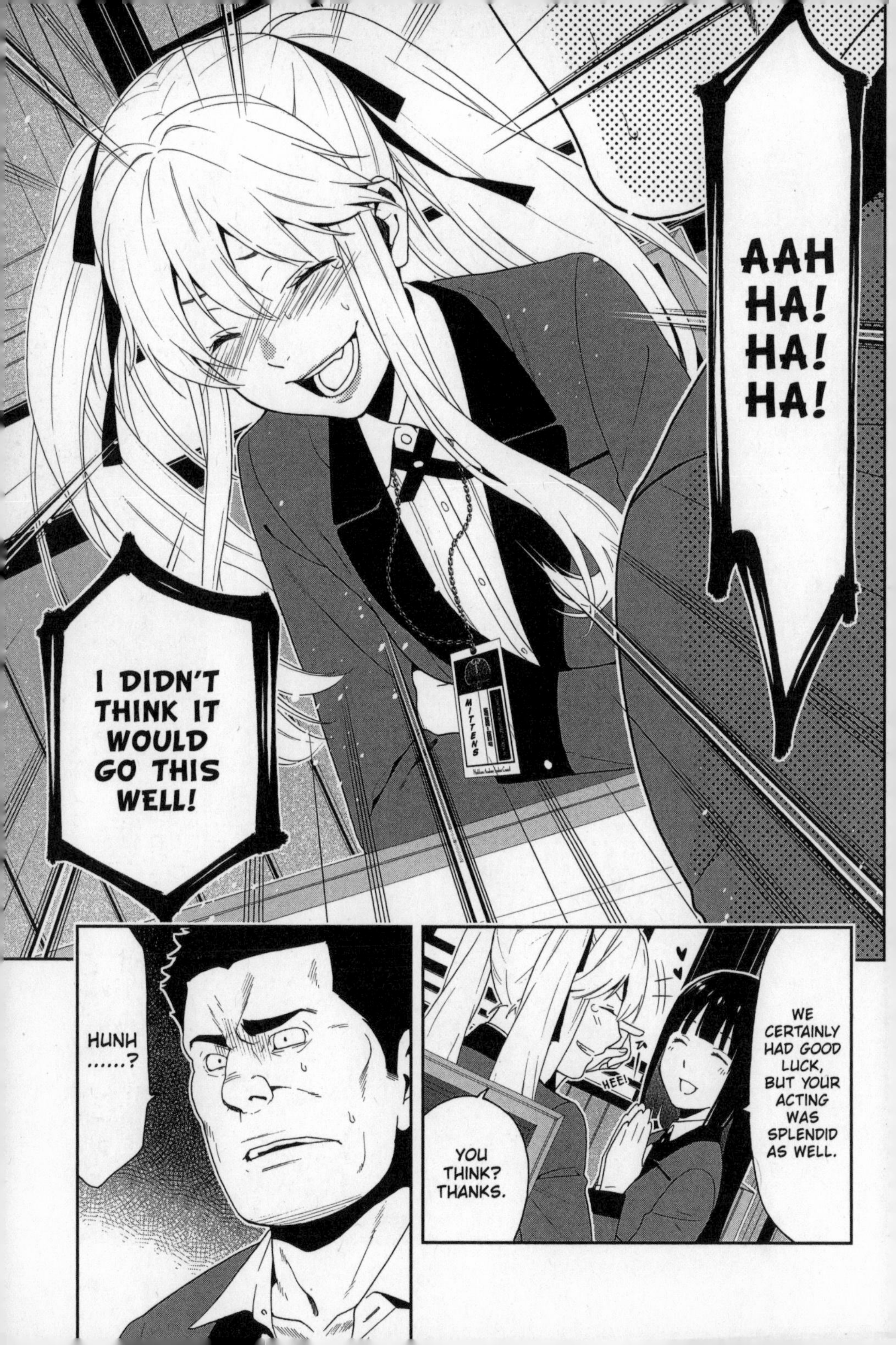
AAH HA! HA! HA!
I DIDN'T THINK IT WOULD GO THIS WELL!
WE CERTAINLY HAD GOOD LUCK, BUT YOUR ACTING WAS SPLENDID AS WELL.
HEE!
YOU THINK? THANKS.
HUNH ......?

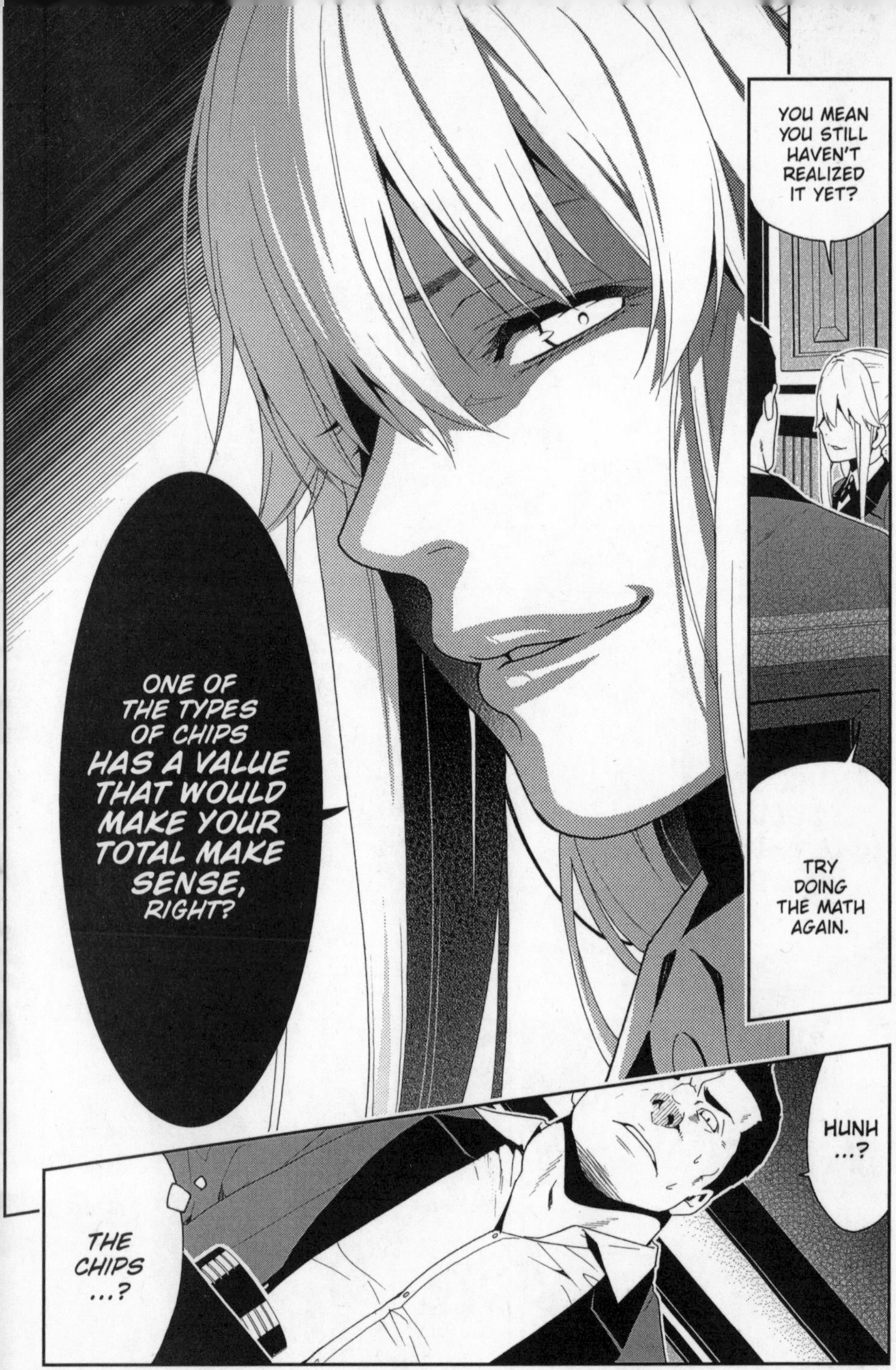
YOU MEAN YOU STILL HAVEN'T REALIZED IT YET?
TRY DOING THE MATH AGAIN.
ONE OF THE TYPES OF CHIPS HAS A VALUE THAT WOULD MAKE YOUR TOTAL MAKE SENSE, RIGHT?
HUNH ...?
THE CHIPS ...?

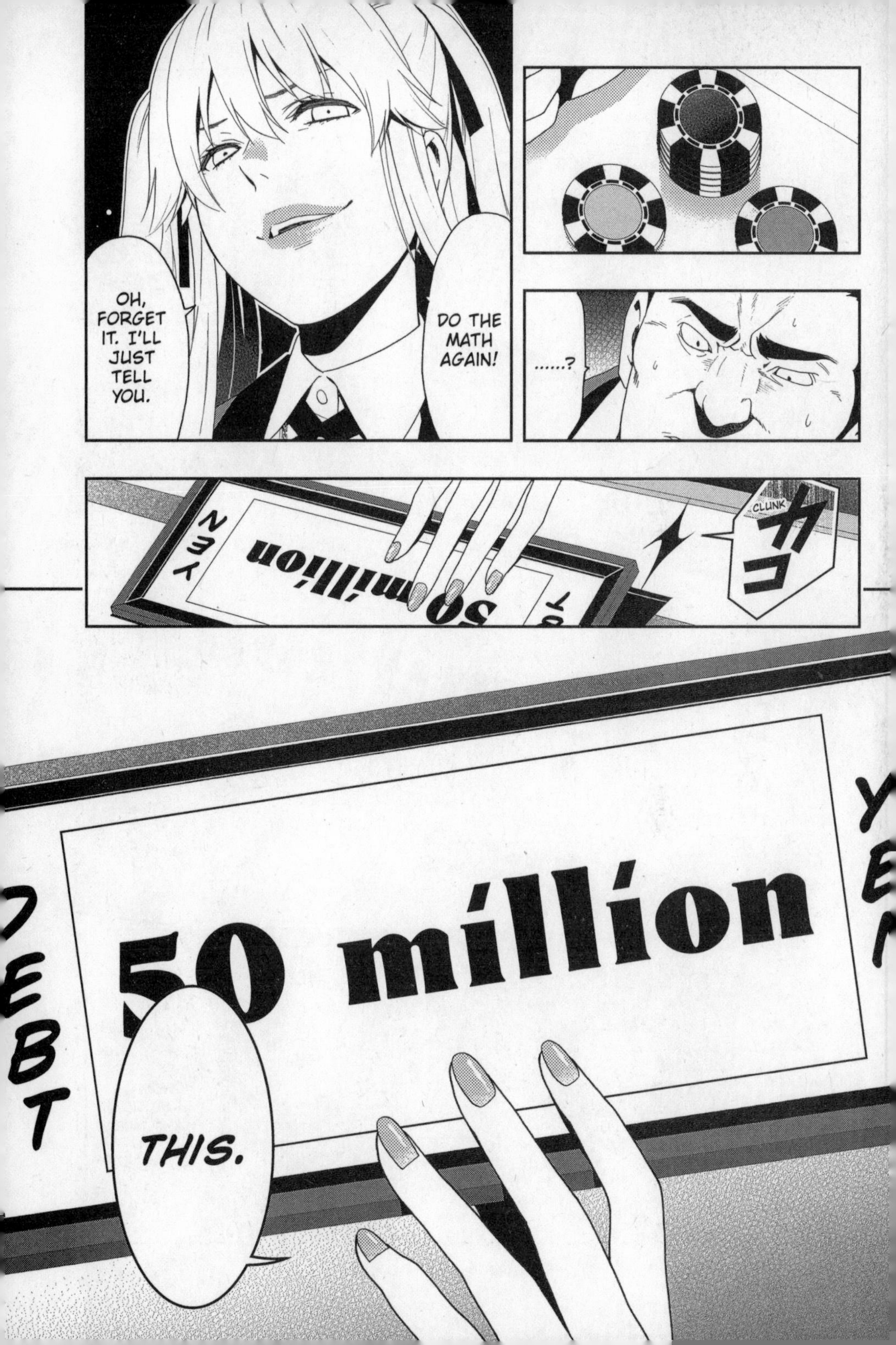
......?
DO THE MATH AGAIN!
OH, FORGET IT. I'LL JUST TELL YOU.
CLINK
YEN
50 million
YEN
50 million
DEBT
THIS.

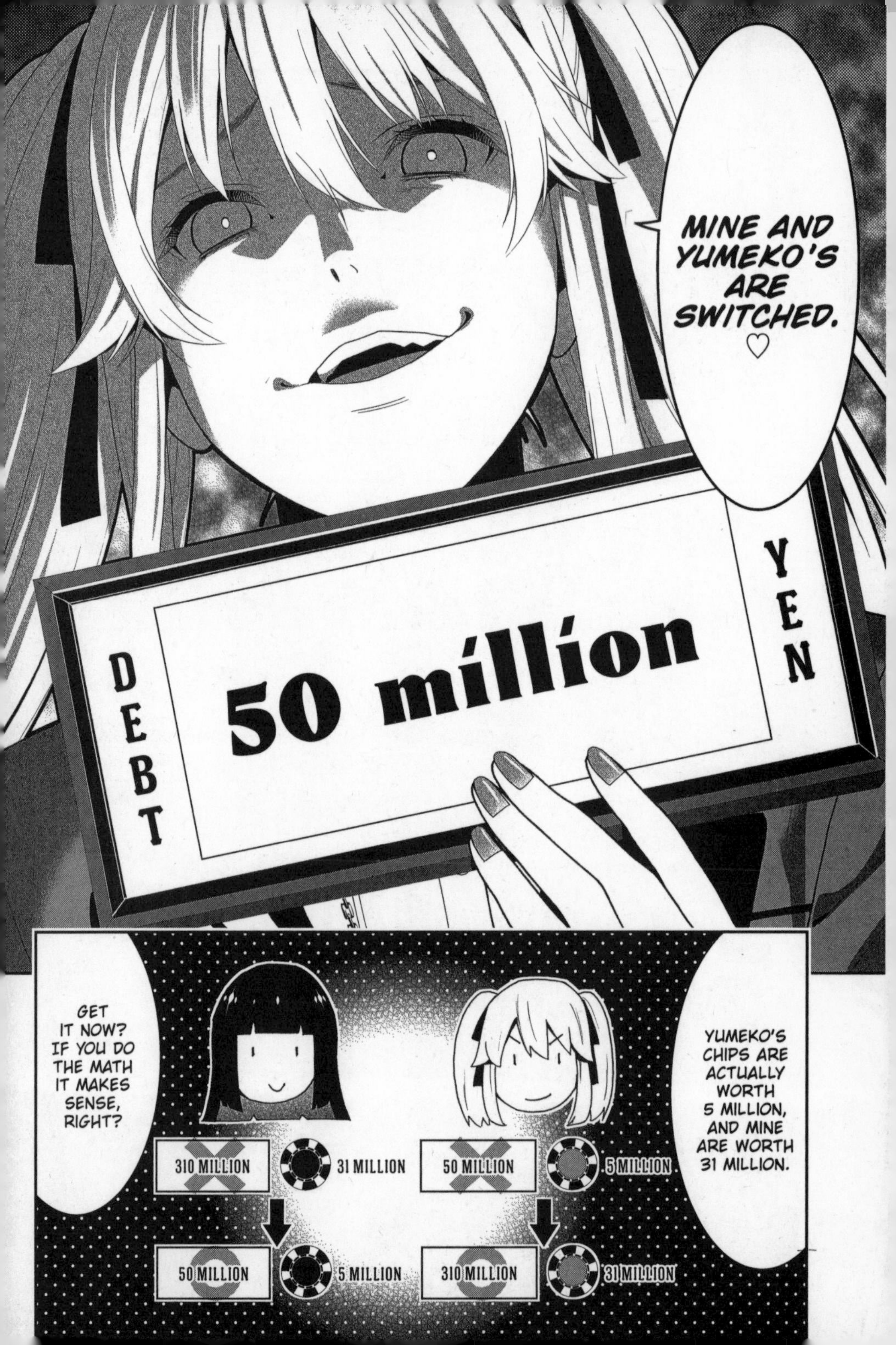
MINE AND YUMEKO'S ARE SWITCHED. ♡
DEBT
50 million
YEN
YUMEKO'S CHIPS ARE ACTUALLY WORTH 5 MILLION, AND MINE ARE WORTH 31 MILLION.
GET IT NOW? IF YOU DO THE MATH IT MAKES SENSE, RIGHT?
50 MILLION
5 MILLION
310 MILLION
31 MILLION
310 MILLION
31 MILLION
50 MILLION
5 MILLION

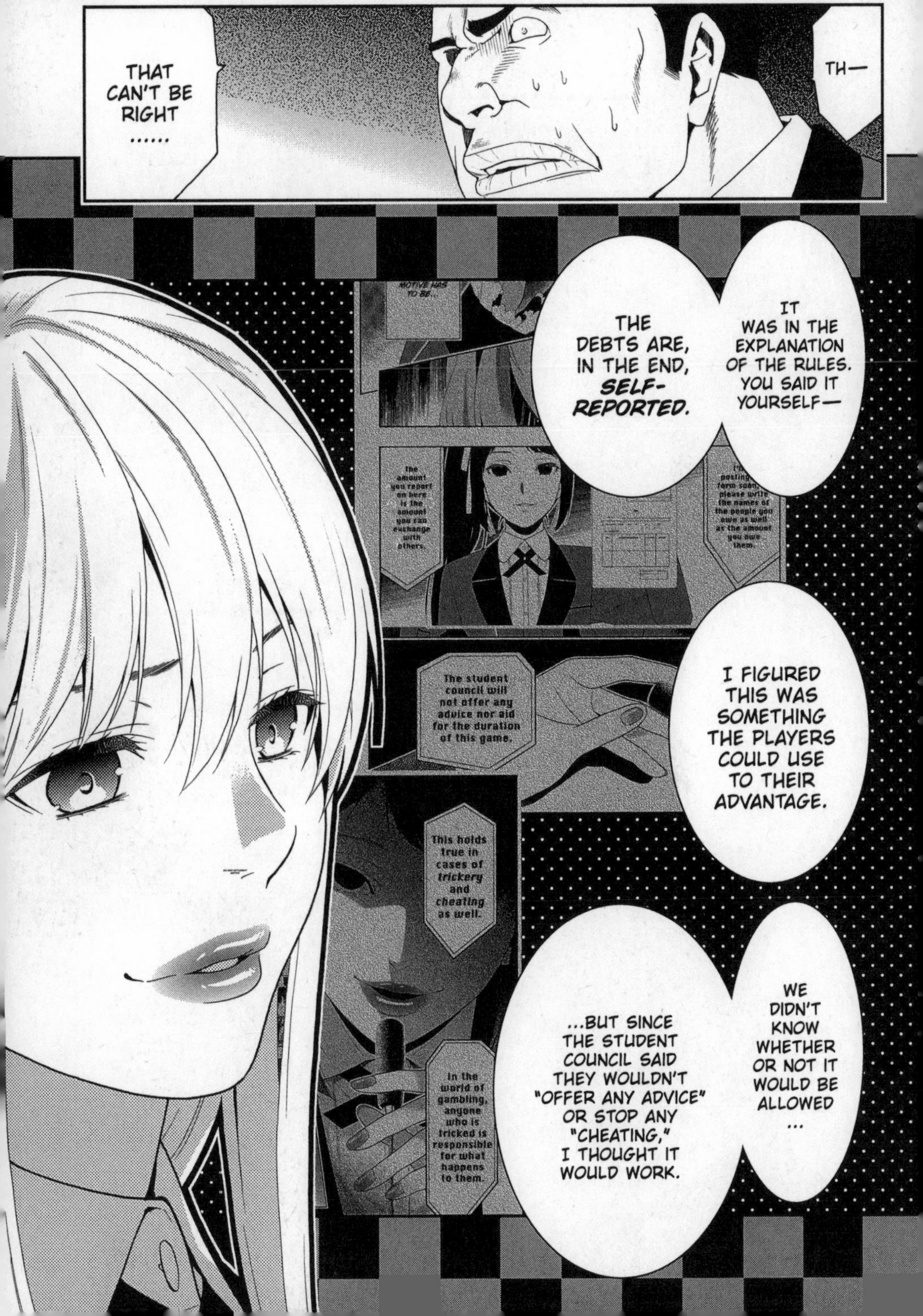
TH—
THAT CAN'T BE RIGHT ......
IT WAS IN THE EXPLANATION OF THE RULES. YOU SAID IT YOURSELF—
THE DEBTS ARE, IN THE END, *SELF-REPORTED.*
MOTIVE HAS TO BE...
posting form soon; please write the names of the people you owe as well as the amount you owe them.
The amount you report on here is the amount you can exchange with others.
I FIGURED THIS WAS SOMETHING THE PLAYERS COULD USE TO THEIR ADVANTAGE.
The student council will not offer any advice nor aid for the duration of this game.
This holds true in cases of *trickery* and *cheating* as well.
WE DIDN'T KNOW WHETHER OR NOT IT WOULD BE ALLOWED ...
...BUT SINCE THE STUDENT COUNCIL SAID THEY WOULDN'T "OFFER ANY ADVICE" OR STOP ANY "CHEATING," I THOUGHT IT WOULD WORK.
In the world of gambling, anyone who is tricked is responsible for what happens to them.

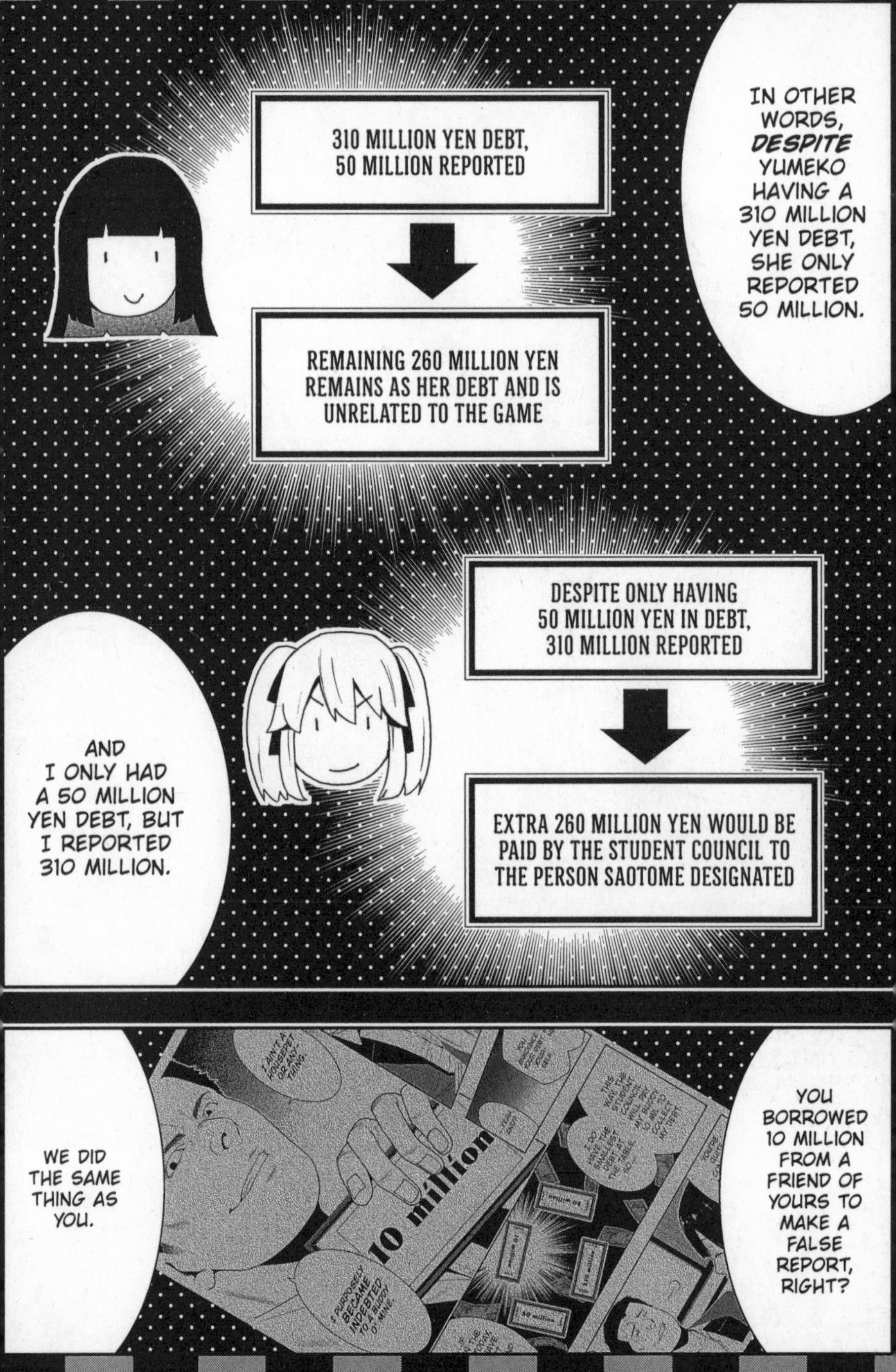
IN OTHER WORDS, DESPITE YUMEKO HAVING A 310 MILLION YEN DEBT, SHE ONLY REPORTED 50 MILLION.
310 MILLION YEN DEBT, 50 MILLION REPORTED
REMAINING 260 MILLION YEN REMAINS AS HER DEBT AND IS UNRELATED TO THE GAME
DESPITE ONLY HAVING 50 MILLION YEN IN DEBT, 310 MILLION REPORTED
EXTRA 260 MILLION YEN WOULD BE PAID BY THE STUDENT COUNCIL TO THE PERSON SAOTOME DESIGNATED
AND I ONLY HAD A 50 MILLION YEN DEBT, BUT I REPORTED 310 MILLION.
YOU BORROWED 10 MILLION FROM A FRIEND OF YOURS TO MAKE A FALSE REPORT, RIGHT?
I AIN'T A HOUSEPET OR ANY-THING.
I DO HAVE THE SMALLEST DEBT AT THE TABLE, SO...
10 million
I PURPOSELY BECAME INDEBTED TO A BUDDY O' MINE.
WE DID THE SAME THING AS YOU.

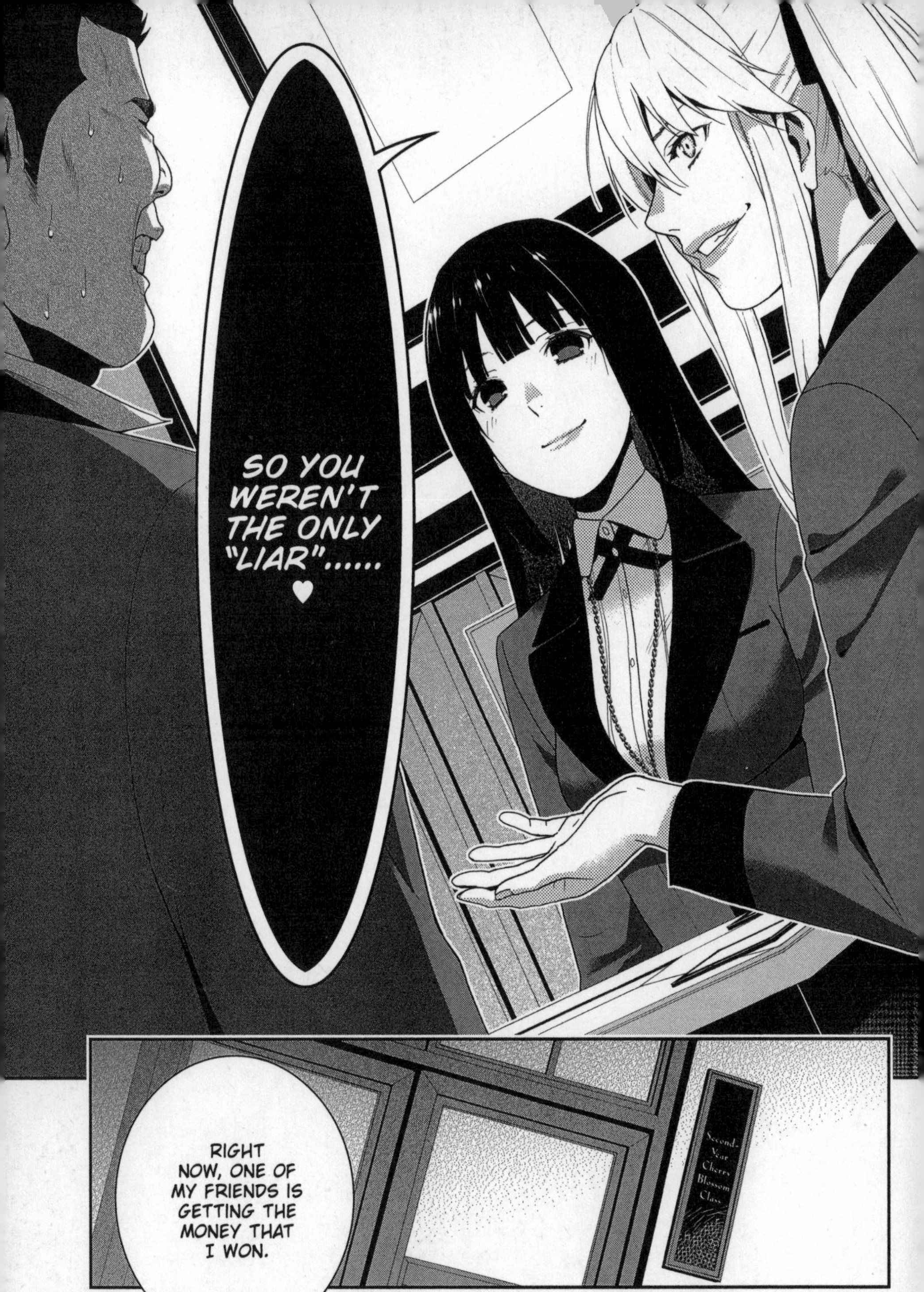
SO YOU WEREN'T THE ONLY "LIAR"...... ♥
RIGHT NOW, ONE OF MY FRIENDS IS GETTING THE MONEY THAT I WON.
Second-Year Cherry Blossom Class

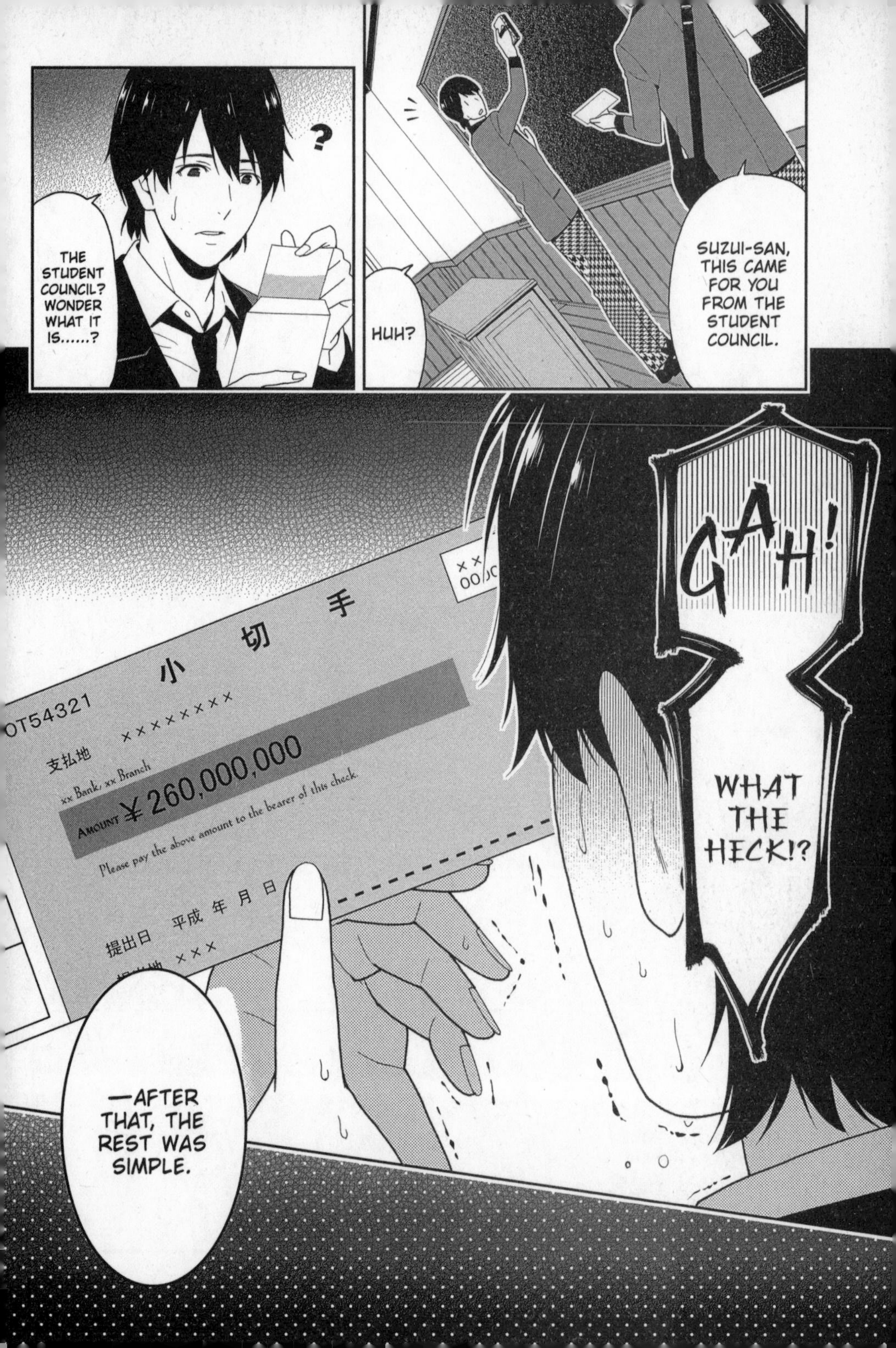
SUZUI-SAN, THIS CAME FOR YOU FROM THE STUDENT COUNCIL.
HUH?
THE STUDENT COUNCIL? WONDER WHAT IT IS......?
GAH!
WHAT THE HECK!?
小切手
OT54321
支払地 ××××××××
xx Bank, xx Branch
AMOUNT ¥260,000,000
Please pay the above amount to the bearer of this check.
提出日 平成 年 月 日
×××
—AFTER THAT, THE REST WAS SIMPLE.

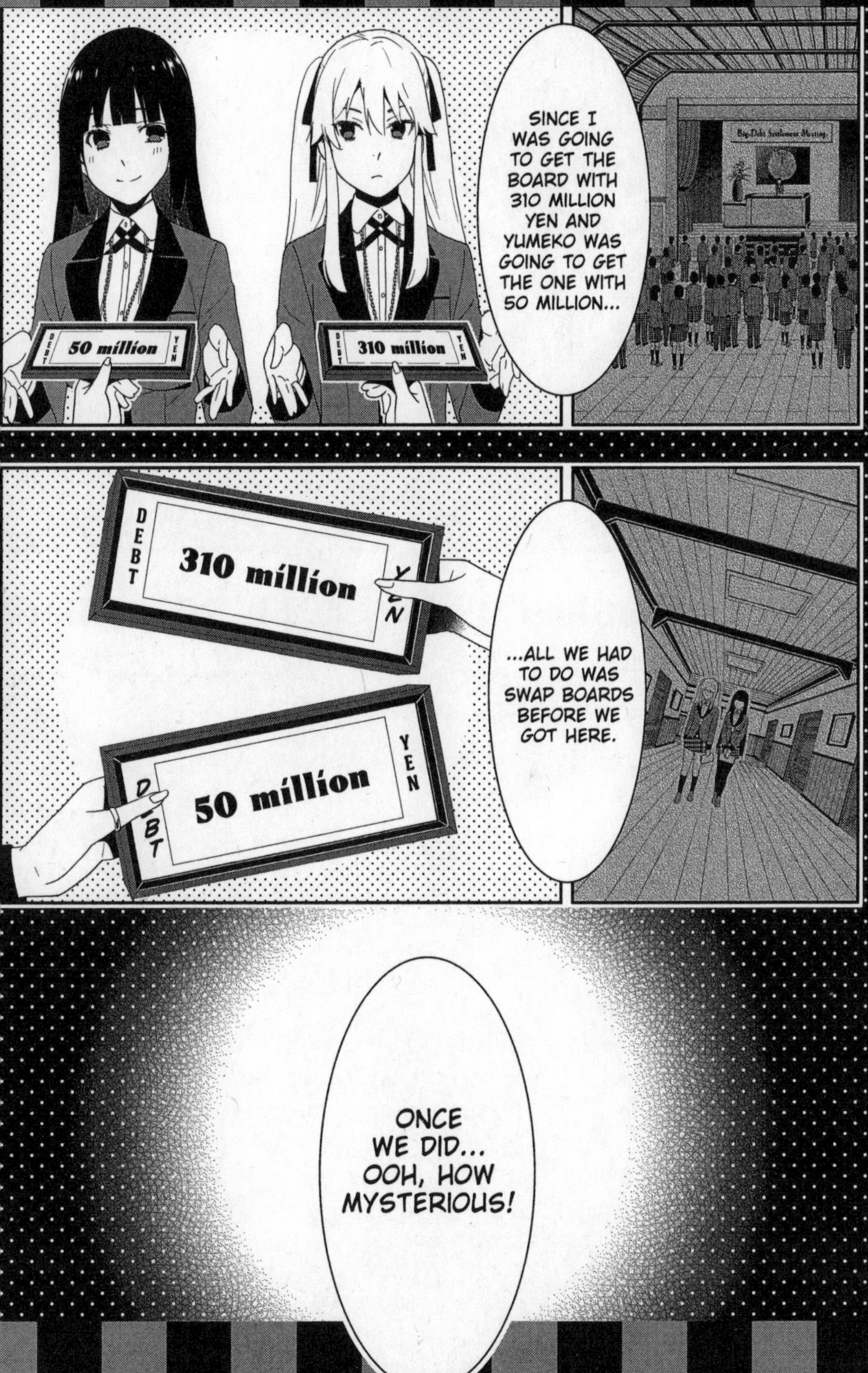
SINCE I WAS GOING TO GET THE BOARD WITH 310 MILLION YEN AND YUMEKO WAS GOING TO GET THE ONE WITH 50 MILLION...
Big-Debt Settlement Meeting
DEBT 310 million YEN
DEBT 50 million YEN
...ALL WE HAD TO DO WAS SWAP BOARDS BEFORE WE GOT HERE.
DEBT 310 million YEN
DEBT 50 million YEN
ONCE WE DID... OOH, HOW MYSTERIOUS!

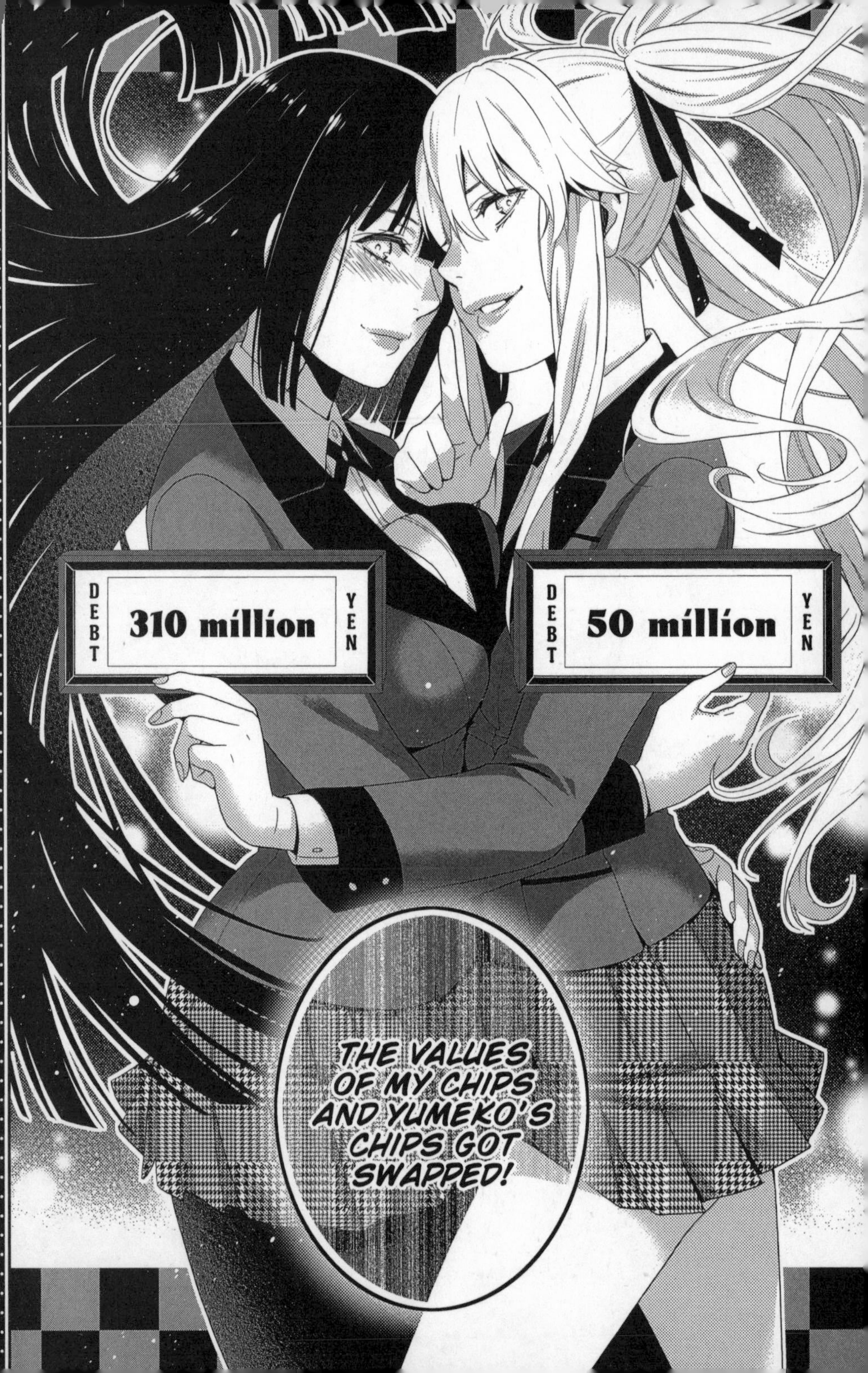
DEBT 310 million YEN
DEBT 50 million YEN
THE VALUES OF MY CHIPS AND YUMEKO'S CHIPS GOT SWAPPED!

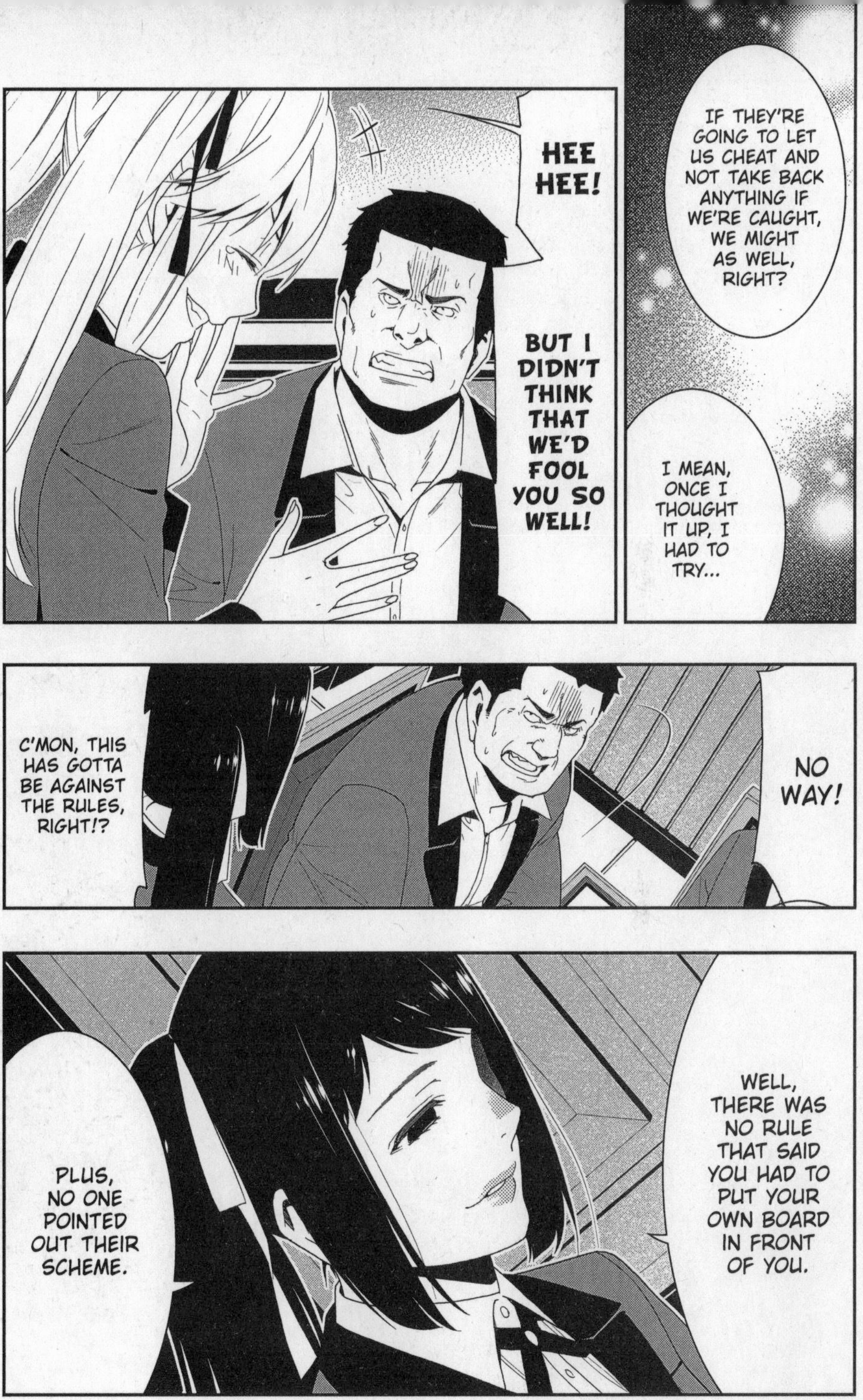
IF THEY'RE GOING TO LET US CHEAT AND NOT TAKE BACK ANYTHING IF WE'RE CAUGHT, WE MIGHT AS WELL, RIGHT?
I MEAN, ONCE I THOUGHT IT UP, I HAD TO TRY...
HEE HEE!
BUT I DIDN'T THINK THAT WE'D FOOL YOU SO WELL!
NO WAY!
C'MON, THIS HAS GOTTA BE AGAINST THE RULES, RIGHT!?
WELL, THERE WAS NO RULE THAT SAID YOU HAD TO PUT YOUR OWN BOARD IN FRONT OF YOU.
PLUS, NO ONE POINTED OUT THEIR SCHEME.

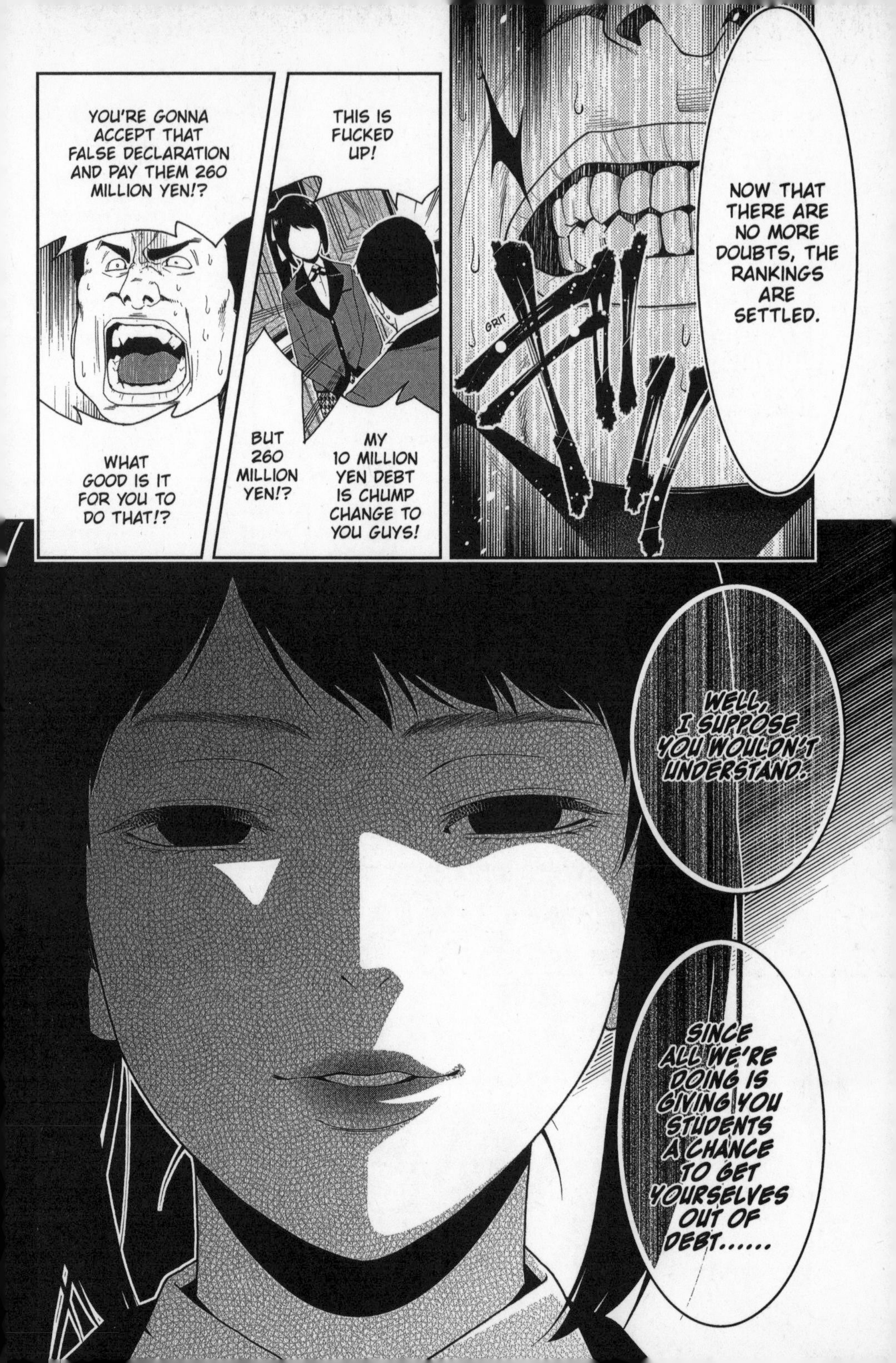
NOW THAT THERE ARE NO MORE DOUBTS, THE RANKINGS ARE SETTLED.
GRIT
THIS IS FUCKED UP!
MY 10 MILLION YEN DEBT IS CHUMP CHANGE TO YOU GUYS!
BUT 260 MILLION YEN!?
YOU'RE GONNA ACCEPT THAT FALSE DECLARATION AND PAY THEM 260 MILLION YEN!?
WHAT GOOD IS IT FOR YOU TO DO THAT!?
WELL, I SUPPOSE YOU WOULDN'T UNDERSTAND.
SINCE ALL WE'RE DOING IS GIVING YOU STUDENTS A CHANCE TO GET YOURSELVES OUT OF DEBT......

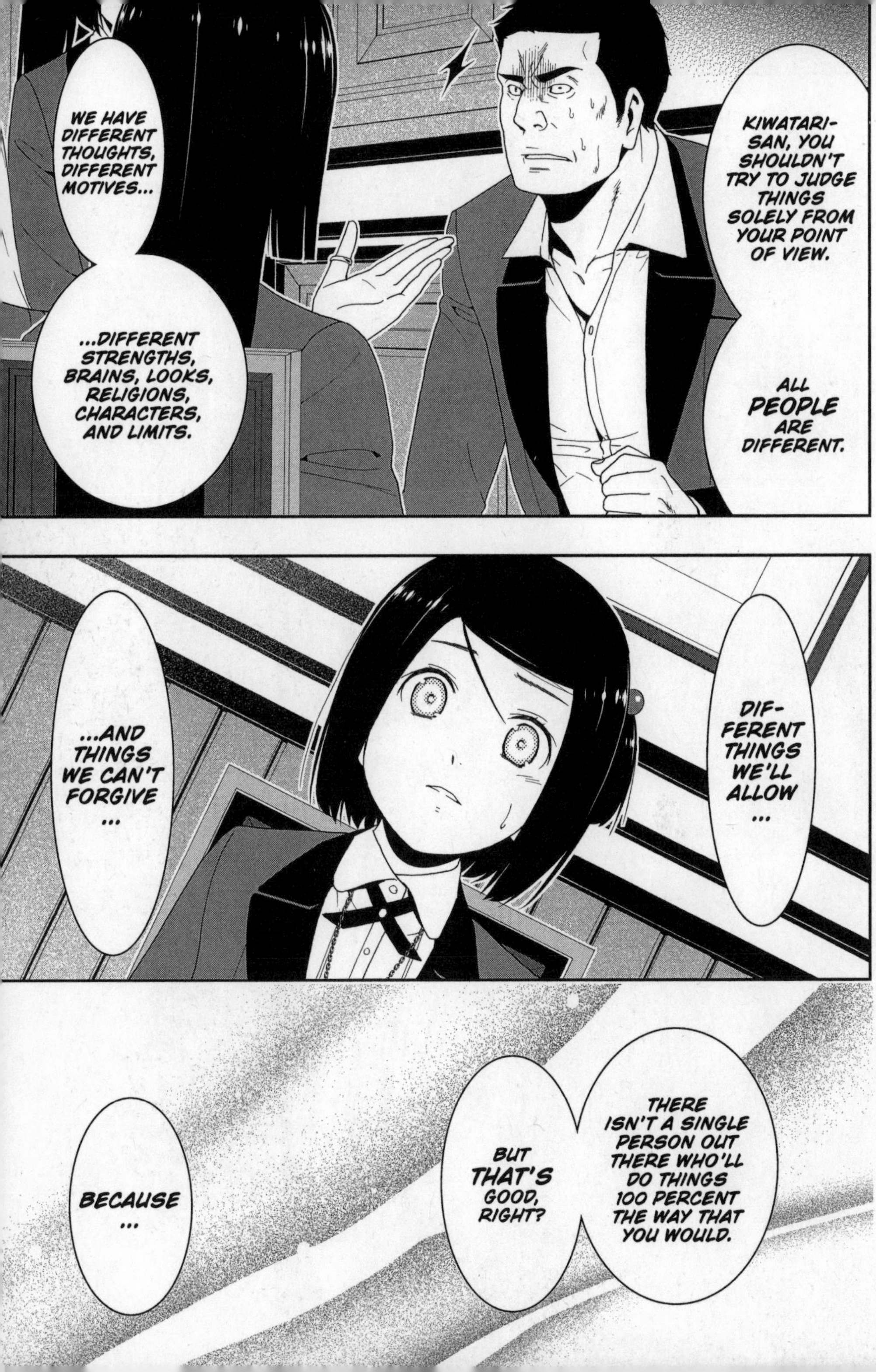
KIWATARI-SAN, YOU SHOULDN'T TRY TO JUDGE THINGS SOLELY FROM YOUR POINT OF VIEW.
ALL PEOPLE ARE DIFFERENT.
WE HAVE DIFFERENT THOUGHTS, DIFFERENT MOTIVES...
...DIFFERENT STRENGTHS, BRAINS, LOOKS, RELIGIONS, CHARACTERS, AND LIMITS.
DIF-FERENT THINGS WE'LL ALLOW ...
...AND THINGS WE CAN'T FORGIVE ...
THERE ISN'T A SINGLE PERSON OUT THERE WHO'LL DO THINGS 100 PERCENT THE WAY THAT YOU WOULD.
BUT THAT'S GOOD, RIGHT?
BECAUSE ...

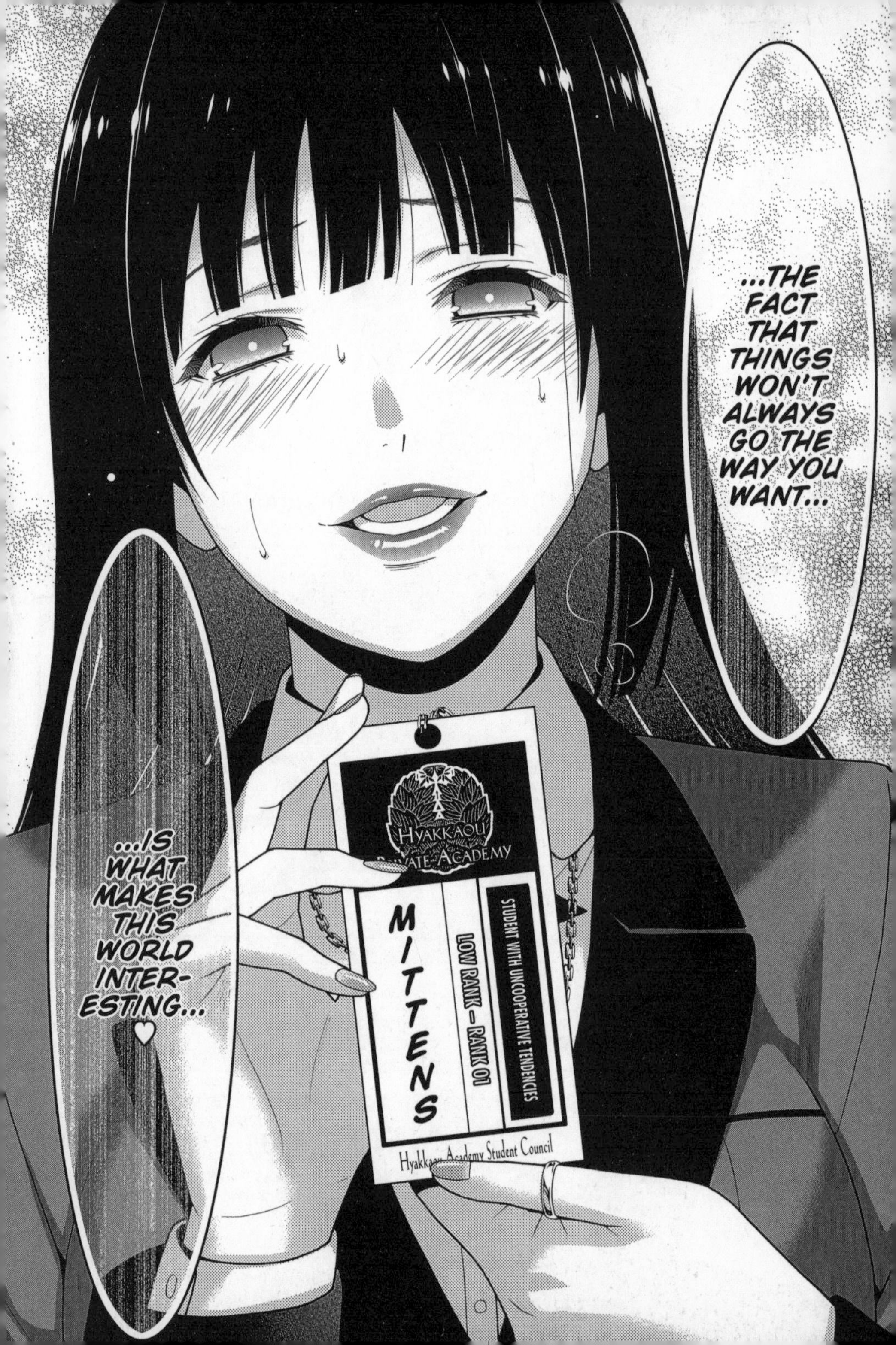
...THE FACT THAT THINGS WON'T ALWAYS GO THE WAY YOU WANT...
...IS WHAT MAKES THIS WORLD INTER-ESTING...♥
HYAKKAOU
MITTENS
LOW RANK - RANK 01
STUDENT WITH UNCOOPERATIVE TENDENCIES

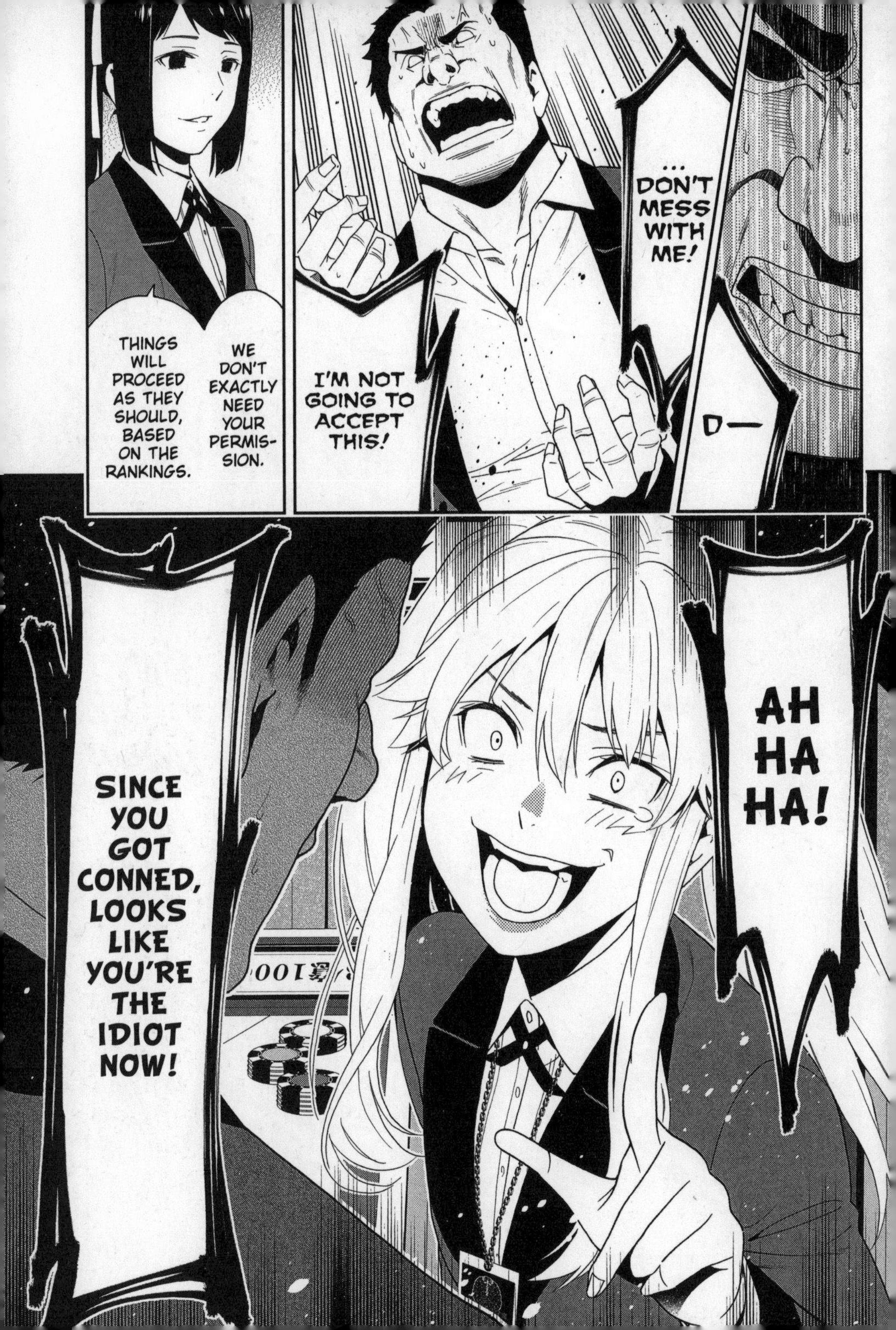

... DON'T MESS WITH ME!
D—
I'M NOT GOING TO ACCEPT THIS!
WE DON'T EXACTLY NEED YOUR PERMISSION.
THINGS WILL PROCEED AS THEY SHOULD, BASED ON THE RANKINGS.
AH HA HA!
SINCE YOU GOT CONNED, LOOKS LIKE YOU'RE THE IDIOT NOW!

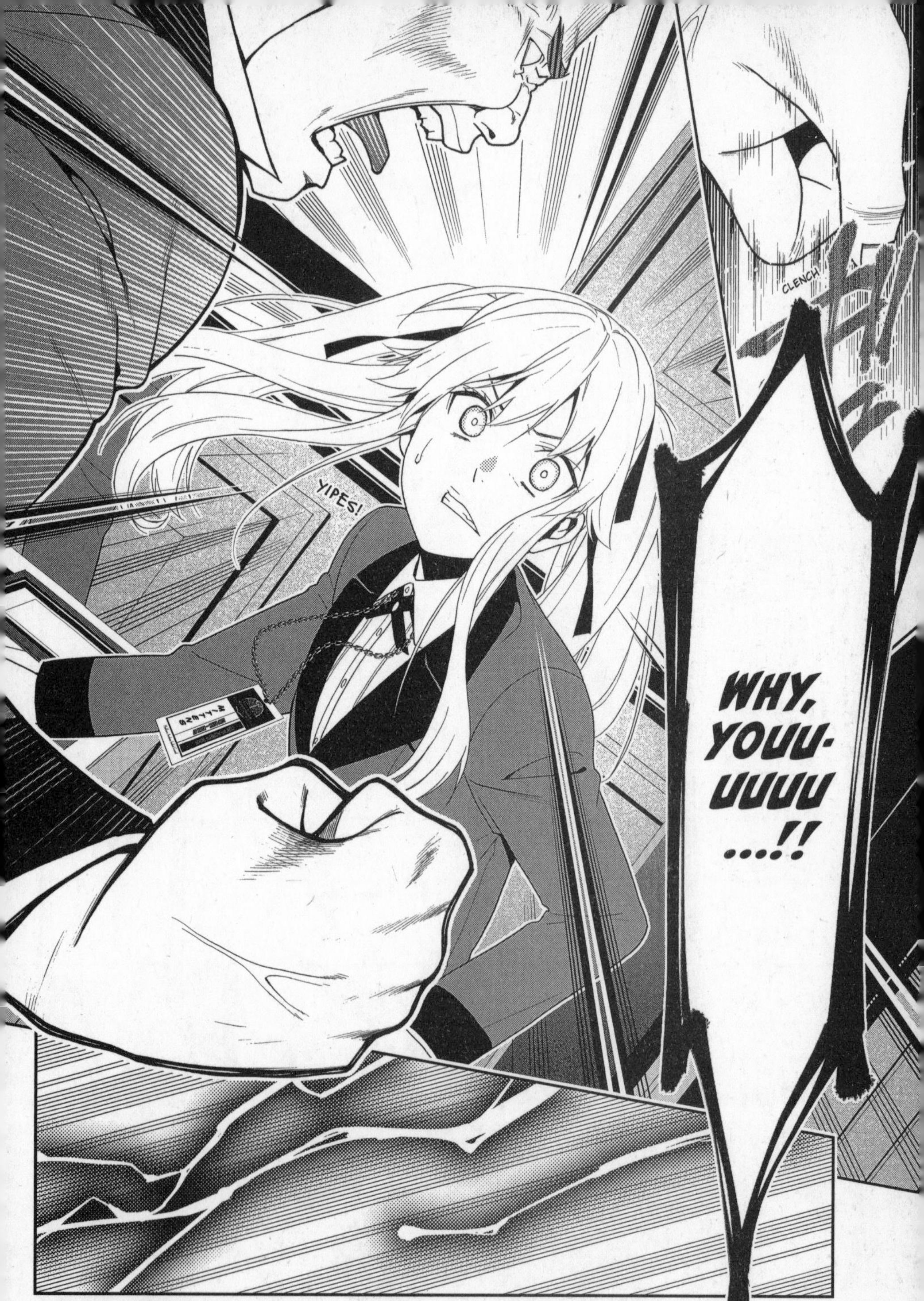
CLENCH
WHY, YOUUU-UUUU ...!!
YIPES!

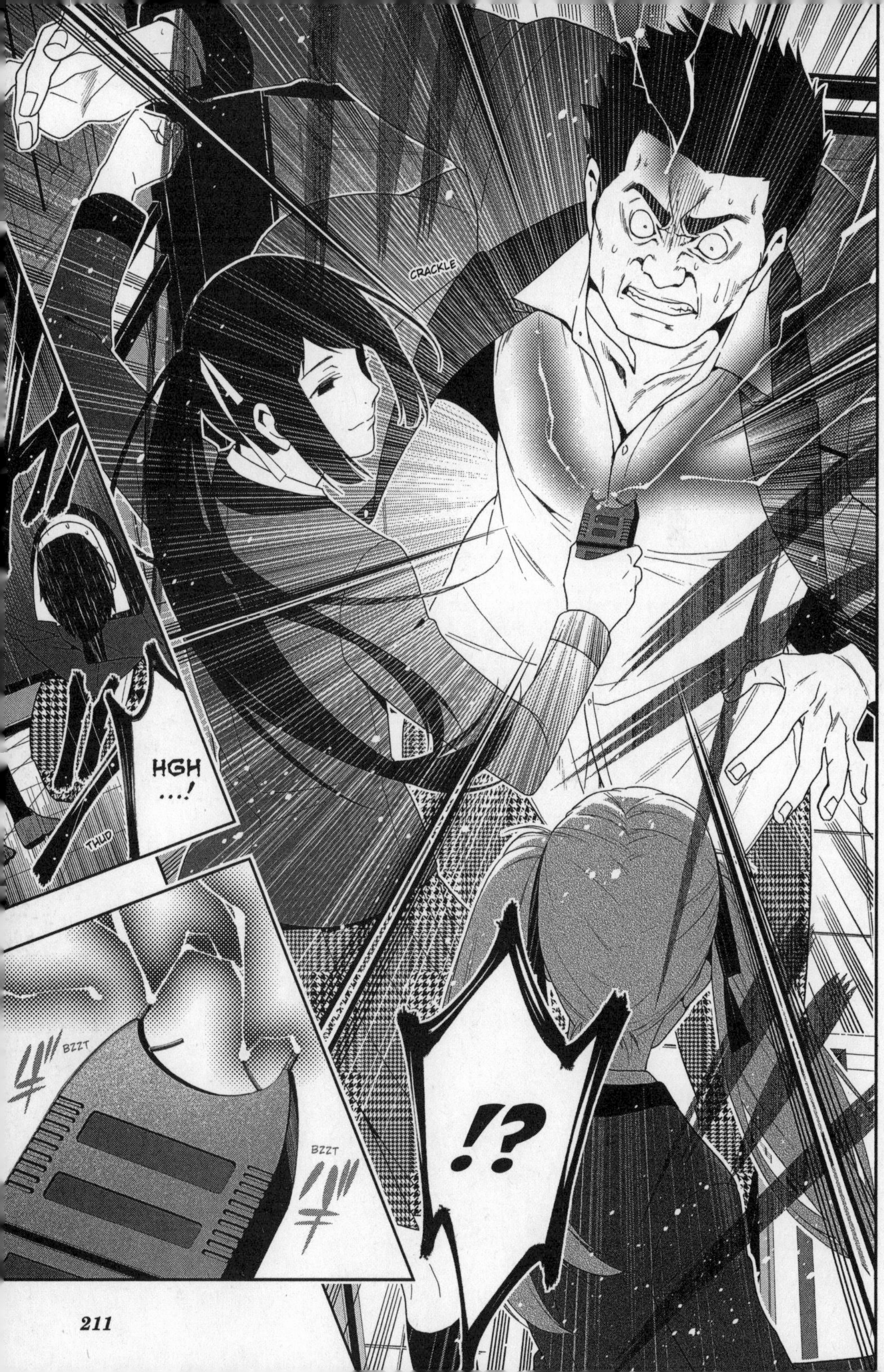
CRACKLE
!?
HGH ...!
THUD
BZZT
BZZT

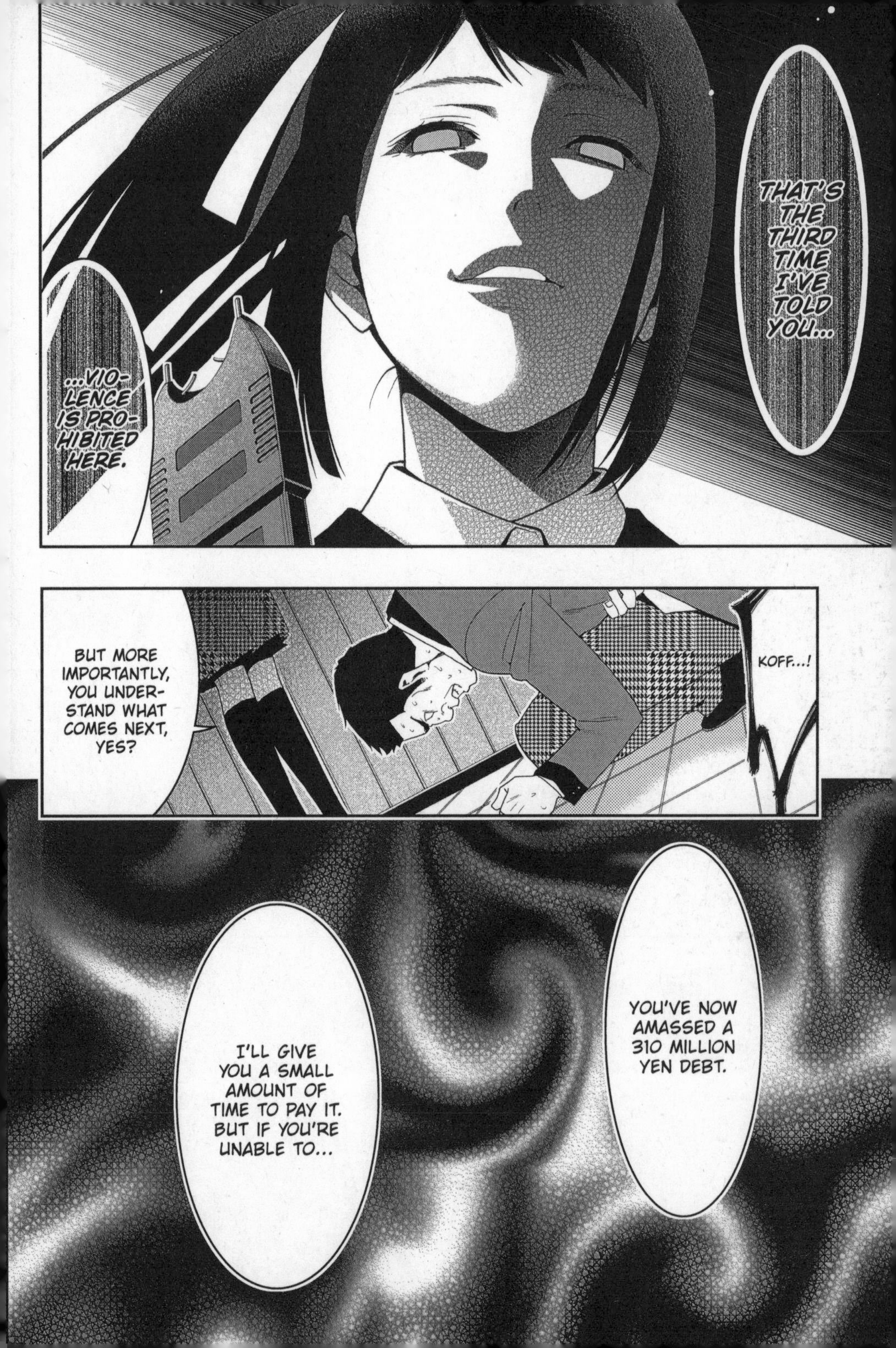
THAT'S THE THIRD TIME I'VE TOLD YOU...
...VIO-LENCE IS PRO-HIBITED HERE.
KOFF...!
BUT MORE IMPORTANTLY, YOU UNDER-STAND WHAT COMES NEXT, YES?
YOU'VE NOW AMASSED A 310 MILLION YEN DEBT.
I'LL GIVE YOU A SMALL AMOUNT OF TIME TO PAY IT. BUT IF YOU'RE UNABLE TO...

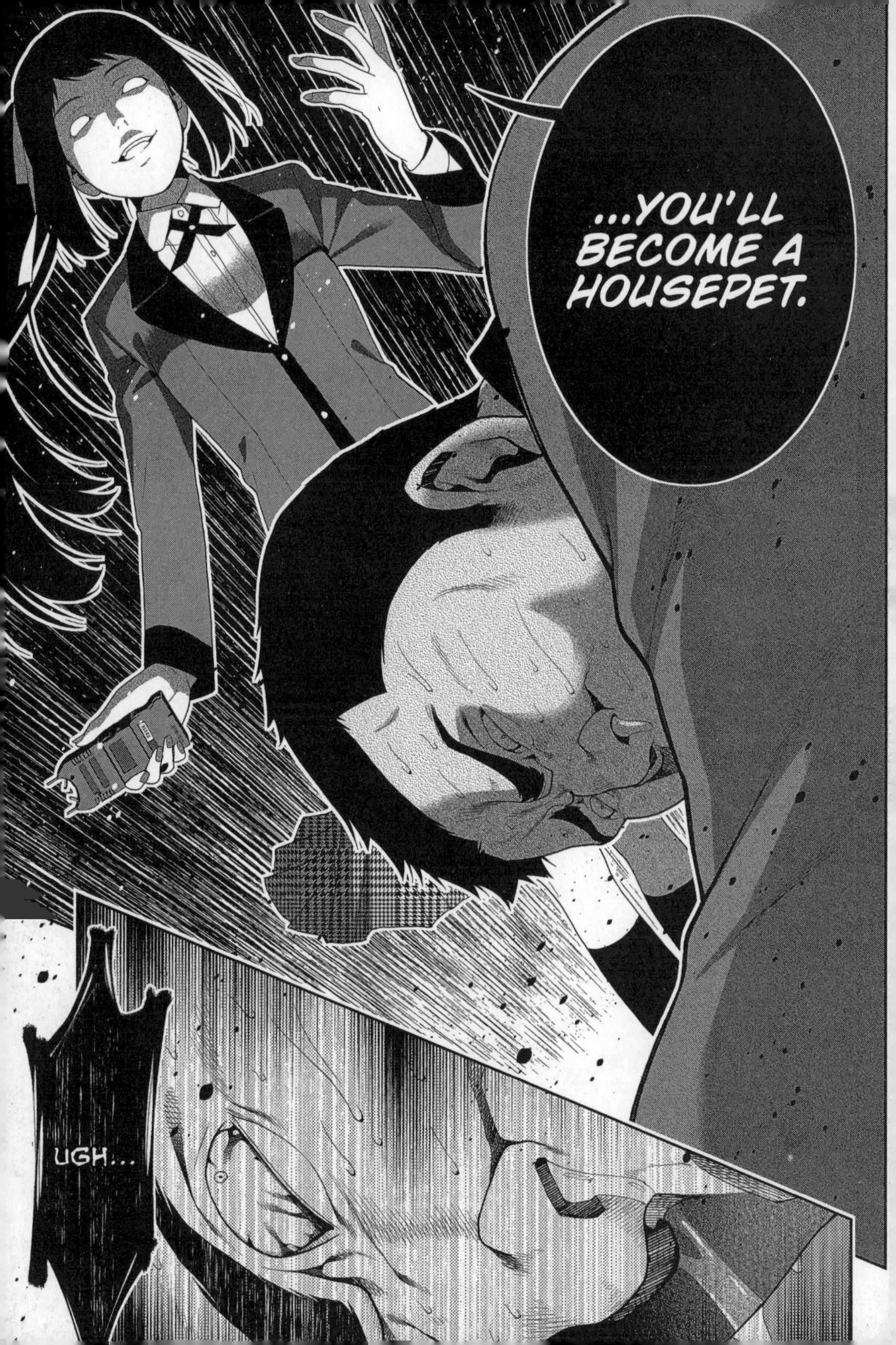
...YOU'LL BECOME A HOUSEPET.
UGH...

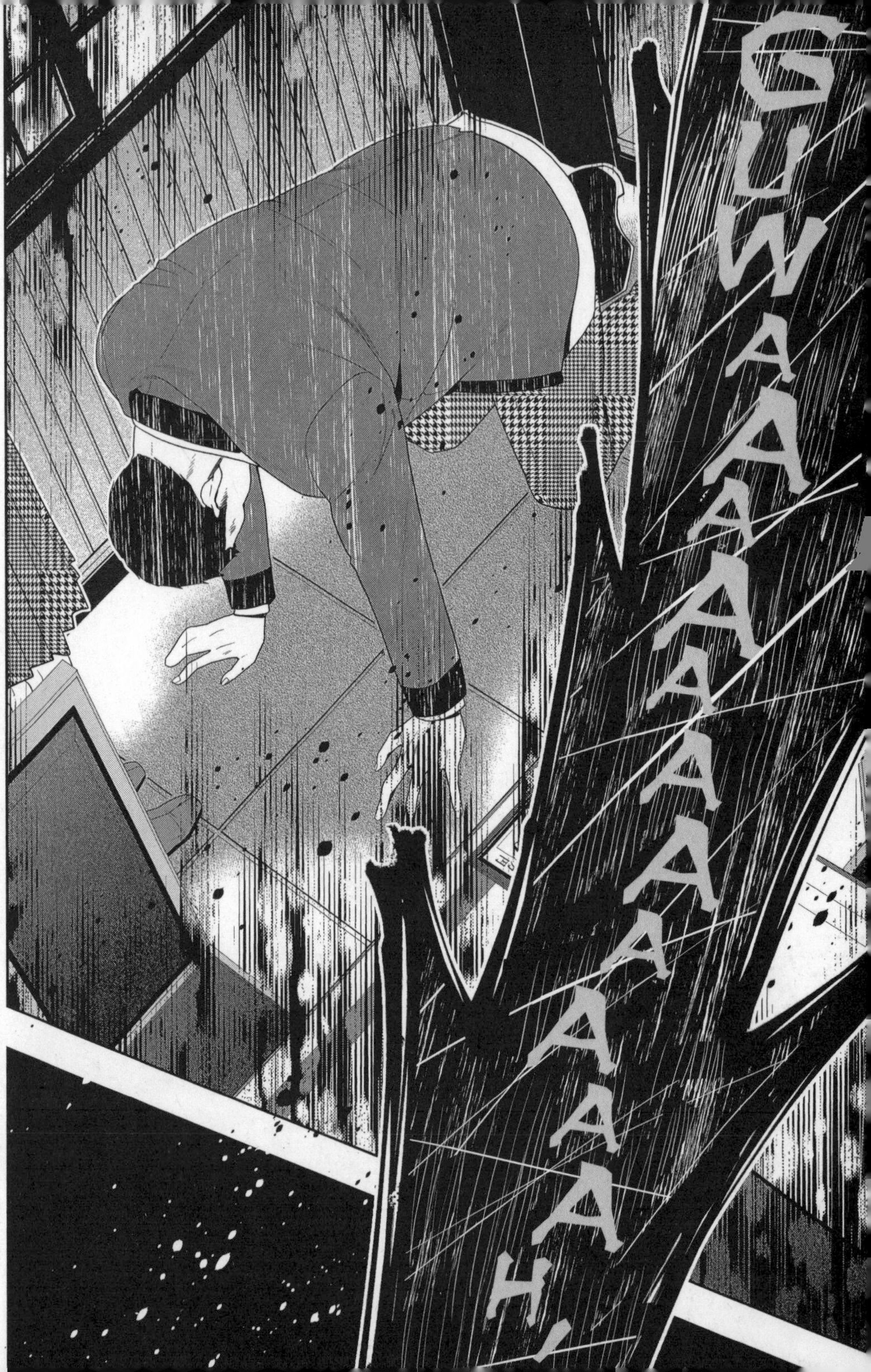
GUWAAAAAAAAAAAH!

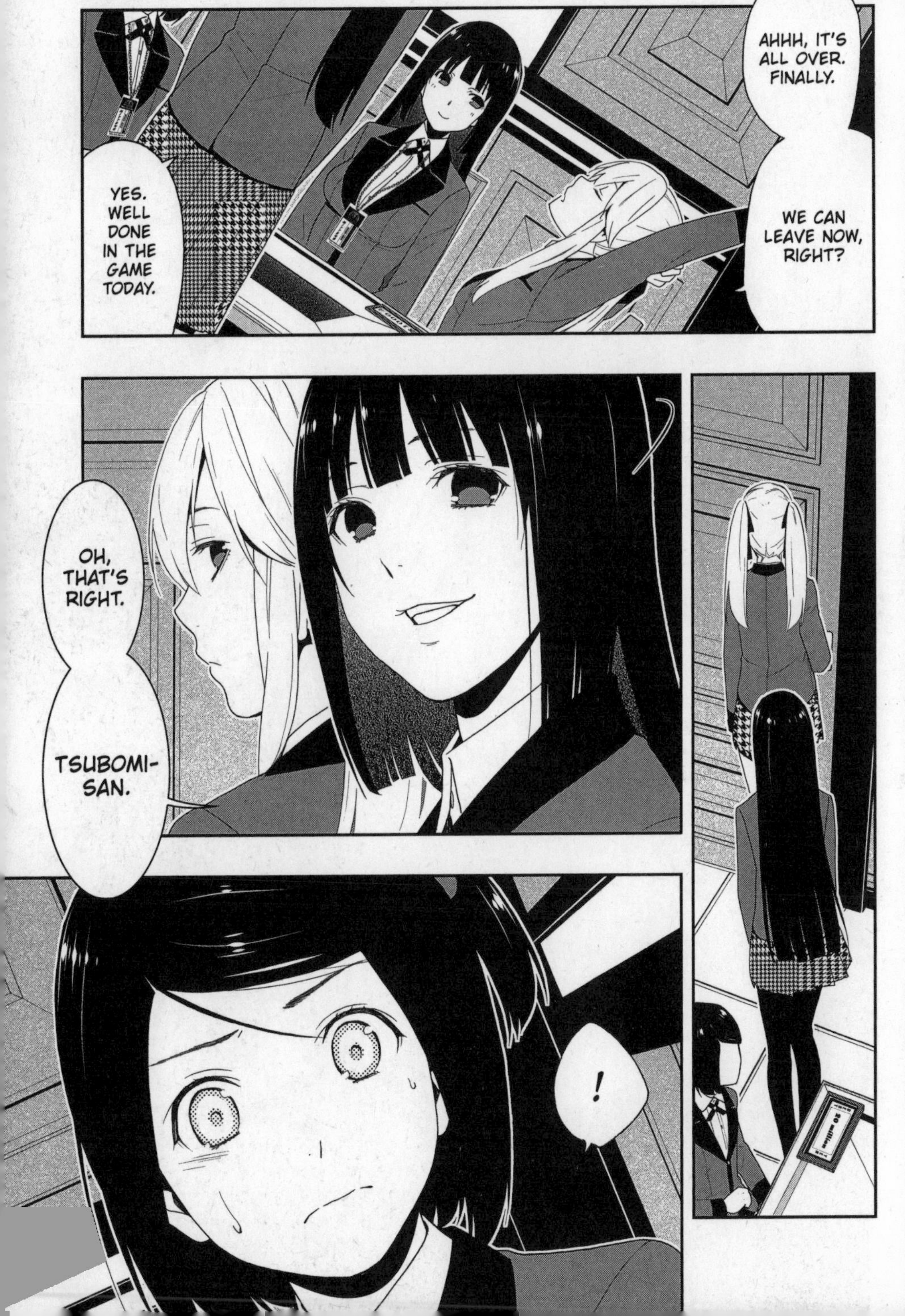
AHHH, IT'S ALL OVER. FINALLY.
WE CAN LEAVE NOW, RIGHT?
YES. WELL DONE IN THE GAME TODAY.
OH, THAT'S RIGHT.
TSUBOMI-SAN.
!

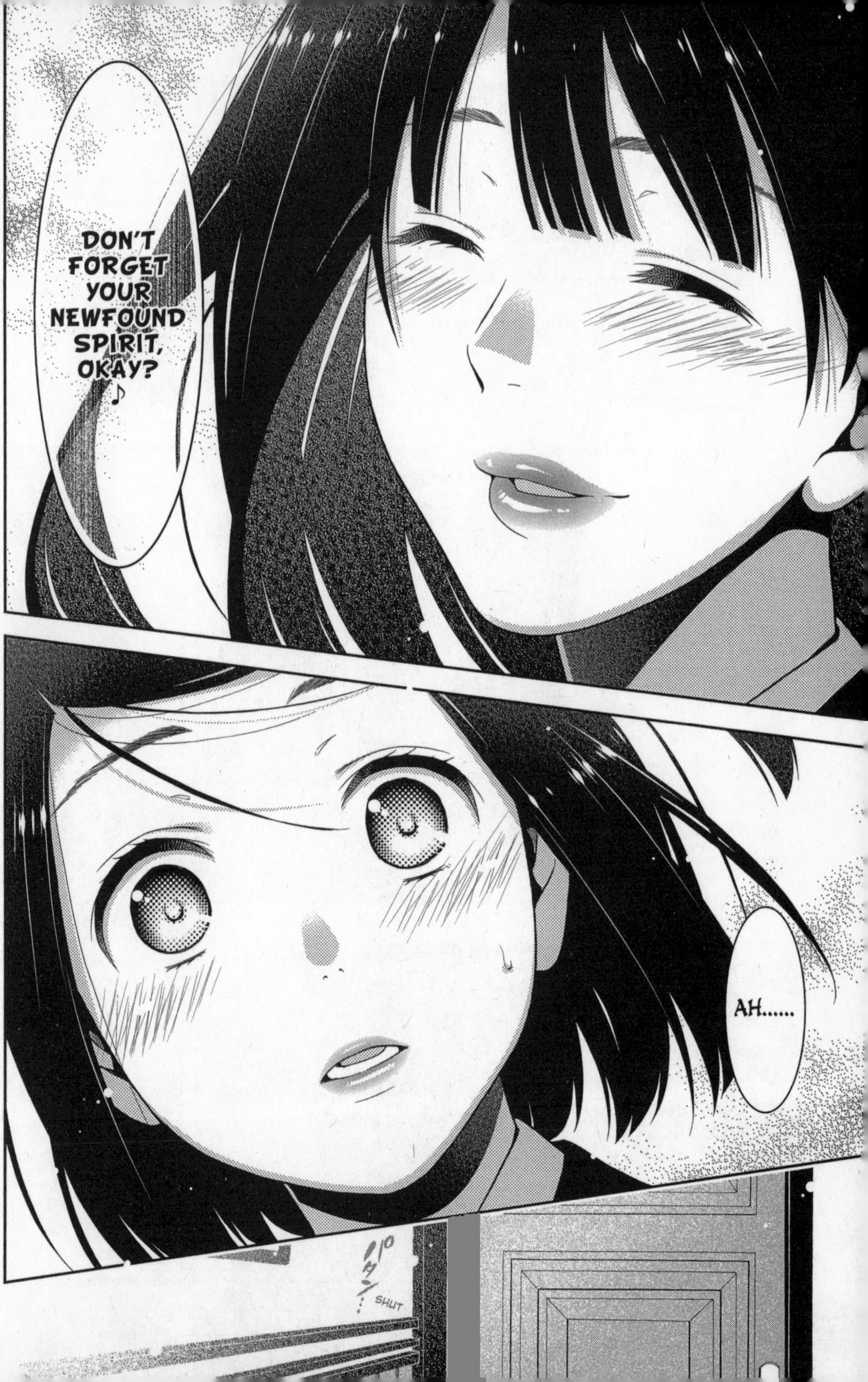
DON'T FORGET YOUR NEWFOUND SPIRIT, OKAY? ♪
AH......
パタン…
SHUT

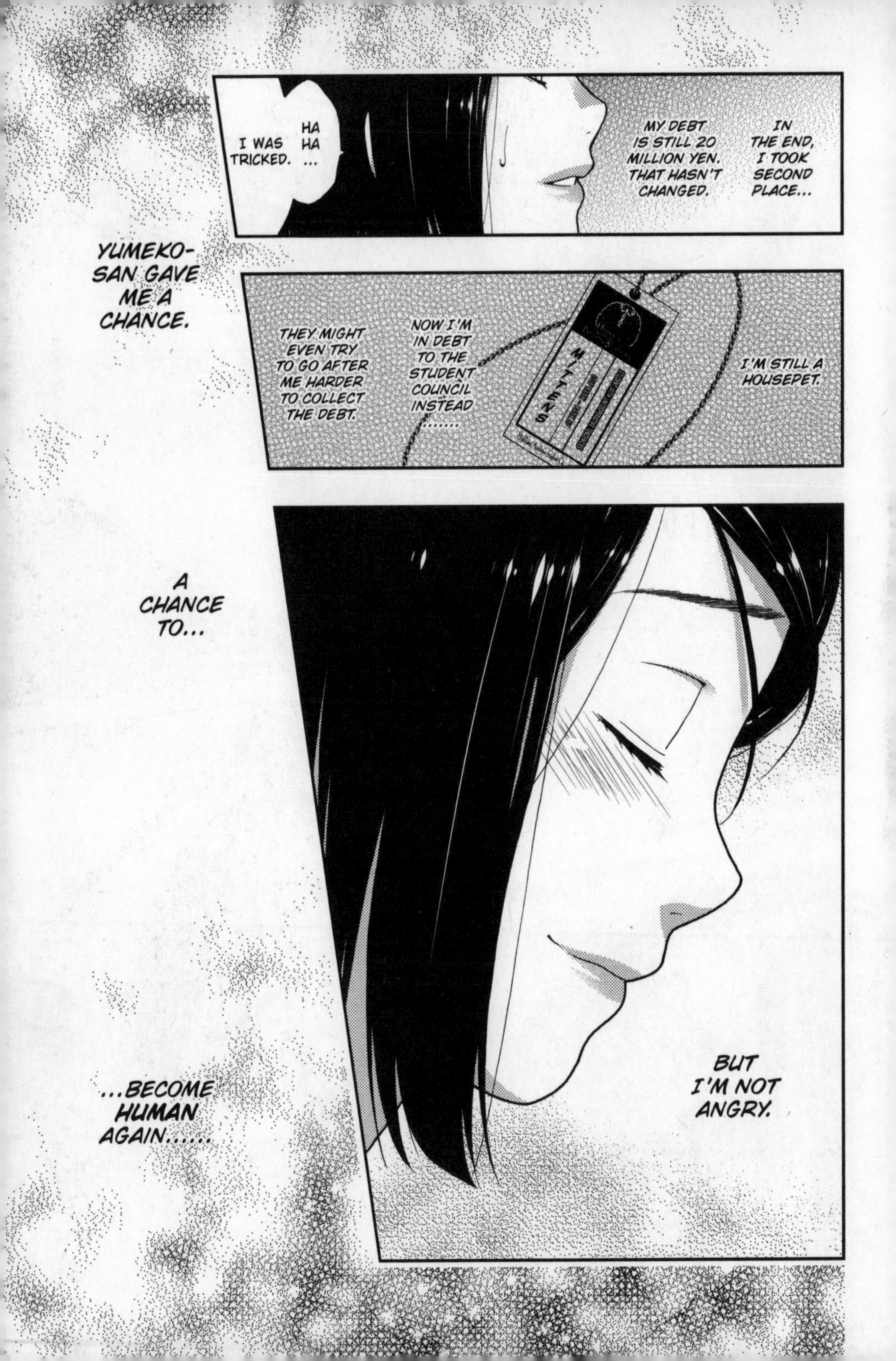
IN THE END, I TOOK SECOND PLACE...
MY DEBT IS STILL 20 MILLION YEN. THAT HASN'T CHANGED.
HA HA ...
I WAS TRICKED.
I'M STILL A HOUSEPET.
MITTENS
NOW I'M IN DEBT TO THE STUDENT COUNCIL INSTEAD......
THEY MIGHT EVEN TRY TO GO AFTER ME HARDER TO COLLECT THE DEBT.
BUT I'M NOT ANGRY.
YUMEKO-SAN GAVE ME A CHANCE.
A CHANCE TO...
...BECOME HUMAN AGAIN......

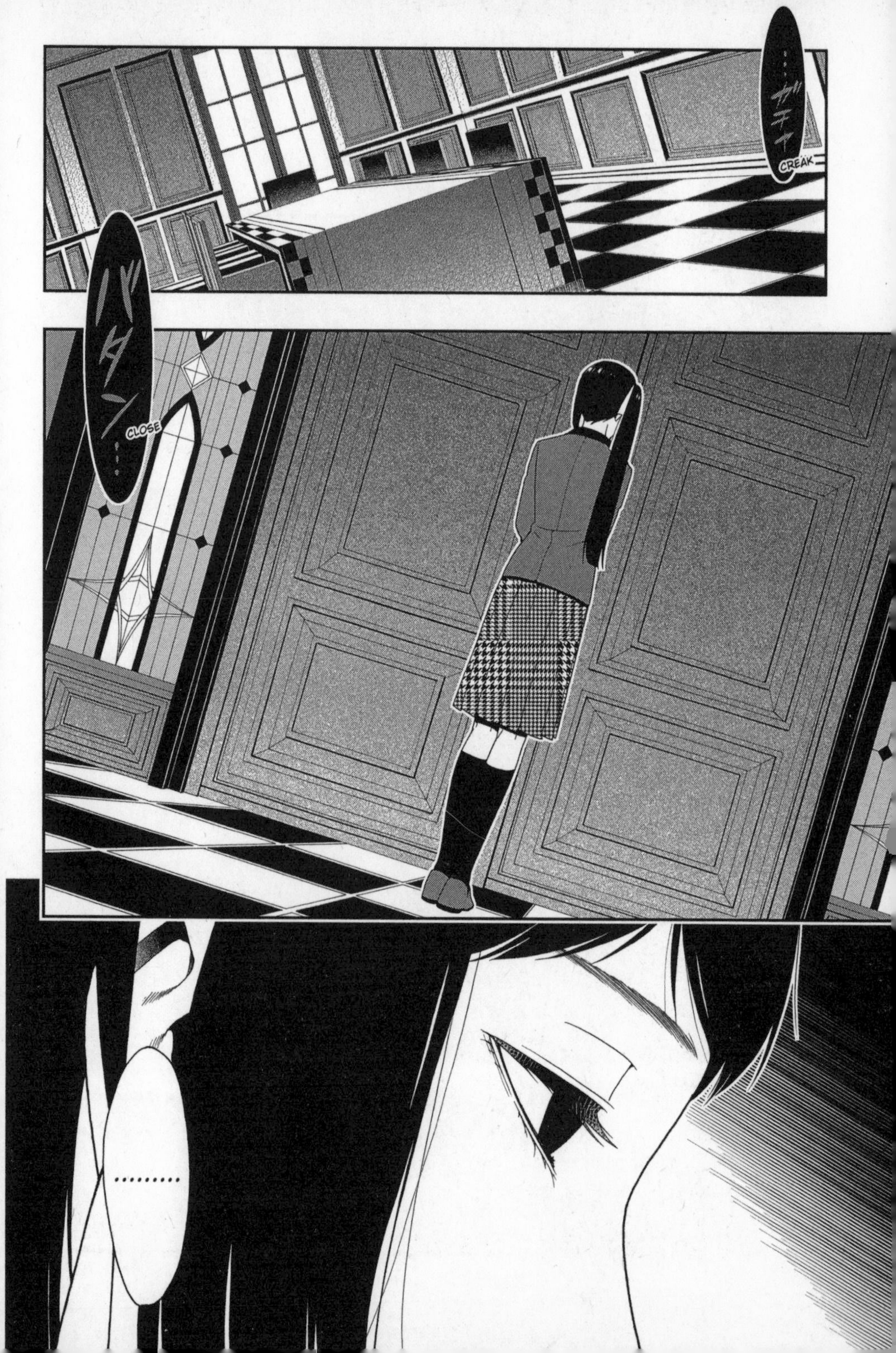
…ガチャ
CREAK
バタン…
CLOSE
....

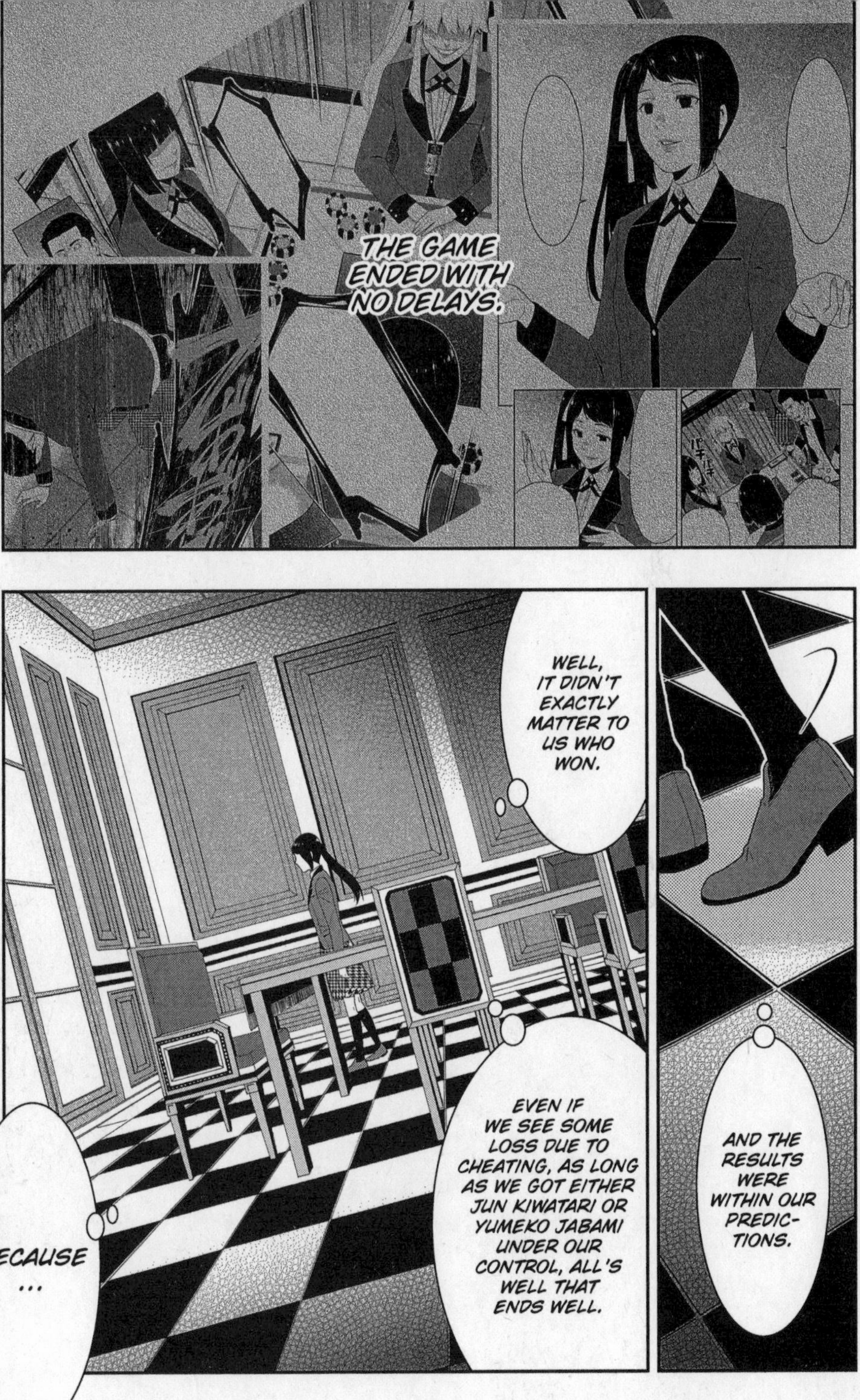
THE GAME ENDED WITH NO DELAYS.
AND THE RESULTS WERE WITHIN OUR PREDICTIONS.
WELL, IT DIDN'T EXACTLY MATTER TO US WHO WON.
EVEN IF WE SEE SOME LOSS DUE TO CHEATING, AS LONG AS WE GOT EITHER JUN KIWATARI OR YUMEKO JABAMI UNDER OUR CONTROL, ALL'S WELL THAT ENDS WELL.
BECAUSE ...

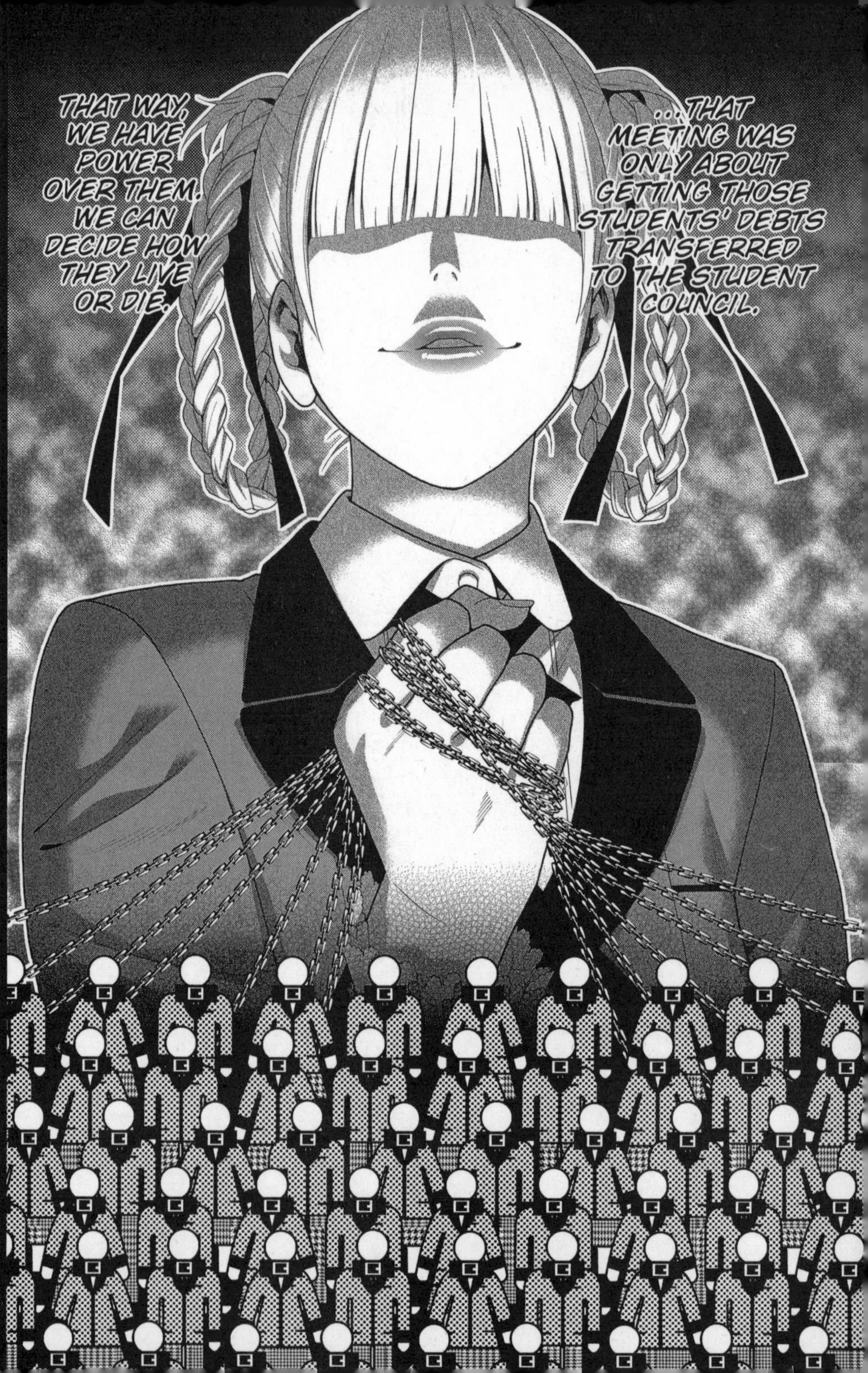
...THAT MEETING WAS ONLY ABOUT GETTING THOSE STUDENTS' DEBTS TRANSFERRED TO THE STUDENT COUNCIL.
THAT WAY, WE HAVE POWER OVER THEM. WE CAN DECIDE HOW THEY LIVE OR DIE.

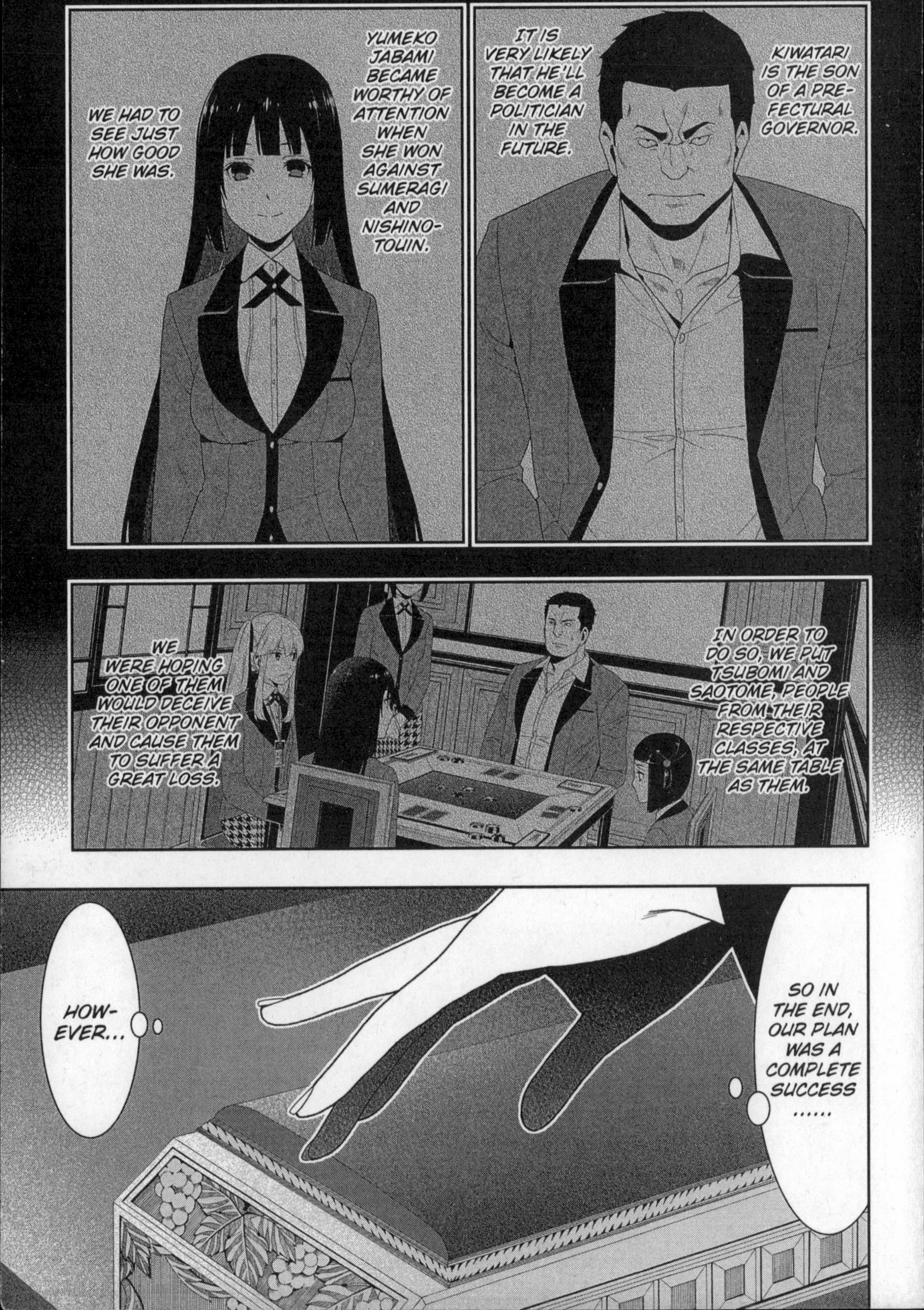
KIWATARI IS THE SON OF A PRE-FECTURAL GOVERNOR.
IT IS VERY LIKELY THAT HE'LL BECOME A POLITICIAN IN THE FUTURE.
YUMEKO JABAMI BECAME WORTHY OF ATTENTION WHEN SHE WON AGAINST SUMERAGI AND NISHINO-TOUIN.
WE HAD TO SEE JUST HOW GOOD SHE WAS.
IN ORDER TO DO SO, WE PUT TSUBOMI AND SAOTOME, PEOPLE FROM THEIR RESPECTIVE CLASSES, AT THE SAME TABLE AS THEM.
WE WERE HOPING ONE OF THEM WOULD DECEIVE THEIR OPPONENT AND CAUSE THEM TO SUFFER A GREAT LOSS.
SO IN THE END, OUR PLAN WAS A COMPLETE SUCCESS ......
HOW-EVER...

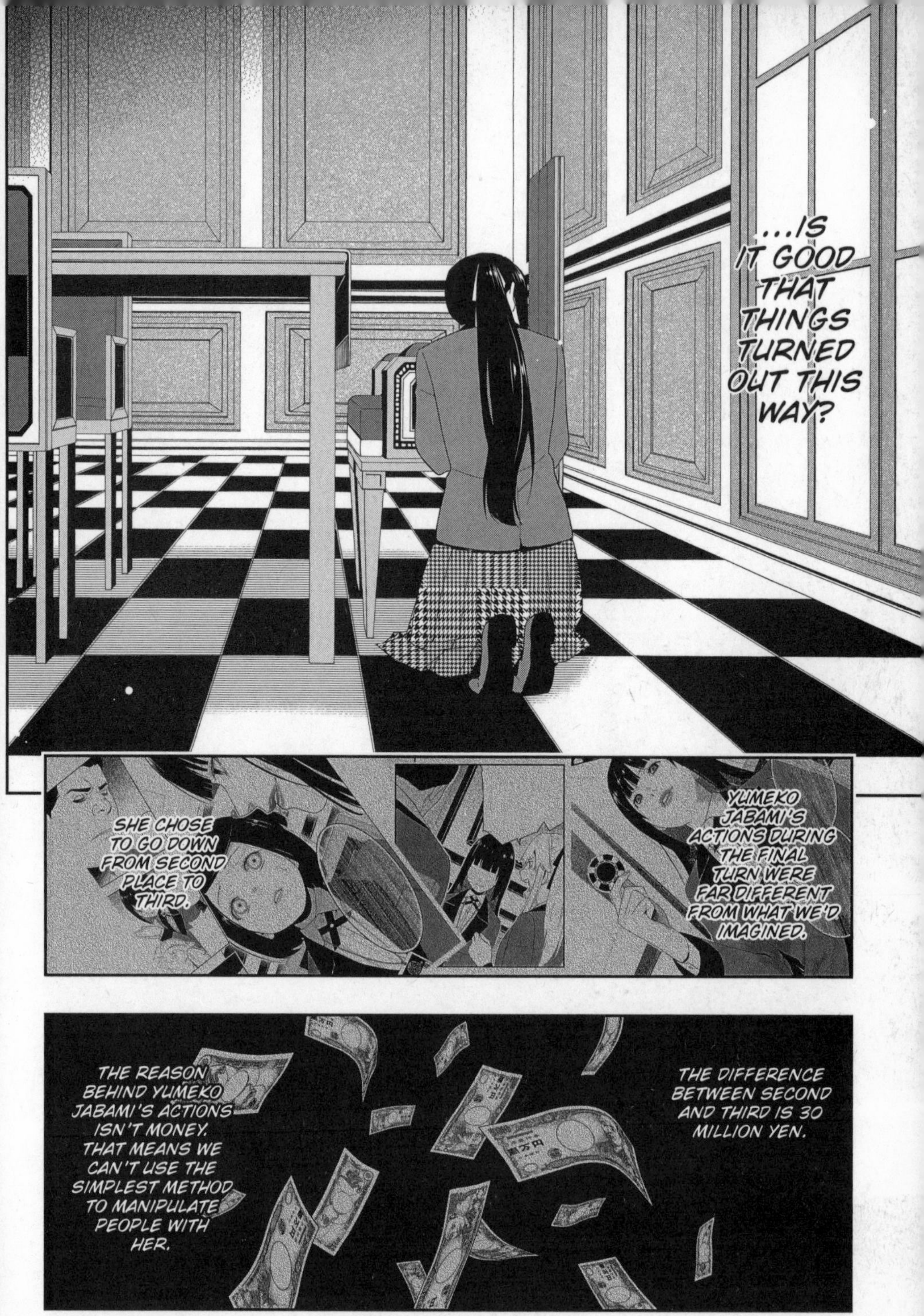
...IS IT GOOD THAT THINGS TURNED OUT THIS WAY?
YUMEKO JABAMI'S ACTIONS DURING THE FINAL TURN WERE FAR DIFFERENT FROM WHAT WE'D IMAGINED.
SHE CHOSE TO GO DOWN FROM SECOND PLACE TO THIRD.
THE DIFFERENCE BETWEEN SECOND AND THIRD IS 30 MILLION YEN.
THE REASON BEHIND YUMEKO JABAMI'S ACTIONS ISN'T MONEY. THAT MEANS WE CAN'T USE THE SIMPLEST METHOD TO MANIPULATE PEOPLE WITH HER.

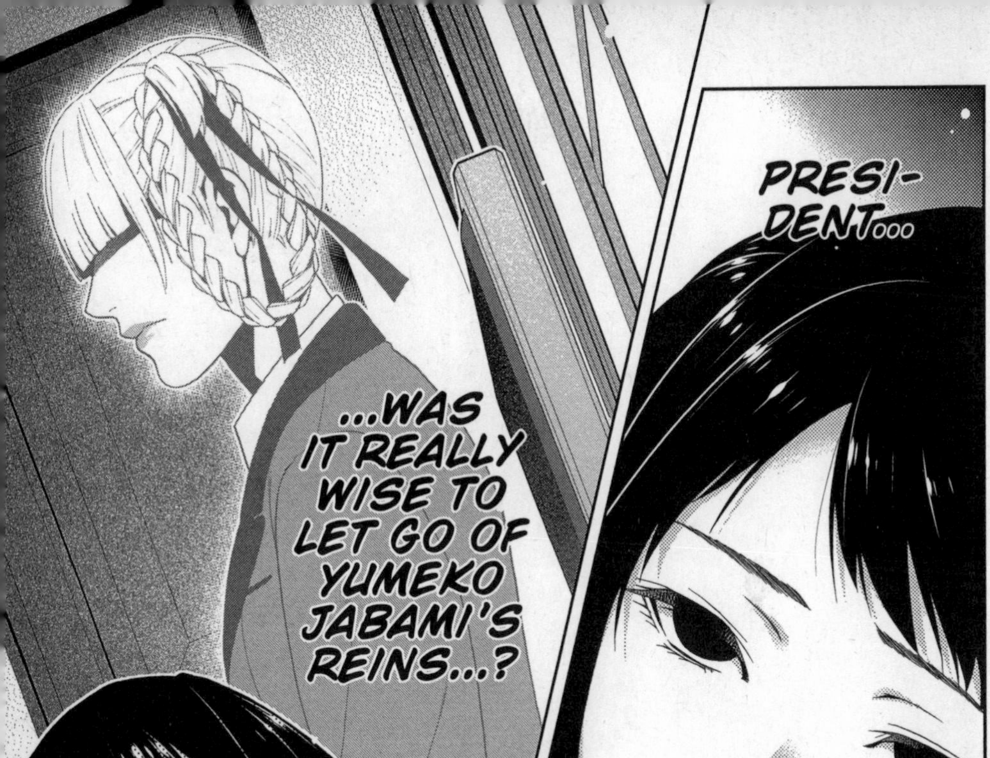
PRESI-DENT...
...WAS IT REALLY WISE TO LET GO OF YUMEKO JABAMI'S REINS...?

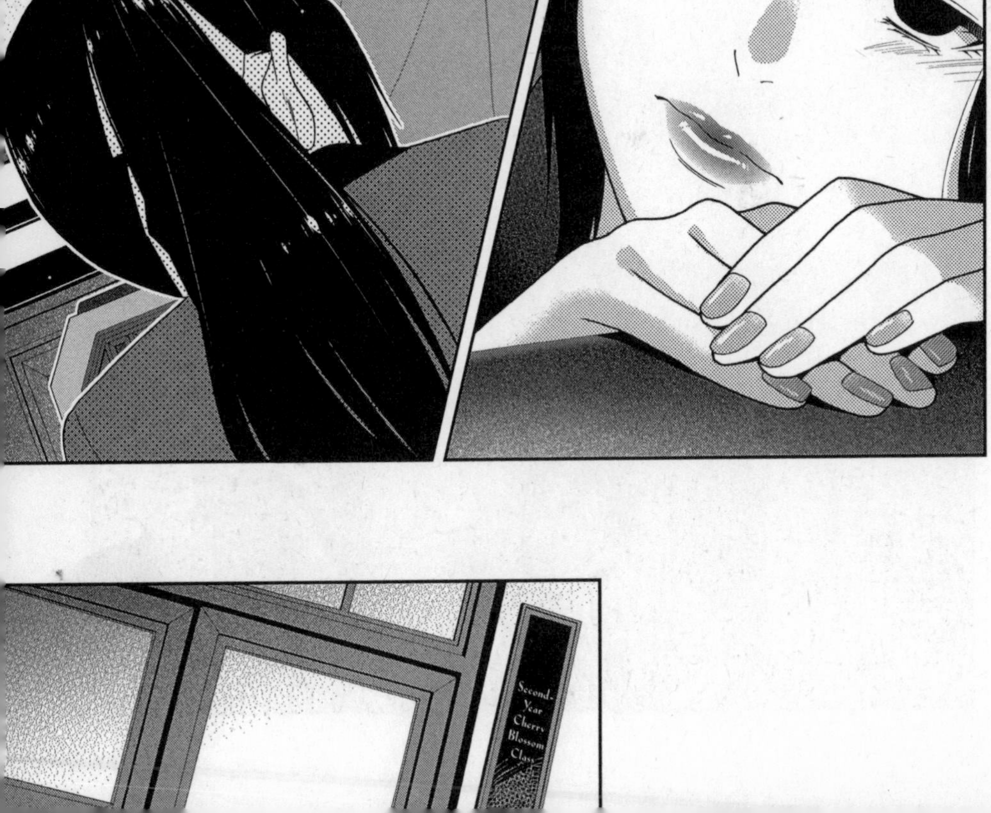
Second-Year Cherry Blossom Class

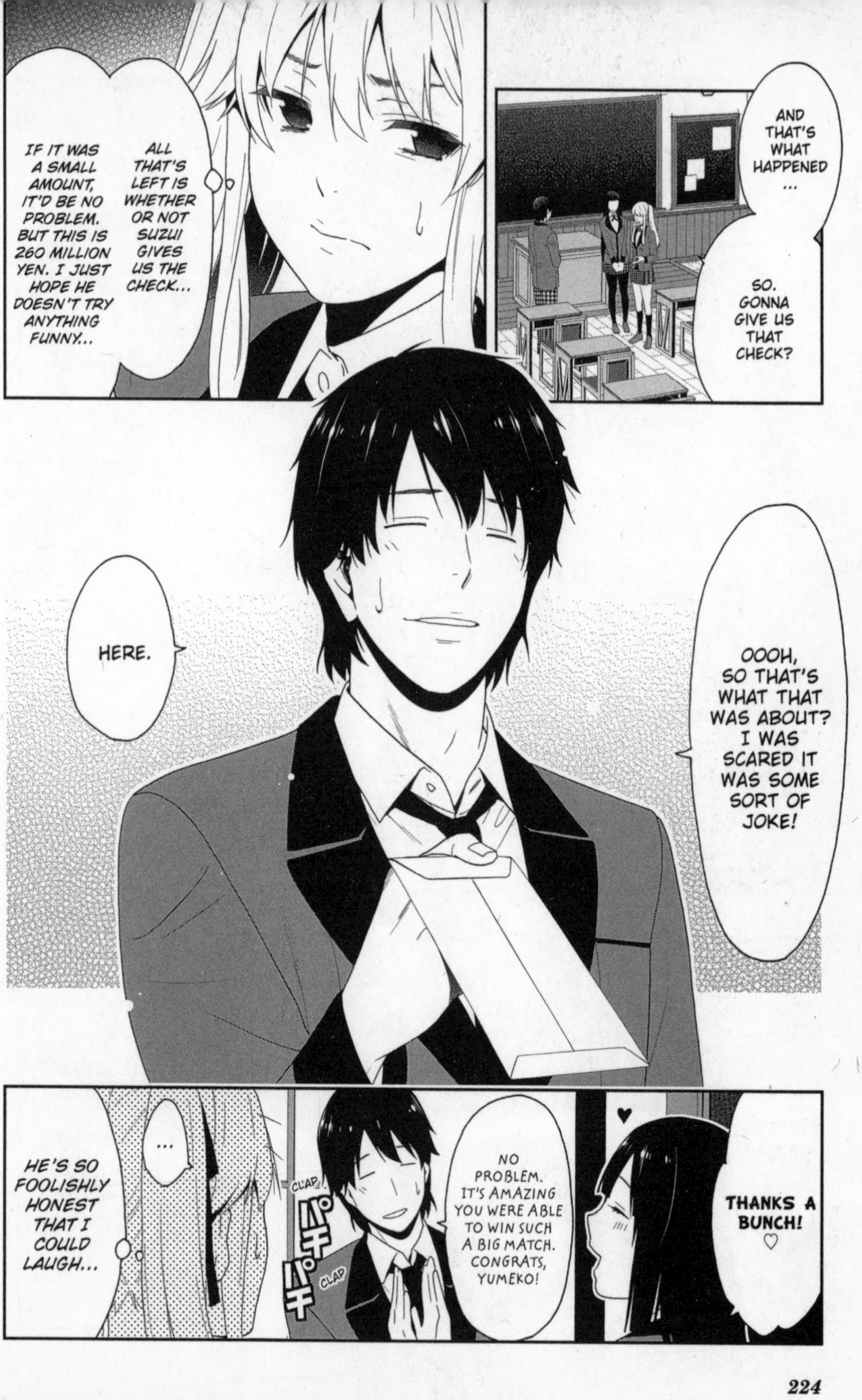
AND THAT'S WHAT HAPPENED ...
SO. GONNA GIVE US THAT CHECK?
ALL THAT'S LEFT IS WHETHER OR NOT SUZUI GIVES US THE CHECK...
IF IT WAS A SMALL AMOUNT, IT'D BE NO PROBLEM. BUT THIS IS 260 MILLION YEN. I JUST HOPE HE DOESN'T TRY ANYTHING FUNNY...
OOOH, SO THAT'S WHAT THAT WAS ABOUT? I WAS SCARED IT WAS SOME SORT OF JOKE!
HERE.
THANKS A BUNCH! ♡
NO PROBLEM. IT'S AMAZING YOU WERE ABLE TO WIN SUCH A BIG MATCH. CONGRATS, YUMEKO!
CLAP
パチ
パチ
CLAP
...
HE'S SO FOOLISHLY HONEST THAT I COULD LAUGH...

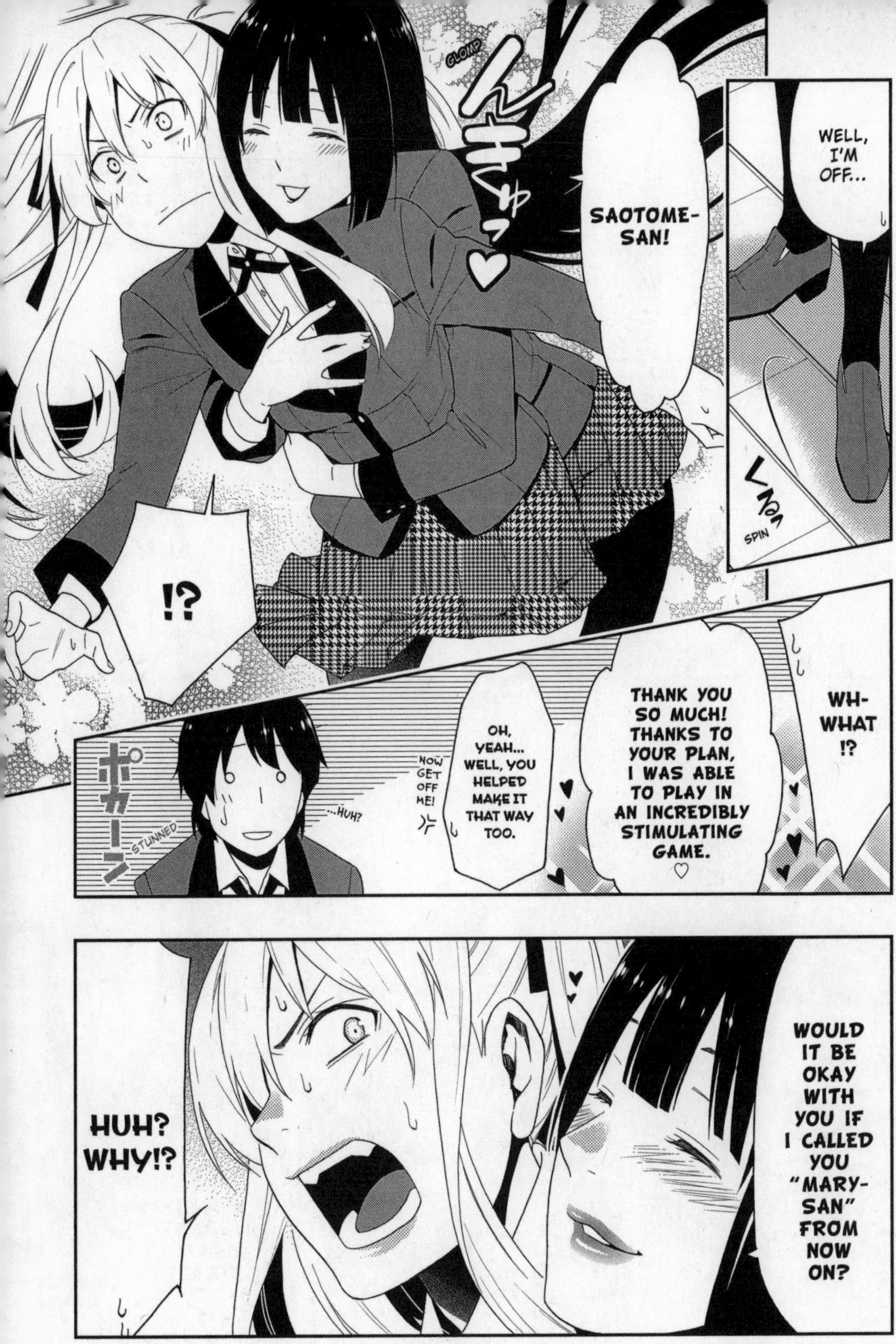

WELL, I'M OFF...
SPIN
GLOMP
SAOTOME-SAN!
!?
WH-WHAT!?
THANK YOU SO MUCH! THANKS TO YOUR PLAN, I WAS ABLE TO PLAY IN AN INCREDIBLY STIMULATING GAME. ♡
OH, YEAH... WELL, YOU HELPED MAKE IT THAT WAY TOO.
NOW GET OFF ME!
...HUH?
STUNNED
WOULD IT BE OKAY WITH YOU IF I CALLED YOU "MARY-SAN" FROM NOW ON?
HUH? WHY!?

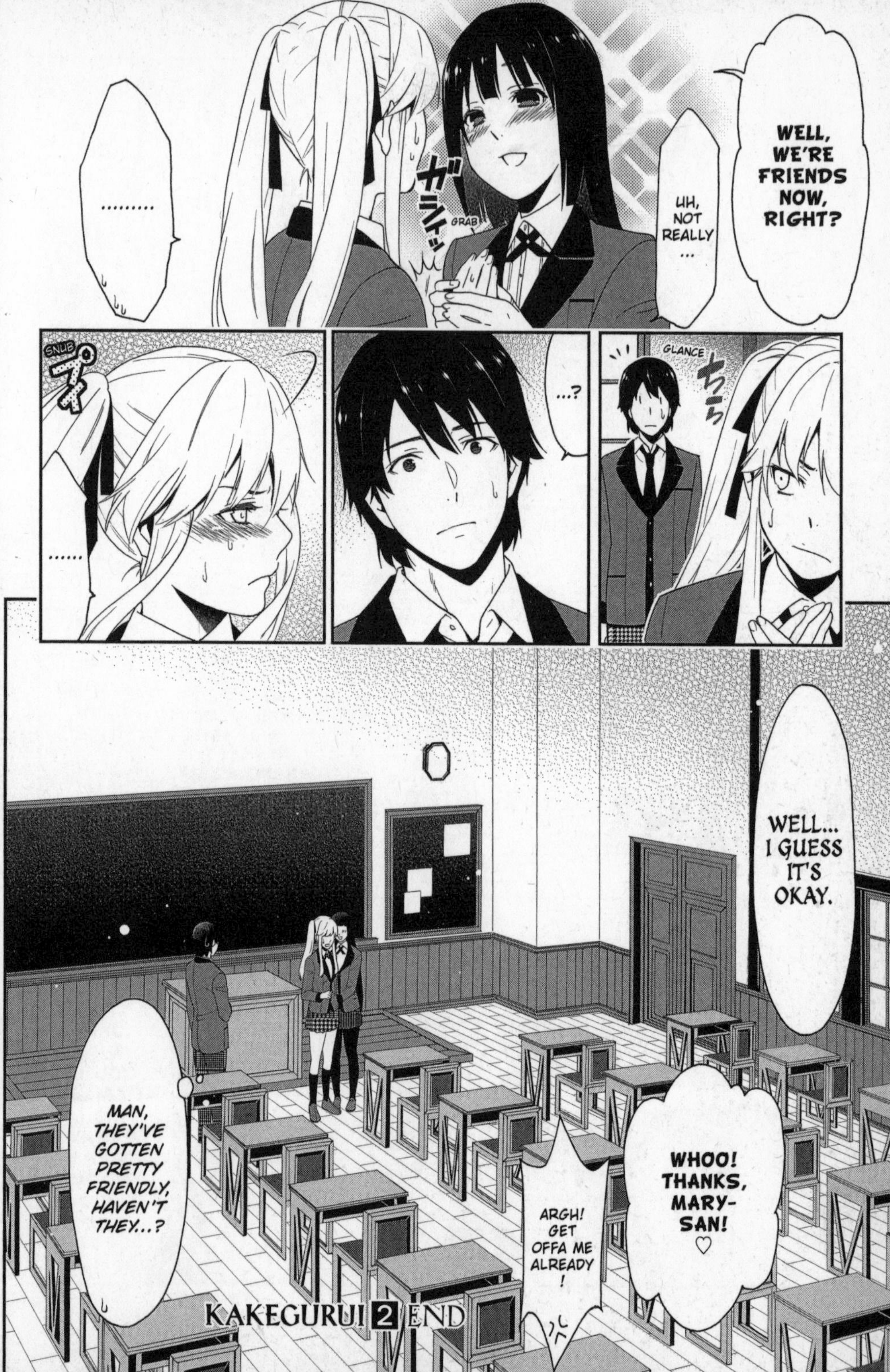
WELL, WE'RE FRIENDS NOW, RIGHT?
UH, NOT REALLY ...
GRAB
....
GLANCE
...?
SNUB
......
WELL... I GUESS IT'S OKAY.
WHOO! THANKS, MARY-SAN! ♡
ARGH! GET OFFA ME ALREADY!
MAN, THEY'VE GOTTEN PRETTY FRIENDLY, HAVEN'T THEY...?
KAKEGURUI 2 END

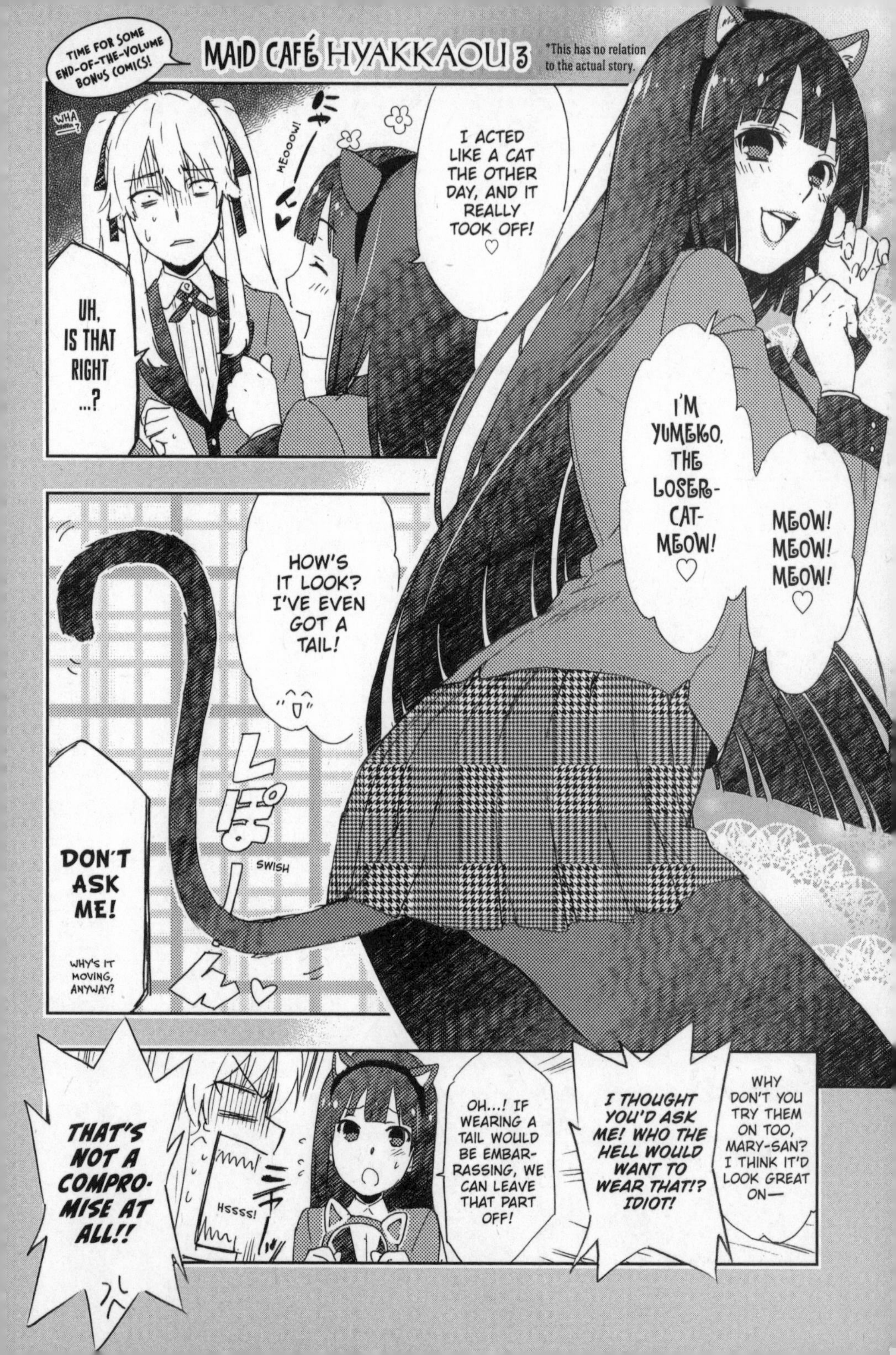
TIME FOR SOME END-OF-THE-VOLUME BONUS COMICS!
MAID CAFÉ HYAKKAOU 3
*This has no relation to the actual story.
I'M YUMEKO, THE LOSER-CAT-MEOW! ♡
MEOW! MEOW! MEOW! ♡
I ACTED LIKE A CAT THE OTHER DAY, AND IT REALLY TOOK OFF! ♡
MEOOOW!
WHA
UH, IS THAT RIGHT ...?
HOW'S IT LOOK? I'VE EVEN GOT A TAIL!
SWISH
DON'T ASK ME!
WHY'S IT MOVING, ANYWAY?
WHY DON'T YOU TRY THEM ON TOO, MARY-SAN? I THINK IT'D LOOK GREAT ON—
I THOUGHT YOU'D ASK ME! WHO THE HELL WOULD WANT TO WEAR THAT!? IDIOT!
OH...! IF WEARING A TAIL WOULD BE EMBAR-RASSING, WE CAN LEAVE THAT PART OFF!
HSSSS!
THAT'S NOT A COMPRO-MISE AT ALL!!

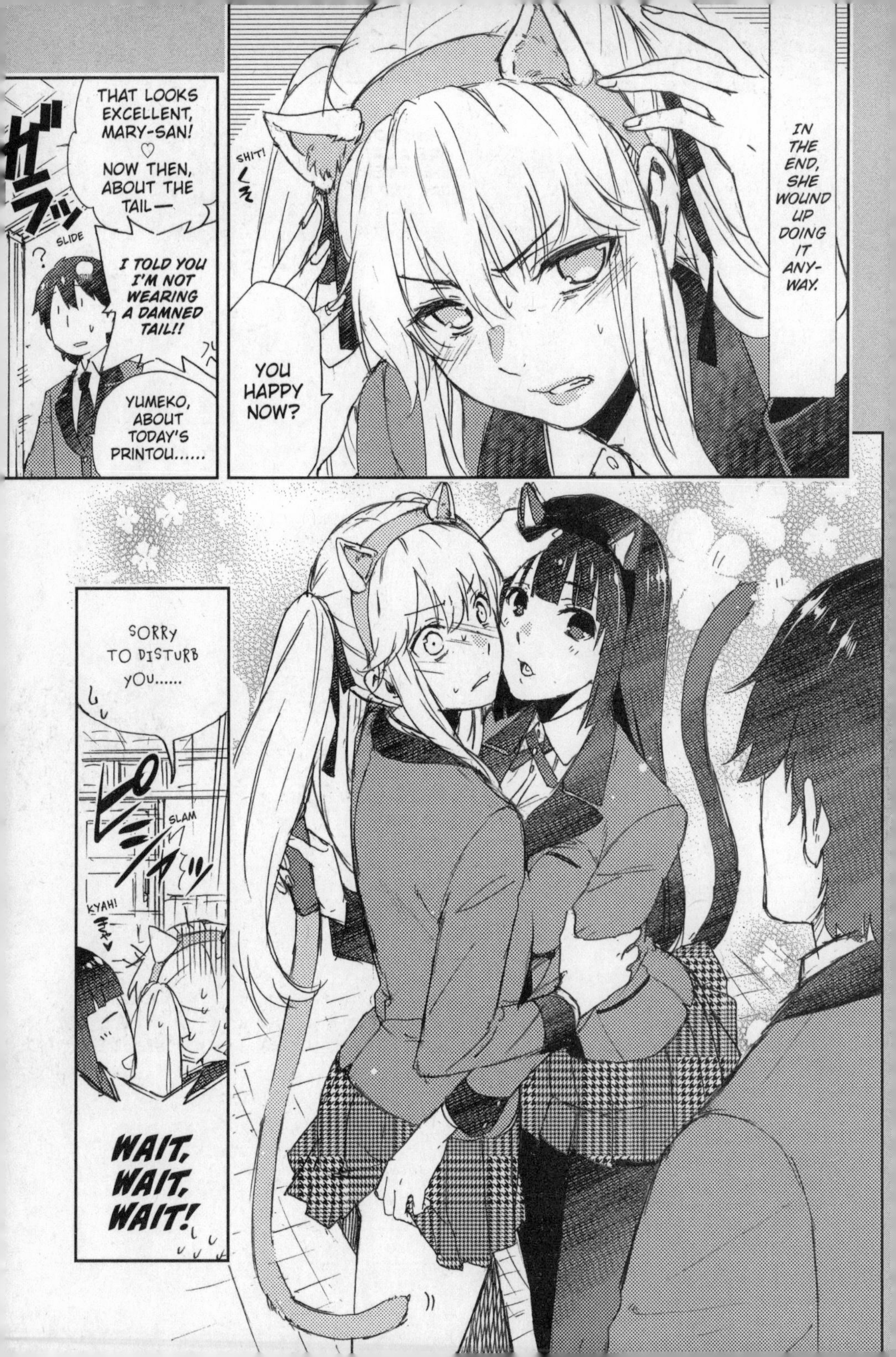
IN THE END, SHE WOUND UP DOING IT ANYWAY.
SHIT!
YOU HAPPY NOW?
THAT LOOKS EXCELLENT, MARY-SAN! ♡ NOW THEN, ABOUT THE TAIL—
SLIDE
I TOLD YOU I'M NOT WEARING A DAMNED TAIL!!
?
YUMEKO, ABOUT TODAY'S PRINTOU......
SORRY TO DISTURB YOU......
SLAM
KYAH!
WAIT, WAIT, WAIT!

GAMBLING, THAT IS MY RAISON D'ÊTRE.

Indian Poker is pretty fun on its own. But when you start betting chips, it becomes a much more fun and strategic game. (In Japan, gambling is illegal [Article 185 of the Penal Code], so do not bet money when playing.) Two-Card Indian Poker not only involves betting chips but also public and private cards. That introduces a new aspect to the game. I think it would be a fun variation to actually play. What do you think? If you were to play with the sort of scheme Yumeko came up with, it would be a really easy poker game to play.

TWO-CARD INDIAN POKER

Thank you very much for reading *Kakegurui* Volume 2. As I said in Volume 1, I'm going all out with my hobby in this. It's full speed ahead! I have nothing but thanks for both the staff at *JOKER* for letting me write everything I want, and the people who read this manga, filled to the brim as it is with my hobby. Every now and again when I was writing the script, I'd go, "I wonder if this plotline is any good...? This seems a bit too overboard...Nah, but I really like it." But then because of the support of all of you, the "GO" sign in my heart would turn on. Again, it would make me very happy if you were to get into this series for the long haul. So many people helped me out in Volume 2 as well. It's been about half a year since this series got serialized, and I still find myself shockingly impressed every time with the quality of the artwork of Naomura-sensei and his assistants. My editors, Sasaki-sama and Yumoto-sama, keep helping me improve the quality of the manga. Sorry for not getting things until you guys tell me multiple times! There are so many other people who helped me that I couldn't write them all here, so I'll just use this space to say thank you to all of them. Oh, and thanks to Tanaka for loaning me a toothbrush recently. I'll give it back soon. Please pick up Volume 3 as well!

Homura Kawamoto.

Afterword

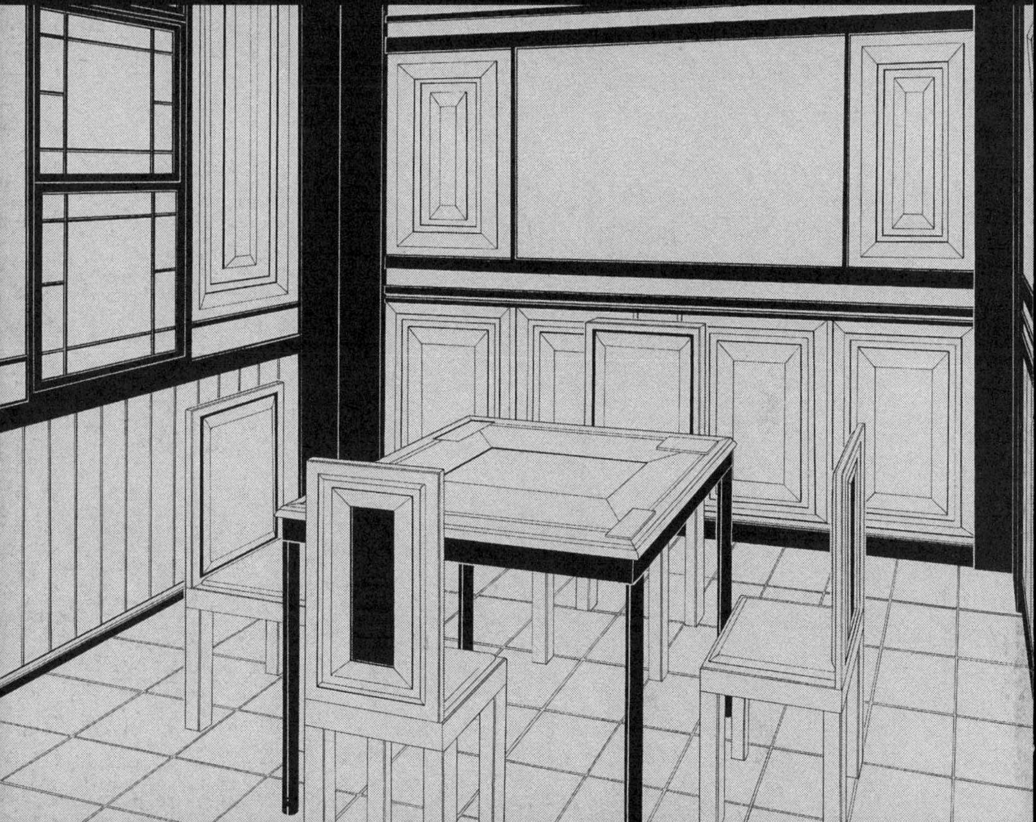

Thank you for picking up Volume 2 of *Kakegurui*.
I have terrible luck and I'm bad at strategy and bluffing, so I think I'd lose big in the Two-Card Indian Poker game that was in this volume.
Also, my assistant pointed out to me that there were big changes in how I drew Kiwatari. So I apologize for that. (*bitter laugh*)

SPECIAL THANKS

My editors • Kawamoto-sama • Imoutoko • H1-sama • H2-sama

Toru Naomura (artist), December 2014

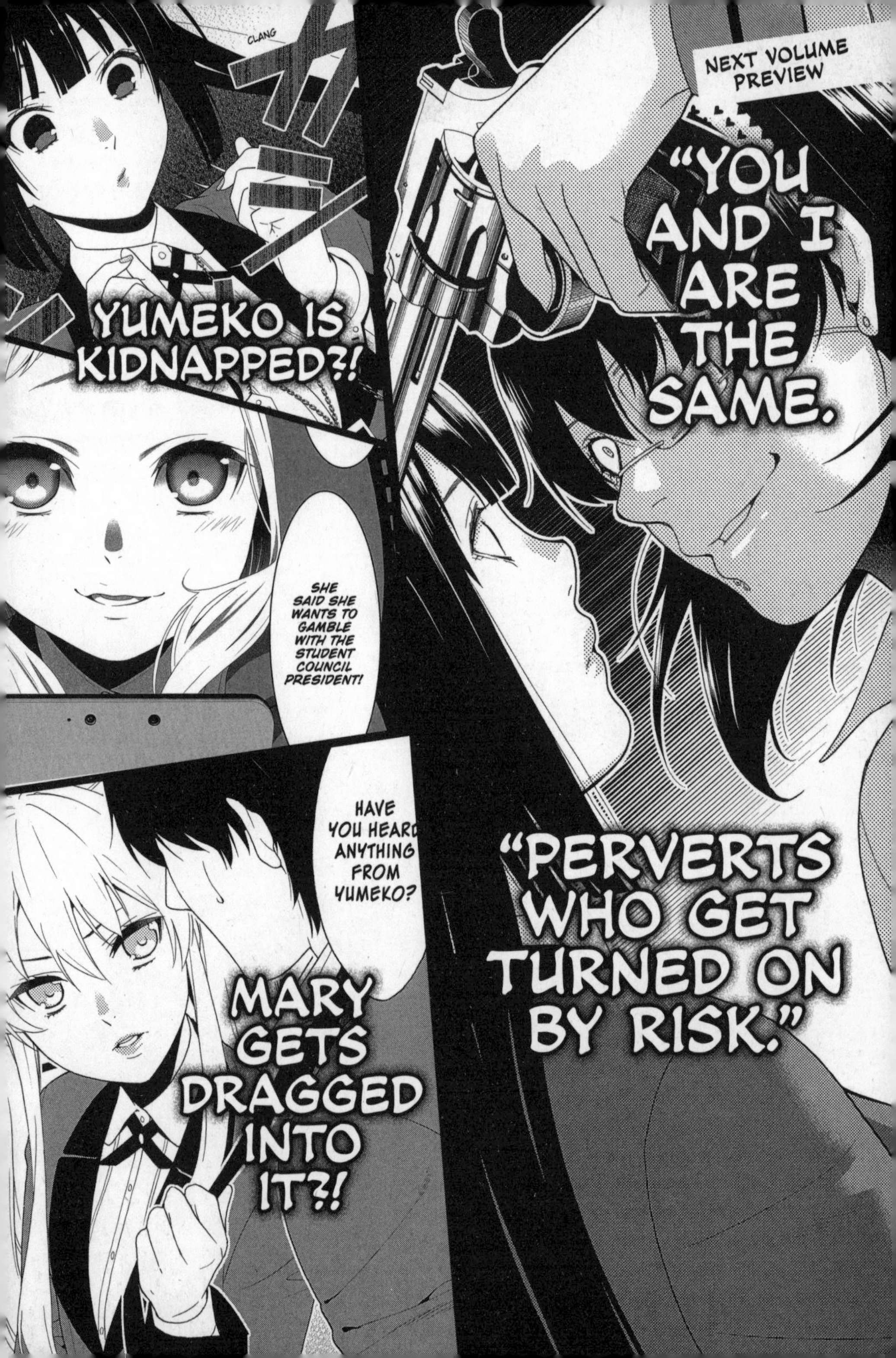
NEXT VOLUME PREVIEW
"YOU AND I ARE THE SAME.
"PERVERTS WHO GET TURNED ON BY RISK."
CLANG
YUMEKO IS KIDNAPPED?!
SHE SAID SHE WANTS TO GAMBLE WITH THE STUDENT COUNCIL PRESIDENT!
HAVE YOU HEARD ANYTHING FROM YUMEKO?
MARY GETS DRAGGED INTO IT?!

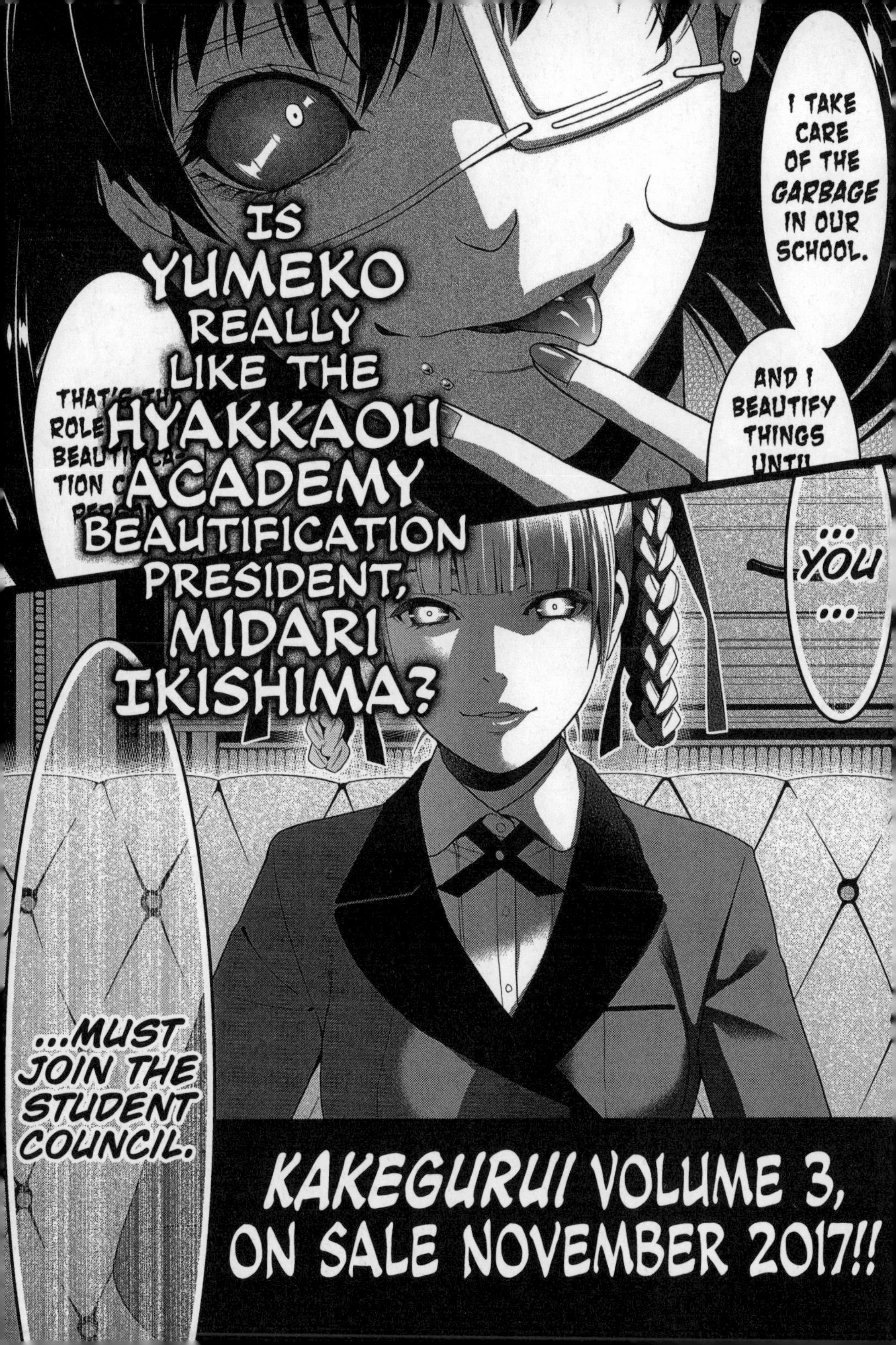
I TAKE CARE OF THE GARBAGE IN OUR SCHOOL.
AND I BEAUTIFY THINGS UNTIL
IS YUMEKO REALLY LIKE THE HYAKKAOU ACADEMY BEAUTIFICATION PRESIDENT, MIDARI IKISHIMA?
...YOU...
...MUST JOIN THE STUDENT COUNCIL.
KAKEGURUI VOLUME 3, ON SALE NOVEMBER 2017!!

COMMON HONORIFICS

no honorific: Indicates familiarity or closeness; if used without permission or reason, addressing someone in this manner would constitute an insult.

-san: The Japanese equivalent of Mr./Mrs./Miss. If a situation calls for politeness, this is the fail-safe honorific.

-sama: Conveys great respect; may also indicate that the social status of the speaker is lower than that of the addressee.

-kun: Used most often when referring to boys, this indicates affection or familiarity. Occasionally used by older men among their peers, but it may also be used by anyone referring to a person of lower standing.

-chan: An affectionate honorific indicating familiarity used mostly in reference to girls; also used in reference to cute persons or animals of either gender.

-sensei: A respectful term for teachers, artists, or high-level professionals.

-senpai: A suffix used to address upperclassmen or more experienced coworkers.

Yen conversion: While exchange rates fluctuate daily, a convenient conversion estimation is about ¥100 to $1.

Hyakkaou Private Academy: In Japanese, *hyakkaou* means "one hundred flowers"—thus, all the classrooms in the school are named after different kinds of flowers.

Fido/Mittens: In the original, male housepets are called "Pochi"—a common Japanese name for dogs—and female housepets are called "Mike"—a common Japanese name for calico cats, which, due to genetics, are nearly always female.

Yumeko Jabami: The Japanese kanji that make up Yumeko's full name have interesting meanings. *Yume* means "dream" and *jabami* means "to eat a snake."

Loser-cat: In Japanese, a common word for "loser" is *makeinu*, which literally translates to "loser-dog." So in this volume, "loser" female housepets are called *makeneko*, or "loser-cats."

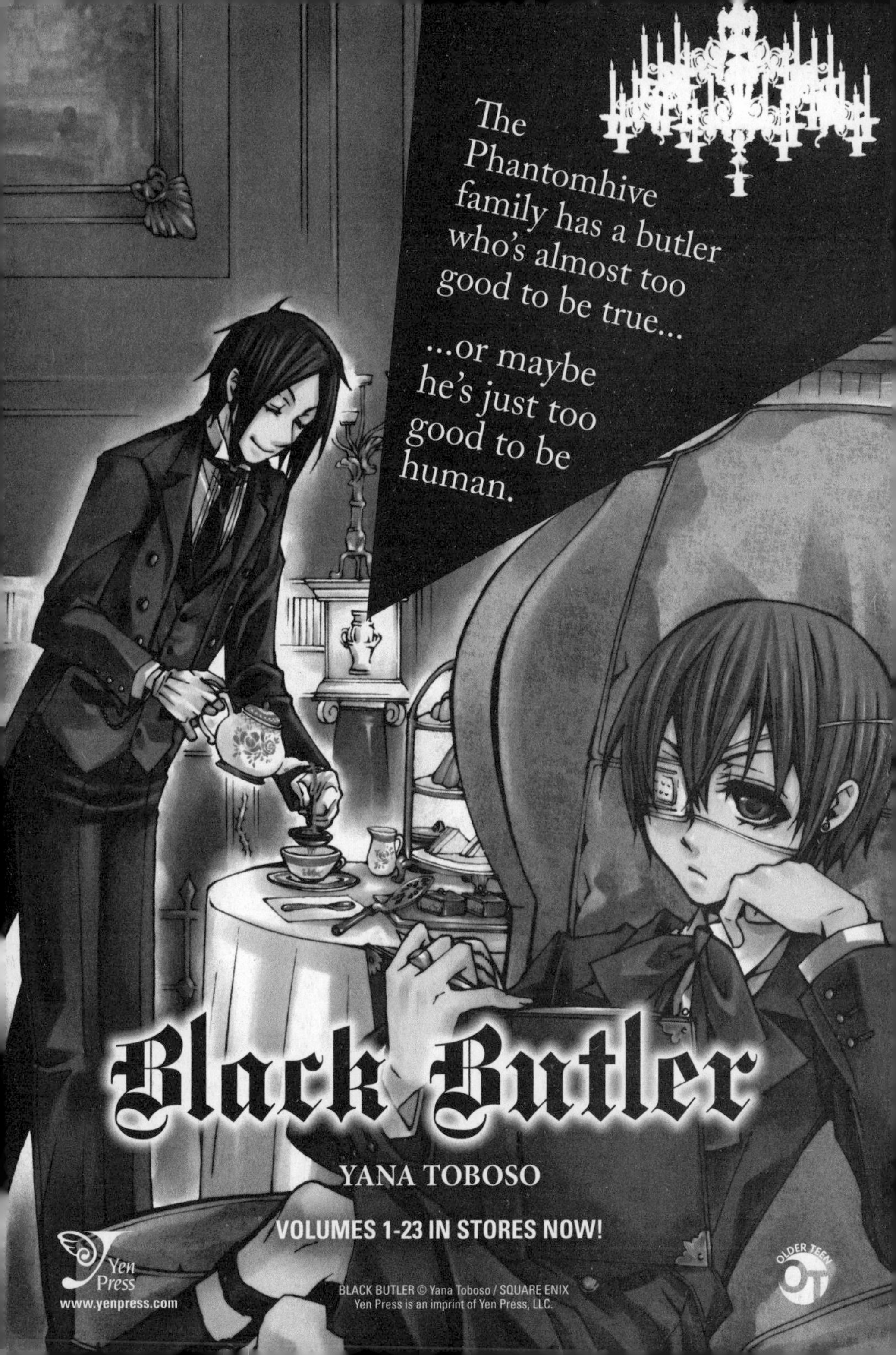
The Phantomhive family has a butler who's almost too good to be true...
...or maybe he's just too good to be human.
Black Butler
YANA TOBOSO
VOLUMES 1-23 IN STORES NOW!
Yen Press
www.yenpress.com
BLACK BUTLER © Yana Toboso / SQUARE ENIX
Yen Press is an imprint of Yen Press, LLC.
OLDER TEEN
OT

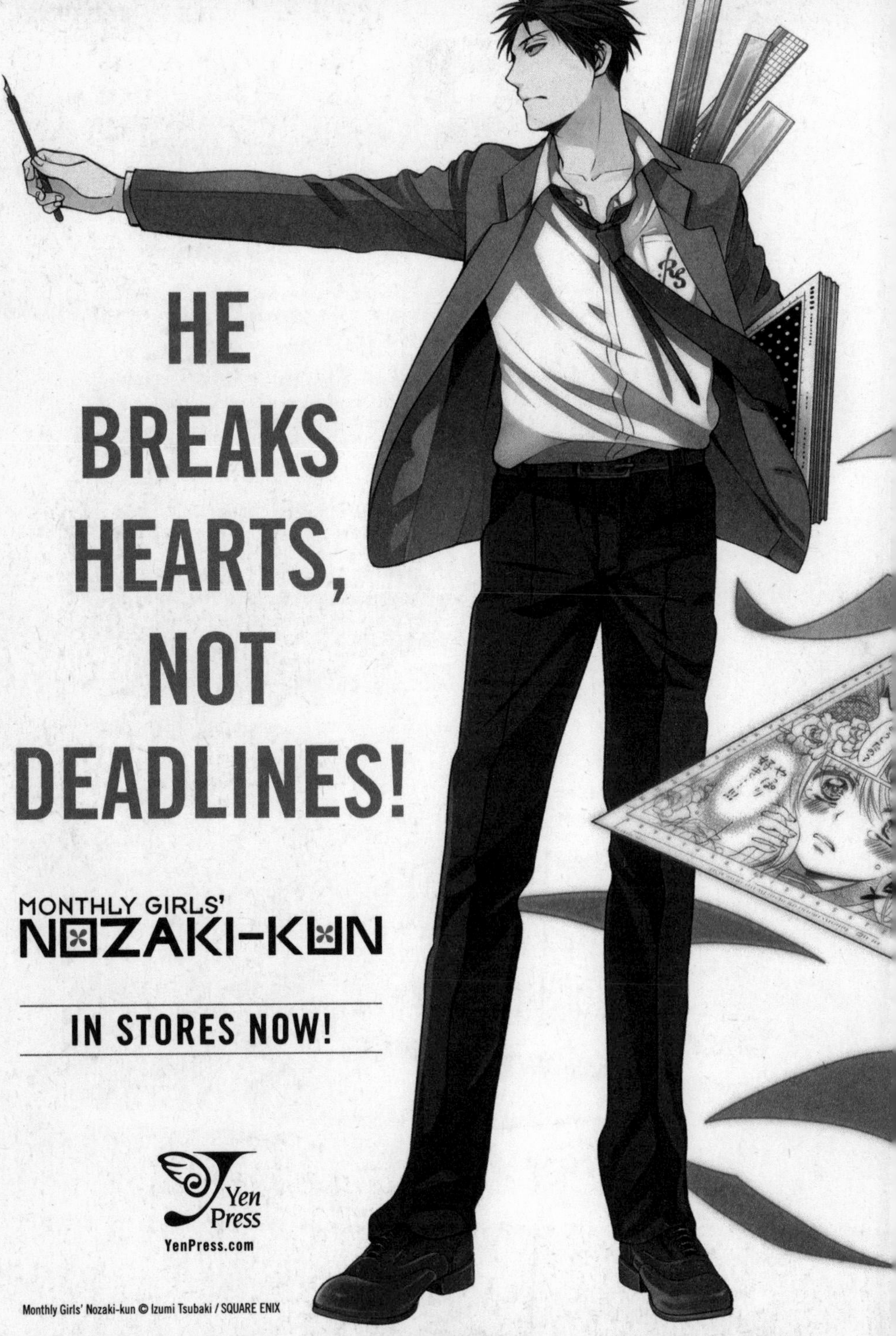

HE BREAKS HEARTS, NOT DEADLINES!
MONTHLY GIRLS' NOZAKI-KUN
IN STORES NOW!
Yen Press
YenPress.com
Monthly Girls' Nozaki-kun © Izumi Tsubaki / SQUARE ENIX

②

STORY: **Homura Kawamoto**
ART: **Toru Naomura**

Translation: Matthew Alberts
Lettering: AndWorld Design,
Anthony Quintessenza

This book is a work of fiction. Names, characters, places, and incidents are the product of the author's imagination or are used fictitiously. Any resemblance to actual events, locales, or persons, living or dead, is coincidental.

KAKEGURUI Vol. 2 ©2014 Homura Kawamoto, Toru Naomura/SQUARE ENIX CO., LTD. First published in Japan in 2014 by SQUARE ENIX CO., LTD. English translation rights arranged with SQUARE ENIX CO., LTD. and Yen Press, LLC through Tuttle-Mori Agency, Inc.

English translation ©2015 by SQUARE ENIX CO., LTD.

Yen Press
1290 Avenue of the Americas
New York, NY 10104

Visit us at yenpress.com
facebook.com/yenpress
twitter.com/yenpress
yenpress.tumblr.com
instagram.com/yenpress

First Yen Press Print Edition: September 2017
Originally published as an eBook in August 2015 by Yen Press.

Yen Press is an imprint of Yen Press, LLC.
The Yen Press name and logo are trademarks of Yen Press, LLC.

The publisher is not responsible for websites (or their content) that are not owned by the publisher.

Library of Congress Control Number: 2017939211

ISBN: 978-0-316-56298-0 (paperback)

10 9 8 7 6 5 4 3 2

BVG

Printed in the United States of America